Kern's Movers & Shakers

by Camille Gavin and Kathy Leverett

THE KERN VIEW FOUNDATION
BAKERSFIELD • CALIFORNIA

Library of Congress Catalog Card Number 87-090869
ISBN 0-9618770-0-6

Book and jacket design: Claire Maeder
Production design: Ann Pridgen and Christine Williams

First Edition

Acknowledgements

The Kern View Foundation gratefully acknowledges the following underwriters who have contributed support to the publication of Kern's Movers & Shakers.

Borton, Petrini & Conron — One of Kern County's pioneer law firms, Borton, Petrini & Conron was formed in 1923 in Bakersfield by Fred E. Borton and James Petrini. The lawyers were joined in 1933 by Harry M. Conron. Today the firm has more than 60 attorneys. It has become the largest law firm in the Central Valley, between Sacramento and Los Angeles, with officers in ten California cities. Borton, Petrini & Conron has been a leader since its earliest days, particularly in laws pertaining to oil and gas, real estate, water, and transportation.

The firm is equally well known for its numerous former associates who have gained distinction as members of the judiciary. These include P.R. Borton (the son of Fred Borton), a Kern County Superior Court judge from 1964 to 1981; George A. Brown, the Presiding Justice of the Fifth District Court of Appeal since 1971; Walter H. Condley, a former Municipal and presently a Superior Court judge; Roy Gargano, who after serving as Kern County Counsel and then as a Superior Court Judge, went on to become an Associate Justice of the California Court of Appeal, Fifth Appellate District.

Rayburn and Joan Dezember — Ray and Joan Dezember gratefully acknowledge the support of the community which has allowed American National Bank and Central Pacific Corporation to grow and prosper over the past 23 years. The Dezembers recognize as well the dedication of the 11 individuals who made up the bank's founding Board of Directors: Martin C. Erreca, Chairman, John L. Blackwood, Baptiste Borda, Floyd D. Burcham, John S. "Stu" Hagestad, O.D. Handel, Albert D. Lum, Peter J. McCart, Fernelly I. Roberts, Ernest D. Wattenbarger and Dr. Harry Wong.

Occidental Exploration and Production Company — Occidental Petroleum Corporation, the Los Angeles-based parent company of Occidental Oil and Gas Corporation, was organized in 1920 and merged with Gene Reid Drilling Company of Bakersfield in 1959.

Contel — The third largest independent telephone company in the nation, Contel serves 20 Kern County communities and has its Western Region headquarters located in Bakersfield. Contel has been a part of Kern County since 1961, when it bought Central Western Telephone Company from telephone pioneer Jack P. Maguire and several local partners.

Jim Burke Ford — One of the largest Ford dealerships in the United States, the company is owned and operated by Jim Burke and is located at 2001 Oak Street, Bakersfield.

Brock's — A family-owned department store since 1899, Brock's is located in downtown Bakersfield, Valley Plaza Regional Shopping Center and soon in the East Hills Mall.

KGET-TV 17 — Kern Golden Empire Television applauds those who have made a difference in Kern County.

Price Waterhouse — Celebrating our association with Kern View and our fifth year of business in Kern County.

Clay Diversified Inc. —The parent company of four Steak, Seafood, Salad Sizzlers throughout Bakersfield has been owned and operated by Meg and Wayne Clay since 1979.

Authors Page

A great many people have provided invaluable assistance in the creation of Kern's Movers & Shakers.

While it would be impossible to recognize all of them, we do wish to thank in particular the following individuals.

Denny Kline, public affairs officer at the Naval Weapons Center, and members of his staff were extremely helpful in supplying information for portions of the chapter on aviation and science. Material for this section also came from Don Haley of the Edwards Air Force Base public information office and Dr. James Young, base historian.

Oil writer Bill Rintoul graciously shared his vast personal knowledge of the petroleum industry as well as his extensive files. Dr. Phillips Dunford furnished material for the section on health and medicine as did Dr. Thomas Larwood.

Many cloudy historical issues were clarified with the help of author-historian Harland Boyd. The lists of elected officials in Kern County could not have been completed without the assistance of Bernice Blake of the county Elections Department.

The Kern County Library's historical collection has been a major source overall. John Walden and other members of the Beale Library reference staff pointed out many bits of information that might otherwise have been overlooked. Professionals at other institutions who provided assistance include Christy Gavin and Jim Segesta of the Cal State Bakersfield Library, and Dawn North, librarian for *The Bakersfield Californian.*

Many individuals were generous in supplying photographs. However, our two main sources were the Kern County Museum and *The Bakersfield Californian.* For making it possible to reproduce photos from these files we are indebted to Museum Director Carola Rupert and Robert Bentley, *The California's* managing editor. Dave Fanucchi loaned pictures from the Bob Elias Hall of Fame.

Eloise Lambert edited much of the copy for the manuscript and made many useful suggestions. In addition, she aided in the research and writing of certain segments. Barbara Macnair and Julie Durick also assisted with the research.

Graphic artist Claire Maeder, the designer of Kern's Movers & Shakers, has been a key figure from the beginning. Her background and experience (she has designed three books for Texas Monthly Press) proved to be of inestimable value. The production design was carried out by Ann Pridgen and Christine Williams, two dedicated participants in making this publication a reality.

We are most grateful to the members of the Editorial Board. These individuals aided in the selection of the "movers and shakers' and also read portions of the manuscript in progress. For their yeoman service in reading the final manuscript — within a short period of time — we especially thank Barbara Macnair, Edward Simonsen, Mark Raney and John Hicks.

Our final note of thanks goes to Ray Watson, who conceived the idea for Kern's Movers & Shakers more than a year ago. His unflagging enthusiasm, support and encouragement as well as his confidence in our abilities has sustained us throughout.

Camille Gavin and Kathy Leverett
September 1987
Bakersfield, California

Kern's Movers & Shakers

Table of Contents

Settlers in the Kernville area welcomed the goods — and the gossip — that Andrew Brown's wagons brought to their ranches.

A man of great vision, Edward F. Beale developed the Tejon Ranch, south of Bakersfield, more than a century ago. A gift from his estate established the Beale Memorial Library in the early 1900s.

Schoolteacher Marianna Bohna, whose grandfather, Christian Bohna, settled on Kern Island in 1860, grew up in Woody and taught in the Bakersfield schools for many years.

Edward M. Kern's companions on the first leg of John C. Fremont's 1845 expedition to the West included such famous mountain men as Kit Carson, Old Bill Williams and Alexis Godey.

1
In the Beginning

"One of (Fremont's) chief aides was a painter from Philadelphia, a virile hotspur with a temperament matching his deep red hair."

Robert V. Hine, *In the Shadow of Fremont*

A first-rate mover and shaker was Edward Meyer Kern.

In fact, he sets the standard for this book. Like his name, which is derived from the Anglo-Saxon word meaning seed or kernel, Ned Kern is the vibrant core.

Most people think of the man for whom Kern County was named simply as John Charles Fremont's topographer. Nothing more.

But there is more, much more, to be said of this 19th century artist, scientist and fun-loving adventurer. The few weeks in the winter of 1845-46 that Kern spent in this region, existing on a diet of acorns and mule meat, marked the starting point of a truly remarkable career of outstanding service to his country.

Ironically, much of what is known today about Edward M. Kern's romantic career might have remained a mystery had it not been for the plumbing problems of a country hotel in Dingman's Ferry, Pennsylvania. In 1958, more than a century after Kern's death, the owners of the hotel, Mr. and Mrs. Fred Cron, found it necessary to move some boxes in the cellar to clear a path to the offending pipes. The boxes contained the journals, letters and sketches of Edward M. Kern.

Life magazine, which subsequently published portions of Kern's diary, reported that as the Crons "emptied the contents, they realized they had uncovered a treasure trove of history."

A further and somewhat disappointing bit of irony lies in the fact that upon making the discovery, the Crons contacted the Kern County Library in the hope that the institution would be interested in buying Kern's papers for its historical collection. Unfortunately, the library lacked the funds to make the purchase. Much of this original material now is held, under the title *Fort Sutter Papers,* by the Huntington Library in San Marino, California.

During his short life — Kern died in 1863 following an epileptic seizure, one month after his 40th birthday and less than three years before Kern County was established — the Philadelphia native played a vital role in shaping America's westward frontier. He even had a part in opening up trade with the Far East.

You can read about Kern's achievements, along with those of other early explorers and settlers, in the section of biographical sketches that follows this brief historical overview. However, to give you an idea of his importance in terms of both American and Kern County history, the topographer's contributions include:

- providing the U.S. government with graphic and factual information about previously uncharted areas of the Great Basin and California
- serving as commander of Sutter's Fort
- surviving Fremont's disastrous attempt to find a railroad route over the Rocky Mountains
- unveiling, through his maps and sketches for the U.S. Bureau of Topographical Engineers, the New Mexico Territory

- playing a key role in two U.S. Navy expeditions to the Far East and returning to San Francisco on the first Japanese ship ever to visit the United States.

Indeed, the people of Kern can take pride in Edward Meyer Kern, the man who unknowingly gave his name to their county.

John C. Fremont, who first passed through the region in 1843-44 with the famous frontiersmen Kit Carson and Alexis Godey, is perhaps the most famous of the early explorers. But "the pathfinder," as Fremont is familiarly known, was not the first, nor was he the first American citizen to enter what is now Kern County. That honor goes to Jedediah Strong Smith, considered by many historians to be the greatest of the 19th century mountain men.

Jed Smith's explorations in 1827 were followed in 1834 by those of Joseph Reddeford Walker, the discoverer of Walker's Pass, the present-day link, via Highway 178, between the desert area and the Kern River Valley. Walker entered the pass from the east, after crossing the desert and stopping to take on water at

Joseph Reddeford Walker, who discovered Walker's Pass in 1834 (the present-day link between the Kernville area and the Mojave Desert), later became one of John C. Fremont's most trusted scouts.

Indian Wells, near Inyokern.

Two notable Spaniards preceded the Americans: Commander Pedro Fages, in 1772, the first European to enter the area, and Father Francisco Garces, a trailblazing priest who came four years later. The diaries of their travels provide the first written accounts of Kern County's history.

Thousands of American Indians — mainly Yokuts and Piute — were the first known inhabitants of Kern County. Members of these tribes served as guides for the early explorers. Their numbers diminished rapidly after the white man's arrival.

Prospectors, drawn by the lure of gold, were among the county's first settlers in the 1850s. Richard Keyes, the founder of the once-thriving town of Keyesville, arrived in 1853, three years after California was admitted to the Union. By 1856, Abia Lightner had in-

---

Prospectors, drawn by the lure of gold, were among the county's first settlers in the 1850s.

---

stalled the first quartz mill there, using an ox team to haul the heavy equipment over the rugged roads from San Francisco, including a final stretch over Greenhorn Mountain, by way of a road built by William P. Lynn, for whom Linn'sValley is named although spelled differently.

That same year, James M. Glenn established Glennville, in an area that drew a number of families in the next decade, including the Woodys and Bohnas. Settlers such as Walker Rankin also began to establish ranches in Walker's Basin and the nearby South Fork area.

Farther to the south, John Brite and his family were putting down roots in the Tehachapi area, soon to be followed by the Cuddebacks and the Cummings. Edward Fitzgerald Beale was acquiring the first of the four Spanish land grants that ultimately would make up his immense Tejon Ranch, and Henry Miller, who owned large tracts of land throughout the San Joaquin Valley, also was becoming a major force in the economy.

Christian Bohna, who came in 1860, one year before the beginning of the Civil War, was the first permanent resident of Bakersfield. The leading Bakersfield pioneer, though, was Colonel Thomas Baker, the town's visionary founder, land reclaimer and surveyor.

Still, for those bent on quick profits and an exciting life, the mountainous area of Kern County was the place to be in the 1860s. Keyesville, the original center of mining activity in the county, soon was replaced by Kernville, the site of the Big Blue Mine.

Havilah, the first county seat, was named by Asbury Harpending, a professed Confederate spy who claimed to have pocketed $800,000 in one year's time. Harpending, who made his profits by selling real estate rather than gold mining, is just one of the more colorful characters in Kern's long line of movers and shakers.

Starting with Delano in 1874, the Southern Pacific Railroad established a number of towns in Kern County within the next few years as it extended its route through the valley, over the Tehachapi Mountains and across the Mojave Desert. The stations provided commercial as well as transportation opportunities for farmers, ranchers and miners already living in the area.

KERN COUNTY MUSEUM

The first Delano station agent was Daniel Cecil; Emile Chauvin the first postmaster. Among those on hand to greet the railroad in Delano were Joel McMillen, James T. Clark, George Dyer, Archibald Leitch, John B. Hockett and Harry Quinn, whose son John R. Quinn later became Los Angeles County tax collector.

Drugstore owner Robert Trewin was Mojave's first postmaster in 1876. Elias Cohn, the Wells, Fargo and Company agent, also ran a general store in partnership with Edward Green of Tehachapi.

A quarter century later, the Santa Fe Railroad was the impetus for other permanent settlements in the county.

Shafter pioneers included N.E. Vandem, Harry and John Scarroni, Frederick W. Haag, Frederick E. Mannel and Fred Dequine. Wasco's first families were those of William A. Smith, E.B. Root, W.G. and A.J. McCombs, John Brittain, J.E. Anderson, Manuel Pimental, Tipton Matthews and Nathan Taussig.

The oil boom, which began about 1900, caused the formation of Taft and other places on the West Side. Once known as Boust City, for E. J. Boust — founder of Producers Guaranty Oil Company — the town went through a series of name changes before Harry Hopkins dubbed it Taft.

At about the same time, a few ranchers and dairy farmers were eking out a living in the area around Ridgecrest, originally called Crumville. But the northeastern part of Kern County lay largely dormant until the 1940s when the U.S. Navy chose China Lake as the site for its weapons testing center.

A common quality bonds all of the early explorers and settlers. Vision, foresight, an ability to inspire others, and a dogged determination to make a better life for themselves and others are its chief elements. It is the stuff of which movers and shakers of every generation are made.

Baker, Thomas — Today, with gasoline pumps, fast food restaurants and motels available in handy clusters along every major freeway, it's hard to imagine what "Baker's field" must have meant to travelers in the 1860s. For one thing, it meant a fairly large spread: Colonel Thomas Baker's original land grant amounted to 87,000 acres.

But more than anything it meant to travelers-who felt lucky if they covered 35 miles in a day's time, the promise of hay for their horses, cool well water to quench thirsts, and inside the home of Bakersfield's founder, a hot meal and perhaps a bed for the night. And all for free.

With that kind of hospitality, it's easy to see why Baker's field was a welcome sight. Yet the colonel (he earned his title in the Iowa state militia and also had served in both the Iowa and California legislatures before coming to the area then called Kern Island) was also a good businessman. He knew that if he gave people what they wanted and needed, they just might stay

around for awhile. And when it comes right down to it, that foresight more than anything else is what puts Thomas Baker in the ranks of the movers and shakers.

As one of his contemporaries, Benjamin Brundage, put it: "The colonel was the pioneer and did all that was in his power to induce immigrants to settle on the rich alluvial lands of this part of the San Joaquin Valley."

In reclaiming the land and making it tillable, Baker hired Indians to dig canals and build levees to help corral the meandering and sometimes rampaging Kern River. He also laid out the town's original plan and set aside land for a civic center in the same area where those buildings are today.

By constructing a road from Bena (now a Southern Pacific signal station near the Highway 58 Caliente cutoff, 12 miles east of Bakersfield) Baker expanded the market for farmers in the area. The roadway, which wound its way across creeks and up rigorous grades to Walker's Basin and Havilah, set up an important commercial link between the farmers in the lowlands and the miners in the mountain areas.

In 1872, a typhoid epidemic struck Bakersfield and Baker was one of those who died from the disease. His widow, Ellen, later married Ferdinand Tracy. (Ferdinand's nephew, William Tracy and his wife, Fannie, are the forerunners of the Tracy family that lives and farms in Buttonwillow.) The colonel's son, Thomas A. Baker, became a sheriff of Kern County. One of his direct descendants, Harold Brewer, died this year; another, Lawrence N. Baker, still lives in Bakersfield. Brewer's son, Chris, is a historical consultant and recently published, with Don Pipkin, a book on East Bakersfield.

Beale, Edward Fitzgerald — Truly one of the giants in western American history, Edward Fitzgerald Beale is known best in Kern County for his development of Tejon Ranch and for his family's many contributions to Bakersfield, most notably the gift that established the Beale Memorial Library in 1900 at Chester Avenue and 17th Street.

He was admired in his time for his many achievements as a Mexican War hero, explorer, superintendent of Indian Affairs in California, rancher and politician. "Beale successfully pursued a personal El Dorado of adventure, status and wealth," says Gerald Thompson in *Edward F. Beale & The American West.* "In so doing, he mirrored the dreams of countless Americans of his day."

Beale was the first to reach Washington with the official news — and nuggets to prove it — of the gold strike at Sutter's Mill. He is known also for being the leader of the U.S. Camel Corps, one of the more peculiar experiments in American history.

The general (while settling Indian problems in 1856 he had the rank of brigadier-general in the state militia) was one of the first to suggest a canal route across Central America. He lived in the nation's capital for about 20 years — in Decatur House on Lafayette Square, now a historical monument — and became a close friend of President Ulysses S. Grant. In 1876-77, Beale served as U.S. minister to Austria-Hungary.

As the founder of Tejon Ranch, which before his death amounted to just under 270,000 acres, he was much respected in Bakersfield. In 1888, at a marathon banquet — it began at 8 p.m. and lasted until four the next morning — Beale, who was known in his time as "Mr. California," was hailed by the leading citizens of the town. He was recognized for his contributions to the state and the region, including his efforts to encourage railroad entrepreneurs to bring a line into Bakersfield proper after the Southern Pacific bypassed it and started a new town at Sumner, now East Bakersfield.

Few pioneer families have given as much to Bakersfield, in a financial sense, as the Beales. Following Beale's death in 1893, his wife, Mary, and son, Truxtun Beale (for whom Truxtun Avenue is named), provided the money for three large civic additions: the city's first

---

Fremont gained title to the Mariposa grant, the largest Spanish land grant in California, made a fortune from his gold mine there, then lost his money and the land.

---

public library, the clocktower (dismantled after the 1952 earthquake, its reproduction now stands at the Kern County Museum) and the Greek amphitheater at Beale Park.

Bohna, Christian — Considered the first permanant settler in Bakersfield, then called Kern Island, Christian Bohna arrived with his family in February 1860. After living for a time in Thomas Fitzgerald's abandoned house the Bohnas built a larger home of cottonwood tree logs thatched with tules in the vicinity of 24th and P streets. Following the flood of 1861, Colonel Thomas Baker appeared on the scene and offered Bohna $200 for his house and the rights to 160 acres. Bohna accepted and moved, with some members of his family, to Oregon.

One of Bohna's daughters, Sarah Louise, and her husband, Dr. Sparrell Woody, a graduate of St. Louis Medical School, left the valley floor and established the town of Woody in the Glennville area. Dr. Woody was named foreman of Kern County's first grand jury. The couple's son, Stonewall A. Woody, was elected county auditor in 1907 and held the position for many years. Both the Bohnas and the Woodys have many descendants in Kern County; many have made valuable contributions over the years.

Brown, Andrew — Due mainly to its liberal policy of credit, the A. Brown Company was a household word in the Kern River Valley and a major force in its economy for nearly a half-century.

Little cash exchanged hands at the stores Andrew Brown established in the 1860s in Kernville and Weldon. Farmers, ranchers and their employees charged their purchases, settling up once or twice a year when crops were harvested or livestock sold. Many a hopeful miner was extended the same opportunity.

The company's delivery wagon also served as a means of communication. In addition to conveying goods to isolated areas, the driver carried messages from one ranch to other and could always be counted upon to bring the latest news gathered in his travels throughout the community.

Andrew Brown, who was born in Donegal, Ireland in 1829, raised wheat and livestock on his large ranch in the South Fork area. He also built a sawmill and a flour mill. In time, he acquired extensive real estate holdings in Los Angeles. After his death, in 1909, his interests in the Kern River Valley were managed by his wife, Alice, the daughter of Judge Joseph W. Sumner, and his sons, Andy and Sumner Brown.

Fitzgerald, Thomas — Thomas Fitzgerald, an expert rifleman and hunter who served with John C. Fremont, may have come to the county first as early as 1834. In 1859, he built an adobe trading post in Glennville. The structure, situated near the Kern County Fire station in the mountain community, is the oldest known adobe still standing. Fitzgerald also had a small hut on Kern Island (present-day Bakersfield) which he used as a hunting lodge. Christian Bohna lived in this structure when he first arrived in 1860.

Fox, Joe — In Ridgecrest terms, Joe Fox is a pioneer, for he came there more than 50 years ago when the town barely existed. Pat Farris, publisher of the *Inyokern News Review,* says, "Everything that happened in the early days, Joe Fox set in motion."

Fox and his wife, Bessie, came to the area in 1934. He and his sons dug by hand the first water wells for their ranch, using a winch and bucket. It was the beginning of Ridgecrest's present water system. Elizabeth Hise, president of the Historical Society of the Upper Mojave Desert, said that the Foxes, fearing retaliation from the existing water supplier, dumped the dirt far out in the desert. The society plans to place a marker on the site of the original Fox wells.

In the 1940s, when the Navy came to China Lake, Joe Fox began subdividing land for homes and donated large portions to various churches. He also gave the land for the USO building and for the James Monroe School.

Fox was active in numerous civic organizations and helped establish Camp Owen. His sons, Larry and Elliot Fox, still live in the area.

Fremont, John Charles — Kern, the name we now know so well, first appeared officially on a map published by the U.S. government in 1848. It is John Charles Fremont who put it there.

The name appears twice on the map that records Fremont's surveys in 1844-45 of Oregon and Upper California: It denotes the river that rises in the Sierra and, following its westward course, the lake on the west side of the San Joaquin Valley into which it then drained. Fremont named both in honor of his topographer, Edward M. Kern, who actually had done the mapping during the winter of 1844-45. Twenty-one years later, when the county was formed, Kern was the chosen name.

Fremont was called "the pathfinder" in his day but "pathmarker" might have been a more suitable nickname. For the surveys he did for the U.S. government in the 1840s provided some of the first accurate maps of the previously explored trails in the West, as well as scientific data about the region's wildlife and natural resources. In doing so, he provided the goverment with the kind of information it needed to encourage westward expansion.

One of the most controversial figures in American history, Fremont's career was marked with a number of highs and lows. He gained title to the Mariposa grant, the largest Spanish land grant in California, made a fortune from his gold mine there, then lost his money and the land. He was court martialed by the Army in 1848 — convicted but later pardoned by President Polk. The national respect and admiration he gained in his earlier western expeditions turned to shame and disgrace following his disastrous attempt to find a trans-

Hopkins pointed to the president's picture and said, "Name it Taft."

continental railroad route across the Rocky Mountains in the winter of 1848-49. Yet in 1850 he became one of California's first U.S. Senators and in 1856 was the Republican Party's first presidential nominee.

Although Fremont never lived in Kern County he once owned a sizeable portion of the San Emigdio Ranch, which he bought in 1853 for $2,000. The pathfinder spent his last years living in the West but died in 1887 in New York.

Godey, Alexis — A fur trapper and frontiersman, Alexis Godey had traveled throughout much of the West before joining John C. Fremont's expedition of 1844. From then on, Godey became a lifelong friend of Fremont. It was Godey who rescued Edward M. Kern and other survivors of Fremont's disastrous trek across the Rockies in 1848.

In the mid-1860s, Godey, a native Missourian of French-Canadian descent, settled in Kern County. For a short time he was engaged in sheepraising with Edward F. Beale at Tejon Ranch (Beale dissolved the partnership when he became dissatisfied with the frontiers man's handling of money) and Godey later owned a portion of San Emigdio Ranch. Godey, along with Pablo Galtes and others, was instrumental in laying the groundwork for the first Catholic Church in Bakersfield.

Hopkins, Harry A. — Although Harry Hopkins' life was filled with notable achievements, he is remembered chiefly for giving the city of Taft a respectable name.

Initially, the town was known as Boust City, then Moro. However, a Wells Fargo office in San Luis Obispo County had a similar name. So, hoping to avoid confusion, the Southern Pacific Railroad added the letter "n" to the word, making it Moron. This only made matters worse. The townspeople objected for obvious reasons and the government said it wouldn't do because a post office in Colorado had the same name.

Then along came Harry Hopkins, whose appointment in 1909 as the town's first postmaster was made by President Howard A. Taft. While discussing the problem with the Bakersfield postmaster, R.A. Edmonds, Hopkins pointed to a picture of the president on the wall above Edmonds' desk and said with conviction, "Name it Taft." So it became and so it has remained.

Hopkins, who came to McKittrick in 1904 to manage the Chanslor-Canfield Midway Oil Company, was one of several businessmen who formed Taft's water company and its first ice delivery service. He served as mayor from 1914 to 1917.

In 1932, as chairman of the California Highway Commission, Hopkins was instrumental in the construction of Highway 33 between the Cuyama Valley and Ojai. Pete Gianopulos of Taft recalls attending the barbecue that celebrated the opening of the road.

Kern, Edward Meyer — Edward M. Kern, John C. Fremont's topographer and the man for whom Kern County is named, had an uncanny knack for spending the yuletide season in unusual and sometimes hazardous situations.

Kern welcomed the Christmas season of 1845, during which he mapped (and nearly drowned in) the river

The site of Alexis Godey's former residence now is owned by the Coca-Cola Bottling Company.

which also bears his name, on top of Walker's Pass with other members of Fremont's Third Expedition to the West. In his diary, the 21-year-old artist and scientist described his impressions of the Joshua trees, mistakenly referred to as "yucas," that lit the darkness:

"Our Christmas Eve was spent in a most unchristmaslike manner ... The guard had set fire to a number of Yuca trees, lighting up the scene most beautifully. I lay a long while in my bed watching the distant fires ..." Kern wryly noted that on Christmas Day, "We dined, by way of change, on one of our old travel-worn mules, instead of a horse ..."

One year later, the Philadelphia native was at Sutter's Fort, serving as commander of the post. His responsibilities that winter included organizing the first relief effort to rescue the doomed Donner Party.

The winter of 1848-49 was a tragic time for Kern, one that would leave him with bitter feelings for Fremont, the leader he once admired. As a member of Fremont's ill-timed and poorly planned fourth expedition across the Rocky Mountains, he was one of the fortunate few who survived. The rest died from exposure and starvation.

But the following year found him in good spirits, celebrating the holiday season in lively style in Santa Fe, New Mexico, with other members of the Odd Fellows Lodge. However, the fact that he is credited with preparing the first map of the New Mexico Territory for the U.S. Topographical Engineers shows the more serious side of his work during that time.

Perhaps the most unusual of Kern's Christmases occurred in Japan in 1859-60, while he was serving in the U.S. Navy. Using his scientific training and artistic skills, he charted the newly opened trade routes in the northeastern Pacific and made watercolor sketches to illustrate the people and the culture of the then-unknown empire of Japan. Kern's ship was wrecked off the coast of Japan and he and other members of the crew were stranded there for several months.

As always, Kern landed on his feet. He made a triumphant return to San Francisco on March 17, 1860 aboard the Kanrin Maru, the first Japanese vessel ever to visit the United States. More than a passenger, Kern also assisted with the navigational chores on the trip across the Pacific.

Owing to a lack of congressional funding, much of Kern's work never was published. Yet he played a chief role in giving the American government the factual knowledge it needed to encourage westward expansion and to open even wider the door to the Far East. Many of his field notes, letters, and watercolor sketches are held by the Huntington Library in San Marino and the U.S. Navy. The National Portrait Gallery of the Smithsonian Institution also has several of his oil paintings.

A life-long bachelor, Kern's Sutter's Fort journals show that he fell in love with a woman there — unfortunately she was already married. He had no known descendants.

Lightner, Abia T. — Like many of the early settlers in the Kern River Valley, the elusive promise of gold drew Abia Lightner to the area. But Lightner brought

As the proprietor of the Onyx Store east of Kernville, William Scodie often found himself the victim of armed robberies at the hands of such notorious bandits as Tiburcio Vasquez.

something else besides himself: a stamp mill, with which to refine the quartz. In 1858, Lightner began ranching in Walker Basin. His daughter, Lavinia, married Walker Rankin; descendants of their large family still own property in the area, including the popular guest ranch operated by Helen Rankin.

Petersen, Neils Peter — In 1863, Neils Peter Petersen gave up the sea for the land. And a wise choice it turned out to be for the enterprising Dane.

Within 10 years after he went to work at the Big Blue Mine, N.P., as he was familiarly known, had a good-sized ranch and was the owner-operator of the Kernville Hotel. (*The Havilah Miner* said it was "first-class".)

A short time later, he started a harvesting service, using a mobile, steam-powered threshing machine, and began operating a stage line that even now, more than a century later, runs regularly between Kernville and Bakersfield.

Initially passengers rattled along the Kernville-Caliente road in semi-enclosed "mud wagons' drawn by four-horse teams. Ever the pioneer, Petersen switched to automobiles in the early 1900s — with mixed results.

Because of a scarcity of spare parts and skilled mechanics, the first "bus," a Cadillac touring car, soon was put out to pasture on the Petersen ranch. The Cadillac was replaced, says Kernville historian Bob Powers, by a "Stanley Steamer that blew up in Havilah three days after it was put into operation." In 1912, after laying a succession of cars to rest on his ranch, Petersen sold the Kernville Stage to Charles Hand and William Tibbets.

The present owner of the Kernville Stage and Freight Line is Tom Bailey of Fresno.

Petersen, who sailed the seas on merchant ships and in the U.S. Navy from the time he was 14 until he was 23, served his adopted country well. In 1902, Petersen was appointed to the Kern County Board of Supervisors. Elected in 1904, he served until 1909. Members of his family still living in the mountain area include Amos Petersen and his daughter, Patsy; Walter "Boss" Petersen and his son, Jake; and Thelma Petersen Frazier of Glennville. Amos's daughter, Barbara Ridarte, is a resident of Bakersfield.

Scodie, William — William Scodie, a native of Prussia, was the first proprietor, in 1861, of the Onyx Store. One of the Kern River Valley's treasured landmarks, the present structure replaced the original one made of adobe. In addition to the store, Scodie's Station, as Onyx then was known, included a barn, a stable and a blacksmith shop. Life was far from peaceful in the early days and Scodie successfully survived a number of armed robberies. In 1875, the intrepid storekeeper, along with a man named Morris Jacoby, was tied up by members of the notorious outlaw Tiburcio Vasquez's gang and relieved of $800, a change of clothes and a string of horses.

As a boy, Scodie went to sea as a cook on a merchant ship and worked in the same capacity in Chile and in Australia before coming to California. He opened a hotel in Keyesville in 1855 and operated it for five years before moving to Onyx. Scodie died in 1898 at 71. He was married twice, the first time to an Indian called White Blanket.

Smith, Thomas Hooper — Thomas H. Smith, one of the early ranchers in the South Fork, has many descendants in the Kern River Valley. In 1863 Smith began building ditches to bring water from the river for use in irrigating his crops, as did John Nicoll and George Clancy. Smith's daughter, Henrietta, married Jim Powers; they were the parents of 14 children. In 1900, Powers was employed as forest ranger by the U.S. Department of the Interior. His territory included the mountanious region and extended as far as Little Lake in the Mojave Desert.

Stevens, Elisha — A trapper, explorer, soldier, Indian agent and farmer, Capt. Elisha Stevens was widely recognized as kind, caring and generous. *In the Heart of the Golden Empire*, Richard C. Bailey notes that Stevens welcomed Ellen and Thomas Baker with a gift of two hogs, six hens and a rooster. "The family never forgot the kindness."

Stevens first came to California in 1844, when he guided a wagon train from Missouri to the Sacramento Valley, the first to cross the Sierra Nevada successfully. The route, which became known as the California Trail, was the same one taken by the Donner Party. The captain (he served in the war with Mexico and helped make California a part of the United States) explored other parts of the San Joaquin Valley. In 1850, he farmed in the San Jose area where Stevens Creek bears his name. Stevens came to Kern Island in 1860 and had

a farm in the vacinity of Bakersfield Memorial Hospital. He died in Bakersfield in 1887 at 84.

Sumner, Joseph Warren — Judge Sumner, as he was known to everyone in the Kern River Valley, was justice of the peace in Kernville for 40 years, from 1870 to 1910, one year before he died at 92. In those days, justices received no salary. Instead they got their pay from the fines they charged for offenses and Sumner was noted for his creativity in finding ways to collect his pay.

Explorer Elisha Stevens, an early settler on Kern Island, welcomed Thomas and Ellen Baker with gifts that the newcomers must have found useful: two hogs, six hens and a rooster.

He is equally known for his ownership of the Sumner Mine, later called the Big Blue Mine. (The manner in which the mine was unearthed is one of the favorite stories in Kern County history: A prospector named Lovely Rogers discovered it in 1860 while looking for a stray mule.) The Big Blue was the most productive and profitable mine in the area for the next 25 years. It attracted even more miners and investors to the area, many of whom settled in the Kern River Valley.

Yen Ming, who came to Kern County in 1874 as a railroad laborer, later owned a farm on present-day Ming Avenue and became known as "The Chinese potato king."

Using a stack of crates as his podium, Lloyd W. Frick addresses an early meeting of Calcot Ltd.

The superintendent of Tejon Ranch for many years, J.J. Lopez led a historic sheep drive from Kern County to Wyoming in the 1870s.

Jack Pandol checks the potential yield in the grape vineyards owned by Pandol Brothers, a Delano corporation that operates on an international scale.

2
Fertile Fields

"With the breaking up of large holdings of land and the coming of small farmers...Kern County will become one of the chief sources of food supply in the West."

Wallace M. Morgan, *History of Kern County*

Agriculture in Kern County has undergone vast changes since the first farms and ranches were established in the 1850s and 1860s in the mountain and valley regions.

But it rarely has been uneventful.

Consider, for example, this banner headline in the June 15, 1915 edition of *The Bakersfield Californian:* "Chinese gets $10,000 for his potato crop: Keester and Smith sell Yen Ming's spuds for $1.57 1/2 per 100 pounds."

After noting that the contract represented the highest purchase price for the season, the article went on to say, "No rancher in Kern County raises more potatoes than does Yen Ming. His place just a few miles from this city is one of the most valuable tracts in this section of the state ..."

The newspaper writer, of course, meant "valuable" in terms of its agricultural productivity. Little did he know that the area surrounding Ming's farm one day would become the site of the Valley Plaza Regional Shopping Center.

And surely he would never have imagined that eventually, through modern farming methods and complex irrigation systems, huge areas of "desert" land — then covered with sagebrush and inhabited mainly by jack rabbits — would be brought under cultivation or that

the expertise of Kern County agricultural leaders would become known throughout the world.

All of that growth was a long way in the future in those pre-World War I days. And even more so in the Civil War days when settlers began moving into Kern County. Yet even then farmers and ranchers were eager to find ways to increase their yields and improve their livestock.

In 1862, when the Bakersfield area was known as Kern Island, Alexander McCray introduced short-horned Durham cattle. By breeding the new stock with the wild and scrawny herds brought here by the Spaniards about 40 years earlier, he was able to produce better quality beef. The cattle industry already was thriving in the mountainous areas, where the ranchers (many are mentioned in the first chapter of this book) had established herds in the 1850s to serve the mining camps. Before long, ranchers such as the Cuddebacks of Tehachapi would graze their livestock in the Mojave Desert as far as Randsburg, digging wells and erecting windmills to provide water for their herds.

Solomon Jewett and his brother, Philo, the sons of a Vermont sheepraising family, brought purebred Merinos to Kern County in the 1860s and cross-bred them with flocks that had been established by the early Californians. As historian Harland Boyd notes, the Jewetts "not only improved their own flocks, but through the sales of blooded sheep, they helped improve the quality of flocks throughout the West."

In the next century, Philo's son, Hugh Jewett would become a prominent farmer in the Arvin area. (A noted philanthropist, Jewett's name can be found in association with many organizations listed in the chapter titled, "Catch the Vision.")

A wide number of families of French and Basque descent became involved in sheepraising in various parts of the county. Among the earliest were J.B. Berges, A.P. Eyraud, Andre Vieux, the Faure brothers, Jules Villard, Leon Bimat, Pierre Lambert, Anton Pauly, Vincent Mon, Louis Clerou, John Iriart, the Gerard brothers, Juan Ansolabehere and "Big Mike" Ansolabehere, Leonard Bidart, Thomas Echenique, Martin Etcheverry, Pascal Eyrhabide, Gregorio Mendiburu, Domingo Othart, to name just a few. Many of these pioneers formed the core of the Kern County Woolgrowers Association.

More than a century ago, independent farmers began forming associations in an effort to pool their knowledge and to increase the market for their crops. The first Granges (then called the Patrons of Husbandry) were organized in 1874.

In 1914, the Kern County Farm Bureau was established, with Fred Hall as its first president. The agency, which today has about 1,400 members and is managed by Loron Hodge, also provides research and educational information and has a scope and influence that is nationwide.

Farmers' wives also have established associations to help educate the public about agriculture. Winifred Pandol of Delano is serving her second term as a vice president of California Women for Agriculture. Among other things, CWA has published a book on agriculture for third and fourth graders that is used in schools throughout the state.

The CowBelles, formed in 1946 as an auxiliary to the Cattlemen's Association, changed its name this year to the CattleWomen's Association. Peggy Morosa, who as 1987 "CowBelle of the Year" is the last to hold that title, says, "Our job is to promote the beef industry and we feel we will be taken more seriously with the new name." Cotton Wives helps promote that industry by sponsoring the annual Maid of Cotton competition.

Attempts to raise cotton began in the 1860s. However, it would not be until the 1920s that cotton would become a leading crop in Kern County and the West. This prominence came about through the introduction of the Acala strain, which was developed at the U.S. experimental station in Shafter under the direction of W.B. Camp. The one-variety cotton law was enacted by the California Legislature in 1925.

Two years later, area cotton farmers formed the California Cotton Cooperative Association (now the Bakersfield-based Calcot, Ltd.) in an effort to increase sales and broaden their market. Among the organizers were C. R. "Dick" Shannon and Lloyd Frick. Current president of Calcot is Tom Smith.

Owing to the large number of livestock, alfalfa was a major crop right from the start, in the mountainous areas and on the valley floor. In the 1870s, Henry Miller planted huge tracts of alfalfa in the Buena Vista area. The German-born cattleman irrigated his fields with overflow water from the Buena Vista Lake Bed, into which the Kern River empties.

Irrigation long has been a necessity in our semi-arid county. And water — particularly its ownership — has been the source of many legal conflicts. The most historic one was the lengthy court battle *(Haggin & Carr v. Miller & Lux)* of the 1880s between two legendary figures: James B. Haggin and Henry Miller. The ultimate decision, and the Miller-Haggin Agreement that followed, is a landmark in California water law.

In the past 25 years, great quantities of formerly barren land have become productive as a result of the Central Valley Project and other water programs. Many people have taken leadership roles in the development and management of water resources, including legislators whose contributions are included in the chapter titled "Law Makers and Keepers."

Among those not mentioned elsewhere, or in the biographical sketches that follow this introduction, are Mary Collup, the current president of the Water Association of Kern County, William E. Moore, Jr., a former president of Tejon Ranch; Jerry Cappello, president of the Wheeler Ridge-Maricopa Water Storage District and its engineer-manager, Arnold Rummelsberg; Milo E. Hall, who heads the North Kern Water Storage District; Gene Lundquist of Calcot; Cliff Trotter, engineer-manager of the Arvin-Edison Water District; businessman Roland Curran and Hal Sparks, whose voice was heard for many years on the radio program, "On the Water Front."

The potato industry began to flourish about 1920 in the Shafter area. And about 10 years earlier, James B. McFarland, founder of the town that bears his name, introduced pump irrigation. He also was instrumental in the formation of the McFarland Creamery.

Grapes and tree fruit were established early in Kern County. By the 1880s, apple orchards were thriving in Tehachapi. English families who settled in the Kern

Tom Akers, Jr. of Calcot became the first U.S. cotton salesman to visit the People's Republic of China in 1973. Here he takes time out from his duties to visit the Great Wall.

Give SOUTHERN LIVING for Mother's Day—and save $$$$!

Send a one-year (12 issues) gift subscription of SOUTHERN LIVING to each of the following, and bill me later for $17.95 per gift—a savings of $4.00 off the regular subscription rate of $21.95. I understand this special gift rate can be used only by subscribers to SOUTHERN LIVING.

Special gift rate for SOUTHERN LIVING® subscribers only!

GIFT #1

Name _____

Address _____

City/State/Zip _____

Sign card: _____

GIFT #2

Name _____

Address _____

City/State/Zip _____

Sign card: _____

YOUR NAME

Name _____

Address _____

City/State/Zip _____

Southern Living®
P.O. Box 830119
Birmingham, AL 35283

This offer good in the states of AL, AR, AZ, CO, DC, DE, FL, GA, KS, KY, LA, MD, MO, MS, NC, NM, OK, SC, TN, TX, VA, and WV. All other subscriptions, $24.00/yr.

SLAU7PI

County Land Company's short-lived Rosedale colony grew several kinds of fruit in the 1890s. Orchards later were planted by growers in Wasco, McFarland, Shafter, and in the Arvin-Lamont area.

Vineyards were planted before 1900 in Delano, now known as the "grape capital of the world." The grape industry would see a rapid expansion in the Arvin area, particularly after 1920, when the DiGiorgio Corporation began its operation there.

There can be little doubt the pioneer farmers would be astounded by today's billion dollar ag industry and the diversity of crops grown here. As ag writer Tim Heinrichs puts it, "Kern County agriculture includes everything from exotic kiwi fruit garnishing the upscale salad bar to mundane field corn sliced into silage and served as a dairy herd's main course."

One thing that hasn't changed: the caliber of people involved in agriculture. Farmers and ranchers are by their very nature visionaries, well-known for their unwillingness to give up even in the toughest times — and there have been plenty of those. Over the years, the movers and shakers who have risen from the fertile fields of our county are a bountiful crop in their own right.

Agnetti, Louis — A pioneer grain and farm equipment dealer, Louie Agnetti was born in Arizona in 1900 and came with his parents to Bakersfield when he was six months old. As a young man, he started the San Joaquin Grain Company, a feed mill at 14th and D streets. (The building now houses the Golden Empire Gleaners, a voluntary organization that distributes produce and other foods to a number of local agencies.)

Agnetti and his wife, Doreta, later bought the Allis-Chalmers Agency and renamed it the San Joaquin Tractor Company. Louie was the president. The couple soon took in Sam Tobias as a partner, and because he was a good salesman, made Tobias vice president and general manager. (Tobias also was a noted philanthropist and fund-raiser — the football field at Garces High School is named Tobias Field in his honor.)

An organizer of the Italian Heritage Dante Association, Agnetti was the recipient of the group's first Columbian Award in 1964. Before his death in 1985, he donated money for a fountain in the association's park.

Amenta, Harry — A graduate of the University of Baltimore Law School, Bakersfield resident Harry Amenta first became associated with agriculture in the 1930s with the DiGiorgio Fruit Corporation in Florida. He came here in the late 1940s as a troubleshooter for the Bakersfield Dehydration Company, which later was absorbed by DiGiorgio. During World War II, Amenta was chief of the War Food Administration's dehydrated food division.

Using Bakersfield as a base, Amenta organized the International Fertilizer and Feed Company in association with several businessmen. The company's first project was the purchase and processing of several thousand pounds of Kern County potatoes for the manufacture of whiskey by Schenley. International Fertilizer became the parent company for about a dozen other firms connected with the agriculture industry.

Amenta served on the 1963 Kern County Grand Jury, and the same year was appointed by President John F. Kennedy to the first trade mission to Mexico. The agribusinessman also has been an advisor to Bakersfield Junior Achievement and cochaired the building committee for Our Lady of Perpetual Help Catholic Church. He is the recipient of the Italian government's Order of Cavaliere. Harry's brother, Sam Amenta, is manager of the Italian Heritage Dante Association.

Bottorff, Allen — One of California's foremost authorities on water, Allen Bottorff was the first president of the Kern County Water Agency, and from 1960 to 1968 represented the agency as chairman of the State Water Contractors Audit Committee. In 1960, the year the State Water Bond Act was approved by voters, he served as president of the Feather River Project Association, later called the California Water Resources Association.

All of Bottorff's water-related positions were non-salaried and during this time he raised cotton and alfalfa on his farm near Buttonwillow. Following his two terms on the water agency board, Bottorff continued to act as a consultant and in 1973 was a speaker at the Kern County Business Outlook Conference. In 1956, the Indiana native was named "Farmer of the Year" by the Bakersfield Kiwanis Clubs. Now retired, he makes his home in Bakersfield.

Burtch, Lewis — Jack rabbits drove former Kern County agricultural commissioner Lewis Burtch into public service. For a number of seasons, Burtch's small farm in the Weedpatch area suffered an infestation of the lively and voracious hares. So in 1923, he took a part-time job with the county agriculture office to help solve the problem.

The Nebraska native, who served for 29 years and was agricultural commissioner when he retired in 1951, was widely respected for his persistence in standardizing the growing and handling of crops. Burtch, who died in 1960 at the age of 70, was instrumental in the formation of the Kern County Seed Potato Association.

Camp, S.A. — The annals of Kern County farming are filled with success stories and one of them is that of Saul Camp, who arrived in 1923, almost penniless, and died 34 years later a multi-millionaire. In addition to his vast farming and ginning operations, the South Carolina native developed one of the foremost horse racing stables in the nation — at one time there were 38 Camp horses running at Santa Anita under the supervision of Joe O'Brien — and numerous business interests, including an auto dealership.

Saul Camp, the older brother of W.B. Camp, first worked for the Kern County Land Company and his wife, Nellie, cooked for the field hands. In 1925, the couple invested their savings in a small farm in the Shafter area and with their son and daughter, worked the fields themselves. Within a short time, Saul Camp

Joe O'Brien, who managed S.A. Camp's stables for many years, is considered one of the outstanding harness racing drivers of all time. OBrien also developed a large training facility in Shafter.

formed a farming partnership with Lawson Lowe and Harry West. The company was called Camp, West and Lowe. When the partners bought a large parcel of land at Highway 99 and Lerdo Highway, they named it Cawelo. In 1947, Camp formed his own company with his son, James Y. Camp.

At various times, Saul Camp worked in concert with a number of other farmers, including Kenneth Mebane and Bill Lachenmaier.

The California Assembly passed a resolution recognizing Camp's contribution to the state's agriculture industry. In 1956, the Shafter Chamber of Commerce named him its "Man of the Year."

Today the S.A. Camp Companies is devoted mainly to real estate development. Attorney James S. Camp, the son of Jim and Betty Camp, is the president. Saul's daughter, Willene, the wife of vice president Donald Hart, is a director as was her mother, 96-year-old Nellie Camp. Fred Carlisle, Jr., a non-family member, is the secretary-treasurer.

Camp, Wofford Benjamin — One of the many honors W.B. "Bill" Camp received in his lifetime was the Horatio Alger Award, presented to him in 1984 by Dr. Norman Vincent Peale in the grand ballroom of the Waldorf Astoria Hotel in New York. Perhaps more than any other recognition he attained in his lifetime, the

"rags to riches" award personifies the life of Camp, who is credited with being chiefly responsible for the modern cotton industry in Kern County and California.

Camp, who paid his first tuition at Clemson College with the money he had earned picking cotton as a boy in his native South Carolina, came to California in 1917. He was sent here by the U.S. Department of Agriculture to develop cotton as a crop in the west, for use in the construction of military aircraft. When World War I ended, he established the government experimental station at Shafter. (He was assisted in his selection of the site by Dick Stansbury, agricultural inspector in the area.) The idea of growing cotton was unpopular in California at the time — agronomists considered it a "poverty crop."

But Camp set out to prove the experts wrong.

One of the strains developed at the station was a productive, long-staple variety called Acala, named for the area in Mexico where it first was found. Through the leadership of Camp, and others, the California one-variety cotton law was passed in 1925.

In the 1930s, Camp held a position with the U.S. Chamber of Commerce. In 1936, the farmer founded W.B. Camp & Sons. Camp's sons by his first wife, the former Georgia App who died in 1943, are Don Camp, who now manages the farming operation, and Bill Camp, Jr., a Southern California real estate developer. In 1956, W.B. Camp married Louise Wise, the widow of a South Carolina cotton farmer. Bill and Louise Camp served on the national board of Freedoms Foundation. The farmer died in 1986 at the age of 92.

Cattani, Arnold T. — Vineland-Arvin area farmer Arnold Cattani is well-known for his work in agriculture and cattle-raising and for breeding outstanding thoroughbred racing horses. ("Arksoni" became a famous handicap horse in the mid-1960s.)

Cattani came to Kern County as a child with his Italian-born parents, Peter and Henrietta Cattani, who bought a farm in the Vineland district. In 1925, after his graduation from Bakersfield High School, where he was a member of Howard Dickson's Agriculture Club, Arnold formed a farming partnership with his brother, the late William L. Cattani. The Cattanis built their first cotton gin in Vineland in 1938 and over the next 20 years erected or acquired several others before selling their ginning operation to Producers Cotton Oil Company in 1957. The brothers also were instrumental in developing the Wheeler Ridge area.

In 1972 Arnold Cattani turned over his farming interests to his son, Arnold Cattani, Jr., who has an MBA from Harvard Business School. The senior Cattani continues to manage the family's 12,000 acre cattle ranch in the Tehachapi Mountains.

Over the years, Cattani has given encouragement and support to his fellow farmers and to many community organizations, including the Arvin Women's Club. He donated the land for the Oakley Memorial Hall at Twin Oaks and the Kern County Fire Station at Loraine. He is married to the former Corinne Kovacevich. Their daughter, attorney Maryellen Cattani, is general counsel for the Transamerica Corporation in San Francisco.

Chavez, Cesar — Union organizer Cesar Chavez has made an impact on agriculture that will not soon be forgotten. And although many growers disagree with his policies and tactics, more than a few have a grudging respect for the president of the United Farm Workers of America.

It was Chavez who brought farmworkers' rights into the mainstream of American consciousness starting in 1962 when the Yuma, Arizona native formed the National Farm Workers Association. This group was merged in 1966 with the Agricultural Workers Organizing Committee of the AFL-CIO to form the United Farm Workers Organizing Committee of Delano. The result was the now-famous Delano grape strikes of the late 1960s, which drew national attention from the media and the interest of numerous political leaders, including Senator Robert Kennedy.

Through Chavez's persistent efforts — and those of Bishop Roger Mahoney of Stockton (now the archibishop of Los Angeles), Governor Jerry Brown and Rose Bird, who wrote the legislation and was then a state agricultural official — the Agricultural Labor Relations Act was enacted. The law gave farmworkers a number of rights, ranging from health insurance to the prohibition of the use of the short-handled hoe. The UFW also built Agbayani Village in Delano, a housing development for elderly Filipino workers.

The 60-year-old Chavez and his wife Helen, now live at La Paz — the Spanish word for "peace" — his headquarters in Keene. In 1986, Chavez was one of those awarded the Ellis Island Medal in connection with the 100th anniversary of the Statue of Liberty.

Denison, Burt M. — Burt M. Denison established the first commercial pear orchard in Tehachapi in 1909, in association with his brother-in-law, Charles A. Lee, a former Kern County Recorder. Denison also had an interest in a Burbank canning factory. His Bartlett pears bore the label, "T-HACHA-P," which later was patented by the Tehachapi Fruit Growers Association.

Denison came to Tehachapi in 1888 as the station agent for the Southern Pacific. A few years later, he and his brothers-in-law, Dan and Jack MacFarlane, established the Oak Creek Lumber Company and operated a saw mill and box factory. Denison was instrumental in the formation of the California Pine Box Company, manufacturers of orange crates.

Dickson, Howard K. — During his lifetime, Howard K. Dickson was saluted as "Mr. Kern County Fair." And with good reason: he started it in 1925, with a group of 30 agriculture students and the pigs they raised.

Actually, the fair — and more specifically, the Junior Livestock Auction which today is the largest of its kind

ALAN FERGUSON/THE CALIFORNIAN

United Farm Workers president Cesar Chavez travels throughout the county but makes his home at "La Paz," his headquarters in Keene, southeast of Bakersfield.

in the world — began in 1920, one year after Dickson came to Bakersfield to teach in the high school's newly formed agriculture department. Raising pigs — one for each boy — was their first project. Some students lacked the money to participate, so Dickson asked banker Angus Crites to loan them the money. Crites did — with a handshake as the only collateral.

The first Purebred Swine Sale was held in May 1920. The profits from this sale were used to form the 15th District Agriculture Association, whose chief function is that of putting on the annual fair that now involves hundreds of youths and draws thousands of visitors each year.

Dickson served on the fair board for the next 50 years and was honored throughout the state and the nation for his services. He also is credited with securing the funding for the grandstand at the fairgrounds. When it was completed, it was named the Howard K. Dickson Pavilion.

At a banquet celebrating the ag teacher's half-century with the fair, cattle rancher Kenneth N. Mebane expressed the thoughts of many former students when he said, "Howard Dickson has been an inspiration to hundreds of boys and girls and has influenced an unbelievable number in the fields of agriculture. He was tough, but we learned ... there were no shortcuts or compromises."

Dickson, a native of Watsonville who did his academic work at the Berkeley and Davis campuses of the University of California, retired from teaching in 1960 but continued to be active until his death in 1975 at the age of 83. The teacher's son, Dr. Robert Dickson, was a well-known Kern County veterinarian.

Enns, Paul I. — In 1983, President Reagan appointed Shafter-area farmer Fred Enns to a six-year term on the 13-member Federal Farm Credit Board. The board is the policy-making body for two agencies: The Farm Credit System, composed of borrower-owned agricultural lending institutions, and the Farm Credit Administration, an independent federal agency charged with supervising and regulating the system.

Enns starting farming in Kern County in 1946 and served for 31 years on the Production Credit Association board of directors, including 12 as chairman. He also has given many years of service as a member of the 11th District Farm Credit Board and the Stockholders Advisory Committee of the Federal Intermediate Credit Bank in Berkeley. At the time of his presidential appointment, he was president of the Rosedale-Rio Bravo Water Storage District.

Etcheverry, John F. — John Etcheverry, a native of Rosedale and a member of a pioneer Basque family, has risen through the ranks of Tenneco West to become a senior vice president. He is known internationally as a pioneer in the development of linear irrigation. Bob Hartzell, executive vice president of the California Association of Winegrape Growers, has described Etcheverry as "one of the most creative thinkers I've ever met and an excellent farmer."

In 1986, upon the retirement of Tenneco West chief executive officer Tristan E. G. Krogius, Etcheverry assumed the bulk of Krogius' responsibilities but not the title. Etcheverry's duties include the supervision of Tenneco's food processing, farming and land development divisions. The executive has served on the boards of the California Table Grape Commission, the California Almond Board and Winegrowers of California.

Frick, Forrest — Forrest Frick began farming in the Arvin-Lamont area in 1919 and for more than 50 years was a leader in water development in Kern County by way of the Central Valley Water Project and the state water plan. He was a key figure in obtaining federal and other types of funding for the construction, in 1966, of the $46 million canal and distribution system that serves the Arvin-Edison Water Storage District. Frick also was instrumental in providing the community of Lamont with its first swimming pool.

Frick served the Arvin-Edison water district as president from 1942, when it was formed, to 1971. In 1987, his son, Howard Frick, was elected to the post. Forrest Frick, along with Frank Jeppi and Henry J. Brandt, provided the $100,000 that established the Bakersfield Rotary Foundation. Now 93, Frick was honored this year for his 51 years as a Rotarian.

Helping young people learn about agriculture was Howard K. Dickson's lifelong vocation. The Bakersfield High School teacher founded the Junior Livestock Auction in 1920 and was its guiding force for the next 50 years.

Frick, Kenneth — The son of pioneer farmer Forrest Frick, Kenneth Frick presently is the state executive director of the Agriculture Stabilization and Conservation Service of the U.S. Department of Agriculture. From 1969 to 1977, Frick was the federal administrator of the USDA agency. During his service in Washington, D.C., he headed the U.S. delegation of the International Cotton Advisory Committee in its meetings of the ICAC's 46 member nations and received a presidential citation from President Gerald Ford.

Giumarra, Joseph — Joe Giumarra, a native of Sicily who now is 88, made his first visits to Kern County in the 1920s to buy produce for the fruit stand his father, Salvatorre Giumarra, had in the Los Angeles wholesale market.

"I bought a truck and went to the Imperial Valley, buying cantaloupes; to Bakersfield and Arvin to get good early grapes," Joe says. "It was awfully dangerous going on the old Ridge Route in those days."

The Giumarras came to North America from their native Sicily in 1912. They first sold fruit from a pushcart in Toronto, then worked at various jobs in Detroit and New York City. By the time they arrived in Los Angeles in 1920, they had saved enough money to buy the truck and, a few years later, were able to send for Joe's mother and the rest of the family — his sister Esther (since married to Dominick Corsaro) and his brothers, Fred, George and John. (The fruit stand was the nucleus of Giumarra Brothers Fruit Company, which now is the largest wholesale produce firm in Southern California.)

In the 1930s, the Giumarras began buying small farms in the Edison area, one parcel at a time. Today, the family farms 15,000 acres and is the biggest grower/packer/shipper of table grapes in the United States. Giumarra Vineyards winery was established in 1946. It sold only bulk products until 1975 when the family began bottling wines under their own label.

Joe Giumarra still is a working member of the operation, as are George Giumarra and Dominick Corsaro. John Giumarra was active until his death in 1986. Joe's son, Sal, is president. His son Al is a vice president as are the other sons of the founders: George Giumarra, Jr., Robert Corsaro, and John Giumarra, Jr. Gary Giumarra, the son of John, Sr., also is involved in the management.

John Giumarra, Jr., a graduate of Stanford Law School, was chairman of the 1983 convention of the United Fruit and Vegetable Association in Anaheim which drew more than 5,000 people from all parts of the world. His wife, Pamela, chaired the conference's women's division.

Haggin, James Ben Ali — In 1850, James B. Haggin, then 29, gave up his law practice in his native Kentucky and came to California to seek his fortune. And a fortune it turned out to be, for Haggin, who was one of the founders of the Kern County Land Company, left an estate of $15 million when he died in 1914 and at one time owned, with his partner, Lloyd Tevis, an estimated 400,000 acres in Kern County.

Unlike many other pioneers of the gold rush days, Haggin (whose middle name was the maiden name of his mother, the American-born daughter of a Turkish physician) was a shrewd investor. Shortly after coming to San Francisco, Haggin formed a partnership with George Hearst, Marcus Daly and Tevis. Together, they developed the famous Homestake gold mine and the Anaconda copper mine.

Haggin and Tevis began buying land in the Central Valley in the 1870s and developed extensive irrigation projects, including the one which used Kern River water in this county. The cattle ranchers objected — in particular, Henry Miller and William Lux — to the diversion of water to farmlands. In the 1880s, the legal issue of riparian rights was bitterly contested on both sides. The case eventually was carried to the California Supreme Court and the Legislature, where a law was passed that recognizes, even today, that irrigation is a public necessity.

Haggin's headquarters in Kern County was the Bellevue Ranch on Old River Road (now the site of Tenneco West's headquarters). Haggin developed an extensive horse-breeding farm in Lexington, Kentucky, and also raised thoroughbreds at Bellevue, which he visited often. Bakersfield residents enjoyed watching the land baron and his retinue debarking from his railway car at the Santa Fe (now Amtrak) station, then climbing into the procession of horse-drawn buggies that conveyed the party to his ranch.

Hair, Mickey — Mickey Hair grew up on his family's farm in Buttonwillow, where he raised champion steers as a 4-H project, and became a leading agribusinessman in helping underdeveloped nations of the world employ modern farming technology.

After 21 years of family farming (his grandfather, Hardy H. Hair, Sr., and father, Curtis T. Hair were Buttonwillow pioneers), Hair joined Honolulu-based Hawaiian Agronomics International in 1974 and spent the next 10 years in Indonesia. His responsibilities included the development and management of a 5,000-hectare rice estate, an irrigated and mechanized farm that included processing and storage facilities. Since the workers spoke no English, Hair became fluent in the Indonesian language, as did his wife, the former Betty Lou Mageors.

In 1986, the Shafter High School and Bakersfield College graduate was hired by Resources International of Fresno to help redesign and develop a large farming operation in the Middle East kingdom of Jordan. But

Inspecting potato test plots at the Shafter Experimental Station in the 1940s are Tom Hankins, manager of the Kern County Seed Potato Growers, W.B. Camp, Ed Peters and J.C. Jacobsen, Jr., president of the Kern County Seed Potato Growers.

KERN COUNTY MUSEUM

unfortunately, he was unable to complete the assignment. The 55-year-old Hair died of heart disease in Amman on June 20 of that year.

Harrison, George J. — The success of the California cotton industry is due in large part to the efforts of George Harrison. As an agronomist at the USDA Cotton Experimental Station at Shafter, he developed the Acala 4-42 strain of cotton in 1939. Harrison, a native of Texas who previously had worked for 14 years at a similar lab in Arizona, came to Kern County in 1934.

Houchin, C. Elmer — A key figure in the agriculture development of Kern County, Elmer Houchin also was a leader in oil, real estate and finance.

Houchin was one of the first to make raw lands productive by using large-scale leveling operations and extensive irrigation systems. At the time of his death in 1953, his ranches comprised 100,000 acres. In addition, he had large cattle holdings, operated five cotton gins and a number of grain warehouses, and kept a fine stable of racehorses. He also had major oil interests in the Paloma field and auto dealerships in Taft, Delano and Bakersfield.

Houchin came to Kern County in 1908 when he was 22. After working for Miller & Lux for five years, he bought the Pioneer Market in Taft. He soon began buying land. He laid out the townsite of Buttonwillow, donating lots for the construction of Community Baptist Church, a community clubhouse and the county branch library. In 1945, he purchased a 300-acre site north of Bakersfield's 24th Street from the Kern County Land Company and developed Westchester for residential, business and commercial use. He established the Houchin Community Blood Bank in Westchester in 1951 as a memorial to his mother.

Kovacevich Park was a gift to the people of Arvin from fruit grower John J. Kovacevich and his sisters, Mary Malovich, Corinne Cattani and Madeline Trino.

His brothers were agricultural leaders too. Lester Houchin served as president of the Buena Vista Water Storage District, and Okey W. Houchin also farmed in Buttonwillow. Several of their descendants still farm in the area.

Jacobsen, Jacob Christian, Jr. — J.C. "Jake" Jacobsen, who is of Danish descent, had farmed in Idaho before coming to Tehachapi in 1940. His efforts to bring supplemental water to the Tehachapi Valley began two years later.

"Those who were willing to open their eyes knew we had a serious overdraft in the late '40s," Jacobsen says now. "The future of the whole valley could be in jeopardy. We were losing about 20 feet of water each year in overdraft."

As a city councilman from 1944 to 1952 (and mayor for six years), Jacobsen was instrumental in the formation of the Tehachapi Soil and Water Conservation District. He was a founding director of the Tehachapi-Cummings Valley County Water District in 1963 and

served for about 10 years. It is through his efforts, and those of other leaders, that supplemental water now is pumped 3,200 feet over the mountain from the California Aqueduct for distribution by the Tehachapi-Cummings agency. This arrangement was made possible in part by a $2.5 million bond issue approved by 90 percent of the voters in the area in 1971.

Until his retirement from farming in 1973, Jacobsen had a sod farm and was involved for 20 years with a USDA seed testing program. Agriculturists from around the world visisted his acreage. He also went to other countries as an observer. His farm supplied the turf for San Francisco's Candlestick Park and for most of the football fields in the San Joaquin Valley, including Bakersfield College's Memorial Stadium.

He is a former president of the Kern County Seed Potato Growers Association and the Kern County Potato Growers Association, and has been an advisor to several state agencies. Jacobsen is a former trustee of both the elementary and high school district boards in Tehachapi. Jacobsen Junior High is named for him. He has been honored as an "outstanding citizen" by the County of Kern and the Tehachapi Chamber of Commerce.

Jeppi, Frank — (See "The Plus Factor")

Kennedy, J. Russell — When Russell Kennedy joined Calcot (then called the California Cotton Cooperative Association) in 1944, he already had a national reputation in the industry. The Texas A&M graduate previously had been the head of the U.S. Department of Agriculture's cotton classing operation for the western states, which was based in Dallas. He also had served with the USDA in Washington, D.C.

At the time Kennedy was named manager, the cooperative had been undergoing a variety of problems for a number of years. Kennedy proposed a plan — one that was considered radical at the time — that would put Calcot on a sounder footing. Among other things, the reorganization provided that members would be advanced only the amount that could be borrowed on their cotton and that Calcot would no longer purchase cotton in the open market or from other growers. Kennedy's marketing concepts proved successful and by 1949 Calcot was growing faster than the cotton industry. It had moved into its present complex on Brundage Lane in Bakersfield and had vastly increased its warehouse space. By the time Kennedy handed over the reins of leadership to G.L. "Sam" Seitz in 1971, Calcot had become a recognized leader in the United States and throughout the world.

Kennedy and his wife, Aileen, also gave their time and energy to many community organizations.

Kirschenmann, Wayne — Wayne Kirschenmann was born in Shafter and now farms in the Arvin-Lamont-Edison area. He has been a leader in promoting better relations within the potato industry and with the railroads. Kirschenmann Enterprises Inc. grows 13 different crops but the company's primary product is potatoes, which are shipped all over the United States and Canada. The label, "Edd's Sno-Wite," is named for Wayne's father, Edd Kirschenmann, who came to Kern County about 1930.

Wayne Kirschenmann and his wife, Virginia, presently are restoring 19 houses in Di Giorgio to provide adequate rental housing for people who live and work in the area. The Kirschenmanns recently purchased the old Di Giorgio home and gave it to the California Living Museum.

The Kirschenmann family — some spell the name with one "n" — is a large family, and many of its members live in Kern County.

Kovacevich, John J. — Currently, 77-year-old John Kovacevich is best known for his development of the popular red table grape, Flame Seedless. The Arvin farmer first began growing the grape in 1940 when Dr.

George Nickel, Jr., water expert, farmer and developer of Rio Bravo Resort, is the grandson of cattleman Henry Miller, a mover and shaker throughout California in the 19th century.

GREGORY IGER

John Weinberger of the USDA Experimental Station in Fresno gave him a few cuttings to test. From those few pieces, Kovacevich developed 120 vines and for three years was the only one growing the new variety. Today the Flame Seedless is grown by many and is exported to Mexico and Chile. Kovacevich also gave the grape its name, which occasionally is used incorrectly. "It irritates me to hear it called 'Red Flame,' ... that is not the right name."

Incidentally, during his speedboat racing days — he set four world records between 1937 and 1940 — the grape grower dubbed his craft the "Muscat Kid."

Truly one of the giants of California agriculture, Kovacevich is noted for being both opinionated and fair-minded. Although he disapproves of organized farm labor, he was one of the first growers to meet with Cesar Chavez. Kovacevich served eight years on the State Board of Agriculture. He has been a member of the board of directors of the California Grape and Tree Fruit League since its inception in 1936 and was president in 1949-50.

A native of Fresno whose father and grandfather came to the valley from Yugoslavia in the 1900s, Kovacevich began farming in the Arvin area in 1928. His present operation includes about 1,200 acres of table grapes and tree fruits.

Although he and his wife, Beverly, who is the sister of Supervisor Mary K. Shell, make their home in Bakersfield, the Kovacevich family has been active in the Arvin community. In 1976, the grower and his sisters, Corinne Cattani, Mary Malovich and Madeline Trino, donated the five-acre Kovacevich Park. They later were honored by the Arvin Chamber of Commerce. Kovacevich's sons, John and Michael, and one of his daughters, Mary Anne Bek, are involved in the farming operation. Another daughter, Jayne Ellen, teaches high school in northern California.

Lopez, Jose Jesus — J.J. Lopez, as he was familiarly known, is one of the legendary figures in the history of Tejon Ranch and the sheep industry. A member of one of California's oldest families, Lopez was born in 1853 on his father's ranch in the San Fernando Valley. (It later became the site of the final dam in the Los Angeles Aqueduct.)

Lopez came to the Tejon in 1874 and for the next seven years was the overseer of Edward F. Beale's estimated 60,000 head of sheep. During that time, a period of severe drought, the intrepid sheepherder drove several thousand head of sheep from Kern County to Wyoming. Although many were lost on the way, about 8,000 of the initial number survived the long trek. Author Mary Austin immortalized Lopez and his remarkable feat in her book, *The Flock.*

Later, Lopez was made superintendent of the cattle operation and in 1902 was named manager of the Tejon. He retired in 1909 when the Beale family sold the ranch, but was rehired in 1912 by the new owners and continued as superintendent for several more years. Lopez lived out his long life on his ranch near Tejon and as late as the 1930s was a popular figure in Frontier Days parades. The major-domo and his wife, the former Mary Winter, had one daughter, Margaret Pearl.

Mettler, Emanuel H. — Shafter farmer Em H. Mettler often was called "the father" of the Kern County potato industry. The South Dakota native planted

Since coming to Tehachapi, apple grower John Nunes has become an active member of the mountain community and his spearheaded many civic projects.

his first potatoes on a 90-acre plot in 1920, with a yield of 90 sacks per acre. Through the use of commercial fertilizer, an innovation in those days, Mettler continued to increase his yields, ultimately gaining an output of 300 sacks per acre. He was a leader in the development of the seed potato program as well as a number of modern farming techniques, such as improved harvesting equipment and marketing procedures. He started the first packing shed operation in 1934 and was a pioneer in the use of sprinkler irrigation.

A community leader, Mettler served for many years on the Richland School District board and was a director of the Shafter Branch of the Bank of America. The farmer, who died in 1970 at the age of 82, was married to the former Pauline Schnaidt. There are many other members of the Mettler family in Kern County, a number of whom still are involved in farming.

Miller, Henry — One of the truly legendary figures in both Kern County and California history, Henry Miller, a native of Germany, first came here in the 1860s. The cattle rancher , who at one time owned vast tracts of land throughout the Central Valley, began buying property and raising livestock in the Buena Vista area in association with his San Francisco partners, William Lux and James C. Crocker.

The development of water was one of Miller's chief interests. He has earned a place in history for the compromise he worked out with James B. Haggin. After a lengthy court battle, and as a result of the Miller-Haggin agreement of 1888, the Riparian Water Right Law of California was established. (Nearly 75 years later, Miller's great-grandson, George W. Nickel, Jr., a farmer and the developer of Rio Bravo Tennis Resort in northeast Bakersfield, would become one of the leaders in the development of the Buena Vista Aquatic area.)

Stories abound about Miller, who remains a controversial figure to this day. It is said that he gained title to much of his land by placing a rowboat on top of a wagon and driving the rig over wide expanses. (The reclamation law stated that any land which could be traversed in one day by a boat became the property of the "rower".)

Although Miller left a large estate when he died in 1916, it became dissipated through mismanagement, and litigation ensued in an effort to remove the trustees of the Henry Miller Trust. George Nickel, Jr., who came into the business in 1939, is credited with restoring a substantial portion of the estate. In 1954, Nickel took over the control of 30,000 acres in the Buena Vista Lake area and converted them to agricultural use. He is well-known as an independent thinker on the subject of water issues.

Ming, Leong Yen — Yen Ming was one of thousands of Chinese who were brought to California by the Southern Pacific Railroad as laborers for the construction of its tracks through the Central Valley. Ming arrived in 1874 and helped build the historic Tehachapi Loop, then started farming and became a leading potato grower in Bakersfield. Ming Avenue, then called Ming Road, is named for him. (His son and daughter-in-law, George and Mary Ming, have resided on Ming Avenue for many years.) He also operated a produce company in Taft and at several locations in Bakersfield; the Kern County Land Company was one of his major customers.

In 1912, Yen Ming hired a Chinese teacher from San Francisco to start the first school for Chinese children in the Bakersfield community. Ming also sent money to his own village in China so a school could be built there.

Moore, David L. — In April of this year, Arvin potato grower David Moore was named president and chief executive officer of the Western Growers Association. The influential Irvine-based association represents the interests of its 2,600 members who grow and pack more than 90 percent of the fresh vegetables raised in California and Arizona. Many of its affiliates are located in the San Joaquin Valley.

Moore's responsibilities include both domestic and foreign operations. At the time of his appointment, the 55-year-old farmer said that environmental issues, particularly those involving the use of pesticides, are a key concern. "It will be somewhat of a battle to ship good-looking vegetables that are clean of contaminants."

A graduate of Bakersfield High School and the University of Southern California, the new CEO grew up in Arvin. His father, John Moore, came to the area in the 1920s, having earned his grubstake in the mines of Nevada. David is the owner of White Wolf Potato Company, which ships potatoes to potato chip manufacturers, and farms about 3,500 acres in California and Utah. John Moore, who is named for his grandfather and is the eldest of David and Priscilla Moore's children, currently manages the company. The Moores now make their home in Corona Del Mar.

Nunes, John — Although John Nunes has been in the Tehachapi area only a short time, he is known as a leader, not only in the apple industry but in the community at large. Nunes has been an enthusiastic supporter of the Tehachapi Apple Festival and has donated land for civic improvement projects. He also operates a turf farm and holds a patent on a machine he developed for the harvesting of turf.

Pandol, Jack — One of the more colorful farmers to spark the Kern County agricultural scene, Delano grower Jack Pandol is as well-known internationally as he is locally. The family-owned Pandol Brothers Inc., of which Jack is the most vocal partner, does more than $100 million in sales annually, with exports and imports of commodities involving five continents.

In the 1970s, Pandol was a strong opponent of the proposed nuclear plant near Wasco, a plan which ultimately was defeated by a voter initiative. Observing that the water which would have been needed for cooling purposes at the plant could have irrigated thousands of acres of farmland, Pandol called it "a waste of the valley's lifeblood . . . something God could never forgive."

Much in demand as a speaker on a variety of topics, Pandol was a guest lecturer at the Harvard Business School a few years ago. The latter engagement both pleased and surprised the agribusinessman who often refers to himself as "a poor, dumb Slav."

Although the only truthful portion of that phrase is the word "Slav," Pandol likes to point out that he never attended college, even though his father urged him to do so. When Jack began working on the farm, after finishing high school and a stint in the military, his father said, "There are no more Sundays — [you work] seven days a week." Says Pandol, "I think he was trying to break me and hoping I would go to school."

Pandol, his brother Matt Pandol, and other family members have been pioneers in introducing innovative marketing, management and production methods. The Pandols are active members of the Delano community and well-known for the excellent barbecues they prepare personally.

Patterson, Frederick D. — Tehachapi apple grower Fred Patterson established the first commercial orchard there and is a leader in the industry as well as in his community. The owner-operator of Patterson Orchards and president of Orchard Management Service, he also sells approximately 5,000 bare root trees annually for C & O Nursery and is third in sales in California for the company, which is based in Wenatchee, Washington.

A native of St. Paul, Minnesota who came to Kern County in the 1930s, Patterson was active in obtaining federal funding for the Tehachapi Watershed Project. He has served on the boards of the Tehachapi-Cummings Water District and the Tehachapi Resource Conservation District. A three-term president of the Tehachapi Unified School District, he was instrumental in urging the district to provide its water needs by digging its own well. As a result, the district now saves an estimated $25,000 each year in water costs.

Patterson is a founding director of Sierra National Bank, the community's only independent bank, and continues to serve on its 13-member board. He and his wife, Laviece, have been Tehachapi residents since 1960.

Perelli-Minetti, Antonio — This pioneer Delano winemaker landed in New York in 1902, almost penniless but with a degree in enology earned in his native Italy and in his pocket, a few grape cuttings.

Over the next 74 years the vintner, who drove his own car daily to his vineyards almost until the time of his

---

"It was desert country, nothing but screech owls, rabbits by the thousands and coyotes."

---

death — in 1976 at the age of 94 — had a remarkable career in the industry.

Perelli-Minetti came to Delano in 1927, after working for a number of California wineries. He also had founded, then lost, several wine companies of his own, including one in Mexico where his vineyards were destroyed in the revolution of 1910. Describing his impressions of Delano at the time of his arrival, Perelli-Minetti once said, "It was desert country then, nothing but screech owls, squirrels, rabbits by the thousands and coyotes."

Buying alkali land a few parcels at a time, the vintner turned it into a rich and fertile vineyard by neutralizing the soil with the refuse from the winery. Fifty years later, the vineyards of "Don Antonio" totaled 2,500 acres. The corporation he and his sons controlled also included a wine bottling plant and a 150,000-barrel brandy warehouse.

At the time of the patriarch's death, the company's management team included his sons Fred, William and Mario. Another son, Dr. Antonio Perelli-Minetti, Jr., is a Bakersfield psychiatrist. A daughter, Jean, is an attorney in Southern California. The winery is now in the process of being sold.

Peters, E. J. — The founder of Maple Leaf Enterprises, E. J. Peters came to the Wasco area in 1920, with his father, Simon Peters, who started farming in the Maple area. E.J. became a leading potato farmer and served three years as the president of the National Potato Council. He also built KWSO, the first radio station serving Wasco and Shafter. Peters was involved in a number of community activities and for three years was president of the Kern Council of the Boy Scouts. Douglas Peters and Edward Peters now are the owners and operators of Maple Leaf Enterprises.

Pomeroy, Harold L. — As the first manager of the California Planting Cotton Seed Distributors, from 1925 to 1936, Harold Pomeroy was a key figure in establishing the policies for the one-variety cotton law. Through the efforts of Pomeroy and other leaders, the association gained the broad cooperation of all sectors of the cotton industry, which resulted in the successful implementation of the far-reaching program. Pomeroy also served the Cotton Seed Distributors as president from 1939 to 1961, and headed the Western Growers Association for 20 years.

Now 92, the Massachusetts native began farming in the Weedpatch area in 1914 and at one time was the county's horticultural commissioner. In the 1930s he developed a farm enterprise in the Arvin area in association with Charlie Scharpenberg and had agricultural interests in the Arvin area in association with Charlie Scharpenberg and Hugh Jewett. Pomeroy has given a great deal in terms of time and money to a number of civic organizations, including the Rotary Club.

Pyle, Stuart — Considered one of the most knowledgeable water experts in the state, Kern County Water Agency manager Stuart Pyle is on a first-name basis with key legislators and has served as a World Bank consultant to under-developed nations.

A native of Napa who earned his degree in civil engineering from Marquette University, Pyle and his wife, Virginia, came to Bakersfield in 1973. He previously had worked for the state Department of Water Resources for 19 years. After leaving the state agency, Pyle spent three years in East Pakistan, where he was project manager for a private company engaged in water development under contract to the World Bank and the U.S. government. He subsequently held a position with the Water Resources Council in Washington, D.C.

Pyle is often tapped by the media throughout the state for expert opinions on water issues and in 1986 was a guest speaker on the subject at conferences in India and Greece. In his role as manager of the Kern County Water Agency, Pyle advises the agency on the allocation of water supplies and the decisions, particularly in dry years, have been disputed by some water districts. The control and ownership of agricultural water has been a hot issue in Kern County since the 1880s and the situation continues today.

Kern County Farm Bureau Presidents

Fred H. Hall	1914-15	Henry J. Bartell	1952-53
J.H. Waters	1915-16	Curtis Graves	1953-55
George H. Peters	1916-19	Kenneth Wegis	1955-57
Joe J. Duel	1919-21	Jack Thomson	1957-59
F.W. Brewster	1921-22	Victor S. Cerro	1959-61
Larry B. Nourse	1922-23	John C. Hershey	1961-63
H.W. Mellen	1923-25	Robert L. Smith	1963-65
A.E. Hoagland	1925-27	Stanley E. Willis	1965-67
C.P. Morgan	1927-28	Howard R. Frick	1967-69
Walter E. Haag	1928-29	Jerry L. Cappello	1969-71
Joseph Schneider	1929-30	Robert H. Wegis	1971-73
Tom Martin	1930-33	Fred L. Starrh	1973-75
Forrest Frick	1933-35	Warren G. Carter	1975-77
Andrew H. Walker	1935-37	Peter Van Dam	1977-79
Walter E. Haag	1937-38	C. Joel Thomson	1979-81
Andrew S. Heimforth	1938-40	Barton L. Bussell	1981-83
Frank Stockton	1940-41	Frederick A. Wegis	1983-85
Ernest G. Buerkle	1941-50	Clinton Shick	1985-87
Loren Voth	1950-51		

Roberts, Hollis — Like hundreds of other refugees from the Dust Bowl, Hollis Roberts, the son of a Texas farmer, came to Kern County during the Depression years of the 1930s. In the next 40 years, the outgoing, cigar-chewing Roberts built one of the largest agribusiness empires in the world.

Even though the farmer often was the subject of controversy — and in the 1970s lost most of his holdings after filing for Chapter 11 bankruptcy — he was well-liked and admired for his honesty.

Roberts served for several years as president of the Kern County Fair Board. In his final years, his own company, the McFarland-based Roberts Farms, Inc., owned 12,500 acres in Kern County and farmed another 20,000 acres in Arizona.

Rudnick, Oscar — Oscar Rudnick fled his native Russia at the age of 14 to escape the Czarist government's

---

Rudnick often expressed his appreciation for the "privilege" of living in America.

---

practice of conscripting Jewish boys to 25 years of service in the Russian army. He arrived in the United States in 1904 and came to Kern County in 1918.

Rudnick had a number of occupations before he purchased the Kern Valley Packing Company on South H Street in 1922. (He later acquired the Piute Packing Company, now the site of the Bakersfield Auto Mall.) As a Watkins Products' salesman, he travelled by horse and buggy from Los Angeles through the Mojave Desert to Carson City, Nevada. He developed lifelong friendships, and later business associations, with farmers and ranchers in the area.

In 1932 Rudnick bought the historic Onyx Ranch in partnership with Arthur J. Alexander. Today the ranch, comprising 365,000 acres — 300,000 are leased from the Bureau of Land Management — is owned by his descendants. (In all, Rudnick had 12 children: six daughters and five sons by his first wife, Libbie, who died in 1951, and a daughter by his second wife, Dr. Sophie Loven Goldman Rudnick.

He formed the M & R Sheep Company with Gregorio Mendiburu in the eastern part of the county in 1936. The operation included farming, as many as 100,000 sheep, feed lots and a pellet mill. The ranch later was sold and a portion of it became the community of California City. By 1948, Rudnick, partly in association with others, had major landholdings in California, Arizona and Oregon.

Rudnick, who died in 1959, often expressed his appreciation for the "privilege" of living in America and took an active interest in youth organizations. For many years he and his company, Kern Valley Packing, were primary financial supporters of the Junior Livestock Auction at the Kern County Fair.

Sandrini, Lido — A pioneer farmer and cattleman in the Delano-McFarland area, Lido Sandrini came to the United States from Italy as the infant son of Ugo Sandrini, arriving about 1911.

Initially, Ugo Sandrini worked as a dairyman, delivering milk in the McKittrick-Maricopa area by using a wagon and a team of horses. He later formed a partnership with his sons, Lido and Lester. Today, Sandrini Brothers is a diversified farming and cattle operation which also includes Lido's son, Richard Sandrini.

Lido Sandrini, who attended Pond elementary school and is a graduate of Delano High School and Bakersfield College, long has been a leader in agriculture and in community affairs. He served for 22 years on the Delano High School board of trustees and for 12 years was chairman of the Delano Parks and Recreation Commission. He was the chairman of the Delano 50th Anniversary celebration in 1974 and has headed the Delano Harvest Festival committee. He is a former director of the Federal Land Bank and, on his retirement, his brother Lester was elected to the board.

Ugo (in 1969) and Lido (in 1977) Sandrini are the only father-and-son who have received the Italian Heritage Dante Association Columbian Award. In 1975, Lido was recognized by the president of Italy for his civic activities and community service in the U.S. and was awarded the title of "Cavalieri."

Starrh, Fred L. — In addition to managing his family-owned Starrh & Starrh Farms, Fred Starrh is highly involved in the agriculture industry at both the state and national levels.

During the California cannery strike of 1978, Starrh, who then was managing the vegetable acreage of SVG Farms, dramatized the effect of the strike on farmers by shipping a load of tomatoes to the White House. The delivery of the tomatoes received national media attention.

Starrh is a past president of the 96,000-member California Farm Bureau Federation. In 1985 that organization presented him with its Distinguished Service Award. He has been chairman of the California Acala Cotton Board, vice president of the Western Cotton Growers and a director of the National Cotton Council. For several years he was co-chairman of the buyers' committee for FFA and 4-H project animals at the Junior Livestock Sale.

The Shafter High School graduate is a Kern High School District trustee and trustee of the Richland Elementary School. He has been chairman of the Shafter Parks and Recreation District and is a director of the

Shafter Historical Society. The farmer and his wife, Nancy, a public health nurse, have four children. Fred II and Larry are partners in Starrh Farms, as is Jay Kroeker, the husband of their daughter, Carol. Another daughter, Anne, is an agribusiness major at Fresno State.

Tracy, Fannie C. — In her time, Fannie Tracy was known as the "Buttonwillow Bird Lady," due to the successful but short-lived ostrich industry she initiated about 1910. (Ostrich plumes for ladies' hats were much in demand; the wholesale price was about $35 a pound.)

A graduate of the Normal School in San Diego, she taught in Kern County schools before her marriage in 1904 to farmer William Tracy. Starting with a pair of ostriches she obtained in Arizona, Fannie developed a herd of about 200 of the feisty, long-legged creatures. In *The Tracy Saga,* published in 1962, she relates many of her adventures in raising the unusual birds.

Her enterprise aroused the interest of *Los Angeles Times* publishers Harrison Otis and Harry Chandler, who then owned the Tejon Ranch. At one time there were about 500 South African ostriches on the Tejon.

The descendants of Fannie and William Tracy still farm in Buttonwillow. The ostrich is not one of their products.

Waterman, Ward — In 1958, Ward Waterman, along with his partner, Harold Loomis, founded the alfalfa seed company that has become W-L Research, Inc., a Bakersfield-based subsidiary of the Tejon Ranch Company.

In doing so, Waterman and Loomis established the first proprietary alfalfa seed company in the world devoted solely to developing genetically improved alfalfa varieties. Previously, all such research had been done by the U.S. Department of Agriculture and state experimental stations. Today, W-L is one of the largest companies of its kind in the United States and maintains research stations in Maryland, Wisconsin and Washington as well as in Bakersfield.

Willis, Stanley — Stan Willis, who farmed in the Arvin-Lamont area, was a leader in the farming industry, regionally and nationally. The owner of S.E. Willis Co., he served as president of a number of organizations, including the Kern-Delta Water District, Kern County Farm Bureau, California Planting Seed Distributors and the National Cotton Council. Active in community affairs, Willis served the Lamont Lions Club as president and was a member of the Kern County Grand Jury. He also was a key figure in the Junior Baseball Association and the Boy Scouts. A licensed pilot who often surveyed his crops from the air, Willis was killed in an airplane crash near Rancho and David roads in 1981.

Zaninovich, Martin J. — A native of Dinuba, Martin Zaninovich began farming in the Delano area in 1946 in partnership with his cousin, Vincent M. Zaninovich. (There are many Zaninoviches in the area and as Martin puts it, "It's not a family — it's a clan.") Today their vineyards and cold storage facilities are operated as Jasmine Vineyards Inc.

A respected leader in the farming industry, Martin Zaninovich is the president of Californians for Labor Law Reform and a board member of several trade associations, including the California Table Grape Commission, California Grape & Tree Fruit League, California Chamber of Commerce and South Central Farmers Committee. He also is a director of the Delano Growers Grape Products.

He has been recognized by his peers with the Garfitt Award from the United Fresh Fruit and Vegetable Association and the Mentors Award from the California Grape and Tree Fruit League. A founding member of the Cal State Bakersfield Foundation board, he now is one of its two honorary members.

Zaninovich and his wife, the former Margaret Surjak, make their home in Delano with their son, Jon. They have two married daughters, Katina, who resides in Santa Barbara, and Sonya, of San Francisco.

KERN COUNTY MUSEUM

James Curran, founder of Bakersfield Sandstone Brick Company, supplied the materials for the mansion William S. Tevis built in Stockdale.

A cattle rancher and former resident owner, Johnny McNally acts as master of ceremonies for just about every civic and sporting event that takes place in the Kernville area.

In 1935 Cyril Haworth the founder of the Orange Belt Stages, used this stretch limousine to take passengers to various points in the southern San Joaquin Valley. The firm, which originated in Bakersfield in 1918, also provided charter service for oil field companies.

3
Dollars & Sense

"Weill's general store was an exciting place for a child. How I loved digging into the giant cookie jar.."

Lawrence Weill, *Lawrence Weill's Bakersfield*

Kern County's pioneer business leaders were individualists who nonetheless quickly found their way into the mainstream of community life.

Thrift, hard work, tremendous energy and an unswerving faith in the county's future were their hallmarks.

Henry J. Brandt, who later became one of Bakersfield's most influential businessmen, worked for several years as a blacksmith before saving enough money to start his first enterprise. Others accumulated their nest eggs while clerking in stores, tending sheep or digging ditches.

Most of those born in non-English speaking countries — and there were many who were — learned to speak, read and write the language. Although few had much formal education, they saw to it that their sons and daughters had the benefit of schooling.

Despite their strong streak of individualism, many of the early entrepreneurs were generalists in terms of the goods and services they provided.

The merchant who offered groceries, buttonhooks and Levi Strauss overalls at his general store usually operated several satellite enterprises.

One of Delano's first merchants, Emile Chauvin, also ran a hotel and a livery stable. The Frenchman established his businesses in an ideal location — directly across from the train station on High Street (then called Front Street). Next door, at Ygnacio Valencia's combination barbershop and saloon, customers could, presumably, quench their thirst while being shorn.

Banks as we know them were virtually non-existent, so extending credit was a common way of doing business. For years, accounts were kept in handwritten ledgers, recalls 98-year-old Lawrence Weill, whose father, Alphonse Weill, was one of Bakersfield's pioneer merchants and leading businessmen.

"In an office at the rear of the store, I remember the bookkeepers working at narrow, sloping desks, mostly in a standing position, although stools were available for their use," said Weill in *Lawrence Weill's Bakersfield.* "At first there were no typewriters, telephones or adding machines, and light came from kerosene lamps."

With their skill in handling money and their familiarity with the community, many store owners were the key figures in establishing the first banks. The Bank of Tehachapi, founded in 1892, had its office at the rear of Jacob Asher's store. Asher was named president of the bank, which opened with $10,000 in its capital account.

Today, getting a bank loan requires a detailed financial statement and a thorough examination of the applicant's credit rating. Such was not the case in pioneer times. "Banking practices," says author Judy Barras, "were largely governed by the banker's knowledge of an individual and his standing in the community, as well as his reputation for industry and integrity. A loan was usually based on those assets rather than on tangible security."

Seeking funds from out-of-town financial institutions was difficult at best. After the disastrous fire that destroyed the entire business section of Bakersfield in 1889, three business leaders — Henry Jastro, Hugh A. Blodget and Solomon Jewett — went to San Francisco to seek help in rebuilding the town but were turned down by every bank they visited. Ultimately, a loan that allowed Bakersfield to arise from the ashes was secured from a San Francisco money lender named Daniel Meyer.

About 20 years later, a group of Bay Area businessmen who were soliciting business for their city made a formal presentation to Bakersfield leaders. After hearing what the San Franciscans had to say, Alphonse Weill stood up and reminded them that when Bakersfield had needed help, the vaults of "the City" had been slammed shut.

Even in the earliest times, the members of the business community banded together to find ways to encourage the county's growth and development. The Bakersfield Club, formed in the 1870s, actually was the city's first Chamber of Commerce. A Board of Trade was organized in 1902. Delano formed a similar trade group in the early 1900s. Its leaders were Ben Thomas, W.T. Boone and H. Hawley.

However, the efforts of these early chambers of commerce were devoted strictly to the particular community they served. In recounting Delano's beginnings historian Cecil Dyar complained, "Bakersfield newspapers [of the 1880s] did their best to pacify the citizens of their city by not publicizing the business boom going on in Delano."

Some of the individuals responsible for the "boom" were Charles Tyler, who built the first grain storage warehouse in Delano in 1888; John J. Schlitz, a grain dealer; C.A. Weaver, proprietor of the Delano Hardware Company; as well as Columbus "Lum" Dorsey and N.R. Mitchell who ran a blacksmith shop. Harry Quinn, who got his start raising sheep, would become, in 1908, the president of the community's first bank. In later years, the town's leaders would include Frank Panero, Millard Gibson, Lauren Billings and Ernest J. Girard.

Commercial enterprises in Taft in the early 1900s included Cox & Foster's Bakery, and the Taft Furniture & Hardware.

In Tehachapi during those years, Henry Downs and Peter D. Greene were among the leading merchants.

Still, Bakersfield was the center of commerce for the county. And a remarkable number of Bakersfield businesses still are operated by descendants of the founders of these enterprises. Many are included in the biographical sketches that follow.

Among others are Dewar's, which had its beginnings when James Harvey Dewar opened his first candy shop at 17th and Chester in 1909. Located at 1120 Eye Street since 1930, the business now is directed by the founder's son, James, and, grandson, George Dewar. Jim Snider runs the city's oldest bicycle shop, established on Baker Street in 1904 by his grandfather George Snider. Luigi Lemucchi, whose popular East Bakersfield restaurant is filled with sports memorabilia, has been in business for 56 years. North of Luigi's on Baker Street, is Saba's men's clothing store, still operated by the sons of the founder, Mike Saba.

Several Bakersfield businesses that began in the late 1930s or in the post-World War II years have been in continuous operation by the same individual or family.

Charles Everett opened his Green Frog Market in 1939. Ben Stinson III, assisted by his mother, Mary, runs Stinson Stationers, the office supply firm started by his father, the late Ben Stinson, Jr., in 1947. Sparkle Cleaners owner Richard K. "Stubby" Newman, who began as a route driver for a cleaning establishment in Taft, later bought the company and moved his now-thriving business to Bakersfield about 40 years ago.

Just as in any other field of endeavor, the business world of the 1980s is a much more sophisticated affair than it was a century ago. Advanced college degrees are as common as computers. One thing that hasn't changed is the commitment entrepreneurs have to the community.

As their biographical sketches indicate, their participation is seen in countless organizations and in service clubs such as the Rotary, Kiwanis and Lions. (The Bakersfield Rotary — at 67, it is the county's oldest — recently honored 12 of its most senior members. Two of the dozen, Lawrence Weill and Carlton W. Minner, have been active for more than six decades.)

Over the years, there has arisen a greater recognition that in order to attract new business and industry to the

Security Pacific Bank executive Sheryl Barbich, who grew up in Delano, served as moderator of the 1987 Kern County Business Outlook Conference and is active in many community organizations.

county, cooperative efforts are necessary.

At the same time, the business leaders of today are no different from their pioneer counterparts when it comes to their individualistic nature. Getting ahead in business still requires plenty of hard work, a willingness to take calculated risks and perhaps more than anything else, the kind of personal integrity that earns as much respect as it does profits.

Babcock, Constance — Babcock's Book Shop is one of the mainstays of the downtown Bakersfield business section. And so is its owner, 77-year-old Constance Babcock. A staunch supporter of the area's revitalization, Babcock says, "For a while I was getting discouraged but I think there has been a change in attitude. There's a resurgence of optimism in the downtown area."

Babcock opened her business at 1619 19th Street in 1952 — on a slim budget, but with a solid background in her field. She previously had worked for two book stores, including one owned by Julia Babcock, a former Kern County Library director. (Constance married one of the librarian's relatives.) Constance Babcock is noted for her encouragement of local authors and for her willingness to special order books for patrons. Her daughter, Carol Hageman, is assistant manager. She is married to Ed Hageman, chairman of the industrial education department at Bakersfield College.

Barbich, Sheryl — During the 20 years she has been in the banking business, Sheryl Barbich has become a major figure in the industry. She also is a strong role model for women in many professions. As vice president and manager of the Bakersfield Business Banking Center of Security Pacific National Bank, Barbich is the bank's top-ranking executive in the area — male or female. The center handles commercial accounts of $1 million or more.

The daughter of Harry and Shirley Roberts, Barbich grew up in Delano. Upon her graduation from the University of California at Davis in the late 1960s, she was hired by Security Pacific for its then-new management training program. She was one of only two women in the 11-member group of trainees. Since then, her career has moved steadily upward.

The executive is much in demand as a speaker and was moderator of the 1987 Business Outlook Conference. She is a member and former chairman of the Golden Empire Transit board and has served on the Kern County Board of Zoning Adjustment and the Bakersfield Memorial Hospital Foundation board. She has held state offices in the California Bankers Association. Barbich is a past president of Bakersfield Branch of American Association of University Women and has held a post in AAUW's state division. In 1982, she cochaired the supervisorial campaign of a fellow AAUW past president, Pauline Larwood, who became the first woman elected to the Board of Supervisors.

Lou Barbich, Sheryl's husband, the son of a Delano farming family, is the senior partner in Barbich Longrier & Company, certified public accountants. He served as president of the California Society of Certified Public Accountants in 1985-86.

Bergen, Harold — As Bakersfield City Manager from 1966 to 1981, Harold Bergen was at the forefront of one of the city's greatest periods of growth and development. During his tenure, the city's geographic area tripled in size and the population doubled. Known for his single-mindedness, Bergen said at the time of his retirement, "Most managers worry too much about keeping their jobs. You can't do a good job trying to please everybody."

One of Bergen's major achievements was the city's acquisition of water rights from Tenneco West for $17 million. Now 57, Bergen is engaged in land development. His wife, Barbara, was the volunteer coordinator of the profitable gift shop operated by the Dorian Society in connection with the Armand Hammer Art Exhibit at Cal State Bakersfield's Madigan Gallery in 1987.

Blodget, Claude Raymond — A pioneer builder and real estate developer, Claude Blodget was a charter member of the Bakersfield Board of Realtors when it was formed in 1905. He served the board as president in 1938 and was instrumental in the formation of the Multiple Listing Service in 1947.

The businessman was known for his fair-mindedness. His granddaughter Claudia Blodget-Lusich, who continues the family tradition as the owner of her own real estate firm, recalls that her grandfather often said, "If you're not ethical, then you couldn't possibly be a Blodget."

A member of the first Kern County Union High School graduating class in 1893, Blodget attended Stanford University after serving in the Spanish-American War. His wife, Viola, was principal of Williams School for 20 years. Their son, Kirby S. Blodget, was a partner in the pioneer firm until his death in 1979.

Brandt, Henry J. — **(See "The Plus Factor")**

Brock, John, Sr. — John Brock is the chairman of the board of Brock's Department Stores, which has been owned by members of his family since 1900. Like his father Malcolm Brock, who died in 1962 at the age of 84, John Brock has taken a major role in the city's business development and is an active supporter of many community organizations.

Known for his pragmatism and his optimism, Brock often recalls, with his characteristic wry humor, the evacuation of Brock's Chester Avenue store following the earthquake of 1952. During the nine months involved in restoring the damaged structure, customers were served in a huge circus tent erected on a parking lot in the Westchester area. Presently, Brock's is engaged in the construction of East Hills Mall, a joint venture with the Hahn Corporation of San Diego. Upon completion, the mall will become the second largest retail development in Bakersfield. (Valley Plaza Regional Center, where Brock's also has a store, is the largest.)

A dedicated supporter of community organizations,

Brock's 1975 "Party of the Year" stands out as one of most innovative fund-raisers ever held in Kern County. (Some still call it the "Party of the Century.") Staged as a pre-Bicentennial event, the one-night gala was coordinated by Brock's vice president Angela Schiebel and involved dozens of non-profit organizations. The affair drew about 4,000 guests who enjoyed food and entertainment on all four floors of Brock's downtown store. The proceeds were given to the Junior League for its construction of a children's museum adjacent to the Kern County Museum at 3803 Chester Avenue. The facility later was named the Lori Brock Children's Museum in memory of the daughter of John and Gladys Brock. The businessman also headed a major fund drive for the Boy Scouts in the 1970s and has taken a leading role many other groups.

John Brock, Jr., is president of the department store. Also involved in its management is William Colm, Jr., the son of John Brock, Sr.'s sister, Bette.

Brown, Vander — As president of Western Greyhound Lines, Vander Brown heads the nation's largest inter-city bus line's operation in 11 western states. The son of Mr. and Mrs. Vander Brown, Sr., the executive was well-known in local football circles as a fullback with the Drillers in 1965. He and his wife, the former Jo Ann Britt, are residents of Dallas, Texas.

Burcham, Floyd — A native of Beggs, Oklahoma, Floyd Burcham first came to California in the 1930s with his parents, then settled in Kern County following his Army service in World War II. At first, times were not easy for the future businessman. As Olympics promoter Bill Chisholm has said, "If Floyd gets a wistful look when passing a haystack, chances are he's recalling

Born in Alaska, department store executive John Brock, Sr. came to Bakersfield in 1920 when his father, Malcolm Brock, acquired the store founded in 1900 by the Hockheimer brothers, who were relatives of the Brock family.

During the nine months involved in restoring the damaged structure, customers were served in a huge circus tent erected on a parking lot in the Westchester area.

---

the two weeks he spent sleeping in one when he first landed in Arvin."

Burcham soon invested in a war surplus store in Bakersfield. It was the beginning of his two "blocklong emporiums." Today, Floyd's is a corporation, with retail outlets selling hardware, office furniture, canvas goods, plants and gardening supplies.

A former welterweight boxing champion, Burcham has been active in organizing teams for youths in all areas of sports. (An avid tennis player, he spends much of his leisure time on the courts he built at his ranch in Glennville.) He also participates in Kiwanis Club activities.

Burke, James — Ask auto dealer Jim Burke what he's proudest of, and he's likely to say, "I'm a native — so is my wife, Bebe." Burke's great-grandparents settled in the mountainous Eugene Grade area northeast of Bakersfield in the 1860s. His grandfather, Walter Burke, became a prominent Kern County cattle rancher.

The businessman is president and owner of Jim Burke Ford and the Certified Leasing Company, and co-owner with Dan Hay (the husband of Burke's daughter, Michele) of Jim Burke Lincoln Mercury Mitsubishi. Burke entered the automobile business in 1949, after his graduation from Stanford, when he became associated with Haberfelde Ford, which was founded in 1913. During his 38 years in the business, Burke has held leadership positions in organizations associated with the industry and has received many top awards.

Burke is a staunch supporter of the public schools. (His aunts, Nora and Theresa Burke, were pioneer schoolteachers.) "I believe that we must do all that we can for education," he says. "It is our primary resource for growth and development."

He is a founding director and past chairman of the Cal State Bakersfield Foundation. In the 1970s, Burke ably guided the Kern High School District's desegregation committee, which developed the Master Plan for Student Enrollment. When state funds for elementary school were cut after the passage of Proposition 13, his company made it possible for thousands of school children to visit Pioneer Village by paying their admissions. Each year, high school students are provided valuable business experience through the Ford Dimension program. The Beautiful Bakersfield Committee recognized Burke in 1985 with its Education Award.

The auto dealer has taken leadership roles in many civic organizations and has been general chairman and moderator of the Kern County Business Outlook Conference. He is a past chairman and board member of Mercy Hospital.

Auto dealer Jim Burke's roots in Kern County go back a long way. His great-grandfather, Daniel Burke, a native of Ireland, settled in the Greenhorn Mountain area in 1864.

Carpenter, Ralph — Delano insurance man Ralph Carpenter has been a major force in his adopted community and in the county as a whole. Carpenter, who graduated from the University of Arizona in 1937 with a degree in journalism, first came to the area in 1945 as business manager for the *Delano Record.* Shortly after his arrival, he chaired the March of Dimes campaign, raising $7,500 when Delano's population totaled only 4,500.

Carpenter served for 20 years on the Kern County Board of Trade, including two terms as president. The Board of Trade generally is credited with bringing Frito-Lay to the county. The food chip manufacturer made its decision to locate here during Carpenter's 1982-83 term. Carpenter also was involved in the formation of Red Rock Canyon State Park and the Buena Vista Aquatic area, as well as the freeway to Lake Isabella and the extension of Road 155 across Greenhorn Mountain. He has been a member of two Grand Juries.

Carpenter was instrumental in the founding of Bakersfield College's Delano Center and has served two terms on the Cal State Bakersfield Advisory Board. He is a past commander of the Delano Veterans of Foreign Wars and has been president of the Exchange Club and the Kiwanis Club. His wife, Jan, is active in Delano's Music Memorial and other organizations. Carpenter is a

Chartered Life Underwriter for Aetna Life Insurance Company.

Carver, Roy III — The principal developer of the California Avenue office district in Bakersfield, Roy Carver built the glass-walled California Triangle building — from an award-winning design by architect David Milazzo — in 1981. Two years later, Carver completed the Stockdale Corporate Tower at California and Mohawk. The tallest building in Bakersfield, the 11-story structure is headquarters for Shell California Production. Carver Development also constructed and owns the Stockdale Business Center, the Ticor Building, Contel Centre and the Shell Plaza Annex.

The young businessman (he became a millionaire before he was 30) has made major financial contributions to a number of non-profit organizations and has been a supporter of the city's beautification efforts. He underwrote the costs of the city flags produced by the Beautiful Bakersfield Committee and was the first to fly the banner — on one of the three poles in front of the Stockdale Corporate Tower. In 1986, a large metal sculpture he commissioned was installed in the fountain in front of the Shell complex at California and Mohawk. It is the first outdoor sculpture to grace the exterior of any building in the southwest business sector.

Carver and his wife, the former Amy Freeman, now make their home in Newport Beach. His company also owns office buildings in Ontario, La Jolla and Phoenix.

Clay, Meg and Wayne — Owners of the Sizzler restaurants in Bakersfield, including the one at the historic Ice House, Meg and Wayne Clay support the activities of many organizations. Particularly interested in encouraging young people, they are the sponsors of Beautiful Bakersfield's annual Youth award.

Clerou, Vincent Henry — The third of eight children born to pioneer sheepman Louis Clerou and his wife, Lucy, Vince Clerou is one of the more colorful figures in Bakersfield business and sports circles.

Now 77, the owner of Vincent's Cyclery earned his first wages at the age of 7 selling newspapers for *The Bakersfield Californian.* Clerou, who proudly points out that his eighth grade certificate from Washington School is the only diploma he ever earned, ended his formal education in 1925 after three months of high school. Before his employment with Roux and Kuentzel, a sporting goods store, where at the age of 16 he worked 11 hours a day, six days a week, Clerou had a bicycle repair shop in the backyard of his family's home on Niles Street. He worked at various jobs — messenger, window-washer, handyman, drug store deliverer and at one time was an apprentice embalmer.

In 1934, Clerou opened his present business at 1723 18th Street — with $63 in cash, two used bicycles and a parts inventory worth $84.40. Says Clerou, "I didn't regard the business as a gamble. No one was making much money anyway and I figured I could make as much as anybody on my own. My first day I did $6.06 in business."

An avid outdoorsman, Clerou maintains a large selection of guns for hunting enthusiasts and has been a

One of Kern County's most prominent business figures, bank executive Ray Dezember also takes a leading role in the activities of numerous civic organizations.

ROUNTREE PHOTOGRAPHY

leader in Ducks Unlimited. His wife, Ann, whom he married in 1936, has been a nurse for 50 years, including 20 for the Lamont School District.

Coleman, Bryan J. — Bryan Coleman was active in Kern County's business and civic life for more than three decades, compiling an impressive record in the fields of business investment, property management and development, and real estate. He was copartner in The Coleman Company and president of Coleman Properties.

A past president of the Kern County Board of Trade, he was that organization's director-in-charge of the annual Kern County Business Outlook for 14 years. Coleman also served the Bakersfield Chamber of Commerce as president and treasurer. He chaired a special committee that campaigned successfully for a comprehensive study of the city and county by the Stanford Research Institute.

In 1980, Coleman was awarded the White House Presidential Citation for outstanding contributions to the White House Conference on Small Business.

The businessman was one of the organizers of Bakersfield Savings and Loan (now Great Western), as well as of Lytton Financial Corporation, later merged with Great Western. He was one of the founders of the Kern County Broadcasting Company, which developed KERO radio and KERO-TV. Coleman also was instrumental in the formation of North American Title Company, since merged with Transamerica.

His civic activities included the American Legion, the Henrietta Weill Child Guidance Clinic and several other organizations. A member of the board of regents of

Arthur Crites as a youth, worked as a cowboy, a hay thresher and also was a freighter on the Mojave Desert.

St. Mary's College, he was the founder of the St. Mary's Scholarship Fund at Garces High School.

As head of the Coleman Company, the businessman was a major developer in the southwest Bakersfield business district. Bryan Coleman died in 1985. His son, Tom, now is president of the company

Crites, Arthur S. — Pioneer banker Arthur Crites was born on his family's ranch near Caliente in 1879. As a youth, he worked as a cowboy, a hay thresher and also was a freighter on the Mojave Desert. While still quite young, he became a bookkeeper for the Kern County Land Company. Crites began his banking career as an errand boy for the Kern Valley Bank. He later became manager and president of the First Bank of Kern and the Security Trust Company. When those two banks were acquired by the Bank of America, Crites stayed on as an officer until his retirement in 1932.

The banker was a leader in many civic organizations, including the American Legion, which honored him with its Distinguished Citizen Award in 1942. (While in his teens, he served in the Spanish-American War.) Earl Warren, then governor of California, was one of the chief speakers. He was a past president of the Bakersfield Rotary, and also served as district governor, and was among those responsible for securing the financing for the construction of the Masonic Temple.

Crites published his memoirs, Pioneer Days in Kern County, in 1952. Upon his death, in 1957, the California Senate passed a resolution in his honor. The banker and his wife, Nellie, had two children: Emma, wife of the late Harry Conron, a lawyer, and Angus D. Crites.

James Curran — Until James Curran, the founder of the Bakersfield Sandstone Brick Company, began manufacturing machine-formed bricks in 1887, all bricks in the San Joaquin Valley were made by hand. Curran's company soon began supplying the construction needs of the growing Bakersfield community. Business boomed as a result of the fire of 1889, which destroyed nearly the entire business area.

In the early 1900s, William S. Tevis, the principal owner of the Kern County Land Company, joined Curran as a major partner and for a time was president of the brick company. Bakersfield Sandstone provided the materials for the mansion Tevis built on his Stockdale estate, as well as for the tile-topped wall that still borders Stockdale Highway leading to the Stockdale Country Club.

The son of Irish immigrants, Curran was born in New

York City and came to our area in 1881 at the age of 19. Before going into the brick business, he worked for the Kern Island Canal Company. Curran was a prominent member of early business organizations. In 1896, he lost his bid for a seat in the state Assembly by only 118 votes. He was appointed to the Fresno State Normal School board of trustees in 1911.

Curran and his wife, the former Mary Swain of Rosedale, had eight children. Today, the Curran Corporation is headed by the founder's great-grandson, James Curran III.

Dezember, Rayburn — One of the county's most respected civic and business leaders, Ray Dezember was the key figure in the formation of the Bakersfield-based American National Bank. He has served as the institution's board chairman since its inception in 1966. (In 1965, he was listed in Outstanding Young Men of America.) Since 1981, he has been chairman of the board and president of Central Pacific Corporation, holding company of ANB.

Well-known for his dedication to the community's growth and development, Dezember has received honors from many organizations, including the Kern County Board of Trade's Distinguished Service Award in 1974. In making the presentation then-president John Logan said, "Kern County owes Ray Dezember a debt of gratitude for his major contributions to the economy and for his fidelity to community service."

The Whittier College graduate served on the Kern High School District board of trustees from 1972 to 1981. He is a past president of United Way and chaired a citizens committee to study the future needs of buildings and facilities for the City of Bakersfield. He also serves on the board of directors of The Bakersfield Californian, Boys Club of America-Pacific Region, Federal Reserve Bank of San Francisco, the National Center of Financial Services on the campus of the University of California at Berkeley, and VISA U.S.A.

The banking executive's wife, the former Joan Erreca, is equally involved in the community and has been especially active on the board of the Volunteer Center.

Freymiller, Don — In April of this year, Don Freymiller's company, Freymiller Trucking Inc., went public, offering one million shares for sale at $13 a share on the over-the-counter market. The 48-year-old Freymiller made Bakersfield his headquarters in 1980 because of its central location for produce shipments. (About 75 percent of his trailers are refrigerated.) He and his wife, Maxine, started the trucking business in 1968 in Shullsburg, Wisconsin, with a single tractor and trailer. Today, Freymiller Trucking is on its way to becoming one of the nation's top 200 truckers.

Kern County Board Of Trade

Presidents

Alphonse Weill	1903	Joseph M. Gannon	1961-62
Henry Brandt	1917-18	A.B. Newby	1962-63
L.N. Slater	1922-23	George C. Parker	1963-64
Charles L. Taylor	1923-24	Robert C. Marshall	1964-65
Howard Nichols	1924-26	E. Alan Petit	1965-66
E. Curtis Clark	1926-27	Clarence Williams	1966-67
O.A. Kommers	1927-31	Richard Ledwidge	1967-68
A.E. Hoagland	1931-34	Robert W. Bovee	1968-69
Lawrence Weill	1934-35	Ralph Carpenter	1969-70
W. Herndon Hitchcock	1935-39	Bryan Coleman	1970-71
George H. Peters	1939-41	Cliff Hewitt	1971-72
J.R. Anderson	1941-43	Garlan Frix	1972-73
Charles P. Lake	1943-45	John E. Logan	1973-74
F.R. Kalloch	1945-49	David G. Parker	1974-75
A.L. Trowbridge	1946	Robert C. Marshall	1975-76
Cecil Jones	1949-51	Joseph M. Gannon	1976-77
W.F. Reynolds	1951-52	Fred Frick	1977-78
W. Frank Jones	1952-53	Audrey Nelson	1978-79
Clifton Clemens	1953-54	Larry Ramirez	1979-80
A.B. "Tex" Newby	1954-55	Ann Gutcher	1980-81
Clifton Clemens	1955-56	Spencer Lees	1981-82
George W. Lake	1956-57	Ralph Carpenter	1982-83
Gene Winer	1957-58	Bryan Coleman	1983-84
A.B. Newby	1958-59	Donald B. Fester	1984-85
Joseph M. Gannon	1959-60	Patsy Darneal	1985-86
Clifton Clemens	1960-61	Judy Salamacha	1986-87

Gannon, Joseph — A leader in building residential housing, Joe Gannon is probably best known for his development of Bakersfield's College Heights area in the 1950s, in association with Ralph Smith, Jr. During his length career in Kern County, Gannon has had a part in building an estimated 10,000 homes in Bakersfield, and several thousand more in Delano, Shafter and Taft.

The builder learned the construction business during his teen years in the 1920s in Pomona, where he worked as a summer laborer for his brother, William G. Gannon. After attending Notre Dame and the University of California, Joe entered into a partnership in Bakersfield with his brother in 1936. Joe, who bought his brother's interest in 1952, recalls the tough times of the depression years. "We took cars, vacant lots, all kinds of things for down payments."

After World War II, Gannon built the Oak Lane Shopping Center, considered Bakersfield's first shopping center. In the 1950s, he was the principal developer of the retail centers in Hillcrest and College Heights. Gannon also constructed most of the original buildings at Garces High School and has been a major benefactor of that private Catholic institution.

Gannon has served as president of the California Builders Exchange, as well as the Kern County and

---

Elmer Goertz was "a mover, a maker, a man whose life personifies the great American success story."

Bakersfield Builders Exchanges, the Kern County Board of Trade, and the American Red Cross. He and his wife, Margaret, a leader in early childhood education, have opened their home on Panorama Drive for the fund-raising efforts of many organizations. The couple's son, Tim Gannon, now is the president of Gannon Enterprises.

Gay, Dean A. — Dean Gay retired in 1977 as president of the Watson Company, but he still is an active member of the business community as the head of Dean A. Gay Realty and Development.

He joined Watson's in 1952 as a salesman and two years later became a partner. Upon the retirement of the company founder Warde Watson, in 1963, Gay became the sole owner. Seven years later, Gay's firm was merged with Robert D. Watson, a builder and realtor. Watson Insurance Company was formed at the same time and the three companies were combined as the Watson Company.

Gay has served as president of the Bakersfield Board of Realtors, which named him Realtor of the Year in

1965, and as vice president of the California Association of Realtors.

Gillette, Marjorie — The descendant of a pioneer Woody family, Marjorie Gillette is vice president and Kern County manager for Transamerica Title Insurance Company. Gillette, who began her title company career 39 years ago, is the first woman to hold a regional executive position with Transamerica. She also serves on the corporation's President's Advisory Committee.

Gillette was one of the original eight employees of Kern County Title Company when it opened its doors in 1948 and soon was named manager. The firm was acquired by Transamerica in 1962.

The executive grew up in Woody, which her grandfather, Joseph F. Weringer, began developing and subdividing in 1912. Weringer, the owner of a brewery and bowling alley in the 1880s in Bakersfield, also operated the Greenback Copper Mine from 1914 to 1918. Gillette's father, Francis Joseph Weringer, was the postmaster at Woody for 45 years. Her mother, Alda Weringer, who still lives in Woody, was the hamlet's librarian for 50 years and also served 15 years as postmaster.

Gillette is a former board member of the Bakersfield Better Business Bureau. She has been recognized by the National Association of Home Builders as a member of the "Spike Club." She has two sons, Richard and Morgan Gillette.

Goertz, Elmer A. — In 1963, when Bakersfield Savings (now Great Western) dedicated its new seven-story building at 18th and Chester, Elmer Goertz was described as "a mover, a maker, a man whose life personifies the great American success story." When Goertz founded the business in 1948, it occupied a single 20-by-24-foot office space on 20th Street. Within just 15 years, Goertz had built the business into a $100 million organization, one that ranked among top savings and loans in the country — 191st out of 8,000 nationwide.

Opening a locally owned savings and loan was a long-held dream of Goertz, who previously had been an executive with the Bank of America in Bakersfield. His strong right arm in establishing the business was Glenn Stanfield, a prominent businessman who had retired in 1948 as manager of the Bakersfield J.C. Penney store. Stanfield was named vice president of the fledgling financial company and served for many years on the board of directors.

Goertz became a dominant figure in California banking circles and was a civic leader as well. He once said, "Community service is one way to say thank you for the opportunities we have received. I think anyone who has

---

The creamery's fleet of trucks was rolling across the Ridge Route to Southern California.

---

been [involved] in community activities will tell you that he gets far more from it than he gives."

Also instrumental in the savings and loan's rapid growth and expansion during the early years were executives Ray Hammett and Richard Leask, as well as such directors as Lee Froman, George L. Henderson, H.W. "Pat" Kelly, John F. Marten and Monroe Morgan.

Gregory, Jim — A major builder-developer in Ridgecrest, Jim Gregory first came to that city in 1945 when his father, a physicist, accepted a position at the Naval Weapons Center at China Lake. After his graduation from Burroughs High School and Fresno State University, Gregory taught elementary school in Bakersfield and later was employed by the county Probation Department.

After working for a time in the construction industry, Gregory went into business for himself in Costa Mesa in the late 1970s. About 1980, he returned to Ridgecrest. In addition to building residential homes, Gregory also developed the desert community's first shopping center.

Chamber of Commerce manager Pat Farlander says, "Jim Gregory has been the cattle prod — the catalyst — for getting things going here. He showed us we could do something significant in terms of quality housing in Ridgecrest." Gregory has been recognized by the Kern County Board of Trade award for his contributions to the area's economic growth.

Haworth, Cyril C. — In 1918, when Cyril Haworth established the Kern County Transportation Corporation, his bus service filled a vital need in the days when few people owned their own automobiles. Today the company, now known as Orange Belt Stages, still is owned by members of the Haworth family and has become one of the 50 largest bus companies in the United States.

Several transportation firms operated out of Bakersfield in the 1920s and competition was keen. Solicitors, who often represented more than one company, would determine a prospective traveller's destination, then steer the passenger to the appropriate bus. (One of these early day travel agents was "Slim" Binger, a tall slender man known for his energetic sales pitch and his piano playing abilities. The solicitor was related to Leon "Bail Bond" Binger.)

The company founded by Haworth was a principal carrier of passengers to the oilfields. It adopted the name Orange Belt when it began offering the first scheduled runs through the citrus growing areas of Porterville, Hanford and Delano. Bryan Haworth, now retired, managed the company's Bakersfield office for many years. Michael Haworth heads the Visalia office.

Hull, H.G. — In 1912, H.G. Hull, a dairy farmer in the Semitropic area, became the prime mover in forming a marketing cooperative that ultimately would become a highly successful enterprise: the Wasco Creamery. Hull was joined in the venture by Rex Smith, C.C. Hill, Harry Fowler, A.E. Beckes, E.B. Root and Nathan Taussig. (A few years later, H.D. Grundt, P.G. Grundt,

Ridgecrest builder-developer Jim Gregory, shown here with his son, spent a number of years as a schoolteacher and probation officer before entering the construction industry in the 1970s.

Harry Scaroni and R.C. Annin joined the operation.)

With an initial capital of $1,200 the original group obtained a $12,000 loan from a Bakersfield bank to construct the creamery building. Their character was said to be their chief security. By the 1930s, the Wasco Creamery had a plant in Bakersfield and its fleet of trucks was rolling across the Ridge Route, delivering to the Southern California area. The company was dissolved in 1944, with a profit for its investors. The Bakersfield facility was sold to the Creameries of America and later was the home of Peacock Dairy.

Harriet Hull, the founder's daughter, later sold the family's farm and other property to Pacific Yeast Products Inc., which was founded in Wasco by Jerry Sudarsky and Robert Fisher.

Karpe, Robert W. — Bob Karpe, the chairman of the board of Karpe Real Estate Center, first made a name for himself in Kern County in the late 1940s as a star lineman for the Bakersfield High School Drillers and later at the University of California at Berkeley, where he also was class valedictorian.

Thirty years later, he gained an international reputation as the president of the Government National Mortgage Association — or Ginnie Mae as it is commonly known — a financial arm of the U.S. Department of Housing and Urban Development. During his tenure, from 1981 to 1985, Karpe was responsible for opening up a world market for Ginnie Mae securities. The executive visited financial leaders in Germany and other parts of Europe to interest them in buying the certificates. As a result of his efforts, the international marketing of GNMA securities has grown into a major method of financing low and middle income housing. This expansion and other changes he initiated have returned millions of dollars in revenue to the U.S. Treasury.

Bob Karpe, a former president of the Government National Mortage Association (Ginnie Mae), now heads the Bakersfield real estate firm founded by his father, Elmer Karpe, in 1937.

From 1971 to 1975, Karpe was the Real Estate Commissioner for the state of California. In that position, he managed an annual budget of $5 million and more than 250 employees. He also was a key figure in promoting professionalism in the real estate industry. The executive who is noted for his succinctness once said of his tenure in public office: "I enjoyed it. When it was over, I was happy to come back home."

A former president of the California Real Estate Association, Karpe was honored this year at the annual meeting of the 2,500-member organization. He has served as director of the National Association of Realtors. He is a founder of Bakersfield Big Brothers and a past president of the Kiwanis Club.

In 1986, Karpe and his wife, the former Phyllis Henning, built a home in Tehachapi, where the company is engaged in residential development. The main office of the 50-year-old firm founded by his father, Elmer Karpe, remains at 4000 Ming Avenue in Bakersfield. Two of the couple's three children are involved in real estate: Rob Karpe is in the construction business in Tehachapi; Ray is associated with the Bakersfield office. Their daughter, Sandra, resides in Washington, D.C.

Koutroulis, George C. — Since 1954, George Koutroulis of Tehachapi has been the sole proprietor of Koutroulis Department Store. The firm was established in 1919 by his father, Gus Koutroulis, a native of Greece.

Presently a member of the Tehachapi City Council, George Koutroulis served as mayor from 1982 to 1984. He has chaired the Chamber of Commerce Improvement Committee for nine years. In that role, the businessman has been instrumental in the development of Railroad Park, the parking mall, and other beautification projects, including street decorations at Christmas time. He has been a member of the city's planning commission and the Tehachapi Unified School District

board. He served on the 1966 Kern County Grand Jury.

In providing the citizens of Tehachapi with leadership, George Koutroulis is following a family tradition, for his father also served as mayor. In that position, Gus Koutroulis was a key figure in mobilizing community resources after the earthquake that struck the area on July 21, 1952. The strongest shock in California since the San Francisco earthquake in 1906, it registered 7.7 on the Richter scale. Eleven people were killed and about 70 percent of the business section was destroyed. In the reconstruction that followed, the City Council was firm in its commitment to adhere strictly to modern-day building codes.

Lambourne, Charles A. — Considered the dean of the area's travel agents, "Bud" Lambourne opened Lambourne Travel Service in Bakersfield in 1946 and operated the business until he and his wife, Beverly, sold the business in January of this year.

At first, the most difficult task the couple faced was that of convincing potential clients that using the services of an agency involved no additional charges. Mrs. Lambourne says now, "The hardest part was educating the public. People would drive down to Los Angeles to get their steamship or airline tickets because they thought it would be cheaper to get them there."

Both of the Lambournes previously taught instrumental music in the Bakersfield City Schools. They were among the first members of the Kern Philharmonic (now the Bakersfield Symphony) when it was formed in 1947, with Edouard Hurlimann as the conductor. They retired from the orchestra in 1982, although Beverly still teaches cello privately. Six of the seven local cellists now playing in the symphony have been her students.

McCarthy, Robert E., Jr. — In serving as president of McCarthy Tank & Steel and McCarthy Construction Company, Bob McCarthy is continuing an 82-year family tradition.

McCarthy's grandfather, William J. McCarthy, who became an apprentice boilermaker at age 16 in Indianapolis, Indiana, founded the company (then called Pacific Boiler & Tank Works) in McKittrick in 1909. Bob's father, Robert E. McCarthy, entered the business after his graduation from the University of California at Berkeley, where he majored in engineering and was student body president. The senior McCarthy became head of the firm in 1933, after the founder's death. At the time, it was a three-man operation. In the next 35 years, McCarthy built the business into a major corporation.

Bob, Jr. joined the company in 1957. A 1949 graduate of Bakersfield High School, where he was student body president, he earned his bachelor's and master's degree in civil engineering at Berkeley. He became president in 1969 when his father died. (His brother, Michael McCarthy also is involved in the business. Their mother, Corinne McCarthy, still lives in Bakersfield.)

McCarthy is a past president of Bakersfield North Rotary, Junior Achievement of Bakersfield, and the California Alumni Club of Kern County. He and his wife, Louise, are the parents of four children.

McNally, John E. — Johnny McNally has been a fixture in the Kernville area for nearly 40 years. He is especially well-known for the sumptuous steak dinners he served at Fairview on the Kern, the restaurant he owned for many years. McNally also maintained a pack station and guided many outdoor enthusiasts into the Kern River Gorge and other parts of the high country before the development of logging roads made vehicular traffic possible.

Today, at 74, he still is a vibrant force in the community. Or, as Kernville Airport manager Gene Nelson puts it, "Johnny McNally is movin' and shakin' all over the place." McNally is most visible — and audible — as the announcer for the annual Kernville Rodeo.

McNally became an emcee by accident about 10 years ago when the professional hired to do the job was unable to fly into Kernville due to weather conditions. Rodeo promoter Cotton Rosser drafted McNally on the spot. He's been at it ever since. McNally also provides his services for high school rodeos, and for Ducks Unlimited dinners and is a key figure in just about every function sponsored by the Kernville Chamber of Commerce. With his typical "Aw, shucks" attitude, McNally

In 1986 steel company executives Bob and Michael McCarthy, and their associates, won a Beautiful Bakersfield award for their restoration of the historic Ice House Plaza on Chester Avenue.

says, "You can't do everything for yourself. You've got to do something for other people in the world. And all you get is satisfaction."

A cattle rancher, McNally grazes his herd on about 4,000 acres in the Woody and Greenhorn areas. Technically, he's a resident of Tulare County. For 20 years, he was Tulare's only deputy sheriff in the area, covering an area of more than 1,000 square miles.

McNeal, George — Largely due to the efforts of George McNeal, the highways leading in and out of Taft

have been improved and made much safer for drivers. McNeal, a partner for 36 years in McNeal and Shuck Petroleum, first became involved in highway improvement while serving on the Taft Chamber of Commerce board of directors. He was instrumental in the relocation of Highway 33 (Taft Highway) in the Buena Vista

---

"When I got on KERNCOG, I noticed that Highway 119 had dropped off the list. I decided to do something about it."

---

area to a higher and straighter route above the lake. For many years, motorists had been forced to negotiate the tricky curves of the original road that skirted the lake's northern shore.

A few years ago, McNeal took action to bring improvements to Highway 119, commonly known as the Coles Levee Road, between Tupman and I-5. As McNeal puts it, "When I got on KERNCOG, I noticed that Highway 119 had dropped off the list. I decided to do something about it."

McNeal, whose father worked for Standard Oil (now Chevron U.S.A.), first came to Taft in 1925. His company, which distributes petroleum products, has been recognized by the Mobil Corporation with its Pegasus Circle of Excellence Award. He has been a Taft city councilman since 1979. A past president of Rotary, he also is active in the Oildorado committee, Lions, Masons and the Taft Pilots Association.

Maguire, John Patrick "Jack" — In 1970, when Jack Maguire was named president of Contel (then called Continental Telecom Inc.), the company moved its headquarters half-way across the continent to comply with Maguire's desire to direct the company's operation from Bakersfield.

The core of the company, at least the western segment of it, was Kern Mutual Telephone Company, which was founded by the executive's father James Thomas Maguire in 1908. (Both Jack and his brother, James. T., Jr., were involved in the fledgling firm from the time they were youths.)

After buying a telephone company in Corcoran in 1947, Jack Maguire led Kern Mutual into an era of rapid expansion. In the next decade the Stanford graduate acquired approximately 250 small firms in other parts of the valley as well as in the Imperial Valley and Arizona.

In 1961, Maguire and a group of East Coast businessmen joined their interests to form Continental Telephone Corporation, which was based in St. Louis, Missouri. Maguire became senior vice president of the Western Division. The division's headquarters were situated adjacent to Meadows Field, where Maguire kept a company airplane. After his retirement as president in 1976, Contel moved its corporate headquarters to Atlanta, Georgia. (Today, Robert Abrams heads the company's Western Division, which still is based in Bakersfield.)

He was a past president of the California Independent Telephone Association and a director of the U.S. Independent Telephone Association. In 1983, two years before his death, he was inducted into the state association's Hall of Fame.

Well-known for his philanthropy, Maguire once said, "This town has been good to me, so why shouldn't I do something for it?"

Morris, Mervin G. — When Mervin Morris left Delano in 1949 to start what would become a successful chain of department stores, he couldn't use his family name. The reason: it already had been taken by his father, Harry Morris, owner of Morris Department Store.

Instead, he chose Mervyn's, a different spelling of his first name. The young Morris, who worked briefly for his father in Delano, opened his first store in San Lorenzo in 1949. By 1978, when Mervyn's was purchased by the Dayton Hudson Corporation for $290 million, the department store had grown into a chain of 42 stores in California and Nevada with annual sales of $330 million. The *San Francisco Chronicle*, in its announcement of the sale, described Mervyn's as "astoundingly successful."

Mervin Morris was a speaker at the Kern County

Mervin Morris, the son of Harry Morris, one of Delano's early merchants, chose a slightly different spelling of his first name when he founded Mervyn's department stores.

Business Outlook Conference in 1977, a few weeks before the opening of Mervyn's store on California Avenue. Morris lives in the Bay Area but still owns commercial property in Kern County. A number of nonprofit organizations in our area have been recipients of grants from the Mervyn's Foundation.

Jackie Slater, Mervin's sister, and her husband, Morton Slater, now own and manage the Morris Department Store in Delano. Morton Slater served as an interim member of the Board of Supervisors following the death of Supervisor Roy Woollomes.

Nelson, Audrey — Audrey Nelson was the first woman appointed to serve on the Kern County Board of Trade and in 1978, became the organization's first female president. Nelson is the owner-operator of Audrey's Pantry, a popular Ridgecrest restaurant.

Nelson, Blanche Griffin — The founder of the French Shop in East Bakersfield, Blanche Nelson came to Kern County from her native Tennessee in 1920. After operating a beauty shop in Mojave, she moved her business to Bakersfield in 1932. Four years later she opened a dress shop on Baker Street and in 1941 built the present structure at 1820 Baker Street.

Although she herself was not French, Nelson had a deep affection for the culture and couture of France. Hers was the first shop in Bakersfield to offer women's designer clothing in a salon setting. The personal atten-

Before establishing the French Shop in Bakersfield, Blanche Nelson survived a number of financial setbacks, including a fire that destroyed the salon she opened in Mojave in the 1920s.

tion she gave her customers quickly earned her a loyal clientele.

Nelson, who died in April of this year at the age of 94, was joined in the business by her son and daughter-in-law, Richard and Mary Griffin. Today, the family-owned shop is operated by the founder's granddaughter, Melinda McKean and her husband, Rob.

Nichols, Howard — Although Howard Nichols first came to Kern County in 1912 as a railroad worker, it was not until after World War I that he began his meteoric rise as a builder and developer. After being associated with Henry J. Brandt for several years, Nichols set up his own office in 1925. Over the next 40 years, partly in affiliation with Ralph Smith, Jr., he developed a series of residential areas, including Greenacres, La Cresta, the Primavera section near East Bakersfield High School and Hillcrest.

Nichols and his wife, Mamie, built a spacious home in Hillcrest and he was a familiar figure in the area until his death in 1969 at the age of 83. (He often visited the post office with his pet chihuahua on his shoulder. The little dog was a striking contrast to Nichols, who was more than 6 feet tall.)

In 1924 Nichols was a key figure in the establishment of Kern County's first airport. He served on the airport commission for 11 years and was instrumental in its development.

Nichols, who had served as an officer in the Army Engineers in France during World War I, returned to active duty during World War II. He attained the rank of colonel and was decorated for his service. At the close of the war, Nichols became prominent in veterans affairs. He was active in gaining home loans for ex-servicemen and in encouraging East Coast financiers to make investments in the county. In 1956 American Legion Post 26 named him "Man of the Year." He also was a leader in promoting the Shrine Potato Bowl. Colonel Nichols School in northeast Bakersfield is named for him.

Olcese, Louis Virgin — Louise Olcese, whose Italian parents emigrated to California during the Gold Rush, was born in Mariposa County. After arriving in Kern County, he became the well-known partner of Beneditto Ardizzi in the East Bakersfield firm of Ardizzi-Olcese.

Originally a merchandising company, Ardizzi-Olcese also operated as an unofficial bank in the early years, extending credit and loans to sheep ranchers and employees of the Southern Pacific Railroad. (The store was cater-corner from the SP station.) The Ardizzi-Olcese Bank was officially formed in 1917. Four years later that institution, along with the First National Bank of Bakersfield, was acquired by the Bank of Italy, which later became the Bank of America. (Frank Estribou, who was of French descent, was manager of the Bank of America's branch on Baker Street for many years.)

Although Ardizzi-Olcese declared bankruptcy in 1893, a time of nationwide economics depression, the store survived. Olcese acquired a large amount of commercial and agricultural property. He also was a prominent sheepraiser. In 1966 George Nickel, Jr., developer

of Rio Bravo Resort, purchased a 17,000-acre portion of the Olcese Ranch, an area on the Kern River near Rancheria Road originally owned by Solomon and Philo Jewett. At one time the ranch was used as a Boy Scouts camp.

Olcese died in 1929. Two of his nieces, Mrs. Errol Clare and Genevieve Cauzza, were among his many heirs. Several of his descendants still live in Bakersfield.

Pierucci, Leo J. — In April of this year, Leo Pierucci celebrated his 50th year in banking — all in his hometown of Bakersfield. Pierucci now is president and chairman of the board of California Republic Bank, and of its parent company, Cal Rep Bancorp, Inc. Prior to joining California Republic as president in 1984, the executive had spent nearly 45 years with Bank of America. At the time of his retirement from Bank of America, he was vice president and manager of its Chester Village Branch. He received the bank's Outstanding Manager Award in 1977.

Pierucci, whose parents came to the United States from Italy in the early 1900s, has been honored by the Italian government with the Cavaliere Award. He and his wife, Janet, a psychotherapist, are involved in a number of community organizations.

Radoumis, James — As the long-time manager of the Kern County Board of Trade, Jim Radoumis is a fund of information about the business community. But he

Pioneer East Bakersfield merchant Louis Olcese is at the wheel of this right-hand drive "horseless carriage." The son of Italian-born parents, Olcese was fluent in several languages, including French and Basque.

also can be tight-lipped when confidentiality is essential.

Such was the case during the lengthy negotiations that resulted in Frito-Lay's opening a multimillion dollar plant in the Buttonwillow area in 1985. Representatives of the snack chip were determined to keep a low profile. Even Radoumis didn't know for nearly 10 months that the individuals he was dealing with were Frito-Lay executives. As time went on and the "anonymous" representatives were shown sites around the county, there was much speculation about just what or whom they represented. Most thought they were beer producers. "I kind of got a kick out of it," says Radoumis. "Even after I knew they were from Frito-Lay, I didn't tell anybody."

With the Board of Trade as the lead agency, Radoumis also played a key role in locating several other major new industries in the county, including the Carnation Company ice cream plant — the largest in North America — and Manville Forest Products beverage carton plant.

Radoumis began his career with the Board of Trade (then known as the Kern County Chamber of Commerce) in 1941 as director of publicity. (The Bakersfield College graduate previously was sports editor for the old Kern Herald. His byline column, "Bakersfield Banter," appeared for many years in the Los Angeles Times.) After a World War II stint with the Air Force, Radoumis rejoined the agency and in 1952 was named manager.

He has served as manager of the annual Kern County

In addition to developing much of the College Heights area, Ralph Smith, Jr. was a prime mover in obtaining broad community support for the construction of Bakersfield Memorial Hospital.

Business Outlook Conference since its inception in 1958. Radoumis has been recognized in the Congressional Record for his campaign to bring much of the space shuttle program to the county, at Edwards Air Force Base. He is a past president of the California State Fair Exhibitors Association and a member of the statewide Advisory Committee of Economic Development Professionals.

St. Clair, Leonard P. — Leonard St. Clair was the prime mover in the organization of Bakersfield Gas &

Electric Light Company in 1888. Within a year, the firm was supplying gaslight to 52 customers. With the acquisition of a steam generator in 1890 and the installation of a series of poles and lines in the downtown area, the company became the first supplier of electric light in the community. The company was absorbed in 1902 by the Power, Transit and Light Company, which also took over the Power Development Company, the firm that in 1897 built the first hydroelectric plant at the mouth of Kern River canyon. In 1911, Power, Transit and Light was merged with the San Joaquin Light and Power Company. In 1939, San Joaquin was absorbed into the Pacific Gas & Electric Company.

Scribner, William — Pioneer merchant William Scribner was instrumental in the formation of the Bakersfield Water Company in the 1880s. This answered a vital need, for individual wells serving homeowners were becoming polluted with surface water.

For many years the company pumped its water from three 60-foot wells into a storage tank known as Scribner's Water Tower at 17th and Eye streets (the present site of Bank of America's main branch). The wooden tower, one of the few structures that survived the disastrous fire of 1889, was saved by Will Houghton, a member of the volunteer fire department. Carrying a lard bucket, Houghton climbed to the top of the tower, where he scooped water from the tank to douse the hot spots below him. Through a series of acquisitions and mergers, the firm became, in 1927, the California Water Service Company which still serves much of the Bakersfield area.

Shomate, Charles — Charles Shomate literally put Shafter on the map. Shortly after opening the community's first general store in 1914, Shomate spent his off-duty hours riding his bicycle around the countryside, gathering signatures for a post office in Shafter. When the petition was accepted, he became the first postmaster; the office and mail room occupied a corner of his store. Often referred to as a "one-man chamber of commerce," Shomate was always on hand to greet visitors arriving at the train depot, which at the time was a converted boxcar. In the 1920s, the Kernville native sold his business in Shafter and moved to Bakersfield. He later served for many years as Kern County Recorder.

Smith, Ralph Jr. — Ralph Smith Jr. made his mark as a real estate developer but he is remembered best as "the godfather" of Bakersfield Memorial Hospital. As hospital administrator Larry Carr puts it, "Ralph Smith is the one who created it, built it, saw it through its initial phases and into its maturity."

In 1951, Smith joined the group of businessmen and physicians that established the Memorial Hospital corporation. The first president of the board of directors, Smith served in that capacity until 1982, four years before his death at the age of 74.

The son of Ralph and Leota Smith, the developer was born in Bakersfield and attended local schools before graduating from the New Mexico Military Institute in Roswell in 1933. After working in his parents' store for a few years, he entered the real estate business. In the late

1940s he developed the northwest part of Westchester, and in the early 1950s major portions of College Heights.

An ardent outdoorsman, Smith was a key figure in the construction of the Kern River Fish Hatchery. He also was active in Ducks Unlimited and the Fish and Game Wildlife Association.

Tevis, William S. — William Tevis is best known for being one of the principal owners of the Kern County Land Company, but he also was a major partner in the early 1900s with James Curran in the Bakersfield Sandstone Brick Company.

Urner's store offered items that were the electric marvels of the day—washing and ironing machines, vacuum cleaners, radios and even the first electric phonographs.

Construction materials for the 9,000 square-foot home which famed architect Stanford White designed for Tevis's Stockdale estate were supplied by Sandstone. But Tevis suffered financial reverses and the mansion never was completed. Describing the fluidity of Tevis's fortune, Hugh Curran once said, "William S. Tevis was many times a millionaire."

For nearly a decade, the mansion's only occupants were dozens of cases filled with art objects collected in Europe by his wife, the former Mabel Pacheco. (The white Italian marble altar that graces St. Paul's Episcopal Church was given to the parish in memory of her father, Romualdo Pacheco, who once served this area as an assemblyman.)Tevis was an avid outdoorsman and horiculturalist. Many of the trees that shade the residences of "old" Stockdale were planted by the financier. And remnants of his jungle-like bamboo grove can be found at the edge of the parking lot on the east side of Stockdale Country Club.

William Tevis's father, Lloyd Tevis, a former president of Wells Fargo & Co., had made his fortune in several successful mining ventures — the Comstock and the Anaconda, among others — in association with George Hearst and James B. Haggin.

Urner, David E. — In the autumn of 1919, 26-year-old David Urner left the security of a teaching job at Kern County Union High School to venture into the then-untested field of home appliances. A fellow in-

structor, Errol P. Janes, joined Urner in the enterprise but returned to teaching in the 1930s.

Urner's store offered items that were the electric marvels of the day — washing and ironing machines, vacuum cleaners, radios and even the first electric phonographs. The company also introduced electric refrigerators to local homeowners. David H. Urner, the founder's son, notes, "Needless to say, the Union Ice Company was not pleased with this turn of events." In later years, the senior Urner became one of the first 10 retail dealers in the United States of the first automatic washer — the Bendix Home Laundry. Today, Urner's is the largest independent appliance and television dealership in the county.

The appliance pioneer was involved in many community activities. He was elected to the high school board of trustees in 1926 and served for several years. He was a founder of the Merchants Association (now the Credit Bureau) and the Kern County Musical Association. An organizer of the Better Business Bureau, he was its first president in 1954.

An avid tennis player, Urner spent nearly every Sunday on the courts at Jastro Park. He was instrumental in the formation of the Tennis Development Corporation, which built the Bakersfield Racquet Club, and was president of the corporation from 1945 to 1963.

Urner was active in his business until his death in 1980. In addition to his son, David H., other family members involved in its management are his daughter, Margaret, and his grandchildren, Bryan and Brad Urner and Deborah Willman.

Weill Family — (See "The Plus Factor")

Watson, Warde — One of Kern County's most prominent Realtors, Warde Watson established his real estate business in 1942. He previously had worked for the Bank of America for 17 years.

Within the next 10 years, Watson's company became widely diversified. In addition to residential resales, the firm became a major broker for commercial and agricultural property. Watson also became active in subdividing, farm management, appraisals and in assembling large parcels for business and industry.

Watson served as chairman of the Kern County Business Outlook Conference in 1959. A past president of the Bakersfield Board of Realtors, he also has been a director of the California Real Estate Association and the National Association of Real Estate Boards.

Henry A. Jastro chaired the Board of Supervisors for 24 years and was manager of the Kern County Land Company for a half century.

In 1981, Sharon Wallis Mettler became the first woman appointed to the West Kern Municipal Court. The judge previously had served in the District Attorney's office.

Kern County Law Wives member Sue McCoy prepares to guide a Hort School class through the Courts and Administration Building.

Bakersfield attorney Morris Chain often pointed to a crystal ball he kept in his office to illustrate to his clients the unpredictability of legal trials.

4
Law Makers
& Keepers

"Within thirty hours after I obtained the writ I had all of the county records on wheels rolling over the Baker Road toward Bakersfield."

Benjamin Brundage

Law and order always has been a hot topic in Kern County.

In the early days, when Bakersfield was a wild frontier town with wooden sidewalks and countless saloons, justice had to be swift and sure. As the city has grown, so has the county, and the legal system has expanded and become more sophisticated.

Yet, even in the 1930s there were only three superior Court judges. In 1947 when deputy district attorney Norman Main was appointed the fourth judge (by Governor Earl Warren, a 1908 graduate of Bakersfield High School who became Chief Justice of the U.S. Supreme Court), this action marked the first enlargement of the Superior Court in more than 30 years.

Now there are 15 Superior Court judges, plus a court commissioner and a court coordinator. And there are eight Municipal Court judges in Bakersfield, two in East Kern and four in outlying districts.

Bakersfield has been the center of legal action since the county seat was moved from Havilah in 1874. The removal came following a disputed election in 1873 — the results showed that Bakersfield had wrested the county seat from Havilah by eight votes. But the Supervisors from Havilah and Tehachapi said it wasn't so.

The people of Bakersfield brought a suit against the Kern County Board of Supervisors. Successfully arguing their case was a young attorney named Benjamin Brundage, who later served as a Superior Court judge.

Most of the early lawyers migrated here from the East and the Middle West. Their credentials might have been sketchy, but their enthusiasm was genuine.

Many colorful characters enlivened the legal scene. There was the now-anonymous lawyer who always wore a heavy overcoat, even in August. He claimed the wool kept out the heat.

And there was the flamboyant but shrewd detective, A.E. "Cookie" Cook, who had been a member of the New Mexico Rangers. He rendered valuable service for the District Attorney's office, though he was not the inconspicuous gumshoe. He often wore his 13-carat diamond ring and kept his tie in place with a miniature horseshoe studded with diamonds.

Initially, there were three supervisorial districts. The present complement of five was reached in 1884, when two more were established. Resignations were frequent in the early days, some within a few months of the particular supervisor's election or appointment.

In one of its first actions, the Board of Supervisors ordered the construction of a jail and sheriff's office. The building was completed in 1867 and quickly put to use. California's law prohibiting the carrying of concealed weapons was loosely enforced in Kern County, according to historian Harland Boyd, and shooting offenses were common.

The same year, the roof was raised on the new courthouse by volunteers "enlivened by a copious supply of . . . lager."

When the county seat was moved from Havilah to Bakersfield in 1874, the county offices were situated in the Town Hall until a new courthouse was built on the southwest corner of Truxtun and Chester avenues. The land, the present site of Bakersfield's City Hall, was donated by a number of residents, including George B. Chester.

However, there was a delay in the start of construction owing to an injunction brought by representatives of the Southern Pacific railroad. When this dispute was finally settled there was a jubilation in Bakersfield.

"Flags were flown, bonfires were lighted, black powder was exploded, and there were anvil salutes," said Harland Boyd in *A California Middle Border.*

The new courthouse, which took two years to complete, cost $29,999. After the turn-of-the century, it would be replaced by a larger structure on the east side of Chester Avenue, which was in use until the earthquake of 1952, after which the present Courts and Administration building was constructed. Each would be the setting for some of the most famous decisions in both the county's and the state's history.

Kern County's legal and political arena often has been an exciting one. It is filled with a large number of movers and shakers, many of whom have had an impact that stretches far beyond the county's boundaries.

Black, Glenn — In all, Glenn Black served 22 years on the Taft City Council, between 1951 and 1980, and a total of 10 terms as mayor. A successful land developer on the West Side and the Central Coast, Black is a past president of the Taft Rotary Club and has been active for many years in the Taft Oildorado.

Brown, George A. — Former Bakersfield attorney George A. Brown was appointed to the Fifth District Court of Appeal in 1971 and named its Chief Justice in 1972, a position he still holds. Two years ago, Brown was elected by appellate and Supreme Court justices to fill the appellate justice spot on the 23-member board of the California Judges Association.

Brown, an articulate lawyer noted for his extraordinary combination of trial skill and analytical ability, joined the Bakersfield law firm of Borton, Petrini & Conron in 1948 and became a partner four years later. He was associated with the firm until his appointment as a Superior Court judge in 1969.

Browne, H. Monroe — A cattle rancher and former owner of Hartman Concrete and McCoy Tire Company in Bakersfield, Monroe Browne was appointed ambassador to New Zealand by President Reagan in 1982.

Browne served three years in the post. He now is a consultant to the State Department for the Pacific Rim countries and is director of the Presidential Fellowship Committee. During Reagan's term as governor, Browne held several administrative positions. He also was a member of Reagan's "kitchen cabinet," an influential group of Californians who were instrumental in gaining support for Reagan's presidential campaign.

Browne met his wife, the former Mary Frances Ashby, when both were students at Bakersfield High School. He retains an office in Bakersfield, which handles his cattle interests in Texas, and is a member of Stockdale Country Club.

Brundage, Benjamin — Benjamin Brundage was a major figure in two historic cases in the early days of Kern County. As an attorney, he successfully won the county seat for Bakersfield in 1874. Obviously a man of action, Brundage later said, "Within thirty hours after I obtained the writ I had all of the county records on wheels rolling over the Baker road toward Bakersfield."

Ten years later, as a Superior Court judge, he presided over the landmark water rights trial in a lawsuit brought by Henry Miller and Charles Lux against James B. Haggin and William Tevis.

The judge, who had practiced law in Sandusky, Ohio, before coming to Havilah in 1865, spent most of his career in Bakersfield and was an active leader of the community until his death, at 77, in 1911. His son, Benjamin Leonard Brundage, was a Bakersfield city

Appointed to the Fifth District Court of Appeal in 1971, George A. Brown was named Chief Justice the following year. When he was on the other side of the bench, Brown gained a fine reputation for his trial skill and analytical ability.

assessor and the secretary of the first Board of Trade.

Cattani, Maryellen — Arvin native Maryellen Cattani, general counsel and a senior vice president for Transamerica Corporation, is one of the top corporate lawyers in the country. She is a graduate of Garces High and Vassar College.

San Francisco magazine, in its March 1987 issue, recognized the Boalt Law School graduate as one of "Nine Lawyers Who Are Tops in Their Fields — Bar None." Cattani was the only corporate attorney selected for the article.

"Corporate law is a regulatory maze," said Cattani. "I have to figure out what step to make and in what order ... I make sure we follow the rules."

Cattani, described by one Bay Area lawyer as "one tough cookie," recently handled a number of complex

Arvin native Maryellen Cattani, now the general counsel and senior vice president of Transamerica Corporation in San Francisco, combines motherhood with her career as one of the top corporate lawyers in the country.

sales of Transamerica holdings, including Budget Rent-A-Car and United Artists. The 43-year-old Cattani's administrative duties, in addition to her work as general counsel, include making sure the corporation is in compliance with Securities and Exchange Commission regulations.

When she was admitted to the bar in the late 1960s, few law firms were willing to employ women lawyers. However, she was hired by a major Wall Street firm and was one of five females in the 200-lawyer New York company.

Cattani, who gave birth to a daughter in 1986, is married to Goldman Sachs investment banker Bernard Mikell. The lawyer's parents are Arnold and Corinne Cattani, long-time Arvin residents.

Chain, Morris B. — Known throughout the county and state for his skill as a criminal defense attorney,

District Attorney

Ezekiel E. Calhoun	1866-67
Thomas Laspheyre	1868-71
A.C. Lawrence	1872-74
J.W. Freeman	1874-79
V.A. Gregg	1880-82
J.W. Freeman	1883-88
Alvin Fay	1889-92
J.W. Ahern	1893-94
Alvin Fay	1895-98
J.W. Ahern	1899-1903
J.W.P. Laird	1903-10
Rowen Irwin	1911-14
Barclay McCowan	1915-18
Jess R. Dorsey	1919-22
Henry E. Schmidt	1923-26
Ray Bailey	1927-33
Thomas Scott	1933-53
Joseph Wooldridge	1953-57
Kit Nelson	1957-70
Albert Leddy	1971-82
Edward Jagels	1983-

Morris B. Chain was born near Kiev, Russia, the son of well-to-do Jewish merchants. The family fled to America when Morris was 7 years old. He attended elementary school in Bakersfield and graduated from Bakersfield High School and Bakersfield College.

When he finished law school at the University of Southern California, he became a solo practitioner out of necessity. Though he offered to work for free just to gain experience, none of the local law firms would hire him. So he set up shop alone in the Haberfelde Building and borrowed $75 from a relative to buy a car.

By the 1960s Chain had achieved a state-wide reputation. A popular saying was, "If you kill somebody, the first thing to do is phone Morris Chain."

He was the defense attorney in many murder cases. One which attracted national attention was the sensational Spade Cooley case in which the country-western bandleader was on trial for having killed his wife.

In the courtroom, Chain was dramatic and entertaining. Helen Banducci, his secretary for 25 years, recalls that, while he was delivering a closing argument, Chain would invariably stop to pull out a gaily-colored, bandanna-size silk handkerchief, mop his brow, then slowly tuck the handkerchief back into the pocket of his expensive tailored suit.

Chain was the founding president of the Bakersfield chapter of the California Trial Lawyers Association. In 1976, one year before his death, he was given the Kern County Bar Association's Bench & Bar Award, an hon-

Kern County Bar Association

Bench & Bar Awards

Alfred Siemon	1959
Claude Baker	1960
James Petrini	1961
Jim Day	1962
Judge Gordon Howden	1963
Walter Winchell	1964
Harry and Calvin Conron	1965
Philip Wagy	1966
Judge P.R. Borton	1967
Appellate Justice Roy Gargano	1968
S.B. Gill	1969
Judge Frank Noriega	1970
Keith Rahn	1971
Harold Matlock	1972
Bruce F. Bunker	1973
James Vizzard	1974
Thomas P. Daly, Jr.	1975
Morris B. Chain	1976
Judge J. Kelly Steele	1977
John B. Young	1978
County Clerk Vera K. Gibson	1979
Appellate Justice George A. Brown	1980
Ivy W. Person	1981
Thomas R. and Wini Davis	1982
Virginia Heyart and William W. Burke	1983
Judge John M. Nairn	1984
Judge Gerald K. Davis	1985
Oliver Rostain	1986
Judge Marvin E. Ferguson	1987

or which his partner, Milton Younger, said "was much deserved and overdue."

Davis, Thomas R. — Out of the thousands of cases that have come before the Supreme Court in its 200-year history, a federal statute has been overturned slightly more than 100 times. Bakersfield lawyer Tom Davis is responsible for one of those times — the Mendoza case in 1963.

The court's decision in his favor declared a statute of Congress unconstitutional — a statute which took away citizenship of a native-born citizen for having gone to Mexico to avoid the draft during World War II. Davis argued, successfully, that the Constitution states that the government can take away your life for a felony, but there is no provision in the Constitution for taking away your citizenship for the offense Mendoza committed.

In 1982 Davis and his wife, Wini Davis, were given the Bench & Bar Award by the Kern County Bar Association — the first and only time a married couple has won it. Wini is one of the organizers of the Court House Tours, which conduct children and interested adults through the court house while explaining the functions of law. In the past year more than 1,000 schoolchildren (6th through 12th grades) have taken the tour.

Donahoe, Dorothy — One of Kern County's most capable and successful legislators, Assemblywoman Dorothy Donahoe was the author of California's Master Plan for Higher Education.

Remarkably, Donahoe never attended college herself. When she was named the Los Angeles Times Woman of the Year in government, she explained that upon her graduation from Bakersfield High School, "College was out . . . the money went for doctor bills." Donahoe contracted polio as an infant and had three surgeries before she was 3 years old. She was unable to walk without the aid of crutches or braces until she was 15.

However, in her view, her handicap strengthened her and was a key element in her desire to be "a champion of people who have no one else to fight for them."

During her eight years in Sacramento, Donahoe backed legislation that benefited physically and mentally disabled children and adults. She also was a strong supporter of a comprehensive water development plan for California.

Before entering public life, she was registrar of Bakersfield High School for 16 years. She once said that the experience she gained as a local and state officer of Business and Professional Women was instrumental in her decision to become a candidate.

Donahoe, who suffered from bronchial asthma, died of pneumonia in 1960 at age 49. A few days after her death, the Assembly Education Committee, which she chaired, named her Master Plan for Education the Donahoe Higher Education Act and voted it into law.

The principal classroom building at Cal State Bakersfield, the last campus of the State University System, was named Donahoe Hall in 1975.

"Don't ever dare to take your college as a matter of course—because, like freedom and democracy, many people you'll never know anything about have broken their hearts to give it to you."

At the time of the building's dedication, her colleague, state Senator Walter W. Stiern, recalled a statement Dorothy Donahoe often made to young people: "Don't ever dare to take your college as a matter of course — because, like freedom and democracy, many people you'll never know anything about have broken their hearts to give it to you."

Dorris, Grace — Grace Storey Dorris of Bakersfield, the first woman elected to the state legislature from Kern County, made a good name for herself almost as soon as she was seated in the Assembly in 1919.

At the opening session, Dorris, then 31, introduced a resolution urging Congress to pass the 19th Amendment to the Constitution — women's suffrage. (Women in most of the western states, including California, already had the right to vote.)

A short time later, she introduced a bill that would limit the work day of domestic servants to 10 hours. It

---

Dorris was the author of the California Water Storage Act, which became law in 1927.

---

was the first legislation ever to be introduced in California by a woman. Although the bill failed to pass initially, it did become law at a later session.

During her three terms in Sacramento — she was elected again in 1922 and served until 1926 — Dorris was the author of the California Water Storage Act, which became law in 1927. The assemblywoman ardently supported the idea of having a public defender as well as a public prosecutor in the state's courts.

A 1909 graduate of the University of California at Berkeley, Grace Dorris was associated with her husband, Wiley C. Dorris, in his law practice although she was not an attorney. Wiley Dorris was killed in a train accident in 1957. Grace Dorris died in 1968 when she was 81.

Dorsey, Jess R. — Jess R. Dorsey was widely known throughout the state for his dedicated work as a private attorney and for his public service. He was a state senator from 1942 until his death in 1958. Earlier in his career he was an assemblyman and a district attorney. As a senator, he was instrumental in the creation of Isabella Lake and took a leading role in securing state and federal funds to aid Kern County communities following the 1952 earthquakes.

The senator's wife, the former Marian Stokum, was a prominent clubwoman and expert gardener. Their residence at 1028 Q Street in Bakersfield was the scene of many social events. The gracious home, reached by a rustic bridge over the Kern Island Canal, was a showplace inside and out. The house had two features rarely found in local homes at that time: a solarium and an upstairs ballroom with a polished hardwood floor on which guests danced to records played on a large phonograph.

Engle, Clair — Recreation-minded individuals may be familiar with Clair Engle Lake, the reservoir behind Trinity Dam near Red Bluff. But they may not be aware that the man it is named for was born in Kern County and is the only native of this area to become a U.S. Senator.

Clair Engle was the grandson of David Engle, a pioneer rancher in the Granite Station area. The senator's father, Fred Engle, was the brother of Frances Engle Stockton, wife of pioneer educator R.L. Stockton.

Congressman Harlen Hagen, who at the time represented Kern County, proposed the legislation to name the lake in Engle's honor.

Engle lived most of his life in Red Bluff and was appointed to the Senate shortly before his death in 1964. He previously served in the House of Representatives for about 20 years and was active in the development of natural resources. In making the resolution, Hagen said, "That the Central Valley Project exists is in large measure a tribute to [Engle's] legislative ability."

The senator's first cousin, 86-year-old Engle Williams, is a resident of Bakersfield.

Gargano, Roy J. — Considered an authority on water law, Roy J. Gargano was a Superior Court judge for four years before being named to the Fifth District Court of Appeal in 1966, a position he held until his retirement in 1976. Now a consultant to the Kern County Water Agency, Gargano also holds an "of counsel" position with the law firm of Borton, Petrini & Conron. He gives seminars to other attorneys on the complicated subject of water rights.

Considered an authority on water law, Roy J. Gargano, a retired appellate justice, often gives seminars on the complicated matters of water rights to other lawyers.

U.S. House of Representatives

District

District				District			
1	D.C. McHuer, Union	1865-66		7	James C. Needham, Rep.	1899-1902	
1	Samuel B. Axtell, Dem.	1867-70		8	M.J. Daniels, Rep.	1903-04	
1	Sherman O. Houghton, Rep.	1871-72		8	Sylvester C. Smith, Rep.	1905-1912	
4	Sherman O. Houghton, Rep.	1873-74		7	Denver S. Church, Dem.	1913-18	
4	P.D. Wigginton, Dem.	1875-78		7	H.F. Barbour, Rep.	1919-32	
4	Romauldo Pacheco, Rep.	1879-82		10	Henry E. Stubbs, Dem.	1933-36	
4	Pleasant B. Tully, Dem.	1883-86		10	A.J. Elliott, Dem.	1937-48	
6	Henry H. Markham, Rep.	1887-88		10	Thomas H. Werdel, Rep.	1949-54	
6	William Vandever, Rep.	1887-90		14	Harlan Hagen, Dem.	1955-67	
6	William W. Bowers, Rep.	1891-92		18	Bob Matthias, Rep.	1966-72	
7	William W. Bowers, Rep.	1893-96		36	William Ketchum, Rep.	1972-77	
7	Curtis H. Castle, People's	1897-98		20	William Thomas, Rep.	1978-	

While a Superior Court judge, Gargano was appointed to the 21-member California Judicial Council, which makes rules for the court system and represents the judicial branch in the legislature. He is the only member of the Kern judiciary to serve on the council.

In Italy, the judge is known as Sir Gargano. He was knighted in 1985 by the government of Italy with the Order of the Cavalieri for being an outstanding Italian-American.

Gargano's hobby is constructing wooden sailing ships models, including a 36-inch replica of the U.S.S. Constitution.

Gibson, Vera K. — Vera Gibson's 27-year career as Kern County Clerk began in an earthshaking manner. "I was appointed on April 16, 1952," she said, "and it wasn't long before I was in tents out in the parking lot." She had plenty of company — all of the county offices formerly housed in the courthouse. The removal came about as a result of the July 1952 earthquake, which damaged the stately building so severely it had to be demolished.

Gibson's long experience undoubtedly helped her to carry on business, almost as usual. At the time of her appointment, upon the death of Roland "Boots" Veon, she had worked in the Clerk's office for 25 years. Gibson was voted into office at the next election and in every election thereafter until her retirement in 1979. The same year, she became the first woman to receive the Kern County Bar Association's Bench & Bar Award.

Like her sister, Dorothy May Gibson, a retired Bakersfield City School District administrator, Vera remains highly visible in the community. Both are members of the Greater Bakersfield Chamber of Commerce's red-coated corps of Ambassadors.

Gill, S.B. — "Barney" Gill of Bakersfield is the only Kern County lawyer listed in *The Best Lawyers in America.* The book, published in 1987, is the result of a national survey. In all, 7,200 attorneys are included.

The 70-year old Gill has been practicing law for 45 years. He specializes in family law — divorces, custody matters, conservatorships. A graduate of Indiana University, where he was an All-American in track, and Stanford Law School, Gill first came to Bakersfield in 1932 to visit his uncle, Charlie Shuler, and to attend the Olympics in Los Angeles. "My uncle convinced me Bakersfield and California are a couple of the greatest places to live and work," Gill said in an interview with *The Californian's* Michael Trihey. "I believed him and I've never changed my mind."

Hart, Don — One of Bakersfield's more active and outgoing mayors, Don Hart served the city for 12 years, from 1969 to 1981.

Hart was a key figure, along with George Gelman, in securing a four-year state college for Bakersfield. Hart served on the state board of education from 1960 to 1964, and from 1960 to 1968, was a member of the board of trustees (chairman in 1967-68) of the California State Colleges. "The sole reason I got on the State Board of Education," he says now, "was to get that campus." (Hart was the first person from Kern County to serve as state college trustee. Martha Fallgatter, appointed in April of this year, is the second.)

An all-round athlete, Hart won 11 letters in football, basketball, boxing and track at the University of California at Santa Barbara. In 1962 the Bakersfield native was one of four former California athletes named to Sports Illustrated's Silver Anniversary All-America Roster.

Two years earlier, President Kennedy appointed Hart to serve on the Committee for Employment for the Handicapped. He subsequently was reappointed by Presidents Johnson and Nixon.

Internationally, Hart has been recognized by Waseda University, Japan, knighted by the president of Italy and awarded the "Medal of Friendship" by the government of the Republic of China. A strong supporter of Bakersfield's Sister City program, Hart has made nu-

William A. Howell, Sr., shown here with his daughter, Genevieve, who is on his left, built a handsome home for his family that now is the "crown jewel" of the Kern County Museum's Pioneer Village.

KERN COUNTY MUSEUM

merous visits to Wakayama and other parts of Japan. During World War II, he was an Air Force captain and squadron leader in the China-Burma-India theater of operation.

Hart is vice president of S.A. Camp Companies. His wife, Willene, is the daughter of S.A. Camp, a pioneer farmer in the Shafter area.

Harvey, Trice — An Arkansas native who grew up in Tupman and attended Taft schools, Trice Harvey was elected to the state Assembly in 1986 from the 33rd District. He previously served 10 years on the Kern County Board of Supervisors.

Herrera, Frank M. — Labor consultant Frank M. Herrera was Delano's first Hispanic mayor, from 1972 to 1974, after a two-year term as mayor pro-tem. In all, he served 12 years on the City Council and was a member of the Delano Planning Commission for 10 years. In 1974, Herrera played a leading role in the community's Centennial celebration.

Howell, William A., Sr. — A century ago, when few people had the benefit of formal schooling, William A. Howell, Sr. possessed an even more distinctive skill: he knew shorthand.

And so it was that the New Orleans native became Kern County's official court reporter in 1880 at the age of 18. He held the position for the next 36 years and was widely respected for the skill and accuracy of his transcriptions. He also was the county auditor from 1889 to 1894.

Active in the business community, Howell was one of the organizers of the Security Trust Company in 1910. When it merged with the Bank of Italy, which in 1927 became the Bank of America, he was named chairman of the Bakersfield board of directors and served until 1955. He organized the Western Water Works in 1911.

Howell was instrumental in establishing the first

Catholic Church in Bakersfield. He was chiefly responsible for bringing the Sisters of Mercy to the city in 1910 and the subsequent founding of Mercy Hospital. He was a member of the Knights of Columbus and was knighted by Pope Pius XII.

The handsome two-story home that Howell built for his family at the northeast corner of 17th and H streets now is the "crown jewel" of the Kern County Museum's Pioneer Village.

Howell lived until he was 97. He and his wife, Elizabeth, had two children: William A., Jr., an attorney who died in 1978, and Genevieve, a resident of Bakersfield.

Jastro, Henry A. — One of the more powerful figures in Kern County's early history, Henry Jastro was chairman of the Board of Supervisors for 24 years, from 1893 to 1916.

At the same time, he was the manager of the Kern County Land Company, a position he held for 50 years. He also owned considerable property, was a director in two local banks, a stockholder in Bakersfield Sandstone Brick Company, and a powerful force in the Democratic Party.

However, even though his personal, business and political interests were intermingled, Jastro did provide sound leadership for the growing community.

He advised Lloyd Tevis, one of the owners of Kern County Land Company, to provide financial backing for the first hydroelectric plant in Kern River Canyon. This action paved the way for Leonard P. St. Clair's Bakersfield Gas and Electric Company. Under Jastro's direction, KCL acquired the city's water system and expanded it. "These improvements," said historian Richard C. Bailey, "added greatly to the whole area's potential for income and quality of life."

A German-Jewish immigrant, Jastro came to Bakersfield in 1870, established a brewery and married May Baker, a daughter of Bakersfield's founder. Jastro previously had been involved in raising cattle and sheep in California. His association with Kern County Land Company founders James B. Haggin and William Tevis

Judge Robert B. Lambert shared his 81st birthday cake with court clerk Virginia Heyart and Amelia Spaulding.

(Lloyd Tevis' father) began in 1874 and lasted a lifetime.

As a member of the state Board of Agriculture, Jastro was instrumental in founding the California State Fair. He also was a president of the American Cattlemen's Association.

Bakersfield's Jastro Park on 18th Street, a low, swampy area once called Reeder's Lake, was named for him. The land company donated the property and Jastro provided the funds for the bandstand. Architect Charles Biggar designed the structure, which is on the west side of the park near Elm Street.

Kinney, Nick — Taft native Nick Kinney was elected to a seat on the Kings County Board of Supervisors in 1986. Kinney was student body president of Taft College and was active in athletics. A graduate of Fresno State University, he has been a teacher, farmer and businessman.

Lambert, Robert Boyd — During his 36-year tenure, from 1927 to 1963, Robert Boyd Lambert was a dominant figure in the Superior Court. Judge Lambert's colleagues often commented on his legal brilliance, integrity, expeditious handling of cases, photographic memory and dry humor.

As one lawyer said, "If a judge isn't strong, then one or the other of the attorneys will take control of a trial. But with Judge Lambert up there on the bench, there never was any question about who was in command of that courtroom."

Lambert, a graduate of National University Law School (now a part of George Washington University),

---

As a deputy district attorney, Judge Lambert prosecuted the Ku Klux Klan.

---

wrote the charter for the city of Bakersfield in 1914. As a deputy district attorney in Jess Dorsey's office, he prosecuted the Ku Klux Klan and helped drive the racist group out of the county.

In addition to his Kern County service, Lambert was assigned by the California Judicial Council to sit protem in 11 other counties. In 1932 he served temporarily as justice of the Fourth (now Fifth) Appellate District in Fresno. Later he turned down a permanent appointment to that court.

The judge was involved in a number of landmark decisions. Among them are *The People v. Bert Brunwin et al,* which affirmed that whipstocking (slant oil drilling) is a crime; The *City of Los Angeles v. The Owens River Canal Company,* a decision giving shareholders the right to bring action against their own corporation; *John W. Austin v. Robert B. Lambert* — the California

Supreme Court ruled that the peremptory challenge of judges is unconstitutional; *Estate of Emma C. Heard,* a case which found that "lawful issue" includes adopted as well as natural children; *Kern Water Storage District v. County of Kern,* which held that water is a taxable property.

Off the bench, one of Lambert's favorite hobbies was horseracing. "He was considered an expert handicapper," says his daughter, Eloise Lambert. "In that area, however, his judgments were often overruled."

When Judge Lambert died in 1974 at the age of 95, *The Californian's* editorial termed him a "paragon of jurisprudence." Upon the recommendation of the California Judicial Council, an account of his career was included in the 1979 edition of the National Cyclopedia of American Biography.

Larwood, Pauline — In 1983, Pauline Larwood became the first woman elected to the Kern County Board of Supervisors.

She got her feet wet — politically — seven years

As mayor of Delano during the grape boycott, Dr. Clifford Loader had what might be called intimate knowledge of most of the participants. Nearly all of those involved were the dentist's patients.

earlier as a founding board member of the San Joaquin Agricultural Protection Council, a group of farmers and business people who were opposed to the proposed siting of a nuclear energy plant near Wasco. In addition to the possible hazards of having such an installation in Kern County, the plant would have taken water (used for agricultural purposes) from the California Water Project.

To decide the issue, the Board of Supervisors placed

Sheriff

William B. Ross	1866-67
R.B. Sagely	1868-69
William H. Coons	1870-73
William R. Bower	1874-75
M.P. Wells	1876-77
William R. Bower	1878-86
Dallas McCord	1887-88
W.J. Graham	1889-90
Henry Borgwardt, Jr.	1891-92
William R. Bower	1893-94
Henry Borgwardt, Jr.	1895-1902
John W. Kelly	1903-10
Thomas A. Baker	1911-14
D. Boone Newell	1915-22
J. Caswell Walser	1923-34
Edward Champness	1935-38
John E. Loustalot	1939-50
Thomas Kelly	1951-54
Leroy F. Galyen	1955-66
Charles Dodge	1967-74
Al Loustalot	1975-82
Leroy Kleier	1983-86
John Smith	1987-

KERN COUNTY MUSEUM

Charles Dodge, Kern County Sheriff from 1967 to 1974, was the Bakersfield Police Department's assistant chief before his election. His wife, Mary Holman Dodge, also spent many years in law enforcement.

it before the people by calling an "advisory" election in March 1978. The proposal to establish the nuclear plant was defeated by a 75 percent majority.

Larwood, a past president of Bakersfield Branch, American Association of University Women, said her interest in the nuclear issue began when she was part of an AAUW committee that studied such concerns. She later was AAUW's legislative director in Sacramento.

She received no salary but did have a paid, professional lobbyist working under her direction.

"AAUW and the nuclear project — that's how I got into politics," she says now. "If I had not had that experience, I would not have run for office."

Larwood is a former schoolteacher with a master's degree in education from Cal State Bakersfield. She is married to Dr. Thomas Larwood, a Bakersfield internist.

Loader, Clifford F. — One of the reasons Dr. Cliff Loader, who then was mayor of Delano, was able to keep law and order during the grape strike of the 1960s was that everyone trusted him. After all, members of both side of the conflict were the dentist's patients, including Cesar Chavez and most of the farmers.

However, Loader, who now lives in Bakersfield, recalls with amusement — and some frustration — that he failed to convince United Auto Workers president

KERN COUNTY MUSEUM

One of Kern County's longest-tenured sheriffs (1939-1950), Johnny Loustalot began his career as a high school truant officer and also refereed prep games. Loustalot later was appointed Bakersfield postmaster.

Walter Reuther that Delano farmers weren't absentee landowners.

Reuther, one of the influential people whose support Chavez sought, came to Delano before the boycott went into effect. Upon hearing the UAW president tell a group of farmworkers that "all these farmers live in penthouses in New York City," Loader told him it wasn't so and set out to arrange a meeting between Reuther and some of the farmers.

"I called 'Swede' Antonell first," Loader recalled, "and it turned out that Jack Pandol and Martin Zaninovich and their wives were having dinner at his house that night. So I took Reuther over there. He talked to them and I thought everything was OK. But the next day, there he was again, out there telling the crowd that all the farmers lived in New York and didn't care about the farmworkers." (Maybe, having been involved with the auto industry most of his life, Reuther just didn't know a farmer when he saw one.)

Active in his profession, Loader is a past president of the California State Board of Dental Examiners and the American Association of Dental Examiners, a group which named him "Dentist-Citizen of the United States" in 1970.

Natho, Gay Lynne — Bakersfield attorney Gay Lynne Natho received the 1986 Pro Bono Award from the California State Bar Association for her work in representing clients, without charging a fee, particularly in cases of spousal abuse. (Pro bono is short for "pro bono publico," a Latin term meaning "for the public good.")

Ivy Person, executive secretary of the Kern County Bar Association, was born in China where her British parents then were living. She has devoted many years to raising the professional standards of legal secretaries and is a past president of the Bakersfield Chamber of Commerce's Women's Division.

Noriega, Frank — As the son of pioneer sheepman Faustino Noriega, a native of Spain, and his Basque wife, the former Louise Inda, Frank Noriega is fluent in several languages. This ability, as well as his affable nature and knowledge of the East Bakersfield community, made him the ideal person to preside over the Municipal Court in that area, which he did for nearly 40 years.

Judge Noriega's first courtroom in 1934 was on the premises of the garage business he owned on Sumner Street. Noriega spent many hours, outside his official duties as judge, counseling new immigrants. He encouraged them to learn English and to become American citizens.

Like his father, Noriega was a sheepowner and in 1953 was president of the California Wool Growers Association.

He and his family own the Noriega Hotel, which for many years was managed by Grace Elizalde and now is operated by her son, Albert Elizalde, and her daughter-in-law, Janice Elizalde, whose husband was Louis Elizalde. The hotel is noted throughout the state for its Basque food, served in the traditional style with diners seated at long tables.

Judge Noriega, now 82, and his wife, Louise, are residents of Bakersfield.

Palmer, Oran Walker — In 1939, Oran Palmer was appointed Kern's first county counsel, a position he held until 1944. He was responsible for forming the Kern County Public Employees Association, now the largest AFL-CIO affiliated union in the county, and was its president in its early years.

Widely known for his knowledge of water law, the Bakersfield lawyer at one time was the general counsel for 20 of the county's public service districts.

Palmer, a native of Los Angeles, opened his practice in Delano in 1930 and from 1932 to 1935 was the community's city attorney.

He served as district governor of Rotary International, helped start the Kern County Shrine Club and was active in Elks. Palmer also was a member of the governing board of the Bakersfield Symphony. At the time of the attorney's death in 1986, one of his sons, George C. Palmer, a retired associate superintendent of the Bakersfield City School District, said of his father, "His real love was music."

State Senate

District		
4	J.W. Freeman, Dem.	1865-68
4	Thomas Fowler, Dem.	1869-72
4	Tipton Lindsey, Indep.	1873-76
4	Thomas Fowler, Dem.	1877-79
4	Chester Rowell, Rep.	1880-82
36	Patrick Reddy, Dem.	1883-86
36	John Roth, Dem.	1887-90
34	George S. Berry, Dem.	1891-94
34	Sylvester C. Smith, Rep.	1895-1902
32	E.J. Emmons, Dem.	1903-06
32	E.O. Miller, Dem.	1907-10
32	E.O. Larkins, Rep.	1911-14
32	J.L.C. Irwin, Dem.	1915-22
32	John Creighton, Rep.	1923-26
32	J.I. Wagy, Rep.	1927-30
34	J.I. Wagy, Rep.	1931-42
34	Jess R. Dorsey, Rep.	1943-59
34	Walter W. Stiern, Dem.	1960-86
34	Don Rogers, Rep.	1987-

Person, Ivy — Ivy Person, executive secretary of the Kern County Bar Association, is a past president of the National Legal Secretaries Association and twice has served the Kern County chapter as its president. She has been a leader in encouraging professional standards in her field.

Petrini, James — A native of Lucca, Italy, James Petrini was 6 years old when he came to Bakersfield in 1902 with his parents. A champion high school debater, he went on to complete his law degree at Stanford University and in 1922 opened his practice with F.E. Borton, the firm that later became Borton, Petrini and Conron. A genial and gracious individual, Petrini was considered one of the top general trial lawyers in his time.

In 1958 he was vice president of the Board of Governors of the state bar. The Italian Heritage Association honored him with its 1968 Columbian Award.

Petrini died in Newport Beach at 81. His son, John Petrini, is an attorney with Borton, Petrini & Conron. Another son, Joseph Petrini, is a physician in Salinas.

Reed, Theron — Theron Reed of Havilah was Kern County's first Superior Court judge. In the case resulting from the contested election over moving the county seat from Havilah to Bakersfield, Judge Reed disqualified himself, declaring that he was an interested party. Ultimately, the decision in favor of Bakersfield was made by Judge Alexander Deering in Visalia. (Harland Boyd provides a detailed account of this complex historical matter in *A California Middle Border*.)

Rogers, Don — State Senator Don Rogers' first entrance into politics came in 1973 when he was elected to the Bakersfield City Council. Rogers subsequently served eight terms in the state Assembly, where in 1982 he sponsored the initiative to abolish the California

Inheritance and Gift Tax. He was elected to his present position in 1986. A registered geologist, Rogers is a graduate of Louisiana State University and has lived in California for more than 30 years.

Shell, Joseph Claude — Now an independent oil producer, Joe Shell served for 10 years in the state Assembly, representing the 58th district of Los Angeles, and from 1959 to 1962 was Republican floor leader. He was a candidate for governor in the 1962 primary election, losing to Richard Nixon.

State Assembly

District

	Joseph C. Brown, Dem.	1867-68
	E.W. Doss, Dem.	1869-70
	Jeremiah Burckhalter, Dem.	1871-72
	W. Canfield, Indep.	1873-74
	J.A. Patterson, Dem.	1875-76
	W.S. Adams, Dem.	1877-78
	A.B. Du Brutz, Dem.	1879-80
75	A.J. Atwell, Ind.	1881-84
75	R.J. Ashe, Dem.	1885-86
75	George W. Wear, Dem.	1887-90
75	T.A. Rice, Dem.	1891-92
66	E.A. Pueschel, Dem.	1893-94
66	E.J. Emmons, Fusion	1895-96
66	R.C. Dale, Rep.	1899-1900
66	Jess R. Dorsey, Rep.	1901-06
66	Rowen Irwin, Dem.	1907-08
56	William E. Simpson, Dem.	1909-12
56	Witton W. Harris, Dem.	1913-18
56	Grace S. Dorris, Rep.	1917-18
56	Franklin Heck, Dem.	1921-22
56	Grace S. Dorris, Rep.	1923-26
56	Robert Lincoln Patterson, Rep.	1927-32
41	Rodney L. Turner, Dem.	1933-42
39	Thomas H. Werdel, Rep.	1943-46
39	W.E. James, Rep.	1947-48
39	Joe C. Lewis, Dem.	1949-50
39	H.W. "Pat" Kelly, Rep.	1951-59
38	Dorothy M. Donahoe, Dem.	1953-60
38	Jack T. Casey, Dem.	1960-61
28	Jack T. Casey, Dem.	1962-66
39	John C. Williamson, Dem.	1959-62
29	John C. Williamson, Dem.	1962-66
73	Stewart Hinckley, Rep.	1964-66
28	Kent Stacy, Rep.	1966-72
29	William Ketchum, Rep.	1966-72
28	Ray Gonzales, Dem.	1972-74
29	Robert P. Nimmo, Rep.	1972-74
32	Gordon Duffy, Rep.	1974-82
33	William Thomas, Rep.	1974-78
34	Larry Chimbole, Dem.	1974-78
33	Don Rogers, Rep.	1978-86
34	Phillip Wyman, Rep.	1980-
33	Trice Harvey, Rep.	1986-

Independent oil producer Joe Shell served 10 years in the state Assembly. His wife, Mary K. Shell, now a Kern County Supervisor, entered public life in 1980.

Many Kern County students have gained valuable experience as summer interns in Congressman Bill Thomas's office in Washington, D.C. The former Bakersfield College political science professor is serving his fifth term in the House of Representatives.

Shell, a graduate of the University of Southern California who played four years of varsity football and was team captain in 1939, started in the oil industry in 1940, working on rigs. Following World War II military service (he was a civilian flight instructor for the Air Corps and a Navy pilot), Shell returned to the oil business with exploration and production activities in Kern County.

In 1965 he sold his production interests and became a lobbyist in Sacramento for a group of independent producers and small refiners, continuing in that capacity until 1981. He now devotes full-time to Concho Petroleum, the small company he and his wife, Supervisor Mary K. Shell, own and operate near Porterville. The Shells make their home in Bakersfield.

Shell, Mary K. — One of the most popular and visible mayors in the history of Bakersfield, Mary K. Shell was the first woman to hold that position. In 1985 she was elected to the Kern County Board of Supervisors.

As mayor, she initiated Beautiful Bakersfield, a group of citizens who promote the city's beautification, and spearheaded the revival of the Downtown Bakersfield Christmas Parade. She also established the Historic Preservation Commission. In 1981-82 she was the chairman of the Sgt. Larry Pierce Memorial Committee, which erected in Bakersfield one of the first Vietnam memorials in the United States. Pierce, a native of Taft,

In the case resulting from the contested election over moving the county seat from Havilah to Bakersfield, Judge Reed disqualified himself, declaring that he was an interested party.

received the Congressional Medal of Honor posthumously for his action in Vietnam in 1966.

A journalist by profession, Shell was for nine years a columnist covering the state legislature for *The Bakersfield Californian* and Capitol News Service, a syndicated agency serving 100 California newspapers. She got her early training at East Bakersfield High School, where she was editor of the school paper.

In 1975 she received the California Taxpayers Association's "Best Reporting Award" for a story revealing lucrative early retirement benefits state legislators had voted themselves. The law subsequently was repealed as a result of her story, as well as others. The same year, she was recognized by the California Trial Lawyers Association for her column on no-fault insurance.

The supervisor is married to Joe Shell, an independent oil producer and a former state assemblyman.

Webb Lake in the Buena Vista Aquatic area is named for Vance A. Webb, a Kern County Supervisor for 24 years. In 1975, Webb was elected president of the 1,360-member National Association of Counties.

Bakersfield attorney Thomas H. Werdel gained national prominence in 1956 as the vice presidential nominee on the Constitution Party ticket. He previously served as a state Assemblyman and in the U.S. House of Representatives.

Sigel, John — A native of Taft, John Sigel is the law librarian for the California Supreme Court.

Smith, Sylvester C. — As a congressman from 1905 to 1913, Sylvester C. Smith represented Kern County's petroleum interests and was responsible for a bill that strengthened individual, as opposed to federal, ownership of oil lands.

A lawyer by profession, Smith was admitted to the bar in 1886. One year later he became the editor of the Morning Echo, a newspaper founded by independent farmers during the struggle over water rights. Newspapering in those days could be a life-threatening occupation, according to an account of Smith's career in Morgan's History of Kern County.

"One evening a citizen, armed with a gun, rushed into the office exhibiting a clipping from the morning paper that had aroused his wrath. Presenting the gun at the head of Mr. Smith, he demanded that the editor literally eat the offending article ... Still covered with the weapon, Mr. Smith quietly asked a clerk to telephone for the sheriff. As [Smith] resumed writing at his desk, the angry man had time to become ashamed of his fury and the affair ended amicably."

Stiern, Walter W. — [see "The Plus Factor"]

Stockton, Warren — Superior Court Judge Warren Stockton was known as a "cattleman's lawyer," mean-

ing that he had the instincts of a pioneer lawman/cattle rancher whose handshake was as good as a signed contract. The son of one-time superintendent of schools R.L. Stockton, the judge was born at Granite Station in 1892. Judge Stockton spent 23 years on the Superior Court bench, from 1939 to 1963. He handled juvenile court cases for many years and had a reputation for his kindness and compassion in dealing with young offenders.

Stone, William A. — When he was elected in 1983 to a three-year term on the executive board of the California Judges Association, Superior Court Judge William A. Stone of Bakersfield became the first Kern County judge to serve in that capacity. The 23-member body governs the association. It also proposes legislation and provides continuing education for judges.

In the summer of 1939, former Kern County Supervisor Roy Woollomes was in San Francisco, where he flipped the switch that turned on the lights to signal the opening of the World's Fair, held that year on Treasure Island.

Thomas, William M. — Bill Thomas now is serving his fifth term in the U.S. House of Representatives. His district includes most of Kern and San Luis Obispo counties, a portion of the Antelope Valley region of Los Angeles County, and all of Inyo County.

In 1987, the congressman was appointed to the powerful House Budget Committee. Thomas also serves on Ways and Means, and the Committee on House Administration, where he is the ranking Republican on the subcommittees on elections and office systems.

Prior to his election to Congress, Thomas served two terms (1974-78) in the California Assembly. He had been a professor of American government at Bakers-

Kern County Board Of Supervisors

District 1

Henry Hammell	1866-67
D.W. Walser	1868
F.W. Craig	1868-73
A.H. Denker	1873-74
F.W. Goodale	1874-78
William Lightner	1878-80
Alvin Fay	1881-82
R.H. Evans	1883-88
Charles F. Bennett	1889-92
C.J.E. Taylor	1893-1900
J.W. Kelly	1901-02
Neils Petersen	1902-08
William Houser	1909-12
F. Rinaldi	1912
Charles F. Bennett	1913-16
C.C. Paxton	1917-20
J.B. McFarland	1920-28
W.R. Woollomes	1929-48
Ardis M. Walker	1949-52
W.R. Woollomes	1953-64
Morton V. Slater	1964
Leroy M. Jackson	1965-77
Eldon E. "Gene" Tackett	1977-85
Roy Ashburn	1985-

District 3

Samuel A. Bishop	1866
J. M. Brite	1866-73
John Narboe	1874-77
J.M. Brite	1877-80
P.O. O'Hare	1880-82
L. Crusoe	1883-84
J.M. McKamy	1885-90
E.A. McGee	1891-94
Henry Bohna	1895-98
J.W. Shaffer	1899-1902
A.J. Woody	1903-10
John O. Hart	1911-18
Harry Rambo	1919-22
J.O. Hart	1923-34
Jay Hinman	1934-38
Ralph Lavin	1939-46
Leo G. Pauly	1946
Barney L. Barnes	1947-50
Floyd L. Ming	1951-62
David S. Fairbairn	1963-71
Eugene Young	1971-83
Pauline Larwood	1983-

District 2

J.J. Rhymes	1866-69
C.T. White	1870-73
Solomon Jewett	1873-76
T.F. Kerr	1876
T.E. Harding	1876-79
A.J. Halbert	1880-82
G.H. Wheeler	1882
J.M. McKamy	1883-84
John M. Brite	1885
L.F. Gates	1886
J. Fontaine	1888-95
Jeremiah Shields	1895-1902
Lucas F. Brite	1903-18
Ralph Haven	1919-26
J. I. Wagy	1919-26
J. Perry Brite	1927-34
George Parish	1935-38
C.W. Harty	1939-50
John W. Holt	1951-71
David Head	1971-83
Ben Austin, Jr.	1983-

District 4
(Established 1884)

L. Crusoe	1885-88
Alfred Morgan	1889-92
J.W. White	1893-96
T.J. Bottoms	1897-1903
F.H. Corsett	1903-08
J.M. Bush	1909-16
Stanley Abel	1917-40
A.W. Noon	1941-52
Herbert Evans	1952
Vance A. Webb	1953-77
Trice Harvey	1977-86
Karl Hettinger	1987-

District 5
(Established 1884)

G.C. Doherty	1885-87
E.M. Roberts	1887-92
Henry Jastro	1893-1916
H.I. Tupman	1917-20
Ira Williams	1921-28
Richard Ashe	1929-32
Charles Wimmer	1933-44
Charles P. Salzer	1945-50
John Hanning	1951-60
Charles P. Salzer	1961-69
Milton Miller	1969-73
John Mitchell	1973-85
Mary K. Shell	1985-

field College since 1965 and remains on leave of absence from the college.

Turner, Rodney L. — A state assemblyman from 1932 to 1942, Rodney L. Turner introduced the first bill for the Central Valley Water Project. Turner was part owner of the first cotton gin built in Delano.

Warren, Earl — (See "The Plus Factor")

Webb, Vance A. — A member of the Kern County Board of Supervisors for 24 years, Vance Webb has been described as a "giant among pygmies." Although Webb is a large man, physically, the phrase refers to his leadership, particularly in regard to routing the California Aqueduct canal through the West Side near Taft and the establishment of Buena Vista Lake as a recreation area. (Webb Lake, one of the facility's smaller lakes, is named for him.) He also was instrumental in the expansion of the Buena Vista Golf Course.

In 1975, during his final term in office, Webb was elected president of the National Association of Counties, which at the time had 1,360 member counties throughout the United States. He previously headed the County Supervisors Association of California.

Webb's long career of public service began in 1944, when he became a member of the Taft City School District Board of Education.

Werdel, Thomas Harold — Tom Werdel, who spent much of his youth working in the mines, oilfields and farms of Kern County, was the vice presidential nominee on the Constitution Party ticket in 1956. Four years prior, he headed the "free delegation" to the Republican National Convention. Werdel served two terms in the state Assembly before being elected to the U.S. House of Representatives in 1949. He was re-elected in 1951. The Boalt Law School graduate established his practice in Bakersfield in 1936 and was licensed to practice before the U.S. Supreme Court. His sons Terence, Thomas and Charles all are Bakersfield lawyers.

Wong, Delbert — Delbert Wong, a graduate of Stanford Law School, became the first Chinese judge in the continental United States when he was appointed to the Los Angeles Municipal Court by Governor Edmund G. "Pat" Brown. Wong later was elected to the Superior Court, where he served for 23 years until his retirement in 1987.

The son of Earl and Alice Wong, the judge grew up in Bakersfield. He now is a consultant on corporate cases and is active in many Southern California organizations. Earlier this year, Wong appeared on a segment of the television series, "Superior Court."

Woollomes, W. Roy — During his 30 years on the Board of Supervisors, Roy Woollomes of Delano gained considerable respect for his service to the county.

Woollomes, who was a hardware and grocery merchant when he first came to Delano in 1909, was a key figure in convincing the federal government it should establish an Army Air Corps training base (Minter Field — now Shafter Airport) in the county in the early 1940s. As vice president of the Golden Gate International Exposition and World's Fair in San Francisco, he was given the honor of turning on the lights for its opening in 1939.

During his tenure as a supervisor, Woollomes was instrumental in the formation of the North Kern Golf Course and Lake Woollomes.

Active in the civic and youth organizations of his community literally until the time of his death, Woollomes died of a heart attack in 1964 as he was dedicating the Delano Little League Ball Park.

Wyman, Phillip D. — Phil Wyman, a Tehachapi rancher and lawyer, was elected in 1978 to represent the 34th District in the state Assembly. He chairs the Republican Caucus Task Force on Tort Reform and is vice chairman of the Public Employees Retirement System. The 42-year-old McGeorge School of Law graduate was named as one of the "Outstanding Young Men of America" in 1977 and 1979.

Zaragoza, Vincent — Vincent Zaragoza was the first Hispanic member of the Delano City Council. Appointed to the seat in 1954, he was elected on his own in 1956, serving until 1959. At the time, Zaragoza worked in the office of Frank Salsa's Texaco fuel service. He now is engaged in real estate.

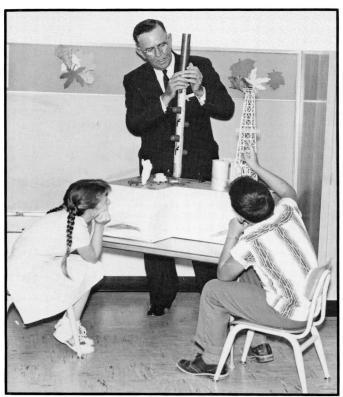

Robert Pyles, the founder of R.M. Pyles Boys Camp, often visited classrooms to explain the workings of an oil field, as he did in his photo taken at a school in Stanton, California, that is named for the former Signal Oil & Gas Co. manager.

Wildcat driller E. A. Bender has been in the oil business for nearly 70 years and also is an inventor of several pieces of drilling equipment. He is shown here with one of his early devices.

Consulting geologist Hy Seiden is all smiles — and with good reason — as he poses next to the Asphalto discovery well with his sons, Stuart and Richard, and a family friend.

5
Lucky Strikes

"You have to stick out your neck and put your money where your ideas are."

E.A. Bender

Glistening yellow gold lured hundreds of prospectors to Kern County in the 1850s. And at least two early mines, the Big Blue in the Kernville area and the Yellow Aster in Randsburg, ultimately would yield millions of dollars in profits for their operators.

Fifty years later, it would be liquid black gold — oil — that swelled the county's population.

Within a few months after Jonathan Elwood and his son, James, drilled their discovery well in the Kern River field in 1899, droves of speculators from all over the country poured into Bakersfield.

Dozens of oil companies were formed. Shares in the fledgling operations were traded on street corners and in the lobby of the Southern Hotel at 19th and Chester.

But even though the location of the petroleum was known, getting it out was no easy matter. The technology was primitive and experienced drillers were in short supply. Oil promoters hired their crews by calling out to the throng that gathered each evening in front of the Southern Hotel, "Are there any oil well drillers in the crowd?"

In recalling the scene, one Kern oil pioneer, George E. von Breyerman, said, "A number of men who did not know the first thing about drilling a well thought, why not take a chance? Six dollars a day is better than skinning mules for a dollar or so."

Though the activity was fervent once it got started, it actually had taken several months for news of the Kern River discovery to reach beyond the confines of the city. Local newspaper editors looked upon the Elwoods' enterprise as nothing more than a publicity stunt and refused to print anything about it.

Finally, Angus Crites, a respected businessman, established the Elwoods' credibility. Curious about what was going on near the banks of the Kern River north of town, Crites visited the site. There he observed the oil well in action, as well as its product, which filled a motley collection of barrels, kegs and cans that formerly had held whiskey, beer or kerosene. Crites reported what he had seen to publisher Alfred Harrell, said Milton McWhorter, the Elwoods' driller.

"Crites told the newspaper men that they had better go up the river and get themselves some oil land," said McWhorter, "because we surely had an oil field. That was what brought out the first news item."

The first oil boom lasted about two years. An oversupply of oil caused the price to drop drastically and many wells were shut down. "The early years of the Kern River field followed a hills-and-valleys pattern that, for better or worse, largely has prevailed through the history of Kern oil," says Bill Rintoul, a respected oil journalist and the author of several books on the industry.

Yet that up-and-down pattern has failed to deter the hopeful. Even today, when wells are drilled only after detailed geological studies have been developed, the movers and shakers of the oil industry are ignited by a certain spirit of adventure.

In the early days, wells were drilled mainly on the information gathered by men known as scouts. Many of the oil pioneers were stubborn about accepting the first academically trained geologists. The "college boys" were considered about as useful as a blazing fire on a hot summer day. Over the years, though, geologists have earned their place and have been responsible for making many major discoveries in the past 50 years.

The larger oil corporations have taken prominent roles in the life of the community as a whole. Many have made, and continue to make, generous gifts to schools and colleges in the area, as well as to numerous non-profit organizations. In recent years, many top oil executives have volunteered their services to many of these groups.

Lloyd Otteman, of Shell California Production, headed the 1986 United Way campaign. David Martin, president of Occidental Exploration and Production, is chiefly responsible for interesting Dr. Armand Hammer, chairman of the board of Occidental Petroleum Corporation, in bringing a portion of his priceless art exhibition to the Madigan Gallery at Cal State Bakersfield early in 1987. Claude Fiddler, a Chevron executive now based in New Orleans, was a leader in the fund-raising efforts of a number of organizations.

Like the pioneers of the oil industry, the early miners were colorful individualists. Stories abound about the exploits of these early prospectors, particularly those in the desert area.

Although individuals certainly were involved in the mining of borax, which began in the 1880s in Death Valley, northeast of Kern County, it is the famous 20-mule teams that are remembered best. These teams brought the product 165 miles across the desert — where temperatures often reach 130 degrees — to the railroad junction at Mojave. (A portion of the trail running through present-day California City has been dedicated as a historical monument.)

The huge 14-foot-long wagons, which were built in Mojave for $900 each, were designed by J.W.S. Perry, a superintendent for the company that operated the Death Valley mine, and a mule skinner named Ed Stiles. When empty, each wagon weighed 7,800 pounds. After being filled with borax, the conveyance tipped the scales at 31,800 pounds. During the six years they were in use — from 1883 to 1889 — the mule teams carried 20 million pounds of borax out of Death Valley.

Borax was discovered in Kern County in 1913, east of Mojave. In 1927, it became a major operation when the Pacific Coast Borax Company (now U.S. Borax) developed a mine and processing plant near the community of Amargo. In 1938, the town became known as Boron.

The mining of gold and other precious metals ceased to be an important part of Kern's economy many years ago. Abandoned mine shafts are the only reminders of the glory days.

Gone too are the wooden oil derricks that dotted the landscape in the county's San Joaquin Valley area. And

it is unlikely that such marvels as the Lakeview Gusher ever will be seen again. (The gusher was well-named: The well near Maricopa blew in out of control in 1910 and over the next 18 months spewed forth an estimated 9 million barrels of oil.)

Today the results produced by the petroleum pioneers are visible in the thousands of pumps that bob their steel heads up and down in front of restaurants and office buildings in southwest Bakersfield, in cultivated fields, and on the barren surfaces on the West Side.

The efforts of these intrepid pioneers, along with those of more recent leaders in the industry, have put our area in an enviable position on the nation's petroleum map.

Only 15 oil fields have been discovered in the United States which have a capability to produce 1 billion or more barrels of oil. Four of those fields are in Kern County: Midway-Sunset, Kern River, Elk Hills and South Belridge.

And if Kern County were a separate state, it would be the fourth largest oil producing state in the country, preceded only by Texas, Alaska and Louisiana.

It takes knowledge and skill to discover the location of the pools, which were formed in prehistoric times and lie hundreds, sometimes thousands, of feet below the surface. Yet a certain amount of pluck and daring is often required to drill the wells that draw the black gold from the earth.

Just as in every other area of science and technology, times have changed. Today, the risks are well-calculated. Even so, the movers and shakers of the oil industry still are those who are willing to take a chance on proving that their instincts are correct.

Bender, Edward A. — E.A. Bender began his oil career in the 1920s working on a Standard Oil pipeline at Elk Hills. By 1962, when he drilled the well that led to the rebirth of the Asphalto field, he had backed about 100 wildcats. Most had been dry or had produced very little oil.

Three years later, the wildcatter reflected on his reasons for drilling the Asphalto well, based on consulting geologist Hy Seiden's detailed study. Bender said, "It couldn't be any drier than some of the wells I've drilled before. You have to stick out your neck and put your money where your ideas are."

Shortly after the discovery, oil writer Bill Rintoul said, "The find was universally hailed as the best of the year in California. Bender himself was acclaimed for his courage in daring to walk where others feared to tread."

Now in his 80s, Bender still is active in the industry as the president of Bender Oil Company. He has invented a number of pieces of oilfield drilling equipment. His latest invention, introduced in 1986 at the Pacific Coast Oil Show at the Kern County Fairgrounds, is a long-stroke pumping unit for deep wells and high volume shallow wells. The unit is the result of more than 20 years of experimentation.

Bender is a former owner of the Bakersfield Airpark on South Union Avenue. He recently sold the airport to the city of Bakersfield.

Bishop, Josie Stevens — One of the more colorful 20th century prospectors in the Mojave Desert, Josie Bishop was known as the "radium queen." She gained the title after discovering the radioactive element on her claim near Cantil in 1937. As a result of her find, Bishop found herself on the cover of Life magazine and gained a place in Who's Who. Noted for her dynamic personality, Bishop's 1940 appearance on the "Believe It or Not" radio show was termed "a howling success."

Born in Silver City, New Mexico in 1875, she later earned a teaching credential at the state normal school. Her father was a frontier sheriff and she wrote magazine articles about some of the outlaws he apprehended — Billy the Kid, among others — and also published her autobiography.

Bishop came to the Mojave Desert with her husband in 1934. From that time on she became a dedicated prospector. She died in a Bakersfield hospital in 1957 as the result of injuries she sustained after falling out of the rear seat of a car during a desert windstorm. In accordance with her wishes, the radium queen was buried in her mine near Red Rock Canyon.

Bradley, W. R. — Ray Bradley, emeritus chairman of the board of Independent Oil Producers Association, has been an oil worker — and lived on oil leases — most of his life.

As the 69-year-old Bradley puts it, "I started out in 1936, at the age of 17, as a weed chopper in the Rosecrans field — at $4.40 a day — and ended up as president of Berry Holding Company." A native of Tennessee, Bradley came to Fellows at the age of 8. (His father worked in the West Side oilfields for many years.)

In the intervening years, he had worked for Barnsdall Oil (now Sun Oil Company), the firm that gave him his first job chopping weeds. At the time of his departure he was the company's production superintendent in the Midway-Sunset field. Bradley joined Berry in 1962 and retired in 1983.

In his present position with Independent Oil Producers, the Taft resident keeps track of legislation affecting independent producers. Les Clark is the manager of IOPA's Taft office. The agency also has an office in Long Beach and employs a lobbyist in Sacramento.

Bradley is a founding director of the Kern Oil Museum in Taft. (Berry Holding donated the building that houses the museum.) He also serves as an advisor to Westec, a Taft College program established to train oil workers.

Church, Victor — Geologist Vic Church, a Ph.D. from the University of Chicago, has been an active member of the oil industry in the San Joaquin Valley for more than 35 years. In June of this year, Church's peers named him an honorary life member of the American Association of Petroleum Geologists. He was saluted at the group's annual meeting in Los Angeles.

The late Jack Beach, cofounder of the Petroleum Club of Bakersfield, and Victor Church were in the forefront of establishing professional organizations for geologists. Each served a term as president of the San Joaquin Geological Society.

Over the years, Church has worked for both major and independent companies, as well as on his own as a consultant. He presently is a partner in G.E.C. Oil & Gas Operations, with Ed Green and Max Eastman. Green, a drilling contractor and independent producer, is the head of Gary Drilling Company. Eastman, a graduate of the University of California at Berkeley, is a petroleum engineer with more than 40 years experience in the industry. In 1984, G.E.C. brought new life to the Semitropic field west of Wasco by employing innnovative drilling and completion methods.

Church is a past president of the San Joaquin Geological Society. He and his wife, Virginia, are active in local organizations, particularly the Bakersfield Community Concerts Association, which he has served as president.

Davis, E.F. "Fritz" — Fritz Davis was a key figure in Shell Oil Company's discovery of the Ten Section field in the Kern Delta area in 1936, which led to a series of new discoveries in Kern County.

In his book, *Spudding In,* Bill Rintoul relates an anecdote that helps the lay person to understand the magnitude of the event. Shortly after the discovery, Sidney Belither, who then was president of Shell, and Davis had visited the initial well and were driving back to Bakersfield. Belither's curiosity was aroused when he spotted, in a farm field, "a blindfolded mule plodding in a resolute circle around a crude wooden contraption that looked as if it had been designed by Rube Goldberg."

Upon being told that the mule was supplying the energy for a water well used for irrigation, Belither "took a long look at the bucolic scene and said, 'We've fixed it today so they can retire that old mule.'"

Davis, a native of Colorado, was a graduate of the University of California at Berkeley where he also earned his doctorate in 1917. Prior to joining Shell in

1922 he operated the university's seismograph station. He was a pioneer in the use of many geophysical instruments, including one developed by a Hungarian physicist, Baron Roland Eotvos. Shell's first trial with the Eotvos, a torsion balance instrument that measured fluctuations in gravity, was conducted in a hut erected in the Lost Hills field, 40 miles northwest of Bakersfield.

Davis was in charge of Shell's exploration department on the West Coast from 1922 to 1947, first as chief geologist, then as vice president in charge of exploration.

Elwood, James and Jonathan — In May 1899, Jonathan and James Elwood, a father-and-son team, completed the first oil well on the banks of the Kern River. The site was on Thomas Means' farm, seven miles north of Bakersfield, where, as in other parts of the county, oil had seeped to the surface for a number of years.

But the Elwoods were the first to successfully drill a well and produce oil for commerical use. Author Bill Rintoul says, "For the first time on the West Coast a vast supply of petroleum light enough to be used as fuel had been discovered close enough to a railroad leading to the great harbor of San Francisco."

The Elwoods' well began flowing at the rate of two barrels a day and soon increased to 15. Their first sale, shipped from the Southern Pacific station in East Bakersfield, netted $1 a barrel. Soon, a number of small companies began drilling wells in the area. By 1901, an estimated 12,000 barrels a day were being shipped from the Kern River field.

Ferguson, Glenn C. — Glenn Ferguson's interest in the McDonald Anticline, 50 miles west of Bakersfield, began in the 1930s when he was a geologist for a major oil company. But it was not until 1950, and after long years of study and testing, that his interest paid off. In the summer of that year, Ferguson, who then was a partner with Irwin W. Bosworth in Ferguson & Bosworth, brought in a producing well in the area. Their discovery well was completed in the summer of 1950 and brought in 500 barrels of 30-gravity oil daily. It set the stage for many important developments in the field, which became known as the Layman area. Ferguson & Bosworth also constructed a gas plant at McDonald Anticline in 1957.

Today, Ferguson, who often is a spokesman for independent operators, is associated with Laymac Corporation. The company's most recent activity is a wildcat in the Bacon Hills area northwest of McKittrick.

Fitzgerald, Tom — In 1957, when Tom Fitzgerald became the first president of the Petroleum Club of Bakersfield, he was a well-known consulting geologist. But the path he pursued to gain that status was a rocky one indeed.

Born on a ranch in Pinole in 1903, Fitzgerald first got into the business as an "office boy" with Standard Oil (now Chevron) in San Francisco in 1922. Transferring to Taft, Fitzgerald worked as a roustabout and roughneck, then as a draftsman in the company's geological department. With the money he had saved, Fitzgerald entered the University of California at Berkeley in 1926. However, his funds ran out after only two years of college. So, back he went to Standard Oil. For the next two years the future geologist was a member of magnetometer survey crews in Texas and Venezuela. He returned to Berkeley and in 1932 received his degree in geology — 10 years after his graduation from Richmond High School.

After finishing at Berkeley, Fitzgerald worked a few months for Standard and then joined Amerada Petroleum Corporation. He subsequently worked in various parts of the San Joaquin Valley and in 1936 opened Amerada's first office in Bakersfield. Two years later he joined Richfield Oil Corporation, staying 10 years. In 1948 Fitzgerald became vice president and chief geologist for Oceanic Oil Company and opened its first office here.

The geologist became a consultant in 1950, sharing offices in the Haberfelde Building with George L. Bradford and William D. Kleinpell. Fitzgerald and his fellow consultants were regular members of the "geologists table," an informal group that met for lunch at the old El Tejon Hotel. Fitzgerald and John H. "Jack" Beach were the co-founders of the Petroleum Club of Bakersfield. Initially the club's headquarters were at the old Bakersfield Inn on Union Avenue. It later moved to the Elks Club and, since 1985, has been housed in Old Church Plaza on Truxtun Avenue.

Hagen, Rudolf — Although miners had been taking small amounts of gold from Red Rock Canyon for sever-

After graduating from high school Tom Fitzgerald worked for nearly 10 years as a roustabout and roughneck to save enough money to pay for his expenses at the University of California, Berkeley, where he earned his degree in geology.

PETROLEUM CLUB

al years before Rudolf Hagen arrived on the scene in 1893, it was he who turned out to be the champion prospector. Hagen and his associates are said to have washed $2.5 million from surface workings in the area. One of Hagen's partners, Charles Canfield, later became a pioneer in the Midway-Sunset oilfield. The long-since abandoned desert town of Ricardo was named for Hagen's son.

Jewett, Solomon and Hugh S. Blodget — The names of Solomon Jewett and Hugh Blodget appear in many places in this book. Both were leading figures in many aspects of Kern County's growth and development.

"The miners worked stark naked, covered with liquid asphaltum."

These two Bakersfield men are included in this chapter on oil and mining because of their performing activities in the community of McKittrick, then known as Asphalto. In 1893, Jewett and Blodget, in association with the Southern Pacific Railroad, formed a company called Standard Asphalt. At the refinery the company built near the S.P. railhead crude asphalt was turned into a product used for paving streets. The tar-like substance was treated with oil from hand-dug wells.

Quarrying the asphalt was sticky business, so the refined crude oil, which the partners referred to as a "distillate," also served as a cleaning agent. "The miners worked stark naked, covered with liquid asphaltum," Blodget said. "At the end of the tour they were scraped with a case knife, or the wooden scrapers used on race horses, and washed in distillate."

Oil also was used to run an engine that produced electricity for what may have been the first electric lights in Kern County. At the time, there were many oil seeps in the area. In 1889 Jewett and Blodget had attempted to drill wells in the Maricopa area, southeast of Asphalto. However, their efforts resulted in only a few shallow wells which provided small amounts of oil.

Kinley, Myron — Myron Kinley, who became known world-wide for his ability to cap runaway wells, became a student of the art at age 16 in Kern County. His first job was less dangerous: as a child, Kinley sold newspapers on Bakersfield street corners.

Kinley learned the well-taming trade from Ford Alexander, a pioneer dynamiter with whom his father, K.T. Kinley, was associated. By the 1940s, Myron Kinley was hailed as the man to find when you had an oil fire. His fame was so great that he became the subject of articles in such magazines as the Reader's Digest and the Saturday Evening Post. (Red Adair of Texas, one of Kinley's proteges, later would become equally famous.)

The veteran Kinley capped several wild wells in our area, including a Pacific Western Well at Belgian Anticline and a Richfield gas well at South Cuyama. A North African well, the Devil's Matchstick, was one of his more notable international feats.

In late summer 1953, Kinley was scheduled to speak and show films of his fire control efforts to members of the San Joaquin Valley Chapter of the American Petroleum Institute at the Taft Petroleum Club. At the last minute, he was called to Iran to put out an oilfield fire and had to postpone his Taft engagement until November 17 of that year.

Kleinpell, Robert — There are many heroic stories regarding people in the oil industry who served their country during World War II. Perhaps the most compelling one is that of geologist Bob Kleinpell.

Kleinpell, the brother of Bakersfield consulting geologist William Kleinpell, had gone to Manila in 1939, two years before Pearl Harbor, as a field geologist for the National Development Corporation. He was captured by the Japanese in 1942. Along with 4,000 other civilian prisoners of war, he was placed in Santo Tomas University, which had been turned into a prison. There the geologist, and other inmates who were qualified to teach college-level courses, organized a school in an effort to sustain themselves mentally.

"Students of all ages who took these courses called themselves the Class of '47, based on their estimate of how long it might be before they were liberated," says Robert N. Hacker, who recounted Kleinpell's experiences in a history of the Pacific Section, American Association of Petroleum Geologists, published in 1985.

Kleinpell taught geology and paleontology at Santo Tomas. In teaching his 20-week courses, the geologist relied solely on his personal knowledge and experience. He had no notes or reference works to draw upon. Yet his students acquired 100 or more pages of notes from

---

Kleinpell, suffering from malnutrition, returned to his brother's home.

---

his lectures, as well as detailed drawings of geologic strata and invertebrate animals.

The prisoners were liberated by American and Filipino forces on February 23, 1945. Kleinpell, thin as a reed and suffering from malnutrition, returned to his brother's home on Oleander Avenue in Bakersfield for a period of rest and recuperation.

Bob Kleinpell later became a professor of paleontology at the University of California at Berkeley. He retired in the 1970s. His book, *Miocene Stratigraphy of California,* published by the National Association of Petroleum Geologists, is said to be of "inestimable value" to California geologists.

San Joaquin Geological Society Presidents

John H. Beach	1946-47	Vincent F. Scury	1968-69
Eugene H. Vallat	1947-48	Ernest W. Rennie, Jr.	1969-70
Robert G. Hutcheson	1948-49	George H. Webb	1970-71
J.J. Bryan	1949-50	Harry R. Feder	1971-72
R. Stanley Beck	1950-51	Robert D. Hoffman	1972-73
W.D. Cortright	1951-52	Ben Leverett	1973-74
Victor H. Church	1952-53	W.F. Edmondson	1974-75
Robert L. Johnson	1953-54	Stanley E. Karp	1975-76
Darrel L. Kirkpatrick	1954-55	John A. Carver	1976-77
Horace E. Harrington	1955-56	Hy Seiden	1977-78
Thomas Wilson	1956-57	Robert R. Morrison	1978-79
Tennant J. Brooks	1957-58	Philip L. Ryall	1979-80
Thomas A. Roy	1958-59	Rex Young	1980-81
Harold G. Billman	1959-60	Eugene C. Tripp	1981-82
Robert A. Nesbit	1960-61	N. Jack Kappeler	1982-83
Richard H. Vaughn	1961-62	Frank L. Amato	1983-84
Wesley G. Bruer	1963-64	Jack H. West	1984-85
Rodney G. Colvin	1964-66	Robert L. Countryman	1985-86
Robert A. Ortalda	1966-67	Kenneth F. Hersh	1986-87
James L. O'Neill	1967-68		

Montgomery, Robert B. — Bob Montgomery started Montgomery Drilling Company in the early 1950s with one drilling rig. Twenty years later, his company had become one of the major firms of its kind in the industry. During the boom years of the 1970s and early 1980s, Montgomery had more than 20 rigs operating in various parts of the United States and Canada.

A graduate of Bakersfield High School and Stanford University, Montgomery worked as a roustabout as a youth. He now is semi-retired and devotes most his time to the management of his business interests in the Porterville area. Montgomery has a cattle ranch there and also owns the adjacent River Isle Country Club. Montgomery's wife, Ruth Ann, is one of the founders of Assistance League of Bakersfield.

Mooers, Frederic — Frederic Mooers, a newspaperman turned prospector, is said to be the discoverer of the Yellow Aster Mine near Randsburg in 1895. His partners in developing the fabulously rich vein of gold were Charles Burcham, a San Bernardino cattleman, and John Singleton, a down-on-his-luck carpenter. A few years earlier, Singleton had built a home in Bakersfield for William Howell but nearly went broke as a result of underestimating his costs. (The Howell house now is in the Kern County Museum's Pioneer Village.)

Singleton apparently was the shaft-building expert in the operation. Burcham, the only prospector in the area who had a team of horses, became the third member of the partnership when Mooers agreed to provide the animals' feed and three barrels of water. Burcham's wife, Dr. Rose Burcham (her vignette can be found in "The Healers" chapter), later became an important member of the operation.

Four years after the bonanza was discovered, Mooers wrote an account of the discovery which was published in the *Brooklyn Eagle*. "We three men," Mooers said, "who were virtually down to our last pot of beans in April 1895 . . . found ourselves the producers last year of $650,000 in gold bullion, which with our new mill will be doubled this year." Over its 47 years of operation, the Yellow Aster netted $16 million.

Nadeau, Remi — Remi Nadeau, a French Canadian, made his wealth by hauling silver — as much as 18 tons a day — from the Owens Valley to Los Angeles by way of Walker's Pass. A massive operation, Nadeau's Cerro Gordo Freighting Company was organized into 80 teams. Two teams made up one caravan of three wagons the size of narrow gauge railroad boxcars, which were pulled by 14 mules, plodding along at two miles per hour. At its height, the Cerro Gordo crisscrossed the desert on a daily basis. The teamsters camped and took on water at Indian Wells and Coyote Holes, a few miles northwest of present-day Ridgecrest.

Nadeau also had business interests in Caliente, Bakersfield and Los Angeles. In the late 1870s the freighter bought a small adobe store at First and Spring streets in Los Angeles. There, in 1884, he built the Hotel Nadeau, said to be the town's first four-story structure. Nadeau died in 1888 at the age of 68. In the next century the freighter's great-grandson, also named Remi Nadeau, would become the author of several books on the Owens River water controversy.

Nahama, Rodney — In recent years, Rod Nahama has become a prominent local spokesman for the oil industry. The geologist, who is a partner with Frank

Weagant in Nahama and Weagant, an exploration and production company, has held leadership positions in a number of organizations related to the oil industry. He has been an officer of the San Joaquin Geological Society and is a former board member of the California Independent Producers Association and the Independent Producers of America. He is a current member of the Bakersfield Chamber of Commerce. Nahama, who earned his bachelor's degree at UCLA, moved to Bakersfield in 1958 after completing his master's at the University of Southern California. His wife, Lily, is a member of the Bakersfield City School District Board.

Pyles, Robert M. — In 1949, veteran oil man Bob Pyles founded the boys camp that bears his name. In its nearly 40 years of operation, more than 15,000 youths have attended R.M. Pyles Boys Camp near Springville in Tulare County. Then, as now, the major financial support for the camp came from the oil industry.

The establishment of the camp was the realization of a lifelong dream for the founder, who came to know and love the Sierra as a boy in Randsburg. The eighth in a family of 10, Pyles came to Kern County in the 1890s with his widowed mother. The family opened a grocery store in the mining community. In 1904, at the age of 12, Pyles drove the store's delivery wagon, taking orders to customers in the area. The family later moved to Taft and opened a store there. In 1910 Pyles became one of the youngest drillers in oil history on a rotary drilling rig in the area. He was hired in 1936 by Hancock Oil as drilling superintendent. Later he was associated with Southwest Exploration Company in Huntington Beach, a joint venture of Hancock and Signal Oil. With that company Pyles was the manager of an unusual drilling operation that extended under Highway 101 and the beach to pools one mile out in the Pacific.

Pyles was 55 in 1948 when the camp was initiated and, although he had worked for many years, his personal wealth was not great. The camp's initial "angels" were W.A. Smith, proprietor of a supply house in Long Beach, and W.G. McComiskey, owner of Signal Hill Electric Company. The men had approached Pyles about setting up a scholarship fund for needy children in Pyles' name. Instead, he sold them on his idea of a boys camp.

To aid in the selection of the first campers (most were considered juvenile delinquents) Pyles sought the help of the Los Angeles Police Department. The two officers assigned to help him were Julio Gonzalez and Tom Bradley, now the mayor of Los Angeles. Bradley later said, "It was just as exciting for me as it was for the kids. For many of them, it was their first exposure to the great outdoors. In two weeks, those kids gained a whole new perspective on life."

Reid, Eugene C. — Gene Reid grew up in Maricopa, and, at the age of 15 was cleaning bricks and rebricking boilers in the Midway-Sunset field. By 1959 he was the owner-operator of Gene Reid Drilling Company and was considered one of the best drillers in the business. Industrialist Dr. Armand Hammer was one of those who recognized Reid's expertise. In 1957 Hammer, now chairman of the board of Occidental Petroleum Corporation, had become the president and largest share-

holder in Oxy, which then had only a handful of employees but today operates on an international scale. Oxy acquired Reid's company in 1959, in exchange for $400,000 in stock.

When Reid retired as senior vice president of Occidental Petroleum, he had become a multi-millionaire. The veteran driller gave generously to his community, although, at his request, much of his philanthropy was unknown until after his death in 1971 at the age of 68.

One of his major gifts was the $1.2 million he gave to Bakersfield Memorial Hospital. In 1961 Lucile Reid, the oilman's second wife, had recovered from cancer, and he recognized the importance of early diagnosis and treatment. His gift was used to establish a nuclear medicine department at Memorial. The hospital had hoped to name the new unit the E.C. Reid Wing and make a public announcement of his gift. But Reid would have no part of it. Bakersfield attorney Louis Deadrich, a long-time associate of Reid, said, "Gene wanted no labels, no publicity, no fanfare."

Many other non-profit organizations benefited from the oilman's "quiet gifts." One of these was the YMCA.

Installing a miniature derrick in the garden of their penthouse at 21st and Oak streets seemed natural for pioneer driller Gene Reid and his wife, Lucile.

Reid donated the funds for the construction of the Y's Olympic-sized swimming pool.

Reid's son, E.C. "Bud" Reid, ably led Occidental Exploration and Production Company as president for several years after his father's death. Bud Reid now makes his home in Santa Barbara.

Schmidt, Burro — The desert prospector known as Burro Schmidt earned his place in history for his persistence, not his riches. Schmidt spent most of his life digging a tunnel through a mountain in the Last Chance Canyon area near Garlock. The tunnel, which still can be seen today, is six feet wide, six feet high and 2,000 feet long.

Seiden, Hy — Consulting geologist Hy Seiden is responsible for working out the "play" that resulted in the discovery of the Asphalto field in 1962. But selling

Seiden, Hy — Consulting geologist Hy Seiden is responsible for working out the "play" that resulted in the discovery of the Asphalto field in 1962. But selling his play, an oilfield term describing the creative groundwork that precedes the drilling of an exploratory well, was not easy.

Oil had been produced in the McKittrick area, where Asphalto is located, since about 1900. Few thought that any new discoveries were possible. Seiden, who had given up a position with an oil company to become a consultant in January 1961, spent nearly a year working up his play and another six months trying to find someone willing to drill the well. During this time, Seiden, a New York native who did his academic work at UCLA, held a variety of part-time jobs to support his family — his wife, Ruth, and their two children. In addition to substitute teaching in the Bakersfield City Schools, he was a sales representative for a Los Angeles snack chips distributor and sold swimming pool covers. He also was the booking agent for his sister, Ginny, a professional singer, and his brother-in-law, comedian Dave Barry.

Finally, the geologist approached veteran wildcatter E.A. Bender, who decided to take a chance on Seiden's play. Bender completed the discovery well on December 13, 1962. Oil writer Bill Rintoul says, "Overnight the Asphalto oilfield ceased to be the brainstorm of a stubborn, ambitious geologist and became instead the brightest oil discovery of the year in California."

"Overnight the Asphalto oilfield became the brightest oil discovery of the year in California."

Shuler, Edward H. — The nine years Ed Shuler spent in Bakersfield as vice president and general manager of Getty Oil's (now Texaco) Western Exploration and Production Division convinced him that Kern County is the place to be. Upon his retirement in 1984, the Los Angeles native and his wife, Colleen, decided to make Bakersfield their home.

During his tenure here, from 1973 to 1982, Shuler spearheaded Getty's steam displacement operation, which set daily records for production. The tertiary recovery method increased production of existing wells from 10 percent to well over 50 percent. As Shuler puts it, "We became Getty's 'cash cow.' The Kern River field became the largest reserve anywhere in the world at that time."

In an effort to increase the price of crude oil, Shuler made many speeches around the country and contacted legislators and key officials in Sacramento and Washington, D.C. As a result of his efforts, and those of other industry leaders, the crude oil pricing was de-regulated. He was elected president of the Western Oil and Gas Association in 1978 and re-elected for the 1979 term.

Shuler, who has a master's degree in petroleum geology from the University of South California, joined Pacific Western Oil Corporation, a Getty subsidiary, in 1948. He held a number of management positions before being named vice president of production for Getty's corporate natural resources, headquartered in Los Angeles in 1973. Later that year, he assumed his position in Bakersfield.

Shuler retired in August 1984 as group vice president for three Los Angeles-based Getty divisions: international exploration and production, minerals and Canadian operations. When Getty was acquired by Texaco in February 1984, Shuler was one of those asked to stay on during the transition period.

He now serves on the boards of several local organizations, including Bakersfield Memorial Hospital, Bakersfield Country Club, Boy Scouts and the Bakersfield College Foundation. Colleen Shuler is active in the Dorian Society and Assistance League.

Silcox, John H. — John H. Silcox, who grew up in Standard Oil's 11C camp in Taft, is president of Chevron Overseas Petroleum Inc., a foreign exploration and production subsidiary of the Chevron Corporation.

Silcox joined Chevron (then Standard Oil of California) in 1951, after receiving his bachelor's degree from the University of California at Berkeley, where he also attended graduate school. During the next 30 years, he worked as a geologist with increasing management responsibility for the company's exploration activities in various western states, including a period of residence in Anchorage, Alaska, as exploration manager.

He was named vice president, Exploration, Western Operations Inc., in 1973. Silcox assumed his present position in 1984. He is responsible for directing Chevron's upstream activities in approximately 30 foreign countries. Silcox is a member of the American Association of Petroleum Geologists, the Society of Exploration Geophysicists, and the Commonwealth Club of San Francisco. He represents Chevron as a director of the African-American Institute.

Silcox, his wife, Colleen, and their sons, Clark and Brian, lived in Bakersfield for about 10 years in the 1960s. She taught in the Bakersfield City Schools and was active in Child Guidance Guild and several other organizations. The family also was involved in the Bakersfield Swim Club.

The geologist's father, Donald Silcox, was in charge of Standard Oil's chemical lab in Taft for many years. The senior Silcox and his wife, the former Keith Lee, were well-known members of the West Side community.

Stoner, R.C. "Reg" — Reg Stoner played a key role in the discovery of oil in Saudi Arabia in the late 1930s. Because of his strong belief in the potential for production in the Middle Eastern kingdom, Stoner took what many consider courageous steps to ensure that Standard Oil (now Chevron) would lead the way.

In 1937 the geologist, who earlier had worked for Standard in the San Joaquin Valley, was based in San Francisco as the general manager of production for the company. Stoner was thwarted by a tight budget in his

Geologist John Silcox, who grew up on the Standard Oil lease in Taft, has become one of Chevron's top executives and now is based in San Francisco.

pursuit of uncovering oil in Saudi Arabia. The expenses of such an operation would run into the millions of dollars and he encountered problems when he tried to get money for equipment needed to begin the exploration in Saudi Arabia. Undaunted, Stoner diverted equipment from Standard's operations in California.

The result, on March 4, 1938, was Dammam No. 4, which began flowing oil at a rate of 1,580 barrels a day from 4,727 feet. By April 22, the well had produced more than 100,000 barrels. Subsequently named the Arab Zone, the formation would become the main source of petroleum in Saudi Arabia.

Nearly 40 years later, in its publication chronicling Standard Oil of California's 100-year history, the company summarized the far-reaching effect of Stoner's efforts in Saudi Arabia. "In [1938] the 20th year of its search for oil abroad, [Standard of California] had opened the door to the world's greatest oil treasure."

The Bakersfield High School graduate went to work for Standard about 1913, after his graduation from the University of California at Berkeley, and was one of the first geologists hired by the company. He was responsible for pinpointing a number of major fields in Southern California, including Coyote Hills, Baldwin Hills and Signal Hill.

Suckow, John — Borax was discovered in Kern County in 1913 by Dr. John Suckow. A homesteader, Suckow uncovered the deposits while drilling a water well on his ranch, 30 miles east of Mojave.

It soon became apparent that there were vast deposits of the mineral in the area. In 1927, the Pacific Coast Borax Company developed a mine and processing plant near the community of Amargo. In 1938, the town became known as Boron, which is the name of the fifth element in the atomic table.

Through a series of mergers, the company was absorbed by U.S. Borax. In 1979, U.S. Borax built the world's largest boric acid plant adjacent to its refinery at Boron. The 550-foot pit from which the mineral is extracted is one mile long and one-half mile wide.

Whittier, Max — A legendary Kern County wildcatter, Max Whittier was a primary figure, along with Burton Green, in forming Belridge Oil Company, which discovered the South Belridge field in 1911. He and Green also were partners in the Rodeo Land & Water Company, which developed the city of Beverly Hills.

A native of Caribou, Maine, Whittier arrived in California in 1891 at the age of 21. After working for a time in the lemon groves of Santa Paula for $1 a day, he became a rig hand on a Union Oil crew in that area. In 1894, as a partner in the Hardly Able Oil Company, he drilled an unsuccesful wildcat in Santa Paula. He subsequently had much better luck in the Los Angeles area in association with another oil pioneer, Tom O'Donnell.

Whittier came to Bakersfield in 1899, a few months after oil was discovered in the Kern River field. He profited from the boom and helped found Associated Oil Company. He served as president of Associated, which since has been acquired by Texaco. Whittier also was instrumental in the development of the Midway-Sunset field. That field, along with Beldridge and Kern River, all are billion-barrel fields.

Whitter's great-grandson, Brett Hodges of Santa Barbara, and Tom Van Otteren have produced a 30-minute documentary on the oil pioneer's life. The film was made in 1986 with the cooperation of Shell California Production. The Bakersfield-based company now operates the Belridge properties, which were purchased by its parent corporation, Shell Oil Company, in 1979.

Williams, W. Hampton — Hamp Williams is credited with the discovery of the Joe Walker Mine in 1866. Williams, who previously had prospected — with varying degrees of success — in many parts of Kern's desert and mountain regions, found the rich ledge of gold ore at a site northwest of Walker's Basin. Until its abandonment in the 1870s, due to continual underground flooding in the shaft, the mine was one of the most profitable in the county. Apparently, Williams failed to benefit from those profits. A few days after making his discovery, the prospector and his partner, Blackburn Wyatt, sold their claim to Henry Burdett and Hugh McKeadney for $2,000.

Several other investors were involved in the Joe Walker during its existence. The final owner was Senator John P. Jones of Nevada, who also had interests in the Big Blue Mine near Kernville.

A senior scientist in the physics division of the Naval Weapons Center's research department, Dr. Jean Bennett has won top honors in the highly specialized field of optics.

Cal State Bakersfield professor Duane Blume is a modern-day explorer-scientist. Here he checks some readings during a recent expedition to Mount Everest, the tallest peak in the world.

Hundreds of records have been sent at Edwards Air Force Base Flight Test Center. Scott Crossfield, piloting the Douglas D-558-2, was the first to fly twice the speed of sound (Mach 2) on November 20, 1953.

Janice Brown, who gave up teaching school to become a full-time pilot, joined a select group of aviators in 1982 when she was named one of the winners of the Harmon Trophy for her achievements in solar-powered flight.

6
Horizon Stretchers

"Some people go to the movies to live someone else's adventure. But we thought, phooey, let's go live our own."

Dick Rutan

Over the years, Kern County aviators and scientists have chalked up an astounding number of firsts.

Today, those who challenge the unknown are highly trained professionals with solid reputations in their fields.

But when aviation was in its infancy, a sense of daring was the chief qualification. And the impact was mainly local.

A case in point is Donald McGregor, a Bakersfield newspaper reporter turned parachutist — for one thrilling moment on July 5, 1909.

Clad in a pair of borrowed red tights, McGregor leaped from a balloon that had ascended to a height of 1,500 feet from its starting point at Hudnut Park, in the vicinity of 26th and M streets. His landing was cushioned by the vegetables growing in the garden of a Chinese named Gee Dong.

It was the first parachute jump in the county's history as well as a first for McGregor. On the 50th anniversary of the event, R.E. White, the air show's promoter, recalled McGregor's credentials with amusement. "That reporter sold me a bill of goods. He convinced me he was an experienced aeronaut."

Since that time, scores of records have been set at the Edwards Air Force Base Flight Test Center (the first jet

and rocket planes in America were flown there) as well as at a number of airports in the county.

Mojave Airport, a former Marine airfield now owned by the East Kern Airport District, has become an active center for the development of civilian aircraft, particularly under the leadership of Dan Sabovich, the director. A number of private companies are based at Mojave, including the Rutan Aircraft Factory. It was at Mojave that the experimental Voyager was built and tested before being moved to nearby Edwards AFB for its non-stop flight around the world, piloted by Dick Rutan and Jeana Yeager.

The Kern County Airport System, now numbering eight airports, is a first in itself. In 1925, when Airport No. 1 was established — on a site about one mile west of present-day Meadows Field — it was the first county-owned airport in the nation. Among those who helped make it a reality were Clive Gibson, Eugene B. Duncan, Howard Nichols and Lawrence Weill. (One year earlier, this group of businessmen brought the first air mail service to the county, contracting with the postal department and a Portland, Oregon aviation company.)

The system has become a prototype for other counties throughout the nation. Cecil Meadows, airport superintendent from 1935 to 1957, is credited with providing strong leadership in making the system what it is today. (One of the interesting sidelights of Meadows Field involved the training of Indonesian air cadets in the 1960s. William Rea, then with Pacific Gas & Electric, was instrumental in organizing the program.)

The Kern County Planning Commission completed its master plan for the airport in May 1941, eight months before the start of World War II. But it would be another five years before it could be put into action.

From 1942 to 1945, the airport at Bakersfield was under the control of the U.S. Army Air Forces and no private flying was allowed. The military used the field for basic training, pilot training, pursuit and bombardment aircraft.

Simultaneously, the government established Minter Field. Now called Shafter Airport, the base was named for Hugh Minter — a Bakersfield High School graduate and World War I veteran — who was killed in a midair crash near March Field in 1932. A smaller air training base was placed at Gardner Field near Taft. (As much as a year prior to their opening, military pilots were trained at present-day Meadows Field and many local people were involved in the instruction.)

Despite the seriousness of the task before them, or perhaps because of it, the military enjoyed wide social and recreational contacts with the Bakersfield community. (More than a few airmen met their future wives while stationed at Minter and returned to make their homes here after the war.)

"One day I looked up and there was Jack Dempsey. He was the most gorgeous hunk of a prizefighter I ever saw in a military uniform."

The person responsible for setting up such events was Major Lee Frankovich, who before, and after, his military service was a motion picture producer. As chief of the base's special services, Frankovich brought numerous Hollywood celebrities to entertain at Minter, as well as athletes.

Judy Clausen, presently a contributing columnist for *The Bakersfield Californian,* served on Frankovich's staff during summer vacations while a student at the University of California at Berkeley. "One day I looked up and there was Jack Dempsey," Clausen recalls. "He was the most gorgeous hunk of a prizefighter I ever saw in a military uniform."

Minter servicemen with musical abilities also provided entertainment on the base, and at dances at the Woman's Club and the USO. One of them was Les Herndon, a trumpet-playing member of the Jive Bombers, whose son, Steve Herndon, now is an associate dean

Cecil Meadows, seated in the cockpit of the Jenny he flew during his barnstorming days, was Kern County's first superintendent of airports and a key figure in the system's development.

at Cal State Bakersfield. The Woman's Club hosted a well-attended picnic at Beale Park, spearheaded by club president Georgia Tomerlin.

Women were based at Minter too. These included members of the WAC (Women's Army Corps) and the WASPs (Women Airforce Service Pilots).

Memories of Minter are kept alive through the Minter Air Museum, housed at Shafter Airport. And in 1986 more than 450 (including Col. Carl Pyle, the first commanding officer) attended the first reunion banquet of former Minter-ites. Ed Richardson and Dina Garlow coordinated the event.

The war also was the impetus for the establishment in 1943 — at an airstrip in Inyokern — of the Naval Ordnance Test Station, which has since become the U.S. Navy's largest research, development, test and evaluation activity. Now called the Naval Weapons Center at China Lake, it is a vast complex of laboratories and test-range facilities, covering more than one million acres. The estimated value of its physical plant is a staggering $1,600,000,000.

Often referred to as a military-civilian partnership, the center's working team is made up of about 5,500 individuals from the private sector and about 1,000 military personnel. Close to 2,000 of the cilivians are engaged in science and engineering. Information about much of the work that goes on at the Naval Weapons Center is classified, so the scientific advancements made there are not as well known to the public as those at Edwards AFB.

Kern long has been a mecca for private pilots and its boundaries include more than 60 private airports and landing strips. In June of this year, Rio Bravo Airport, east of Bakersfield, was the site for the start of the 1986 Air Race Classic, sponsored by the Ninety-Nines.

Whether they are public, private or "classified," the individuals who make up the movers and shakers in aviation and science are singular indeed.

Allen, Bryan — Cycling his way through the sky, Bryan Allen set two world records for human-powered flight in aircraft designed by Dr. Paul MacCready, president of AeroVironment in Pasadena.

The first, in the Gossamer Condor, took place over Shafter Airport on August 23, 1977, when Allen completed a figure-eight pattern to win for MacCready the $50,000 Kremer Prize. The historic craft is on display at the Smithsonian Institution's National Air and Space Museum.

Two years later, Allen flew the Gossamer Albatross, an improved version of the Condor, over the English Channel. The cyclist-airman kept the plane aloft for two hours and 49 minutes. This time Allen won for MacCready and his sponsors, the E.I. DuPont de Nemours Company, another Kremer Prize — this time for $100,000.

The Condor initially was tested at Mojave Airport but was moved to the Shafter site because it had a larger hangar and better wind conditions. Kern County residents involved in the trials at Shafter Airport included Vern and Maude Oldershaw, both experienced sailplane pilots and airplane builders; Pete Plumb, Sam Duran and Bill Richardson, who served as principal observer for the National Aeronautic Association.

Amlie, Thomas S. — When Dr. Thomas Amlie was at the Naval Weapons Center, he had a reputation for having little use for what he considered nonsensical red tape. He also was known for his informal attire — especially the red Hush Puppies he usually wore on his feet.

Noted for candor, he frequently appears on CNN (Cable News Network) and other network news programs when a scientific opinion is sought.

Amlie, who has a Ph. D. in electrical engineering, is credited with developing two missiles for the Navy and was actively involved in the Sidewinder program. He served as the center's technical director, a civilian position, from 1968 to 1970 and first came to China Lake in July of 1952 — in time for the Tehachapi earthquake. At the time, he was a naval officer.

Recalling his first impressions of the desert climate and the quakes, Amlie said, "Had I been a civilian, I would have left, but I had no option so I simply had to stay. Of course, by the end of two years when I was released to inactive duty, I had come to love the place."

Since leaving the center, Amlie has worked for the Air Force and the Federal Aviation Agency. He met his wife, the former June Townsend, at China Lake. She earned her Ph.D. in analytical chemistry at Rutgers.

Arnold, Henry Harley, "Hap" — What is now Edwards Air Force Base had its beginnings in September 1933, when U.S. Army Air Corps personnel, under the command of a 47-year-old lieutenant colonel known as "Hap" Arnold, began using the area (then called Muroc Dry Lake) for bombing and gunnery training.

Arnold, who had friends in Bakersfield, made frequent visits to the city and enjoyed hunting game in the surrounding area — in fact, that's what he was doing with Kern County Fire Chief Harold Bowhay on the morning of December 7, 1941. According to one informant, "The Army had an airplane waiting at the airport for 'Hap' and there was a mad scramble on the part of the military to find him. He was a very important guy, even then."

Before his death in 1950, Arnold rose to the rank of four-star general and was Air Force Chief of Staff.

Austin, Carl — The Naval Weapons Center at China Lake is the Navy's primary laboratory for the research and development of geothermal energy resources. Dr. Carl Austin has tenaciously directed that effort for nearly 20 years.

The Coso (Hot Springs) Geothermal project went on line in June 1987 and is expected to meet all of the NWC's electrical needs. For his work in developing the project, Austin has been recognized by Congress, the Department of Defense and the Navy Department. In 1982 he received the center's William B. McLean Award.

Austin, who came to China Lake in 1961, has a doctorate in geological engineering and also teaches geology classes at Cerro Coso Community College. Going on a field trip with the energetic "Doc" often taxes the physical capabilities of students many years his junior.

The geologist raises goats on his farm in the Indian Wells Valley and is concerned, and often vocal, about water issues. "Dr. Austin's voice," says a member of the NWC staff, "is a result of years of speaking over the roar of mining and drilling machinery. His whisper is about the equivalent of someone else's shout."

One of the first scientists to come to China Lake in the 1950s, Dr. Thomas Amlie is noted for his candor and often appears on Cable News Network.

Austin is in charge of mine rescue for the Indian Wells Valley Search and Rescue Group, and also conducts examinations of disputed mining claims for the government. He and his wife, Barbara, co-authored *Common Sense in Desert Traveling,* a guidebook for desert and mine explorers.

Barnes, Florence — The legendary Florence "Pancho" Barnes, a record-breaking aviator in her own right, became a close friend of the test pilots from Edwards Air Force Base.

Her Rancho Oro Verde Fly-Inn Dude Ranch (also known as the Happy Bottom Riding Club) was a favorite gathering place for such notables as Gen. Jimmy Doolittle and Chuck Yeager.

Barnes first became acquainted with the military personnel when she began selling dairy products to the base, which she raised on her farm. Quickly realizing that the facility needed a garbage collector, she contracted for those services too, which in turn stimulated

EDWARDS AIR FORCE BASE HISTORY OFFICE

The parties that Pancho Barnes, second from the right, hosted at her Rancho Oro Verde Fly-Inn Dude Ranch sometimes drew as many as 400 service personnel at one time. Col. Shoup, then the commander of Edwards Air Force Base, is at Pancho's right.

other business: Pancho fed the leavings of the Air Corps mess to her hogs, then sold the end product back to the government in the form of ham and bacon.

Stories abound about Barnes and her unconventional lifestyle. Although she grew up in wealthy circumstances in San Marino, California, she bore few traces of her upbringing. She usually wore men's clothing, was known for her outrageous language and wild parties.

She was married four times — the Rev. Barnes, rector of the Episcopal Church in Pasadena, was her first husband. After leaving the minister, she hopped a banana boat and spent several months as an adventurer in Mexico. Returning to Southern California, she learned to fly and became the star performer of "Pancho Barnes Mystery Circus of the Air." She invested in a variety of

Pancho fed the leavings of the Air Corps mess to her hogs, then sold the end product back to the government in the form of ham and bacon.

financial ventures, many of which periodically left her broke.

But Pancho's achievements in aviation were solid. She participated in many major air races in the 1920s, including the first Powder Puff Derby. One year later she set a new world's speed record for women: 196.19 mph. The previous titleholder was Amelia Earhart.

Barnes died in 1975. Her fourth and last husband still lives in the desert area at Cantil.

Bennett, Harold E. — Dr. Hal Bennett, currently head of the physics division of the research department at the Naval Weapons Center, is recognized internationally for his pioneering achievements in the field of physical optics.

Much of his work is classified. However, the results of his research are said to be vital to the successful use of laser technology in military systems. Among his significant contributions are the development of such instruments as the absolute reflectometer, the optical evaluation facility and the optical functional tester.

The University of Montana graduate, who came to China Lake in 1956, has received every major award given by the center. He also is the recipient of numerous national honors, and has served on the U.S. National Committee of the International Commission for Optics.

Bennett, Jean M. — "Firsts" seem to be a way of life for Dr. Jean M. Bennett, a senior scientist in the physics division of the Naval Weapons Center's research department.

In 1987, she became the first woman to head the 8,500-member Optical Society of America. Earlier in her career, she was the first female to earn a Ph.D. in physics at Pennsylvania State University and the first of her sex to teach the subject there. She came to China Lake in 1956 with her former husband, Dr. Hal Bennett.

Considered one of the outstanding scientists — male or female — at China Lake, Jean Bennett's work is in optics, a field that is as esoteric as it is classified. In 1979 she received the Federal Women's Program Award for the Woman Scientist of the Year.

Blume, F. Duane — Dr. F. Duane Blume may be the only living international explorer-scientist in Kern County.

The Cal State Bakersfield biology professor and director of the college's Center for Physiological Research, has participated in two expeditions to Mount Everest (the tallest peak in the world) in the past 10 years.

Blume was the oxygen officer of the 1971 International Himalayan Expedition to Mount Everest. He helped design a portable oxygen system used by the climbers. In 1981, he served as deputy leader in charge of logistics and finance, and, as senior scientist, on the American Medical Research Expedition to Everest (AMREE).

The purpose of AMREE was to study how healthy individuals respond when faced with extreme oxygen deficiency. During the course of the expedition, experiments tested the functions of the cardiovascular, pulmonary and endrocrine systems at various altitudes, up to and including the summit of Everest: 29,028 feet.

"Interestingly," Blume observes, "the pressure of oxygen on the summit of Everest is at or near the lower limit [needed] to sustain human life, even for short periods. The results of this study may well provide the basis for understanding some of the disease processes seen at sea level."

Blume currently is conducting a comparative physiology study of life-long natives of the Andes in South America and the Himalayas in China-Nepal. He leads a team of seven scientists who are attempting to determine if the natives of the two highest mountain ranges in the world differ in their adaptation to high altitude. Grants from the National Science Foundation and the National Geographic Society have funded his research.

Boyd, Albert — On June 20, 1947 Al Boyd, flying a P-80 Shooting Star, attained a speed of 624 mph. In doing so, he set a world speed record, returning the honor to the United States for the first time in 24 years. Boyd became the first commander of the Air Force Flight Test Center at Edwards Air Force Base, serving from 1949 to 1952. Now deceased, he retired as a lieutenant general.

Brown, Janice — Janice Brown joined a distinguished group of aviators when she was named a winner of the 1982 Harmon Trophy. The award, often called the "Nobel Prize of Aviation, was presented to her by President Reagan at the White House.

The list of previous Harmon recipients reads like a "who's who" of the skies. Among them are Amelia Earhart, Jimmy Doolittle, Scott Crossfield, Howard Hughes and Wiley Post.

Brown was recognized for piloting the world's first successful sun-powered aircraft, the Solar Challenger, in a record-setting flight over the Arizona desert. Then an elementary schoolteacher, she now is director of operations at Rio Bravo Airport.

The pilot became involved with the testing of the lightweight aircraft designed by Paul MacCready when she flew the Gossamer Penguin, the predecessor of the Solar Challenger at Shafter Airport. The designer's son, Marshall, then an 80-pound 13-year old, made the world's first flight powered only by sunlight May 18, 1980. However, it was felt that an adult should fly the

Historic Events At Edwards AFB
(A Selected List)

September 1933 — U.S. Army Air Corps personnel, commanded by then Lt. Col "Hap" Arnold, begin using the Edwards area for bombing and gunnery training.

December 1941 — Permanent training base is established for training Army Air Corps crews.

June 20, 1947 — Col. Al Boyd, in a P-80 Shooting Star, sets a world's speed record — 624 mph — returning it to the U.S. for the first time in 24 years.

Oct. 14, 1947 — For the first time, the speed of sound (Mach 1) is exceeded by then Capt. Charles Yeager.

Jan. 27, 1950 — Edwards AFB dedicated in honor of Capt. Glen W. Edwards.

Nov. 20, 1953 — The Douglas D-558-2, piloted by A. Scott Crossfield, becomes the first aircraft to fly twice the speed of sound — Mach 2.

Sept. 27, 1956 — The X-2 rocket research plane becomes the first aircraft to reach Mach 3, but the pilot, Capt. Milburn G. Apt, is killed when the X-2 goes out of control.

Aug. 22, 1963 — NASA pilot Joe Walker sets a new winged aircraft altitude record of 67 miles with the X-15 rocket aircraft.

March 1, 1965 — An Air Force YF-12A sets nine world speed and altitude records at Edwards — in one day.

Oct. 5, 1967 — Flying the X-15, Major William J. "Pete" Knight sets the world's absolute speed record of 4,250 mph — Mach 6.7.

July 12, 1971 — Col. Edwin "Buzz" Aldrin, the second man to set foot on the moon, is named the new commandant of the Aerospace Research Pilot School.

July 27, 1972 — McDonnell Douglas chief test pilot Irv Burrows makes the first flight of the aeronautics firm's F-15 Eagle fighter.

Dec. 23, 1974 — Beginning of the six-year B-1 bomber test and evaluation program.

Aug. 12, 1977 — First of the five glide and landing tests of the space shuttle prototype Enterprise.

April 14, 1981 — Space shuttle Columbia, lands at Edwards after a 54-hour flight.

July 4, 1982 — More than 500,000 people, including President Ronald Reagan, view the fourth space shuttle landing. (In all, 18 of the 24 successful shuttle missions have landed at Edwards.)

Dec. 14, 1984 — The X-29 forward-swept wing research aircraft flies for the first time in a joint Air Force-NASA program.

Dec. 23, 1986 — After a nine-day round-the-world flight of 25,012 miles, Dick Rutan and Jeana Yeager land the Voyager at Edwards.

demonstration flight at Shafter Airport and the diminuitive Brown was elected.

Brown and Steven Ptacek were the test pilots for the Challenger, setting several altitude, duration and distance records in California and Arizona. In 1981, Ptacek piloted the craft on its 163 mile flight from France to England. Brown was the back-up pilot for the Channel crossing.

Buchner, Les — A long-time flight service operator at Meadows Field, Les Buchner taught many private pilots. Now retired, Buchner lives in Las Vegas. His sister, Carol Buchner Rogers, is a Bakersfield resident.

Burroughs, Sherman Everett, Jr. — Rear Adm. Sherman E. Burroughs, then a captain who had just returned from World War II combat duty in the Pacific, was the first commanding officer at China Lake. It was

Burroughs High School in Ridgecrest is named for Rear Adm. (ret.) Sherman E. Burroughs, the first Naval Weapons Center commander. Burroughs, second from left, was a captain when this picture with Dr. Lauritzen, Cdr. Hayward and Dr. Merle Fowler was taken.

he who established the Naval Ordnance Test Station (now the Naval Weapons Center) in the sparsely populated desert area of eastern Kern County in 1943.

Specifically, the Annapolis graduate (class of 1924) had two missions, both of which he carried out with admirable success: To support the development work of the California Institute of Technology at the facility, and to build a research and development center for the Navy.

In assessing Burrough's achievements at China Lake, a naval spokesman said that the commander's "knowledge of Navy's ordnance needs, particularly aviation [weapons], and his understanding of the kind of work-

An early commander of the Naval Weapons Center, Thomas Connolly, second from the right, went on to become Deputy Chief of Naval Air Operations in Washington, D.C. Also shown in this 1952 photo are Capt. P.D. Stroop, Capt. W. Vieweg, Dr. N.E. Ward and Ted Toporeck.

ing environment needed by civilian scientists and engineers helped lay the foundation for the NWC military-civilian partnership of today."

Now in his mid-80s, the much-decorated admiral and aviator — Silver Star, Legion of Merit, Distinguished Flying Cross, among others — lives on Coronado Island in San Diego. He has kept in touch with the people of Ridgecrest and China Lake over the years. In the summer of 1986, he returned for the graduation ceremonies of Burroughs High School, which is named in his honor.

Connolly, Thomas F. — Vice Adm. Thomas Connolly, who held the rank of captain when he was the experimental officer at the Naval Weapons Center (1952-54), went on to become Deputy Chief of Naval Operations (Air). In that position, he frequently was an outspoken critic of the overall handling of the war in southeast Asia and advocated a halt in bombing.

In a 1967 interview, while serving as Deputy CNO, Connolly noted that more than 75 percent of the air-to-air and air-to-ground weapons then being used in Vietnam were developed at the Naval Weapons center, then called the Naval Ordnance Test Station (NOTS).

"From my job in the Pentagon I get a broad picture of what is going on in air actions world-wide," he said. "Part of NOTS is with me every time I read the daily action reports. The new weapons we worried about then are with us and doing exactly what we intended them to do."

The admiral recalled that, as a project pilot at China Lake, he flew early test firings of the Sidewinder missile with, as he put it, "another little-known NOTS pilot of the time, Lt. Wally Schirra," who later became an astronaut.

Connolly said that he and his wife, Peggy, came to love the desert and the people. "The combination leads me to confess: Those were wonderful, happy days."

Dana, William — Bill Dana, a West Point graduate who grew up in Bakersfield, was project pilot on the X-15 and has been involved in the Space Shuttle program.

As a civilian working for the National Aeronautics and Space Administration's Flight Research Center at Edwards Air Force Base, Dana was the project pilot on the X-15. He attained a top speed of 3,897 mph and an altitude of 310,000 feet in the rocket-powered aircraft, a feat which qualified him as an astronaut.

Dana also was involved in the Shuttle-related manned lifting body flight test program in the mid 1970s. He was awarded NASA's Exceptional Service Medal for his outstanding work. The pilot also received the American Institute of Aeronautics and Astronautics' Haley Space Flight Award for his contributions to the M2-F3 control systems research.

A resident of Tehachapi since 1972, Dana was the grand marshal of the community's Mountain Festival in 1981. His mother, Mrs. Drexler Dana, lives in Bakersfield.

Donnels, Achsa — Bakersfield resident Achsa Donnels, a pioneer female pilot, is a charter member of the Ninety-Nines, an organization of women aviators founded by Amelia Earhart. Donnels no longer flies but is active in the group's Kern County chapter.

Edwards, Glen W. — Edwards Air Force Base is named for Capt. Glen W. Edwards, an outstanding test and engineering pilot, who was killed during the testing of the experimental Flying Wing program. The YB49 he was flying crashed on June 5, 1948.

Edwards grew up in Lincoln, California, a town north of Sacramento, and was a graduate of the University of California at Berkeley. Don Haley of the Edwards public affairs office said the base's namesake was "very well-thought of by his peers. He was a quiet, dedicated pilot who contributed a lot to flight testing in that early period."

Falk, Elynor Rudnick — The founder of Bakersfield Airpark, Elynor Rudnick trained Israeli pilots at the facility from 1946 to 1948. Now owned by the city of Bakersfield, the airport is undergoing a $14 million expansion program. At one time, she also operated a helicopter service in New Zealand.

Fulton, Fitzhugh L., Jr. — "Fitz" Fulton is considered one of the finest multi-engine test pilots in the world. Fulton, who earlier had flown in the Berlin Airlift, arrived at Edwards Air Force Base in 1950. He flew at Edwards continuously (with one year out for a tour in Korea) until 1986 for the Air Force and the National Aeronautics and Space Administration (NASA).

He was a drop pilot for a number of X-series programs and the project pilot for a number of major projects at the Flight Test Center, such as the B-58 and XB-70. In 1960 Fulton, then an Air Force major, successfully landed a B-58 Convair bomber on the Edwards runway. The event was especially significant

---

Naval Weapons Center, China Lake

COMMANDERS*

Rear Adm. Sherman E. Burroughs	1943-45
Capt. James B. Sykes	1945-47
Rear Adm. W.G. Switzer	1947-49
Capt. Walter V.R. Viewig	1949-52
Vice Adm. Paul D. Stroop	1952-53
Capt. R. H. Solier	Aug.-Sept. 1953
Capt. David B. Young	1953-55
Capt. Robert F. Sellars	July-Aug. 1955
Capt. Frederick L. Ashworth	1955-57
Capt. William W. Hollister	1957-61
Capt. Charles Blenman, Jr.	1961-64
Capt. Leon Grabowsky	June-Aug. 1964
Capt. John I. Hardy	1964-67
Capt. Grady H. Lowe	Feb.-Sept. 1967
Capt. Melvin Etheridge	1967-70
Vice Adm. William J. Moran	1970-72
Rear Adm. Henry Suerstedt, Jr.	1972-73
Rear Adm. Paul E. Pugh	1973-74
Rear Adm. Rowland G. Freeman III	1974-77
Capt. Frederic H.M. Kinley	May-Sept. 1977
Rear Adm. William L. Harris	1977-79
Capt. William B. Haff	1979-81
Capt. John J. Lahr	1981-83
Capt. K.A. Dickerson	1983-86
Capt. J.W. Patterson	June-Aug. 1986
Capt. John Alan Burt	1986-

*Rank listed is the highest attained presently or at time of retirement.

TECHNICAL DIRECTORS

Louis T.E. Thompson	1945-51
Frederick W. Brown	1951-54
William B. McLean	1954-67
Haskell G. Wilson	1967-68
Thomas S. Amlie	1968-70
Haskell G. Wilson	1970-73
Walter B. LaBerge	April-Sept. 1973
Leroy Riggs	1973-74
Guilford L. Hollingsworth	1974-77
Robert M. Hillyer	1977-82
Burrell W. Hays	1982-86
Gerald R. Schiefer	1986-

since the craft had blown seven of eight tires on its right main landing gear upon take-off.

Beginning with the Enterprise in 1977, Fulton was the chief 747 pilot for all the tests in connection with the piggy-back procedures of the space shuttle program. From 1981 to 1985 he was the lead pilot on all of the ferry flights that carried the shuttle back to Florida.

Fulton, who retired from the Air Force as a colonel, also is a NASA retiree. Now in his 60s, he presently works for an aeronautical company based at Mojave Airport.

Gianopulos, George — George Gianopulos, who grew up in Taft, has worked for the National Aeronautics and Space Administration's Jet Propulsion Laboratory at California Institute of Technology for more than 30 years. He was director of Mission Control for the Mars Orbiter and Lander. Gianopulos has received a number of achievement awards, including a NASA medal.

Heller, Carl A., Jr. — (See "The Plus Factor")

Holloway, H.H., "Dutch" — In 1919, daring Bakersfield residents paid "Dutch" Holloway to take them up in his Curtiss Jenny biplane. The take-off point was at Alta Vista and Pacific streets, on vacant land owned by Louis Olcese. A large pepper tree that grew there marked the "landing strip." His first female passengers were Mrs. Philip Markle and Mrs. George Crease. The pioneer later operated H.H. Holloway Aerial Service, one of the first commercial flight companies in Kern County.

Daring Bakersfield residents paid "Dutch" Holloway to take them up in his Curtiss Jenny biplane. A large pepper tree marked the "landing strip."

Marr, Kenneth — Kenneth Marr started the first airline in Kern County, operating his "air stage line" between Taft and Bakersfield. His first passengers, on April 5, 1920, were two Maricopa residents, F.O. Shoup and a woman named Dicey Carroll.

The same year Marr, in association with C.A. Pond, offered flights from San Francisco to Los Angeles in an eight-passenger Curtis Eagle. The plane had a pilot and a co-pilot, and advertisements boasted that "the Eagle machine has three motors, any one of which can propel the machine alone, so there is no danger of accidents."

One of test pilot Fitz Fulton's more hair-raising feats came about when he successfully landed a B-58 Convair that had blown seven of the eight tires on its right landing gear upon take-off.

McGregor, Henry — Henry McGregor, a master toolmaker and mechanic, earned his place in Kern County's aviation history in 1911 when he became the first local resident to build and fly an airplane.

McGregor made two flights that day in the Santos Dumont monoplane he had put together from a kit on the second floor of the Bakersfield Garage. Taking off from a point in the Edison area, McGregor, who had no previous experience, reached a speed of 35 mph and rose about 20 feet on his first try. He dragged his feet to brake the plane when it returned to the ground.

His second landing wasn't as happy — in fact, the plane crashed at take-off. McGregor was thrown to the ground, uninjured.

Financial backing for the venture was provided by R.E. White, who later was assistant engineer for the city of Bakersfield, and auto dealer W. E. Drury.

McGregor repaired the Santos Dumont and later was involved in another flying attempt with White, Jess Rodgers and Otto Waneke, who had a Curtiss biplane. Unfortunately, the planes were destroyed when a sudden whirlwind swept across the site at Edison.

In an interview 50 years later, McGregor recalled, "I came out of the tent in time to see one of the planes flip-flopping across the field like a tumbleweed."

The experience convinced the pioneer builder-pilot that his true vocation lay in auto mechanics.

McLean, William B. — Research scientist Dr. William B. McLean invented the Sidewinder missile at China Lake, the weapon that revolutionized air warfare shortly after its introduction in 1952.

But the rumor is that McLean really invented it in his garage. And that may very well be true, in light of a statement he later made regarding his undersea experiments.

"I have one very great handicap in getting ideas executed," said the Cal Tech nuclear physicist, "I can visualize them and see how they'll work, but I have difficulty drawing them. Rather than sketching a new shape for my undersea vehicle, it was much easier to go out to the garage and whittle out a model."

McLean was a member of the founding team of Cal Tech scientists at China Lake and served as technical director from 1954 to 1967. Visitors to the center in the mid-1960s were startled to see the rear of a submarine protruding from a wing of the laboratory — an unusual sight in the desert.

This mini-sub was the Moray, on which McLean worked before moving to the Naval Ocean Systems Center in San Diego. McLean conducted many of the tests of the glass bathysphere in the indoor swimming pool at China Lake.

In 1958, President Eisenhower presented McLean with the President's Award for Distinguished Federal Civilian Service.

Meadows, Cecil — Cecil C. Meadows was one of the key figures in the development of the Kern County Airport System.

Meadows was named superintendent of Kern County airports in 1935. Over the next two decades the system became a prototype for other county-owned facilities throughout the country, and Meadows gained national prominence as an airport executive. He became president of the American Association of Aeronautics Executives and was an officer in the California Aeronautics Association. Locally, he was founder of the Kern County Pilots Association and was a member of the Sheriff's Aero Squadron.

As a pilot, Meadows set a number of records. His achievements include setting the world altitude record for flying without oxygen. He also pioneered the "parachute drop" technique and was the first to successfully use this procedure in rescue operations in California's mountains and deserts.

The native Texan had gained considerable experience as a barnstormer, commercial pilot and instructor in Southern California before coming here. In 1929, he established the Kern County School of Aviation and later organized the Meadows Flying Service. He served as a navigator during World War II.

The pioneer airman died of a heart attack on August 3, 1957. A few days later, the Kern County Board of Supervisors named Airport No. 1 Meadows Field in his honor.

"Rather than sketching a new shape for my undersea vehicle, it was much easier to go out to the garage and whittle out a model."

Mettler, Ruben Frederick — Shafter native Ruben Mettler, who earned his Ph.D. in electrical and aeronautical engineering at Cal Tech in 1949, is the chief executive officer at TRW Inc. (formerly Thompson, Ramo Wooldridge). In 1969-70, he headed the President's Science Policy Task Force and has been a member of the President's Blue Ribbon Defense Panel. He has received numerous professional and civic awards, and in 1980 served as national campaign chairman of the United Negro College Fund. He holds a patent for his interceptor fire control systems. Mettler, the son of Henry F. and Lydia Mettler, resides in Cleveland, Ohio.

Moorer, Thomas Hinman — Time magazine once described Thomas H. Moorer, a former experimental officer of the Naval Weapons Center at China Lake, as "the U.S.'s fastest rising sailor."

The appellation was deserved. At the time, 1965, the 53-year-old Moorer was a four-star admiral, and was commander-in-chief of the Atlantic Fleet, as well as commander of all U.S. troops in the Atlantic and Su-

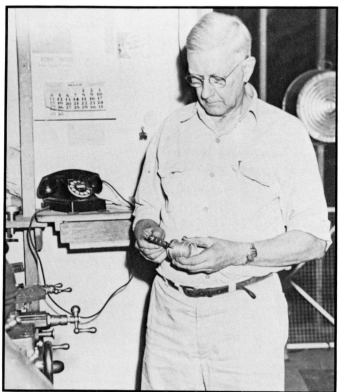

Master mechanic Henry McGregor was the first Kern County resident to build and fly an airplane in 1911. He built the Santos Dumont monoplane on the second floor of the Bakersfield Garage.

KERN COUNTY MUSEUM

John Pearson's fame as the developer of explosive welding techniques extends behind the Iron Curtain. The scientist came to China Lake in 1951, expecting to stay about two years, and has been there ever since.

preme Allied Commander — "NATO's top sailor." Two years later Moorer became Chief of Naval Operations, and in 1970 Chairman of the Joint Chiefs of Staff, a position he held until his retirement in 1974.

The admiral's wife, Carrie, gave birth to two of their four children in China Lake during the time he was stationed at the center.

Paynter, Joan — Cross-country air racing, which combines skills in aircraft handling, navigation, weather assessment and other technical areas, is the ultimate test of a pilot's abilities. Bakersfield pilot Joan Paynter has participated in five such races.

A margin of seconds kept her from winning the four-day, 2,500-mile Powder Puff Derby (now called the Air Race Classic) in 1976. She took second place in the 200-plane competition. Paynter says, "That race was probably the most challenging and nerve-wracking of all I have experienced, in terms of critical weather problems, aircraft mechanical worries and severe turbulence."

A commercial pilot, licensed for single and multi-engine planes, she has logged 4,000 hours since she began flying in 1967. In 1974 she became the owner-operator of PayntAERO, an air charter service. The passengers in her Beechcraft Bonanza have included business people, politicians, patients on medical flights and, on occasion, an injured dog enroute to emergency surgery.

Paynter is active in the Ninety-Nines, an organization of women pilots. In June 1987, the group sponsored the Air Race Classic Start at Rio Bravo Airport.

The pilot is married to architect William Paynter.

Pearson, John — A senior research scientist at the Naval Weapons Center, John Pearson has an international reputation for his development of explosive

welding techniques. His method of joining metals is known as "Pearson welding," even behind the Iron Curtain.

A story often told about the scientist — possibly apocryphal — is that while attending a conference in Europe he was approached by a group of East Germans, who had learned that he was the inventor of Pearson welding. The representatives of the Communist bloc nation told Pearson he should move to their country where he could be "properly honored for his work."

Pearson came to China Lake in 1951 as a research engineer in the physics division of the research department, where he began a long and productive relationship with Dr. John Rinehart, another pioneer in explosives research. Two of the books he co-authored with Rinehart have become classics in their field.

Like many others, Pearson originally intended to make his stay at the Naval Weapons Center a brief one — two years at the most. But in 1984, 33 years after his arrival, he explained, "What kept me here ... was the fascinating work that could be done and the great group of people at China Lake. This is really a way of life, not just a place to work."

Although he retired from civil service in 1980, Pearson continues to head the detonation physics division as a rehired annuitant.

Pemberton, Roy — During his 48-year career as a pilot, Roy Pemberton logged approximately 30,000 hours in the air. At one time, the Bakersfield resident's Pemberton Flying Service had about 16 planes and was the largest operation of its kind at Meadows Field.

The veteran pilot came to Kern County in 1925 from Imperial, California, where he had gone to school with

> "What kept me here...was the fascinating work that could be done and the great group of people at China Lake. This is really a way of life, not just a place to work."

Cecil Meadows. Pemberton's first plane was an open-cockpit, 90-horsepower JN4D. He bought the Jenny for $100. It came in a crate, unassembled.

Pemberton has lost count of just how many private pilots he's instructed. But he does recall that from 1939 to 1942 he trained 500 military airmen under a government contract. When Meadows Field was closed during World War II, he went to Lone Pine and continued working for the military in association with a Bakersfield College aviation program headed by Theron Taber.

In the early days at Meadows Field, Pemberton often took passengers on 20-minute Sunday morning spins. Among his frequent fliers were a very young Mary K. Shell (the supervisor later became a pilot herself) and her grandfather, Harry E. Jaynes.

At least three of his students — Larry Brandvig, Marvin Hort and a man named Rogers — went on to become top intercontinental pilots. One of Pemberton's major aeronautical thrills occurred in the 1950s when Brandvig, who also trained Japanese pilots for Japan Air Lines, gave his former instructor a ride in a huge Convair he was testing. Shortly after Brandvig had the B-36 in the air, headed for the Mojave area, he told Pemberton to take the controls.

With a sense of amazement, Pemberton said, "Here I was, used to flying these old puddle-jumpers, and, when I took a look at the altimeter, here we were at 13,000 feet."

Now 85, Pemberton retired in 1974 and no longer flies. But he still retains a keen sense of what he felt as he flew over the San Joaquin Valley, looking down on the vehicle traffic on Highway 99.

"Here were all those cars down there, all tangled up, moving slow," he said. "And I was sitting up there in the air, and it was all mine."

Rodriguez, Salvador, Jr. — A licensed pilot of the 1920s and '30s, Salvadore Rodriguez, Jr. was the founder of the Mexican Aero Club of Kern County. Ruben Mendoza, in *Herencia Mexicana,* notes that Rodriguez "conducted aerial search and rescue missions during the floods that struck the Tehachapi and Caliente Creek areas in 1932." Soon after this, the pioneering pilot was killed in an airplane crash. His father, Salvadore Rodriguez, Sr., who owned a brick and masonry business, was the club's financial sponsor.

Rogers, Marguerite "Peggy" — Born on a mining claim in Durango, Mexico, of an American mother and a British father, Dr. Peggy Rogers held triple citizenship as a youth. She chose to be an American.

The physicist, who retired in 1980 as head of the systems development department at the Naval Weapon Center but has continued on a contract basis, is known world-wide as an expert in the delivery, development, tactical employment and effectiveness of conventional weapons.

Rogers earned her doctorate at Rice University in 1940 and has received many honors throughout her career, including the U.S. Department of Defense Distinguished Civilian Service Award. The award, which was presented to her by Secretary of Defense Caspar Weinberger, is the highest recognition that can be given by the department to a civilian employee. Rogers is one of only seven women to be so honored since the award was initiated in 1955. As a woman working in a field dominated by men — and as the mother of five children whom she raised following the death in 1957 of her husband, physicist Fred Rogers — she has acted as a role model, and provided encouragement and support, for other females interested in pursuing a career in science and engineering.

The scientist is a close friend of Rear Adm. Grace Hopper — the Navy's oldest and highest ranking female officer at the time of her retirement. The women are said to share the same "Let's get the job done with the least nonsense possible" approach to their work for the Navy.

Despite her heavy work load, Rogers always has been involved in community activities, especially 4H. She also raises and shows purebred Peruvian Paso horses.

Rutan, Dick and Jeana Yeager — The eyes of the world were on Dick Rutan and Jeana Yeager just before Christmas 1986 when they flew the experimental aircraft Voyager on a non-stop round-the-world flight.

The pilots landed the lightweight plane on December 23, 1986 at Edwards Air Force Base, after a nine-day

The record-setting experimental aircraft Voyager that Dick Rutan and Jeana Yeager flew around the world in December 1986 was built and tested at Mojave airport.

flight of 25,012 miles. In doing so, the privately-sponsored craft designed by Burt Rutan set the absolute distance record for non-refueled flight. The feat nearly doubled the previous mileage record, set in 1962 by an Air Force B-52 bomber.

During his career in the Air Force, Dick Rutan, now 48, flew 325 combat missions in the F-100 fighter jet. More than 100 of those missions were over North Vietnam, where he was shot down and rescued on his final one. Rutan has received 16 air medals, the Purple Heart, five Distinguished Flying Crosses and the Silver Star.

At 34, Yeager has had 14 years of experience in engineering design and drafting. She has flown many different kinds of experimental and conventional aircraft.

Both have the kind of pluck and daring that ordinary people find appealing as well as inspiring. A few years ago, when the pilots were involved in testing another lightweight aircraft, the Long EZ, at Shafter Airport, Rutan said, "Some people go to movies to live someone else's adventures. But we thought, phooey, let's go live our own."

St. Amand, Pierre — Regarded by many as a "Renaissance man," Dr. Pierre St. Amand, has made his mark on an array of scientific fields and has a sphere of influence that is world-wide. The Naval Weapons Center geophysicist has for a number of years been listed in Who's Who in the World and in at least 10 other biographical reference works, and has received many distinguished awards.

His work with weather modification has brought him international acclaim, including special recognition from both India and the Philippines for alleviating droughts in those nations. Closer to home, the scientist has spoken out strongly in recent months about what he considers an impending water crisis in the Indian Wells Valley.

St. Amand, who has a master's and a Ph.D. from California Institute of Technology, also is known internationally for his work in seismology.

During his tenure at the Naval Weapons Center he has headed the research department's optics branch, and the earth and planetary sciences division. Now retired, the geophysicist serves as a consultant to the center's technical director. He has several patents in optics and weather modification.

A public-spirited individual, St. Amand was the mayor of College, Alaska, his hometown, from 1946-49. He has continued his public service in Kern County, serving as president of the Ridgecrest Community Hospital board of directors and as a trustee of the Maturango Museum. He and his wife, Marie St. Amand, make their home in Ridgecrest.

Sabovich, Dan — When Dan Sabovich was hired as general manager of the East Kern Airport District in 1972, he "inherited" Mojave Airport, a collection of ramshackle buildings that had been there since the former Marine Corps base was established in 1943.

Under his dynamic leadership the airport has become a center for the design, construction and testing of aircraft, with nearly 150 tenants, including Flight System Inc. and General Electric — companies that handle millions in government contracts. In 1985 the district received a $1.1 million grant from the Federal Aviation Administration to improve the airport's 9,600-foot runway.

Rutan Aircraft Co. also is based at Mojave. And it was

Air Force Flight Test Center
Edwards Air Force Base

COMMANDERS

Maj. Glenn L. Arbogast	July-Dec. 1942
Col. Frank D. Gore	1942-44
Maj. Gen. Robert O. Cork	March 14-31 1944
Brig. Gen. Ralph A. Snavely	April 1-May 1 1944
Col. Gerald E. Hoyle	May-Dec. 1944
Col. Warren E. Maxwell	1944-46
Col. Signa A. Gilkey	1946-49
Lt. Gen. Al Boyd	1949-1952
Maj. Gen. J. Stanley Holtoner	1952-57
Maj. Gen. Marcus F. Cooper	1957-59
Lt. Gen. John W. Carpenter III	1959-1961
Maj. Gen. Irving L. Branch*	1961-66
Col. Ray Vandiver	Jan. 4-16 1966
Maj. Gen. Hugh B. Manson	1966-68
Gen. Alton D. Slay	1968-70
Maj. Gen. Robert M. White	1970-72
Lt. Gen. Howard M. Lane	1972-74
Maj. Gen. Robert A. Rushworth	1974-75
Lt. Gen. Thomas P. Stafford	1975-78
Maj. Gen. Philip J. Conley Jr.	1978-82
Maj. Gen. Peter W. Odgers	1982-85
Maj. Gen. William T. Twinting	1985-

*Branch was killed Jan. 3, 1966, when the aircraft he was landing at the Boeing Company in Seattle, crashed into Puget Sound.

TECHNICAL DIRECTORS

Richard E. Horner	1952-55
Paul F. Bikle	1955-59
Francis H. Richardson	1960-62
Norman V. Peterson	1962-65
Charles W. Oliver	1965-70
Fred M. Stoliker (Acting)	1970-71
Col. Richard C. Lathrop	1971-74
Fred M. Stoliker	1974-81
Alfred D. Phillips	1981-85
Charles E. Adolph	1985-

The growth and development of the Mojave Airport is due in large measure to the dynamic leadership of Dan Sabovich.

there that Burt Rutan designed and built the lightweight experimental Voyager. In December 1986, Dick Rutan, the designer's brother, and Jeana Yeager flew the aircraft on its record-breaking, world-circling flight.

Scatena, Dorothy — Bakersfield's Dorothy Scatena is one of only 1,100 women who served in the WASPs (Women Airforce Service Pilots) during World War II. The female pilots tested planes and helped train military airmen in the program, which ended in 1944. (Adeline Schaefer, a Bakersfield College professor, also was a WASP).

Scatena first was based at Craig Field in Selma, Alabama, and was trained to fly twin-engined B-26 bombers at Laredo, Texas. She was then sent to Minter Field (now Shafter Airport). As a 22-year-old engineering test pilot at Minter she flew planes after they had been repaired. In that position, she determined whether the aircraft was ready to fly, which didn't always sit well with the male-dominated Army Air Corps. Looking back on that time, the former WASP said, "The mere thought of a girl telling men when they could or couldn't fly a repaired plane again bothered them."

Despite their wartime contributions — the WASPs flew a total of 60 million miles — the women were considered ineligible for veteran's benefits. More than 30 years later a number of the former WASPs decided to seek formal recognition. Scatena became an activist in the campaign, which ended successfully in 1978 when the Department of Defense made the WASPs full-fledged veterans, entitled to the same benefits as other former members of the military.

After a hiatus of 35 years, Scatena started flying again in 1981 and checked out in three hours. A major in the Civil Air Patrol, the 64-year-old has her own plane and participates in searches for downed aircraft and other rescue missions.

Yeager, Charles E. — On October 14, 1947, Capt. Chuck Yeager made aviation history when he became

Capt. Chuck Yeager, the first man to break the once-feared sound barrier, dubbed the sleek Bell X-1 experimental rocket plane the "Glamorous Glennis." Yeager made the historic flight on October 14, 1947 at Edwards Air Force Base.

the first to break the sound barrier. He did it at Edwards Air Force Base, flying the Bell X-1 experimental rocket plane.

The direct result of Yeager's accomplishment was the development of the supersonic Century Series of fighter planes, starting with the F-100 Super Sabre.

There is an amusing sidelight connected with the historic event, according to Dr. James Young, the base historian. Just a few days earlier, Yeager had broken several ribs in a fall from the horse he was riding on Pancho Barnes' ranch. Had the flight surgeon known of Yeager's physical condition, he wouldn't have allowed the test pilot to fly.

Yeager's plane, which he dubbed the "Glamorous Glennis," is on display at the Smithsonian Institution. He is a member of the National Aviation Hall of Fame in Dayton, Ohio.

Theron McCuen extended his arm at the groundbreaking for Bakersfield College's first separate campus to indicate the location of the buildings that soon would rise on the then-barren bluff on Panorama Drive. Among the faculty members in the foreground are Dorothy Albaugh, Georgene Bihlman, Richard Tigner and Ysabel Forker.

Thanks to her alphabetical placement, Tina Barnard was the first graduate of Cal State Bakersfield to receive her diploma from founding president Dr. Paul Romberg in 1971.

When she was a student at Lincoln Junior High School in Bakersfield, Ruth Love dreamed of becoming famous one day. The educator has more than fulfilled that ambition.

90

7
The Enlighteners

"The two lasting bequests we can give children
are roots and wings."

Margaret "Peg" Levinson, *Renegade Rip*

The pioneer teachers of Kern County were a hardy lot, accustomed to chopping wood for the school's potbellied stove and dealing with odd circumstances that had little to do with teaching.

Caroline Payne Harris, whose first teaching assignment was at the school in Havilah, recalled. "The playground was not fenced, so it was not unusual to find cattle near the building or lying down at the entrance to the schoolhouse."

And that was in 1911.

Fifty years earlier, there were no public schools or libraries. Children learned their ABCs and their "numbers" from their parents or perhaps in the front parlor of another member of the community who had the benefit of higher education.

Few books suitable for young readers were available, so the early teachers had to be creative in producing instructional materials. Ellen Baker (Tracy), the wife of Bakersfield's founder, fashioned letters from pieces of paper so that her eight pupils could learn the alphabet.

The roots of today's vast public school system were established in 1866, with the formation of the office of Kern County Superintendent of Schools. But the grasp of the first administrator, Dr. Joseph R. Riley, was somewhat tenuous. Riley, a medical doctor, was appointed in August of that year and resigned four months later. It should be noted that the physician practiced 18 years in Bakersfield before moving to Fresno where he became president of the Fresno County Medical Society as well as a successful raisin grower.

Kern's education history is filled with a long line of dedicated teachers who, despite the lack of materials and in some cases, with minimum formal training, managed to instill in their students a love and respect for learning.

A large number of educators, along with school board members and other supporters, have had elementary schools named in their honor. Some of these individuals appear in the biographical sketches that follow. Among the others who have been so honored and the particular school district involved, are:

Ralph Haven — Arvin Union; James Curran, Henry Eissler, Ruth Harding, Caroline Harris, Millie Gardette Munsey, Col. Howard Nichols, Myra Noble, Bessie Owens, Frank West — Bakersfield City; the Cecil family — Delano Union; Woodrow N. Wallace — Kernville Union; O.J. Actis, Charles H. Castle, Sing Lum, Louise Sandrini, Amy B. Seibert, Fred L. Thompson, Wayne Van Horn — Panama Union; Karl F. Clemens, Wasco Union; James B. McFarland — McFarland Unified; Robert P. Ulrich — Mojave Unified; Richard B. Lynch — Muroc Joint Unified; Edward Tompkins, Claude E.

As governor of California, Ronald Reagan was on hand for the groundbreaking ceremonies for the Cal State Bakersfield campus in 1969. Here he greets some of those who attended. State Sen. Walter Stiern, one of the speakers, can be seen in the background.

Wells — Tehachapi Unified.

The first PTAs (Parent-Teacher Associations) in the county were formed about 1910, and the regional Seventh District PTA in 1916. Community leaders in the movement included Mrs. Walter Osborn, Sr., in Bakersfield, and in Shafter, Julia A. Potter and Mrs. Fred Mannel. The PTA was instrumental in establishing hot-lunch programs in the schools and well-baby clinics throughout the county.

The Bakersfield Branch of American Association of University Women, which initially was made up of teachers and librarians, was organized in 1925 with Virginia Lilly French as its first president. The second executive, Betty Smith, the wife of pioneer physician Dr. Joseph K. Smith, said the first meetings were held in the Southern Hotel and at the St. Francis Cafe. Today there are AAUW branches in Shafter and in Ridgecrest, and its membership is made up of women in many professions.

Kern's first libraries were those established by women's clubs. It would not be until the turn-of-the-century that the library became a publicly supported institution. Many intrepid librarians have directed the Kern County Library System, including Julia Babcock, who initiatied — and drove — the first bookmobile. A more modern form of the vehicular system still provides services to citizens in remote areas of the county.

Friends of the Library, support groups whose members raise money to provide supplies for children's programs and volunteer in other capacities, have arisen in the past 25 years. Today, nearly every branch library has a "Friends" group and, following the passage of Proposition 13, many of these organizations became strong advocates in seeking restored funding for libraries.

Another group that has worked with the library in training tutors to help adults to read is the Kern Adult Literacy Council. On its own, the council, which was

formed about 20 years ago, has taught hundreds how to read, using a method developed by missionary Dr. Frank Laubach. Georgia Sykora is the current executive director; Dorothy Parrish heads the volunteer board.

At present, a new multi-million dollar Beale Memorial Library is being constructed to house the central branch and the library system headquarters. The Kern County Library Foundation, a non-profit organization headed by Kern High School District superintendent Don L. Murfin, has launched an effort to raise $1.5 million to provide amenities for the new structure. Campaign co-chairmen are banker Ray Dezember and newspaper executive Jerry Stanners.

Key figures in the development of school libraries include E. Ben Evans and Bernice Braddon at Bakersfield High School; Goldie Ingles, who was for many the Bakersfield College librarian; Dr. Benton Scheide, Cal State Bakersfield's first library director.

Higher education came to Kern County in 1893 when Kern County Union High School was built in Bakersfield. (In the next 25 years, the school would flourish under the leadership of two highly qualified administrators: A. J. Ludden and Herman Spindt.) In 1913 the 13th grade was added in the form of Bakersfield (Junior) College, the second such institution in the state. It would be another 57 years before the county would know the benefits of a four-year state college.

California State College, Bakersfield, a long-held dream of county residents, was approved in 1967 and opened its doors in 1970. The 380-acre site west of Bakersfield was a gift of the Kern County Land Company, now Tenneco West. (Prior to the college's establishment, many teachers earned their credentials at the Fresno State Bakersfield Residence Center, headed by Dr. Claude Varner. That function now is handled by the CSB School of Education.)

In outlining his philosophy for Cal State Bakersfield,

Dr. Philip Wilder, Cal State Bakersfield's first academic vice president, was one of the core group of administrators who planned the new campus. Wilder, now the president of a college in New York, returned to Bakersfield this year for a dinner honoring retiring Arts and Sciences Dean John Coash.

Dr. Paul Romberg, the founding president, said, "As the community [begins to understand that] there must be a free exchange of ideas and thoughts, they will far more appreciate what this institution can be in the development of the region and the community."

Romberg's initial cabinet was made up of academic vice president Dr. Philip S. Wilder, Jr., who now is the president of Hartwick College in Oneonta, New York, Dr. Kenneth E. Secor, now vice president of administrative services; Dr. George Hibbard, dean of students; and Gordon Callison, business manager.

Dr. Clifford Loader, a dentist and long-time mayor of Delano, served as the first chairman of the CSB Foundation. Edgar Richardson, a Kern County native (the town of Arvin is named for his uncle, Arvin Richardson) chaired the college's advisory board of directors.

Education in Kern County has come a long way since the days of one-room schools and McGuffey's Readers. And so has the profession. Its ranks contain leaders whose impact is felt regionally and in more than a few cases, on a much wider geographic scale.

In this 1950s-era photo, the late Kern County Museum Director Richard C. Bailey is shown in front of the reconstructed log cabin of early settler Thomas Barnes. Erected in the 1940s, it was the first structure in Pioneer Village.

Arciniega, Tomas A, — Dr. Tomas Arciniega was named president of California State College, Bakersfield, in 1983 and is one of the few Hispanics to head a public university or college. Arciniega, who has a Ph.D. from the University of New Mexico, serves on the boards of a number of influential national committees, including the Carnegie Corporation of New York Foundation and Independent Sector. IS, as the latter group is known, was formed by John Gardner, the founder of Common Cause, and is a national coalition of 650 corporate, foundation and community service organizations that seeks to promote philanthropy and volunteerism.

Bailey, Richard C. — Helping people learn about the history of our area was a way of life for Richard Bailey. A former schoolteacher, he was the director of the Kern County Museum for 26 years.

Bailey was instrumental in the formation of the museum's Pioneer Village, the recreated frontier town started by his predecessor, Frank Latta. Bailey also was a key figure in establishing the Petroleum Museum, the Lori Brock Children's Museum, the annual Heritage Days celebration and the Museum Alliance. Under his aegis, hundreds of schoolchildren visited the facility and enjoyed the programs on Indian culture presented by Elydia Gilbert, a Yokuts Indian, and Shirley Mac-Fadzean. Delores Heller began organizing the museum's costume collection during the 1970s.

The director often led groups on guided tours of the county, giving on-the-spot lectures that made the history of the particular place come alive for his listeners. Bailey authored several books on local history and at the time of his death was engaged in writing *Heart of the Golden Empire, a* comprehensive history of Bakersfield. Published in 1984, the manuscript was completed

by his wife, Dorothy Bailey, who since has remarried and now lives in Ridgecrest.

Beardsley, Lewis A. — Lewis A. Beardsley was Kern County's fourth superintendent of schools and the first professional teacher to hold that position. At the time of his election in 1874, the New York native was the principal of the only school in Bakersfield and previously had taught in Glennville and in Tulare County.

But the administrator is remembered best for the school district that bears his name. After his four-year term as county superintendent, Beardsley began farming on 160 acres he had homesteaded north of Bakersfield. He donated one acre for the establishment of a school. In 1882 he organized the Beardsley School District and became its first teacher, serving until his death four years later.

The director often led groups on guided tours of the county, giving on-the-spot lectures

Bender, Cora F. McGrann — One of Kern County's pioneer educators, Cora Bender was the first teacher in Walkers Basin in 1877. She retired in 1930 as principal of Washington School in East Bakersfield.

Pioneer educator Cora F. Bender may have been the county's first adult school teacher, by virtue of the evening instruction she gave to a young Irish railroad worker in Caliente in the 1880s.

During her 20 years as principal, Washington School was at Baker and Nile streets, in the heart of a multi-ethnic community. She was known as a stern but fair-minded disciplinarian who insisted, among other things, that the youngsters stand at attention for the daily flag-raising in front of the school. One of her former students, Clemence Mier Lilburn, says, "If the boys were slouching or fooling around, Mrs. Bender would come up behind them and yank them up by the collar." At 5-feet-10-inches, the principal had a distinct edge on the adolescents.

The Mariposa native earned her teaching credential at 16 and later attended the Normal School at Los Angeles (now UCLA). She taught in various county schools until 1890, when she married H. Philip Bender, the founder of the county's first abstract company, the predecessor of today's TICOR Title Insurance Co. Upon his death in 1904, she returned to teaching to support her family of six children. In all, she taught for 39 years.

Bender helped form the Seventh District PTA and the Kern County Historical Society. In 1936, she became the founding president of the Bakersfield Retired Teachers Association and four years later, at age 79, served as the state organization's auditor. Her great-granddaughter, Christy Gavin, is chair of the reference department at the Cal State Bakersfield Library.

Bilas, Richard A. — In March of this year, Dr. Richard Bilas, a former economics professor at Cal State Bakersfield, was appointed to the five-member California Energy Commission. The agency, which has a staff of 400, oversees the siting of power plants, promotes alternative energy development and encourages energy conservation. It also keeps tabs on energy supply and demand. A member of the Libertarian Party. Bilas is well-known locally for his often-critical views of government policy in general, views which have been aired as radio and television commentaries.

Bird, Grace Van Dyke — Grace Bird, the dean of Bakersfield College from 1920 to 1950, was the first woman to head a public junior college in California. And it is she who set the tone and the pattern for Bakersfield College that has continued through the years.

A petite woman with a fine mind and an ability to work well with others, the dean had a number of personal qualities that helped her attract the kind of faculty she needed to establish the high academic standards that remain a Bakersfield College hallmark. In recalling his hiring interview, retired business education professor Dr. Wylie Logan Jones said, "When Grace Bird sat across from you at that desk with a little hat on her head, she could charm a snake right out of a tree."

The dean had a keen regard for the learning process, and was well-known for the personal interest she took in students as well as the staff, the faculty and the Renegades, whose practice sessions she often observed. (At graduations, she handed out each diploma, addressing each student by name — from memory.) Well-acquainted in the community, she was a close friend of farmer W.B. Camp and his first wife, the former Georgia App, and banker Dwight L. Clarke and Mrs. Clarke.

Bird's profession was her whole life — today she would be called a "workaholic." A pioneer in her field, she was instrumental in setting up the framework for junior colleges throughout the state and was respected nationally. Dr. Edmund J. Gleazer, Jr., a former presi-

The energetic and innovative dean of Bakersfield College for 30 years, Grace Van Dyke was highly involved in the cultural life of the community. She was instrumental in the formation of Bakersfield Community Theater and the Kern County Musical Association.

dent of the American Association of Community and Junior Colleges once said, "Grace Bird was one of the wise foundation builders."

A graduate of the University of California at Berkeley — she majored in architecture and minored in French — Bird returned to her alma mater in 1950 to become the university's liaison to the community colleges. In 1976 she was named a Berkeley Fellow, one of the highest honors given by the university. At the same time, Bakersfield College named her its first president emeritus.

An oral history of Bird's life — conducted by the Bancroft Library and funded by a group of her Bakersfield colleagues — was published in 1978. In addition to being a monument to the dean's contributions, the two-volume work is a key source for information about the early history of Bakersfield College. Grace Bird died in 1986 at the age of 94.

Blair, Harry E. — During his 14 years as Kern County Superintendent of Schools, Harry Blair instigated a number of far-reaching programs, which are an accepted part of instruction today, such as pre-schools. Building on the foundation laid by two of his predecessors, Leo B. Hart and Jesse D. Stockton, the administrator

---

"When Grace Bird sat across from you at that desk with a little hat on her head, she could charm a snake right out of a tree."

---

also expanded special education programs for handicapped students. Blair Learning Center was named in his honor after his death in 1977.

In 1964, Blair headed a group of county leaders who went to Sacramento to ask that the Coordinating Council for Higher Education in Sacramento make a favorable recommendation to the Legislature for the establishment of a four-year college in Bakersfield. The superintendent also set up the county schools first office of public information and hired former newspaperman Murray Arnold to run the operation.

Boyd, William Harland — An author and a scholar, Dr. Harland Boyd is a reliable and always-available source for information on Kern County's early history. A dedicated researcher, the 75-year-old Boyd says his interest in California history began when he was a student at the University of California at Berkeley, where he earned his Ph.D. Since coming to Kern County more than 40 years ago, he has devoted most of his research to this area's history. Boyd taught for 27 years at Ba-

kersfield College and upon his retirement in 1973 was given the rank of professor emeritus.

He has written eight books, contributes to the *Encyclopedia Britannica* and is the editor of *Historic Kern,* the Kern County Historical Society's quarterly publication. One of his most significant contributions is *A California Middle Border,* a detailed history of the Kern County area from 1772 to 1880, published in 1972. He currently is doing research for a book that will be a continuation of that history. Assisting him in his endeavors, particularly as an indexer, is his wife, Mary Kay, a retired librarian.

Branson, Margaret — Dr. Margaret Branson, director of curricular services for the Kern County Superintendent of Schools, is well-known both nationally and internationally. She was appointed this year to the National Advisory Committee to the Commission on the Bicentennial of the United States Constitution, and in the past three years has represented our country at two education conferences held in Europe.

Branson, who joined the superintendent's staff in 1981, was instrumental in the organization of the Mock Trial competition in 1982. Her leadership in developing California's framework for the study of history and social science led to the county office's selection, in 1986, as the site of the state's Curriculum Implementation Center for those subjects. She is the author or editor of numerous textbooks.

Castro, Tomas — A native of Mexico who began farming in the Panama-Old River area in 1867, Tomas Castro hired a teacher from Los Angeles (at $25 a month) for the private school he started for his own and other children in the sparsely settled area. This school, according to Dr. Rodolfo G. Serrano of Cal State Bakersfield, was the nucleus of the Panama School Dis-

In 1987, Merlene Jones, a 21-year veteran of the Kern County Superintendent of Schools' Child Development Services, received the Outstanding Professional Award from the California Association of Bilingual Educators.

The nucleus of what is now the Panama School District was formed more than a century ago when Tomas Castro started a school for his children on his farm in the Old River area.

trict, which now serves the heavily populated southwest area of Bakersfield.

Chenoweth, Lawrence E. — Lawrence Chenoweth's background and experience in a number of areas proved to be valuable assets when he became Kern County Superintendent of Schools in 1915. He had been an impresario, managing concerts and musical comedies in the Bay Area, and upon coming to Bakersfield a reporter for (and later part-owner) the Bakersfield *Morning Echo.*

He also had a teaching credential from San Jose State and, from 1907 to 1909, was assistant to the State Superintendent of Public Instruction.

Chenoweth, a master at enlisting wide-based support for his endeavors, was responsible for the formation of six elementary districts and two union high school districts. Ross Harrington, author of a history of the superintendents' office through 1966, notes that "School district organization turned an important corner during Chenoweth's administration." The administrator's foresight is evident also in his development of a school transportation system and his initiation of a countywide purchasing plan.

After resigning his county position in 1928, Chenoweth became superintendent of the Bakersfield City School District, a post he held until his retirement in 1940. But he continued teaching and at the time of his death in 1949 was a professor of education at the University of California at Santa Barbara.

Coash, John — Dr. "Jack" Coash, one of the founding members of the Cal State Bakersfield administrative team, undertook an even greater responsibility when the college's academic structure was reorganized under Dr. Jacob Frankel's direction. At that time, Coash was named dean of the newly formed School of Arts and Sciences, which gathered a wide number of disciplines under one administrative umbrella. He continued in that capacity until he resigned his deanship in 1986. A professor of geology, Coash is known internationally in his field.

Collins, John — A president emeritus of Bakersfield College, John Collins has continued to take an active role since his retirement. Collins currently is president of the BC Foundation board and in 1986 served as acting chancellor of the Kern Community College District during Chancellor James Young's unsuccessful campaign for state senator against Don Rogers.

Compton, John L. — As superintendent of the Bakersfield City School District from 1940 to 1962, John Compton faced, and surmounted, a number of tough challenges, beginning with the teacher shortage caused by World War II. This crisis was followed by the problems of providing adequate services for the post-war "baby boom," temporarily solved through double-sessions until bond issues made it possible to build new schools. Then in 1952 a real disaster struck in the form of earthquakes. The extensive damage resulted in the loss of half of the district's 480 classrooms, and it was back to morning and afternoon sessions again until funding for new construction was secured.

Through it all, Compton was highly regarded by district personnel as well as by members of the community. Ed Freeman, a city schools administrator who once taught at Compton Junior High School (named for the superintendent), said in a recent newspaper interview, "John Compton was a father figure ... He's one of those giants that you just don't see anymore."

Now 86 and living in Laguna Hills, Compton was honored this year by the Kern County chapter of Freedoms Foundation for his role in making the study of American democracy and patriotism a part of the district's curriculum.

John Compton ... "one of those giants you just don't see anymore."

Deal, Bonnye Elizabeth — A school pyschologist and English teacher, Bonnye Deal was director of counseling and testing at Bakersfield High School from 1945 to 1965. The Stanford graduate later was a consulting psychologist for the California Department of Rehabilitation and an adjunct professor at Fresno State University's Bakersfield Residence Center.

Deal was the president of several professional and civic organizations, including Delta Kappa Gamma, the Mental Health Association, the Kern County Pyschological Association, Zonta Club and the League of Women Voters. She also was active in the American Association of University Women and once was a candidate for the Bakersfield City Council. She served for 18 years on the Bakersfield Target Area Program for Child Development — the TAP center in Wasco is named for her. One week before her death in April of this year, the pyschologist was notified that she was the winner of the Child Guidance Clinic's 1987 Blanche and Irma Weill Award.

Gannon, Margaret — A leader in the field of early childhood education, Margaret Gannon is the director of La Cresta Foundation. She also was instrumental in the formation of Warm Line, a volunteer mother-to-mother outreach service. Gannon is the principal author of *Gourmet Parenting,* published in 1985 by Warm Line. In 1986, she was named the first recipient of the Henrietta Weill Memorial Award.

Gianopulos, Pete — A native of Taft, Pete Gianopulos served the Taft High School District for 35 years. He was a counselor for 33 years and for 19 of those years was also director of guidance and pupil personnel services. The administrator has been featured in articles for the National Education Journal and in state publications for school counselors.

Margaret Gannon of Bakersfield, a leader in early childhood education, became the first recipient of the Blanche and Irma Weill Award in 1986. She is married to builder-developer Joseph Gannon.

A two-term mayor of Taft, from 1961 to 1966, Gianopulos is a long-time board member of the Taft Oildorado, the community's salute to itself and the petroleum industry that forms its economic base. He is a former member of the state Democratic Central Committee and the Kern County Water Agency. In 1986 he was named "Citizen of the Year" by the Taft Rotary Club.

Harper, Wilhelmina — A firm foundation for the Kern County Library System's children's program was laid under the leadership of Wilhelmina Harper from 1921 to 1928. The first specialist in that field hired by the library, Harper organized the children's collection and supervised its implementation.

Harper, a native of Maine, gained a national reputation in her field during her 50 years of public service in libraries in New York and California. She also was the author or editor of numerous collections of folk tales. Her book, *The Gunniwolf,* a fanciful tale about a little girl and a wolf-like creature, is a favorite of young readers and adult storytellers alike in Kern County.

Hart, Leo B. — (See "The Plus Factor")

Hofstetter, Vivian — Chipman Junior High School teacher Vivian Hofstetter was named the "Choral Teacher of the Year" in 1987 by the California Music Educators Association for excellence in vocal instruction. She also serves on an international commission of music teachers, which has taken her to Helsinki, Finland, and Innsbruck, Austria, and has taken a group of Chipman School singers on a Sister City visit to Wakayama, Japan. Hofstetter is a former president of the Kern County Music Educators Association.

Hort, Ovillah R. — Ovillah Hort, for whom Bakersfield's Hort School is named, devoted 45 years to the teaching profession and was instrumental in forming the Seventh District PTA and the East Bakersfield High School PTA. After her retirement, she became a leader at Bakersfield Community House, the city's first senior citizens center. She was the first recipient of the Bernice Harrell Chipman Woman of the Year award in 1967. Active well into her 80s, the pioneer teacher died this year at 98. Her son, Marvin "Red" Hort, a retired intercontinental airlines pilot, lives in Burlingame. Her daughter, Jeanne Kamrar is a Bakersfield resident.

Levinson, Margaret — "Peg" Levinson, known for her leadership, warmth and personal integrity, devoted her entire 36-year career to Bakersfield College. She came to the college in 1931 as an English teacher and continued teaching that subject until 1949. She first became an administrator in 1943 and at the time of her retirement in 1967 was dean of instruction.

Levinson had a keen sense of what good teaching entails. She once said, "Teaching is a very immediate, personal relationship . . . there may be just a little mystic in it. When it's effective, something happens between the teacher and the learner that is very real and transcends the exchange of knowledge."

Love, Ruth (Holloway) — For Dr. Ruth Love, a 1950 graduate of Bakersfield High School, getting into the field of education wasn't easy. Although she had wanted to be a teacher from the time she was very young, Love was discouraged from taking college preparatory classes by her high school counselor. At the time, few blacks went on to college and even fewer entered the teaching profession.

But Love persisted and enrolled at Bakersfield College where she was encouraged by such counselors as Dorothy Albaugh and Tom Merson. Love transferred to San Jose State and eventually became perhaps the best-known educator, nationally and internationally, with Kern County roots.

Early in her career, she was a Fulbright exchange teacher in England and director of an Operations Crossroads project in Ghana. In the 1970s she headed the Department of Health, Education and Welfare's Right-to-Read project. Love, who has a Ph.D. from U.S. International University in San Diego, later turned down a cabinet post in President Carter's administration to become superintendent of the Oakland Public Schools.

In doing so, she became one of the few black women to head a public school system in the country and was the only female school superintendent in California. She resigned in 1982 to become superintendent of the Chicago public schools. After a stormy four years, and a number of disagreements with Chicago Mayor Harold Washington, Love left public education and became an entrepreneur. She now heads Ruth Love Enterprises, Inc., a company that produces instructional software and provides consulting services to schools in the United States and other countries.

Holloway-Gonzales Branch Library is named for the educator and then-Assemblyman Ray Gonzales (Since divorced, Love was known by her married name, Holloway, at the time of its dedication.) Her mother, Burnett Love, is a Bakersfield resident.

McCuen, Theron L. — Theron McCuen, a man who ably guided the Kern County high school and junior college district through 25 years of its most rapid growth, has earned and retained the respect of his colleagues and the community at large.

Now 81, McCuen was the head of the then-combined districts from 1945 to 1968. During his term of office the average daily attendance increased from 5,000 to 28,000,

FACT director Ted Murphy instructs a Girl Scout troop on the effects of water pollution and techniques for the preservation of clean water.

the number of high schools grew from five to 15, and Bakersfield College opened its first separate campus on Panorama Drive. In August 1986, the college's administration building was named McCuen Hall. At the ceremony, Mark Raney, a long-time member of the Kern Community College District board of trustees, said, "Theron McCuen personifies the old statement. Theron McCuen was — *is* — a gentleman and a scholar."

McCuen served as president of the California Association of School Administrators and was chairman of a joint committee to develop guidelines for contract negotiations. The superintendent and his wife, Hazel, were part of a group that conducted a 1963 field study of education in Scandinavia and the Soviet Union.

Two of the McCuens' three adult children are directly involved in education and one tangentially. Dr. John T. McCuen is superintendent and president of Long Beach City College. Martha McCuen Miller is a teacher at Van Horn School. And Dr. Peter McCuen, a Ph.D. in mechanical engineering from Stanford, is a major developer of commercial property for high tech industries in Sacramento and a member of the state committee which is reviewing the Master Plan for Higher Education. Thirty years ago, Theron McCuen was a member of the original committee.

Murphy, Ted — As the director of FACT — the Facility for Animal Care and Treatment at Cal State Bakersfield — biology professor Ted Murphy makes possible for hundreds of schoolchildren to gain a better understanding of wild animals. Wounded or homeless creatures are sheltered in the shady site at the southern edge of the campus until they are able to survive on their own.

In 1987 Murphy received an official Iron Eyes Cody Peace Medal from nationally known environmentalist Iron Eyes Cody. (At the same time, Dr. Tom Banks, a veterinarian for the FACT and the California Living Museum, was presented with the John Reed Memorial Conservation Award.)

Kern High School District Superintendents	
E.F. Goodyear	1893-95
J.B. Newell	1896-97
C.C. Childress	1897-1907
C.T. Conger	1907-09
B.F. McComber	1909-13
B.S. Gowen	1913-16
A.J. Ludden	1916-22
Herman A. Spindt	1922-38
T.L. Nelson	1938-45
Theron L. McCuen	1945-68
John W. Eckhardt	1968-77
Gerald S. Degrow	1977-81
Don L. Murfin	1981-

Olson, Harold R. — A superintendent of the Delano Joint Union High School District for 24 years, Harold Olson was a strong leader in education and highly involved in the community. After his retirement, Olson served the California Interscholastic Federation as executive director of its central region. In 1963-64 he was district governor of Rotary.

Pauly, Leo G. — Often described as a man of many parts, Leo G. Pauly began his teaching career in his native Tehachapi in the 1890s and continued in the field until 1917 as principal of the Sumner School in East Bakersfield and as chairman of the board of education. He later became the manager for the Louis V. Olcese Estate — a position he held for about 40 years — and was chairman of the East Bakersfield branch of the Bank of America for more than 30 years. He also served as Bakersfield postmaster, chief of the volunteer fire department, county purchasing agent and was elected to the city council in 1939.

In 1946 one of his former students, Governor Earl Warren, appointed Pauly to the Board of Supervisors upon the death of Ralph Lavin. Pauly was named "Distinguished Citizen of the Year" in 1959 by American Legion Post 26 and received many other honors during his lifetime. The Panama District's Pauly School is named for the pioneer educator.

Powers, Bob — A retired employee of the U.S. Forest Service, Bob Powers has been recording the history of the Kernville area for the past 20 years. Thus far, he has published five books, devoted mainly to the pioneering families of the Kern River Valley. He also teaches an extension course in local history for Cerro Coso Community College. Born in old Kernville — the town now submerged under Isabella Lake — the author is the fifth generation of his family to live in the Kern River Valley. He and his wife, Marjorie, have raised five children there.

Prator, Ralph — Colleagues of Ralph Prator, who served as president of Bakersfield College from 1950 to 1958, credit the Colorado native with being the guiding force that moved BC from being a "junior" college to a community college. Known as an innovator, many of his concepts became realities on the new campus on Panorama Drive. Prator worked effectively to increase the stature of the college in the local area and statewide. He left Bakersfield College to become president of San Fernando State College (now Cal State Northridge). He and his wife, Lois, now live in Camarillo.

Rathbun, Bryce C. — As superintendent of the Standard School District for 28 years, Bryce Rathbun gained wide respect for his pragmatic approach to solving problems. The South Dakota native first taught in the district in the 1930s and, after Navy service during World War II, returned in 1947. He was named district superintendent in 1951, serving until his retirement in 1979. The Rathbun Branch Library in Oildale is named for the administrator, who died in 1986. He was a leader in the activities of the North of the River Recreation District, as well as Freedoms Foundation, the Masons and the Lions Club. His wife, Marilyn, is active in many community organizations.

Richardson, Claude W. — Dr. Claude Richardson's 40-year career in education culminated in his appointment in 1977 as Kern County Superintendent of Schools. During his 11 years of service in that position, Richardson was instrumental in the formation of three far-reaching services: the Schools Legal Service, Self-Insured Schools of Kern and the Schools Service Center, a central transportation and vehicle maintenance system that has become a nationally recognized model.

In 1979-80, the critical years following the passage of Proposition 13, Richardson served as the state legislative chairman of the California Association of County Superintendents of Schools and in 1981 was elected president of the association.

The superintendent had two heart surgeries in 1983. The second cost him the use of his legs so that he was confined to a wheelchair, although he continued to carry out his duties until his death in 1986. Describing that period, John Prueitt of Wasco, then president of the Kern County Board of Education, said, "Claude Rich-

Students in Barbara Leask's third grade class at Wingland School shared her joy in being named the Kern County Teacher of the Year for 1987. Leask has taught in the Standard School District for many years and is the past president of several community organizations.

ardson ... displayed a rare quality of personal courage. He personified the best in American public school tradition."

Rodgers, Glendon J. — Bakersfield High School teacher and counselor Glendon Rodgers made a lasting contribution to education and to Kern County history through the four books he wrote about the area. One of these, *Exploring Kern County,* is used as a supplemental text in the elementary grades. Originally published in 1960, the book was revised in 1985 by Richard L. Rutherford, with the assistance of members of the Beardsley School staff.

When *Exploring Kern County* first was published, Rodgers credited two equally respected educators for pointing out the need for such material: Bruce M. Crawford, who then was superintendent of the Richland

School District, and Evelyn Schiesser of the Bakersfield City School District. The main characters of the engaging and informative book are an 80-year-old Kern County native called "Uncle Jim" and a little girl named Caren, which also happens to be the name of Rodgers' daughter.

Rodgers, who died in 1964, was born in Los Angeles but grew up in McFarland. His wife, pianist Carol Buchner Rodgers, is well-known in musical circles. She is a member of the Bakersfield Symphony and is an accompanist for Foothill High School choral groups.

Rogers, Dora Belle Harris — In the history of the Kern County Superintendent of Schools, only one woman has ever been a candidate for the office: Dora Belle Rogers, who was defeated in the election of 1875. The pioneer teacher was married to Dr. Lewis Stiles Rogers, a Bakersfield physician, and was a leading figure in several charitable organizations.

Romberg, Paul — As the founding president of California State College, Bakersfield, Dr. Paul Romberg possessed a number of personal qualities that ensured that it would become a reality. Romberg was appointed head of the new institution in 1967, three years before its official opening. The Nebraska native and former Marine Corps fighter pilot previously had been vice president of academic affairs at Chico State College.

Dr. Kenneth Secor, who was a member of the founding team of administrators, says, "Even after it was approved by the Legislature, it was touch and go at first whether we would get the campus. I know that it was Paul Romberg's skill at dealing with politicians that kept us from losing the funding." The president was adept at forming positive relationships with all kinds of people, from corporate executives to "ordinary" people, and was readily accepted by the Bakersfield community.

Romberg left Bakersfield in 1973 to become president of Cal State San Francisco, serving there until his retirement. In 1986, one year after his death, the nursing education building at CSB was named in his honor. His daughter, Rory Daniel, lives in Bakersfield.

Rupert, Carola — In her three years as director of the Kern County Museum, Carola Rupert has made sweeping changes at the facility and is chiefly responsible for its being accredited — for the first time — by the American Association of Museums.

More than 100,000 visit the museum and the adjacent Pioneer Village each year. Rupert's persistence in seeking financial support for the museum, particularly that of the Board of Supervisors, has caused some to describe her as a "rabble-rouser." (Those who know Rupert well say the dynamic 33-year-old probably takes more pleasure than offense from the description.)

Rupert presently is supervising a team of workers who are cataloging the 138,000 items in the museum's collection. A native of the Midwest, the director is the niece of Bakersfield's Cotie Wallace.

Cal State Bakersfield Foundation Board of Directors: 1986-87

Tomas A. Arciniega, CSB President
Robert W. Bennett
John M. Brock, Sr.
Bruce F. Bunker
James L. Burke
Warren G. Carter
Curtis Darling
John L. Forney, M.D.
Adeline Frasch
Stan T. Frazier (Treasurer and Manager)
Albert H. Holloway
Edwards Hopple
Jimmie Icardo
Clifford F. Loader, DDS
David R. Martin
Hugh C. Mays (Honorary)
Margaret Moore
Patrick Sansing
Jerry K. Stanners
Jim D. Whitley
Milton M. Younger
Martin J. Zaninovich (Honorary)

Cal State Bakersfield Advisory Board

Bernice Bonillas
Fred H. Carlisle, Jr.
Ralph Carpenter
Kenneth Frick
Christina McClanahan
Gregorio S. Pineda, M.D.
Robert Rodriguez
Judge Carey F. Scott
John B. Sill (Chair)
Thomas W. Smith
Larry A. Valero, DDS

Cal State Bakersfield Presidents

Paul Romberg	1970-73
Jacob Frankel	1974-83
Tomas A. Arciniega	1983-

Bakersfield College Presidents

Paul VanderEike (Principal)	1913-17
Grace Van Dyke Bird (Dean)	1920-50
Ralph Prator	1950-58
Edward Simonsen	1958-68
Burns Finlinson	1968-72
John Collins	1972-83
Richard Wright	1983-

Cerro Coso Community College Presidents

Richard A. Jones	1971-75
Richard S. Meyers	1975-78
Raymond A. McCue	1979-

Taft College Administrators

Robert F. Gray	1922-23
J.T. McRuer	1923-25
John G. Howes	1925-33
Daniel T. Williams	1933-34
Robert J. Parker	1934-35
David W. Reidy	1935-36
John G. Howes	1937-44
Eugene M. Johnston	1944-45
Joseph P. Cosand	1945-50
Garlan A. Basham	1950-75
Wendell L. Reeder	1975-80
David Cothrun	1980-

(Until 1950, the Taft administrators were called principals or deans. The present title is superintendent/president.)

Secor, Kenneth — Dr. Ken Secor's job for Cal State Bakersfield in 1967 was to find and equip an office, within one week's time, for Dr. Paul Romberg, the college's founding president. It was from that office on California Avenue that the plans for the new campus were formed.

Since that time, Secor, who now is CSB vice president for administrative services, has solved countless logistical problems for the college and, as much as anyone, has helped to establish good relations between the campus and the community. Secor is a member of the Kern High School District board of trustees, and is actively involved in Rotary and a number of other organizations. He and his wife, Mary Lou, are the parents of Julie, an audiology specialist for the county schools, and Ken, Jr., a music major at the University of Southern California.

Simonsen, Edward — A native of Oakland, Dr. Edward Simonsen first came here in 1938 as a teacher at East Bakersfield High School. He retired 40 years later as the first chancellor of the Kern Community College District.

Simonsen's administrative career with the district began in 1946, after his World War II service as a Marine Corps pilot. Dean Grace Bird, who hired him, often referred to Simonsen as "my indispensable dean of men." In 1958 he was appointed president of Bakersfield College. Ten years later he became superintendent of the Kern Community College District in 1968 and in 1974 was named chancellor.

His role in establishing Bakersfield's College's first separate campus on Panorama Drive is one of Simonsen's most significant achievements. President Ralph Prator assigned Simonsen the responsibility for the overall planning and development of the facility, which opened in 1956. It was a major step for the college and

Dr. Edward Simonsen, who supervised the construction of Bakersfield College's first separate campus, checks a few figures with Dr. Ralph Prator and painting contractor Art Ferguson in 1954, two years before the facility opened.

for the growth of the community as well, for at the time that area of northeast Bakersfield was a barren wasteland. "When the campus was purchased in 1951," Simonsen says, "that quarter section was out in the boonies and there was no construction around it. I remember seeing an awful lot of rocks." And some skeptics doubted that the school, which then had an enrollment of about 1,500, would ever grow much larger.

Simonsen served as president of the American Association of Junior Colleges in 1972 and earlier headed the League for Innovation in the Community College. He presently serves on the boards of the Kern View Hospital Foundation, the Kern County Assessment Appeals Board and Stockdale Country Club. He is a former president of the Bakersfield Kiwanis Club and has chaired committees for United Way and the Bakersfield Chamber of Commerce.

Since his retirement, the chancellor has acted as a consultant to community colleges in California, Texas, Washington and West Virginia. He and his wife, Marvene, make their home in Bakersfield.

101

Wilson, Eleanor — One of the few female department heads in the history of Kern County, Eleanor Wilson served as Kern County Librarian from 1942 to 1967.

Noted for her ability to work well with others, Wilson

Standard, Ethel Mary — "Tiny" Standard, whose nickname described her short height and small frame, was a pioneer teacher in the Ridgecrest area, one whose concern for students extended beyond the classroom. (A

Stockton had definite ideas about curriculum content and teaching methods. For example: "The reading of nonsense should not be insisted upon either in school or at home. I intend to use my efforts to have the books of

Under the direction of Dr. Joseph K. Smith, chief health administrator from 1921 to 1942, the county's public health services were organized into one coordinated system.

Dr. Juliet Thorner became the first resident children's physician at Kern General Hospital in the 1930s. She has been a leader in increasing the public's awareness about the need for the prevention of child abuse.

In its early years, Mercy Hospital operated a school for nurses. Pictured with the 1917 graduating class are Sister M. Gertrude, the hospital's first superior; Miss Murphy, director of nursing; and Srs. M. Benignus McMahon, Joseph Keane, Gerard O'Shea, M. Ursula Hart and M. Camille Lee.

8

The Healers

"No more delivering a woman on a low cot by lamplight, with a basin of Lysol solution to dip your hands in."

Dr. Lucille B. May

The skill of today's health care professionals, not to mention the medical technology and facilities available, would undoubtedly have caused the pioneer doctors to shake their heads in wonder.

And so would the level of specialization, for the first doctors in Kern County practiced medicine almost as a sideline. As in other parts of California, and like hundreds of others in different professions, it was the hope of making a fortune in gold that lured them here.

Limited training and questionable credentials were the norm, says Dr. Phillips Dunford, a respected Bakersfield physician who is compiling a history of the Kern County Medical Society.

"There was a practice in the frontier areas of a young person's being apprenticed to an established doctor for a number of years and then striking out for himself in the advancing frontier," says Dunford. "Also, the available diagnostic and therapeutic modalities that surround today's doctor were minuscule at best."

So when their hopes of finding El Dorado failed to pan out, most of these early doctors turned to farming or other enterprises. For example, Dr. Charles Bush, who came to Havilah in the 1860s, became the first editor of the *Havilah Courier*.

Some, like Dr. Sparrell Woody and Dr. Issac D. Stockton, were graduates of medical schools. But they too became farmers and apparently practiced little medicine after settling here. Later, when the State Board of Medical Examiners was formed, Stockton was asked to join but refused, saying he wanted "no government in medicine." (In the 20th century, one of his descendants, Dr. Christopher Stockton, would become a well-known Bakersfield physician.)

One early doctor who did make a fortune in gold was Dr. Rose Burcham of Randsburg. Her husband, Charles Burcham, was one of the discoverers, in 1895, of the enormously productive Yellow Aster Mine, and she had provided him with his grubstake.

But another female physician, Lois Worthington, spent her entire career in medicine. In fact, Worthington, who died at 84 in 1959, was still seeing patients until a few days before her death. The physician is especially remembered for providing treatment for members of the Chinese community in Bakersfield during a severe scarlet fever epidemic in the early 1900s.

In 1897 the Kern County Medical Society was formed when 11 physicians gathered in the office of Dr. Charles A. Rogers in Bakersfield. The first president, Dr. R.A. Fergusson, was a graduate of a respected institution, the Royal College of Physicians in Edinburgh, Scotland. Rogers was named vice president and Dr. William H. Cook, secretary. The society was established as a means of exchanging information in order to maintain professional standards, provide continuing education and to educate the public about health matters.

There were few hospitals in the county in the early days and most patients went to them only as a last resort or to recover from badly broken bones, a common occurrence in farming and ranching communities. (Most births took place in the home until well into the 1920s and women were taken to the hospital only when complications arose.)

In 1910 Mercy Hospital was established in Bakersfield by the Sisters of Mercy, a Catholic nursing order founded in 1859 in Ireland. It was the first facility with adequately trained nurses. For a number of years it also was a training school for the nursing profession in Kern County. (The hospital recently celebrated its 75th anniversary and still is owned by the Sisters of Mercy.) Today, those interested in earning a nursing degree can do so in programs offered at Bakersfield College and Cal State Bakersfield.

The County of Kern's health care facilities entered the modern era in the 1920s, largely under the guidance of Dr. Joseph K. Smith, who for many years was the administrator of Kern General Hospital (now Kern Medical Center). Smith also operated the private San Joaquin Hospital, which had its beginnings about 1910 and now is owned by Adventists Health Systems West.

Bakersfield Memorial Hospital was founded by a group of doctors and public-spirited citizens in 1956. Real estate developer Ralph Smith, Jr. was a key figure in the fund-raising and planning for the facility.

Helen Clark and B.J. Thomas were among the leaders who established the Bakersfield Memorial Hospital Auxiliary. The core group also included Alberta Ogden, Hazel Ewing and Florence Clare.

Over the years, many physicians have been instrumental in establishing hospitals or improving health care facilities in their own communities. Among the leaders are Drs. John Montgomery and D.D. Taggart, Delano; Drs. George Garner, John Ellis and J. Dykes Johnson, Taft; Dr. Lynn Gair, Wasco; Drs. Carrol Goss and Vincent Lopez, Arvin-Lamont; Drs. Harold and Madge Schlotthauer, Tehachapi; Dr. Thomas Drummond, Ridgecrest.

Professional mental health care began to come into prominence in the late 1950s when the county established its first clinic for such services at Kern General Hospital.

The field was further advanced with the opening in 1966 of Kern View Hospital, a non-profit corporation which was organized in cooperation with the Bakersfield Memorial Hospital Association and the Mennonite Mental Health Services. Henry F. Brandt, owner of New City Cleaners, was the chairman of the founding board of trustees and served in that capacity until 1974.

The Kern View Foundation was incorporated in 1974 to help provide financial support for the hospital's expanding services. The primary organizers were Mark Raney, the foundation's first president, John I. Kelly and Larry Yoder, hospital administrator. In 1986, Ray Watson,, chairman of the special events committee, initiated the idea of publishing a book that would honor Kern County leaders. The result is *Kern's Movers & Shakers*.

Auxiliaries are a vital part of the operation of many hospitals, providing volunteer services as well as financial support. The Mercy Hospital Auxiliary, founded in 1955, was the first. Yole Antongiovanni was the key figure in its development. Since its inception, members have volunteered approximately 900,000 hours and contributed thousands of dollars, mainly from gift shop profits. The money has been used to buy new medical equipment and expand services.

The Mercy group assisted in the formation of the Bakersfield Memorial Hospital Auxiliary in 1957. Helen Clark was the founder. Lucia Marvin and Mary Louise "Weezie" Ahern initiated the Memorial Auxiliary's first major fund-raiser, a rollicking musical variety show titled, "High Fever Follies." Its cast included doctors, nurses and members of the community at large. In its nearly 20-year history, the auxiliary has donated more than $800,000 to the hospital for the purchase of equipment and furnishings.

Also of longstanding are the support groups formed by the wives of medical, dental and pharmaceutical societies in Kern County. Gladys McKee, the wife of Dr. Keith McKee, was the first president of the Medical Auxiliary in 1929.

Dentists, led by Dr. Clinton Fowler and Dr. Constantine Marsili, initiated the Kern County Dental Society in 1921. Others instrumental in its formation include Dr. Otto Hess of Fellows, Dr. Glen Patton of Taft, and Dr. E.G. Zimmer, Bakersfield.

While the pioneer doctors might have spent an entire day on horseback to reach one of their patients, a number of today's health professionals fly for only hours to remote villages in Mexico to provide voluntary services.

The Flying Samaritans, a group formed in 1980 by Bakersfield veterinarian Dr. Thomas Banks, periodically goes to Baja California. Key physicians in the group are Drs. David Jacobsen, Edward Brown, and William Bezdek. Optometrists in the group include Drs. Ronald Kosh and John Knight. Dentists involved in the Samaritans are Drs. Anthony Tarango, Joe Nunez, Reece McClenny and David Winegar.

Bakersfield ophthalmologist Dr. Ronald Morton is

the founder of the Central Valley Chapter of Surgical Eye Expeditions. The SEE team travels to Mexico several times a year to provide free eye care. Dr. Greg Olson and Dr. Dennis Wetterholm also participate in this group of flying eye physicians.

Many Kern physicians are engaged in the ongoing research into valley fever (coccidioidomycosis), which began as early as 1920. The contributions of many of these practitioners are covered in greater detail in the biographical sketches that follow.

Anderson, Joseph — A chest physician who practices in Bakersfield, Dr. Joseph Anderson is well-known for his contributions to the control of valley fever. He has published numerous papers on the topic and was a member of the Kern County Coccidioidomycosis Study Group during its many years of activity.

He also established the Emphysema Club in affiliation with the American Lung Association of Kern County and has spearheaded many continuing education courses for health professionals.

Anderson, who served as Mercy Hospital's chief of staff in 1984, has been involved with the Lung Association for 20 years. He is a past president of both the county group and its statewide organization, and he has held positions at the national level. In 1985, the American Lung Association of California presented the physician with the Pottenger Award in recognition of his outstanding volunteer service in the control and prevention of lung disease.

Though he is a quiet and unassuming person, Anderson was one of several members of the community who donned an apron in May of this year to participate in the Lung Association's "Celebrity Waiter Luncheon." Anderson served as the international president of the Y's Men (an affiliate of the YMCA) in 1986. He and his wife, Susianna, traveled to every continent during his term in office.

Arbegast, Neil Richard — A cardiovascular and thoracic surgeon at San Joaquin Community Hospital, Dr. Neil Arbegast completed his residency under the world famous cardiac surgeon Dr. Michael DeBakey, at Baylor University in Texas. Arbegast came to Bakersfield in 1970 as chief of surgery at Kern Medical Center. There, he performed the first open heart surgeries in the San Joaquin Valley. In 1972, the University of Maryland Medical School graduate developed facilities for open heart surgery at San Joaquin Hospital. He also has served as the hospital's chief of staff.

At San Joaquin, the 50-year-old surgeon heads a skilled team of hand-picked specialists. Says Arbegast, "I've learned that I have to delegate more of the things I do in order to provide a perfect product in terms of the type of work we do. And that's how we work around here."

Baisinger, Leo F. — Bakersfield eye physician and surgeon Dr. Leo Baisinger was known internationally for his work in ophthalmology. Baisinger, who opened his practice here in 1946, first went to India in 1955, where he spent three months providing ophthalmology services in Mugeli. The eye doctor returned there in 1960 and 1962 to spend similar lengths of time. In 1963, Baisinger again went to India, this time to serve on a voluntary basis for two years as an exchange professor and as head of the ophthalmology department at the Wanless Hospital in Miraj.

During that time he performed surgery on the mother of one of the area's rulers, Sheik Shakhbut bin Sultan, which made it possible for the woman to regain her vision for the first time in several years. Instead of accepting payment for his services, Baisinger asked that the sheik donate medical equipment to the clinic.

In addition to his professional affiliations, Baisinger was active in the community and at First Presbyterian Church. He served 10 years on the Bakersfield City School District board and was a charter member and past president of the Bakersfield Optimists Club. He also was a member of the Greenhorn Mountain Veterans Association.

HAL RANDALL

Chest physician Dr. Joseph Anderson received 1985 Pottenger Award from the American Lung Association of California. Alexander von Hafften, ALAC past president, made the presentation.

The physician died in an automobile accident on Porterville Highway in 1965. His wife, Frances Baisinger, who has been a leader in many organizations, resides in Bakersfield.

Barnard, Marion — Dr. Marion Barnard became chairman of the board of San Joaquin Community Hospital in 1974, a position he holds today. Barnard and his brother, Dr. James Barnard, were among the group of Seventh-Day Adventists who purchased the hospital from Dr. Joseph K. Smith in 1964.

The Barnards were instrumental in developing the first surgical cardiac care facility in Bakersfield outside of Kern Medical Center. When Dr. Neil Arbegast first came here, it was Dr. Marion who interested the vascular surgeon in doing private work through San Joaquin Hospital. And Dr. James is said to have been the first in the Bakersfield area to perform surgery to correct a vascular aneurysm in 1955.

Buckley, Peggy — In her 27 years as a member of the Bakersfield College nursing faculty, Dr. Peggy Buckley has instituted many innovative programs, ones that have benefited students as well as the community at large.

In 1982, two years after completing an Ed.D. in community college administration, she was named director of the associate degree Nursing Program. Recognizing that few spaces were available in the program for licensed vocational nurses (LVNs) seeking to become registered nurses, Buckley established the LVN to RN "ladder" program. She secured a grant to cover the costs of the program. It has proven so successful that it is being used as a model at other institutions.

Buckley has been an innovator right from the start. At the time she was hired in 1960, the school nurse's office was housed in the gymnasium and served mainly athletes. Within a short time, she upgraded her office to a centrally located Student Health Center to serve the health needs of all students on the campus. The center emphasizes illness prevention and health education.

A 1957 graduate of St. Mary's School of Nursing, she continued her education after coming to Bakersfield College. She earned a bachelor's degree in education from Fresno State in 1964 and was certified as a public health nurse the same year. In 1973, she received a master's in education from Cal State Bakersfield.

Buckley was named the 1985 "Nurse of the Year" by the Kern Registered Nurses Society. Three years earlier she received the Distinguished Alumni Award from the California Association of Colleges. She also has served that association as president and is a past president of

Justifiably expressing their optimism at the groundbreaking of Bakersfield Memorial Hospital were R.E. Gignoux, J. Russell Kennedy, board chairman Ralph Smith, Jr., Dr. Harry Lange and Dr. Roderick Ogden.

the Bakersfield College Academic Senate.

Burcham, Rose LeMonte — In Kern County, Dr. Rose Burcham is better known for the part she played in the development of the famous Yellow Aster Mine in the Randsburg area than for her medical skills. For it was she who is said to have provided the grubstake for her husband, Charles Burcham, one of the discoverers of the gold mine. Dr. Burcham, who previously had practiced in San Bernardino, joined her husband at the desert outpost in July 1895. There she became the chief cook, bottlewasher and bookkeeper, and may also have provided medical services for the sparsely populated area.

Burnett, Ralph — In 1958, Dr. Ralph Burnett was instrumental in establishing the Foundation for Medical Care in Kern County and served as president for four years. The second such foundation formed in the United States, it acted as a health financing brokerage firm and provided medical insurance policies for 30,000 county residents from 1958 to 1968. Burnett, president of the California Medical Society in 1967, is the only Kern County physician to have held that position.

Burr, Peter — Vista High School counselor Peter Burr is probably Kern County's best known heart patient. Burr, whose heart had become enlarged and restricted as the result of a respiratory infection, received a heart transplant at the UCLA Medical Center in 1986. The 42-year-old educator returned to work less than three months after the surgery and continues to recover. Burr says he is grateful to the American Heart Association, both the local and the national organizations, for its years of sponsoring research that made his surgery possible. In January of this year, he expressed his appreciation by agreeing to be the honorary chairman of the Bakersfield unit's "Jail or Bail" fund-raiser. Burr, a skilled set designer and technical director, and his wife, Roanne Burr, an outstanding singer and actress, are well-known for their activities with numerous theater groups locally.

Carr, C. Larry — In 1967, at the age of 26, Larry Carr became the youngest hospital administrator in the country when he was appointed to head Bakersfield Memorial Hospital. A graduate of Bakersfield High School, Carr did his graduate work at UCLA and joined Memorial in 1964 under Kevin Hegarty, who then was the administrator. Carr says he expected to be at Memorial only a few years before moving up to a larger hospital. Instead, he has stayed to become a key figure in making the facility the success it is today. Describing himself as knowledgeable in the sciences but inexperienced in administration, Carr says he received excellent guidance and support in the early years from such leaders as founding board chairman Ralph Smith, Jr. and Pete Gignoux, one of the directors.

Clerou, Romain P. — A descendant of one of Kern County's pioneer French families, Dr. Romain Clerou is a familiar figure on the sidelines of the playing field at Memorial Stadium. Clerou has been the team physician for the Renegades since 1946. He is the first and only physician to be inducted into the Bob Elias Hall of Fame.

Although he still is an integral member of the team's medical staff, he turned over his head physician position to Dr. William Baker four years ago. Incidentally, Clerou once played football for Bakersfield College before entering the University of California at Berkeley. He earned his medical degree in 1943 at the Creighton University School of Medicine in Omaha, Nebraska. And, after completing his internship at St. Mary's Hospital in San Francisco and a two and one-half year stint with the U.S. Navy, he returned home to open his practice, which he still maintains.

Drummond, Thomas — Now in his 80s and living in Laguna Hills, Dr. Thomas Drummond is something of a legendary figure in eastern Kern County. The physician first practiced in the Rand mining district, then moved to Ridgecrest in the 1940s. A licensed pilot, he often flew his own plane to treat patients in isolated areas and was highly, and often affectionately, regarded for his devotion to his patients and his profession. Drummond was chiefly responsible for the establishment of Ridgecrest Community Hospital.

Einstein, Hans — In the eyes of his peers, Dr. Hans Einstein is considered the world's foremost authority on valley fever. Currently the director of Medical Services for the Barlow Hospital of Respiratory Diseases in Los Angeles, the physician makes frequent visits to our

---

"We have picked ourselves up off the floor and now it's back to the old drawing board, assuming that funding is forthcoming."

---

area and remains active in the "cocci" study group.

During a recent interview, Einstein expressed his feelings about the results of the Valley Fever vaccine testing program that ended in 1986. "We are all painfully disappointed that after 20 years of lab work and seven years of field work — all voluntary — and $800,000 (half of it contributed by businessmen and citizens of Kern County, the other half by the Legislature) that we have produced nothing for practical use."

But with the doggedness that characterizes all movers and shakers, Einstein said, "We have picked ourselves up off the floor and now it's back to the old drawing board, you might say — assuming that funding is forthcoming."

Born in Berlin, Germany, Einstein came to Bakersfield in 1951 to complete a residency in internal medi-

cine at Kern Medical Center. He subsequently served one year as medical director at the county tuberculosis hospital in Keene and from 1953 to 1956 was the tuberculosis controller for the Kern County Health Department.

While he practiced in Bakersfield, Einstein served as chief of staff at Kern Medical Center and at San Joaquin Community Hospital.

Enns, Russel K. — Shafter High School graduate Russel Enns is director of clinical programs for Gen-Probe Inc., San Diego. A Ph.D. in biochemistry at the University of California at Davis, Enns developed for the company the first FDA-licensed DNA probe assay for rapid diagnosis of infectious diseases.

Before joining Gen-Probe in 1984, he was the director of cell biology research for Alpha Therapeutic Corpora-

Considered the world's foremost authority on valley fever, Dr. Hans Einstein has been a leader in "cocci" research for more than 20 years.

tion in Los Angeles. While there, Enns supervised the company's development and production of Interferon for use in cancer therapy. After completing his doctorate in 1975, Enns went to work for Monsanto Chemical Company in St. Louis, Missouri. During his four years with Monsanto he was a member of one of the first industrial biotechnological projects. Enns and his wife, the former Shirley Morse of Shafter, make their home in Encinitas. She is an occupational therapist.

Forney, Robert — In 1962, Dr. Robert Forney was the coordinator of a poliomyelitis immunization campaign called "Sabin Oral Sundays." It was the first campaign of its kind in the nation. (The pediatrician had trained under Dr. Sabin in Cincinnati in 1939.)

Volunteering their services, health professionals administered the Sabin oral vaccine on a succession of Sundays at county fire stations and at the fairgrounds. In all, two-thirds of the county's population received

"Sabin Oral Sundays," the first polio immunization campaign of its kind in the country, was coordinated by Dr. Robert Forney, a Bakersfield pediatrician, in 1962.

the vaccine that would protect them from the crippling disease. The volunteer force was made up of members of the Kern County Medical Society, Kern County Pharmaceutical Association, Nurses Association, Kern County Health Department and numerous lay people.

Dr. Forney died in 1976. His wife, Sue, lives in Bakersfield, as does his brother, Dr. John Forney.

Frasch, Adeline — Adeline Frasch learned the art of giving as a child in her native South Dakota, where, at Christmas time, she helped her mother deliver gifts of food to friends and neighbors. Later, in Kern County, Frasch would continue that kind of philanthropy but on a much larger scale.

A trained nurse, she came to Bakersfield in 1930 with her late husband, oil man Richard Frasch, and first worked at the women's prison in Tehachapi (now the California Correctional Institute). In addition to providing health care, she taught nursing to inmates.

During World War II, while working as a night supervisor at Mercy Hospital, Frasch observed that there was a lack of coordination between holiday food donors and those who received the gifts. Often there were duplications, and some who were in great need were overlooked.

To help solve the problem, the nurse, and others in the community, set up the Community Council of Metropolitan Bakersfield. The program grew as schools and agencies joined in the effort and ultimately about 1,000 families were receiving food baskets each Christmas.

Describing the way the program works, Frasch said, "Every donor has a problem, and every recipient has a problem. We get them together and work out a compromise."

Frasch, who later worked in the obstetrics ward at Memorial Hospital, chaired the project until 1985, when it was taken over by the Volunteer Center and renamed Christmas Clearinghouse.

Known for her wit as much as for her perseverance, Frasch has been a leader in many civic organization. She was an organizer of the Women's Division of the Chamber of Commerce. One of the original members of the Cal State Bakersfield Foundation board, she still serves as a member of that group. Frasch was instrumental in the formation of Bakersfield's Sister City Program with Wakayama, Japan, and has made many visits there.

Gifford, Myrnie — In the 1930s at Kern General Hospital, Dr. Myrnie Gifford became the first person to suspect that there was a relationship between valley fever and the coccidioidomycosis fungus found in the sputum of patients who had the desease.

As Dr. Thomas Larwood puts it, "Somebody had to make the connection that the common mild condition that made you break out in red bumps, and the terrible fungus that caused ulcers that sometimes killed people, were related. She did it."

Further studies conducted by Dr. Ernest Dickson at Stanford University confirmed Gifford's suspicions that "cocci" and valley fever were one and the same. It was a significant step forward in the treatment of the disease and a stimulus for the research that continues today. Gifford later helped develop the skin test used to detect valley fever.

A graduate of Stanford University Medical School, with a master's in public health from Johns Hopkins, Gifford came to Kern County in 1934 as chief assistant to the county health officer, a position she held until her retirement in 1954. During her 20 years of service, the physician took a leading role in the betterment of community health, particularly that of infants and children. In addition to her valley fever work she is recognized for her efforts to control the spread of tuberculosis and diphtheria.

Generous and warmhearted, she was known to give financial help to many of the Dust Bowl migrants who came here in the 1930s. Gifford died in Oakland in 1966 at the age of 75.

Gillespie, Carolyn Hornkohl — A Stanford graduate who had attended Bakersfield High School, Carolyn Gillespie is the executive director of Western Medical Center, a 248-bed non-profit community hospital in Anaheim. At the time of her appointment in 1983, Gillespie was president of Anaheim Memorial Hospital and previously had served that institution as vice president of operations and chief medical technologist.

Gillespie is one of the few female hospital chief executives in the country, excluding those connected with religious orders. She generally is considered to have put Western Medical Center on a sounder financial basis since becoming administrator and has been instrumental in the hospital's development as one of the major cardiovascular centers in California.

Her parents undoubtedly were her first role models.

Cutting Mercy Hospital's 75th anniversary cake are Mary Rohmiller, Mercy Auxiliary president; Dr. Dennis Wetterholm, chief of staff; chef Angel Diaz; Sister Phyllis Hughes, president; and Jim Burke, chairman of the board.

Frank Hornkohl, who previously had been a chemist for Standard Oil established the first commercial laboratory in Kern County on Truxtun Avenue in 1934. The lab, which he sold in 1967 shortly before his death, tested anything pertaining to chemistry but did no medical work. Elsie Hornkohl, who still lives here, first worked at Kern General Hospital as a supervising nurse. In 1945, she opened La Casa on North Kern Street in Bakersfield. It was the first nursing home (convalescent hospital) in Kern County.

Gillespie's husband, Bill Gillespie, a petroleum engineer, is president of his own consulting company, WINGCO International Inc.

Hard, Suzanne — In the past 15 years, Dr. Suzanne Hard, director of the Indian Wells Valley Association for Retarded Citizens, has taken what was essentially a "non-program" and developed it into a multi-million dollar self-funding agency. Her programs have been used as models throughout the state. She also has made many national presentations — seven in 1987 alone — on sexual abuse prevention for people with disabilities.

Hard, a Ph.D. in humanistic psychology from International College, Los Angeles, is widely involved in the community and was instrumental in establishing a shelter for battered women in Ridgecrest. She was named "Humanitarian of the Year" by the Beta Sigma Phi professional sorority in 1985. The director came to the area in 1966 with her husband, who then was stationed at the Naval Weapons Center.

Hughes, Phyllis — For the past five years, Sister Phyllis Hughes has been the president and chief executive officer of Mercy Hospital. Hughes, 43, who has gained a reputation as an able and efficient administrator, is one of two sisters who are CEOs of hospitals operated by the Sisters of Mercy, a Catholic order. However, she will resign this fall to take a one-year sabbatical to research international health care issues.

During her administration, the 276-bed hospital expanded several departments, increased its technological capabilities through the purchase of advanced medical equipment, increased outpatient services and began operating outreach programs in southeast Bakersfield minority communities. With the opening of Mercy-Richards Child Care Center, the hospital became the first employer in Kern County to provide on-site child care services. The hospital also expanded its child care and health education services in the southwest part of the city at Mercy Center, which has programs for all ages. And in 1985, Mercy celebrated its 75th anniversary in Bakersfield.

Still, Hughes says that, for her, the "people" aspect is the most rewarding part of her job. "The thing I'm proudest of, the thing I hope we've done ... is attract and build the human resources we have. That's the kind of thing that really carries you into the future."

Huntington, Robert, Jr. — During his 25 years at Kern Medical Center, Dr. Robert Huntington gained national respect for his work in forensic pathology and valley fever research. In 1971, Huntington published a

> "The thing I'm proudest of, the thing I hope we've done...is attract and build the human resources we have. That's the kind of thing that really carries you into the future."

paper based on his more than 20 years of study of the disease. Titled, "Human Infection with Fungi, Actinomycetes and Algae," it is considered a definitive work in the field.

Huntington, who retired in 1975 as director of medical services at KMC, also has made significant research contributions in the fields of infectious diseases, neoplastic disease, pathology of trauma, and poisonings. In all, he has written more than 50 articles for scientific and medical journals.

A native of Hartford, Connecticut, and a Phi Beta Kappa at Yale, Huntington completed his internship and residency at New Haven Hospital. He then served at Washington University in St. Louis, Missouri, and at Cornell University in New York. During World War II he was a physician at a number of Navy hospitals. Prior to joining the KMC staff in 1950, he was an associate professor of pathology at the University of Southern California.

At the time of his retirement in 1975, Huntington said, "One of the things that lured me here was the opportunity to pursue my research into valley fever, as well as the chance to make frequent weekend trips to the coast." The pathologist, who now is 79, and his wife, Katherine, maintained a vacation home at Cambria during his time in Bakersfield and made it their permanent home when he retired.

Dr. Belle Lee removed bullets from the victim of a saloon brawl, using the tavern's pool table as her operating arena.

In 1971 the pathologist established the non-profit Huntington Foundation for Medical Education to provide financial aid to medical students from Kern County. Shortly after his retirement, an annual lecture series was established in his honor.

Huntington served as chairman of the California Medical Association's tumor tissue committee and was an assemblyman for the College of American Pathologists. He is a past president of Kern Unit, American Cancer Society and the American Lung Association of Kern County.

Johnson, Laverne C. — Dr. Laverne Johnson, who received her early education in Taft and earned her Ph.D. at Stanford, is known nationally for her research and study of sleep. The psychologist is a chief scientist at the Naval Health Research Center, San Diego and a professor of clinical psycho-physiology. She has written more than 100 journal articles on her findings, and one book, and has contributed chapters for several other books.

Johnson, Royce — Dr. Royce Johnson, who received his medical degree from the University of California at Irvine, came to Bakersfield as vice chairman of the Department of Medicine and chief of Infectious Diseases at Kern Medical Center in 1975. Johnson has been president of the Community Action Committee for Valley Fever Vaccine since 1980 and also served as the Bakersfield site project director for the Valley Fever Vaccine Project. He has co-authored many research findings on coccidioidomycosis and was the chief coordinator of the recent vaccine program.

Kilburn, H. Parley — In Kern County, Dr. Parley Kilburn is known as "Mr. Mental Health" — and with good reason. For nearly 40 years, the psychologist has been energetic and persistent in his efforts to increase the public's awareness of the need for services to help people deal with their emotional problems.

It was he who spearheaded the campaign that result-

ed in the Board of Supervisors establishing a mental health clinic at Kern Medical Center in 1957. The clinic, which was the beginning of today's Department of Mental Health, was an unpopular notion at the time. (Several of the community's leading citizens called the idea "communist-inspired.") He served on the county's Mental Advisory Board for 14 years and was its first chairman.

A key figure in the formation of the Mental Health Association of Kern County in 1950, Kilburn served as president from 1957 to 1962 and again in 1977-78. (The association's Kilburn Center on L Street is named in his honor.) He was instrumental in the formation of the Henrietta Weill Memorial Child Guidance Clinic, Alliance on Family Violence and the Family Service Agency. In the 1960s, Kilburn was, as he puts it, "the expert witness" on June Stiern's "PTA Coffee Time." On the weekly television show the psychologist discussed family emotional problems based on letters sent in by viewers.

Kilburn, who earned his doctorate in education at Stanford, came here in 1950 to accept a position as a counselor at Bakersfield College. He previously had gained a national reputation for his innovative methods as superintendent of a juvenile correctional institution in Utah. Shortly after his arrival, Dr. Ralph Prator, then the president of BC, assigned Kilburn the task of setting up a program of evening classes.

Over the next 21 years, Kilburn — always carrying a clipboard and wearing a friendly smile — became a familiar figure to thousands of night school students as he made his quiet observations of classes in progress. In addition to being dean of the evening division, the psy-

Dr. Parley Kilburn, known in Kern County as "Mr. Mental Health," once joined June Stiern as the co-host of a television show called "PTA Coffee Time."

Kern County Medical Society Presidents

Clarence Compton	1920	Levin N. Osell	1954
E.S. Fogg	1921	Jack M. Hayes	1955
Joseph K. Smith	1922	Ralph W. Burnett	1956
George C. Sabicchi	1923	John K. Coker	1957
P.J. Cuneo	1924	Carl L. Moore	1958
William H. Moore	1925	Robert I. Day	1959
Keith McKee	1926	William H. Moore, Jr.	1960
L.C. McLain	1927	Carrol W. Goss	1961
R.M. Jones	1928	Harold C. Freedman	1962
J.M. Kirby	1929	Thomas V. Reese	1963
E.A. Schaper	1930	Hans E. Einstein	1964
G.E. Bahrenburg	1931	Max H. Newman	1965
Louis A. Packard	1932	John R. Almklov	1966
P.F. Page	1933	Keith W. Spaulding	1967
P.N. Root	1934	James F. Barnard	1968
Seymour Strongin	1935	David S. Ardell	1969
L.H. Fox	1936	Hugh V. O'Connell	1970
H.R. McAllister	1937	M. Martin Clark	1971
Harry W. Lange	1938	Gene A. Anderson	1972
Chester I. Mead	1939	Mortimer Iger	1973
Clarence Compton	1940	Francis A. Matychowiak	1974
Lucille B. May	1941	Dyrel A. Faulstick	1975
J. Headen Inman	1942	David J. Evans	1976
Jack M. Nicholson	1943	Donald J. Sheffel	1977
H.A. Riven	1944	Joseph L. Izenstark	1978
Sophie L. Goldman (Rudnick)	1945	Charles W. Holeman	1979
William H. MacDonald	1946	J. Frank Benedict	1980
James T. Stanton	1947	Theodore M. Badgley	1981
Frederick O. Wynia	1948	Charles S. Ashmore	1982
Robert A. Patrick	1949	Robert C. Marshall	1983
John J. Cawley	1950	George Ablin	1984
Roderick Ogden	1951	Warren E. Simon	1985
George A. Garner	1952	Madan Mukhopadhyay	1986
John E. Vaughan	1953	Samuel Baskerville	1987

chologist also counseled evening students.

Now 83, Kilburn still takes an active interest in community affairs. In 1986, he received the Beautiful Bakersfield Committee's "Humanitarian Award." He and his wife, Winona, make their home in northeast Bakersfield.

Larwood, Thomas R. — Dr. Thomas Larwood is an active member of the valley fever research study group. The physician, who opened his private practice in internal medicine in Bakersfield in 1959, has presented and published many papers on the disease in the past 25 years.

A native of Fresno, he did part of his undergraduate work at Fresno State. (His mother was the first female student body president at the college, then Fresno Normal School.) Larwood earned his medical degree at the University of Southern California Medical School in 1951. After his internship at Los Angeles County Hospital, he came to Kern Medical Center for his residency.

The physician then went to Korea as a Methodist medical missionary. Returning in 1955, he completed a three-year residency in internal medicine. Larwood was the director of the internal medicine department at Kern Medical Center from 1962 to 1965.

For many years, Larwood has been instrumental in providing health education in the schools and the community, through his involvement in the American Lung Association (he is a past president), the American Heart Association and the Cancer Society. He was the chairman of the Interagency Council on Smoking and Health from 1966 to 1977 and has chaired a similar committee for the California Thoracic Society. From 1973 to 1980, he was a member of the Clinica Sierra Vista board of directors.

The physician participates in many community organizations, including the Boy Scouts and Bakersfield East Rotary Club. He is married to Kern County Supervisor Pauline Larwood.

Lee, Belle MacFarlane — One of the first female physicians in Kern County — and, in 1899, the first woman to join the Kern County Medical Society — Dr. Belle Lee first practiced medicine in Tehachapi and often handled emergencies in Mojave. A true pioneer, Lee once removed bullets from the victim of a saloon brawl, using the tavern's pool table as her operating arena. The bartender served as anesthetist.

Lee received her medical degree at the College of Physicians and Surgeons in San Francisco in 1898. She previously had taken nurse's training in Toronto, Canada. She joined other members of her family in Tehachapi in the early 1890s. Her brothers, Dan and Jack MacFarlane, operated the Oak Creek Lumber Company. Her sister's husband, Burt M. Denison, was a leading pear grower and businessman. After her arrival in the mountain community, the physician married Charles A. Lee who served as Kern County Recorder from 1898 to 1922.

In 1904, after six months of post-graduate training in New York where she worked at Bellevue Hospital, Dr. Lee opened an office in Bakersfield. However, according to Dr. Lucille B. May, Lee found there was prejudice toward women physicians. Discouraged, she became a homemaker, although she did provide medical services during the influenza epidemic of 1918.

Lee and her daughter, Winifred Lee Wagner, moved to Los Angeles in 1932 but returned 10 years later and worked at the women's prison in Tehachapi from 1942 to 1953. She died in Berkeley in 1960.

Marshall, Harold — Harold Marshall got his start in the pharmacy business as a youth in Delano. His job then was to pack rock salt around the ice cream at the local drug store fountain each morning before his class

---

The pharmacist, had a reputation for taking a calm, thoughtful approach to problem-solving.

---

at Delano High School. Marshall later enrolled at the University of Southern California and received his pharmacy degree in 1928. After working for other druggists, he went into business for himself in 1935 and became not only a respected pharmacist but a leading member of the community.

The pharmacist, who had a reputation for taking a calm, thoughtful approach to problem-solving, first was elected to the Delano High School board of trustees in the 1940s, serving about 12 years. In the mid-1960s the turmoil in the community brought on by the grape boycott had spilled over into the schools. A group of concerned citizens urged Marshall to run again for a

seat on the board of trustees. He won his bid and served another 12 years.

He received many honors for his civic activities, including the Silver Beaver Award for his work with the Boy Scouts.

Marshall sold his business to Safeway Stores in 1984, one year before his death. The building which now houses Delano Sporting Goods still is owned by his widow, Edwina. Their son, Monte Marshall, also a graduate of the USC Pharmacy School, works for the Safeway Pharmacy. Monte's son, Mylon, is in his third year of medical school at USC.

A great many members of the Kern County medical community have been involved with unraveling the mysteries of valley fever.

May, Lucille B. — An active obstetrician/gynecologist in Bakersfield for 50 years, Dr. Lucille B. May opened her practice here in 1925 after completing her training at the University of California at Berkeley. Although she ultimately gained wide respect and developed a thriving practice, May said the early years were difficult. "It was the Depression years and getting started in practice was very different in those days. People went to a doctor as a last resort . . . no such thing as routine check-ups to keep well. As a new doctor and a woman, it was slow going."

However, three physicians in particular gave her strong support and encouragement: Dr. Joe Smith, Dr. Keith McKee and Dr. T. M. McNamara. As her practice grew, so did the level of sophistication in the field of obstetrics. In the early years, home deliveries were the rule — women went to the hospital only if there were complications. May welcomed the expansion of OB services in hospitals. In the autobiographical notes she wrote before her death a few years ago, she said, "No more delivering a woman on a low cot by lamplight, with a basin of Lysol solution to dip your hands in."

May became the first woman to head the Kern County Medical Society when she was elected president in 1941. (Dr. Sophie Loven Goldman Rudnick is the only other female physician to hold that position.) May also served as chief of staff at Mercy, Kern General and Memorial hospitals.

Seven years after the death of her first husband, geologist Arthur May, the obstetrician married Park Parker, a former Hemet rancher and a producer of the Ramona Pageant. He died in 1980.

Naworski, DE — DE Naworski, who is as singular as her first name, has made great strides in bringing health care to the Kernville area since being named the chief executive officer of Kern Valley Hospital in 1984. Under her direction, the hospital has begun a $13 million expansion and remodeling project funded by a state bond issue. The project will include a 155-bed skilled nursing facility, the first of its kind in the area, which is scheduled for completion in the fall of 1988. The plan also calls for increasing the present number of acute care beds from 27 to 31, an updated radiology department and a new emergency room.

The administrator was instrumental in the formation of the Kern Valley Hospital Foundation in 1986. In its first year, the community-supported foundation has raised more than $250,000 for the hospital. Naworski holds a master's degree in public administration from the University of San Francisco. Before assuming her position with Kern River Valley she was assistant administrator of Bakersfield Community Hospital.

Smith, Joseph K. — Dr. Joe Smith, as he was familiarly known, served as Kern County's chief health administrator for 20 years, from 1921 to 1942. During that time he organized the county's hospital and public health services into one coordinated system. In the depression years of the 1930s, the physician was faced with the difficult task of providing adequate health care for a rapidly increased population brought about by the huge number of Dust Bowl migrants who came to this area. (Between 1935 and 1940 the population of Kern County increased 70 percent.)

A pioneer in valley fever research, Smith was recognized in 1927 by the American Medical Association for his work in that field, in association with Dr. William T. Cummins. Smith also made notable contributions in the diagnosis and treatment of encephalitis.

Smith, who was born in Santa Ana, grew up in Bakersfield and was a member of the Kern County Union High School class of 1910. After receiving his medical degree from the University of Southern California and interning at Los Angeles General Hospital, he served as an Army battalion surgeon in World War I. (The American Legion Post 26 named him "Man of the Year" in 1954.) Upon his return to Bakersfield he entered medical practice with his father, Dr. Samuel F. Smith.

Dr. Joe Smith assumed the position of superintendent and medical director of Kern General Hospital in 1921. The county facility was then on 19th Street. He subsequently was named county health officer. The following year he was elected president of the Kern County Medical Society.

Smith acquired the San Joaquin Hospital in 1937 and continued as its administrator until 1964. When he relinquished his interest in the hospital, he desired that it be taken over by members of the Seventh-Day Adventist Church, and Drs. Marion and James Barnard led the group that responded. Today the facility is owned by the San Joaquin Hospital Corporation and is affiliated with Adventist Health Systems West.

Smith died in 1972. His wife, the former Elizabeth Snyder, still lives in Bakersfield. Their son, Dr. Kent Smith, practiced dentistry in Bakersfield for many years.

Smith, Lee Elton — A 1955 graduate of Taft High School, Dr. Lee Elton Smith served 20 years as a Navy physician. Since his retirement, he has served at the Washington University Medical Center and is a consultant for the Bethesda Medical Center. A proctologist, Smith specializes in colon and rectal cancer. He has been a member of surgical teams who have operated on two presidents — Jimmy Carter and Ronald Reagan — and one Supreme Court justice, Lewis Powell. Smith received his medical degree from the University of California at San Francisco and served his internship at the University of Utah.

Sooy, Francis Adrian — Dr. Francis Sooy, who was chancellor of the University of California, San Francisco, Medical School from 1972 to 1982, attended Taft College before entering the University of California at Berkeley. An otolaryngologist, he pioneered surgical techniques for the improvement of hearing and became internationally known in his field.

Although Sooy was born in Coalinga, he grew up in Taft. His father died of tuberculosis when the future doctor was 3 years old. From that time on his mother, a schoolteacher in Fellows, supported the family.

Sooy drew high praise for his leadership at UC San

Dr. Francis Sooy, who grew up in Taft, pioneered surgical techniques for the improvement of hearing and served for 10 years as chancellor of the Medical School at the University of California.

DAVID POWERS/UCSF

Francisco and was named chancellor emeritus upon his retirement. A licensed pilot, Sooy was killed in an airplane crash near Rio Vista in 1986.

Stringham, E.B. — Affectionately known as "Doc" Stringham, E. B. Stringham opened the first pharmacy in Shafter in 1919. Professional medical services were limited at the time, and the Corcoran native shared with customers his knowledge of health care as he provided for their pharmaceutical needs. Stringham also served the animal population with veterinary services.

The druggist was instrumental in persuading Dr. M. M. Kay, the town's first permanent physician, to come to Shafter in 1920. Kay practiced there until 1941. (Dr. Alvin Gaede was the second medical doctor to arrive on the scene.)

Both Stringham and his wife, Angie, were leaders in Shafter's early development. Today, Stringham's Drug Store on Central Avenue is owned and operated by their daughter, Pat, and her husband, Mert Wiedmann, both of whom are registered pharmacists.

Thorner, Juliet — Dr. Juliet Thorner retired from private practice in 1975, but the pediatrician still works four days a week for the Kern County Health Department. In doing so, she has returned to the place where she first practiced in Bakersfield.

Affectionately known as "Doc" to his customers, pharmacist E.B. Stringham opened a drug store in Shafter in the 1930s. Today it is owned and operated by his daughter and son-in-law, Patricia and Mert Wiedmann.

"Handing a family a new little baby is about the nicest thing in the world."

Thorner, a graduate of Stanford Medical School, came here in 1937 as the first resident children's physician at Kern General Hospital. She quickly became involved in the ongoing valley fever research, particularly in association with Dr. Myrnie Gifford, and her interest continues today.

The pediatrician went into private practice in the early 1940s. She has been recognized for her work with hyperkinetic children. She also was a leader in providing girls with information on menstruation and sexual growth through the seminars she conducted at elementary schools. In addition, Thorner was one of the first members of the medical community to call the public's attention to the prevention of child abuse. She was instrumental in forming the first area committee to study the problem and coordinated several major conferences in the 1970s in association with educational institutions and community organizations. The meetings, which featured nationally known experts in the field, drew a large attendance.

In 1977 the physician established the Juliet Thorner Awards. The annual $1,600 scholarship program recognizes and encourages the academic achievement and potential of girls in sixth grade through high school. In February of this year the California Teachers Association named Dr. Thorner the winner of its 1987 "Friend of Education" award.

Valley Fever Researchers — For more than 60 years, a great many members of the Kern County medical community have been involved with unraveling the mysteries of coccidioidomycosis — a fungus disease commonly known as valley fever or "cocci," which affects the lungs and in its more serious form can be fatal.

And the research continues today. The annual meetings of the local cocci study group are attended by all interested physicians, mainly those in California and Arizona, although it also draws practitioners from other parts of the West.

Dr. Hans Einstein, now considered the foremost authority on cocci in the world, is a key figure in the group. Dr. Norman Levan, a Bakersfield dermatologist, pioneered the research into the industrial aspects of the disease. Both physicians have published numerous papers, as has Dr. Robert Huntington, a former county pathologist.

Other physicians who have contributed in large measure to valley fever research are Drs. Charles Holeman, Ralph Cunningham, Joseph E. Anderson, Royce Johnson, Marco Braschi, Mortimer Iger, George Paulsen, George Ablin, Leroy Smale, J.E. Vaughan, Juliet Thorner, Thomas Larwood, Sophie L. Goldman Rudnick, I.W. Birsner, and C. Ross Hampson, a Ph.D. in microbiology.

Although a practical vaccine to prevent valley fever is yet to be found, much has been done in terms of limiting the effects of the disease. This progress has come about largely through advances in diagnosis and treatment, and through ongoing public awareness programs that inform people what they can do to avoid the disease.

Vaughan, John E. — At the age of 80, Dr. "Jack" Vaughan is still practicing obstetrics because, as he puts it, "Handing a family a new little baby is about the nicest thing in the world."

But in his more than 40 years as a member of the county's medical community, the University of Virginia Medical School graduate has done much more than deliver babies. He was the major force in the establishment of Houchin Community Blood Bank in 1951.

It was Vaughan who approached agribusinessman-developer Elmer Houchin about the availability of a building site for the proposed blood bank. Houchin agreed to donate $50,000 to establish the facility in memory of his mother and subsequently gave another $27,000. Vaughan has served as the president of the Houchin Blood Bank board of directors and presently is its medical director.

The physician also took a major role in the reconstruction of Mercy Hospital following the 1952 earthquake and in the formation of Bakersfield Memorial Hospital.

Vaughan is a former president of the Kern County Medical Society and has been a delegate to both the California Medical Association and the American Medical Association. He has served on the State Board of Medical Examiners for many years. The obstetrician and his wife, Alice, are residents of Bakersfield.

David Ben-Gurion, first prime minister of Israel, greets Charles Katzman, popular BC journalism department chairman, during Katzman's visit to Jerusalem in 1973. Ben-Gurion, 87 at the time, died later that year.

An avidly read syndicated columnist for the **Los Angeles Times,** *Jack Smith reflects his Bakersfield upbringing with his humorous observations on life.*

Ann Gutcher has traveled far since her "Romper Room" days on KERO-TV in 1957. The energetic leader has been highly visible in public relations, marketing, and politics.

118

9
The Pen &
The Lens

"The paper was owned and edited in a fiery manner by Julius Chester, a man who by reason of vitriolic editorials had aroused the enmity of numbers of people."

George W. Wear, *Inside Historic Kern*

he pioneer editors were outspoken, intensely biased, highly competitive, and, as you might guess, relatively short-lived. Those who survived often turned up as the owner or editor of an opposing paper.

Most were fiercely loyal to whatever political faction held their allegiance — or their paycheck. Taking potshots in print at their journalistic rivals was considered fair game.

The competitive spirit gained increased vigor with the "water wars" of the 1880s. On one side of the historic dispute were Henry Miller (the grandfather of Rio Bravo Resort developer George Nickel) and his partner, Charles Lux; on the other, James Ben Ali Haggin and William Tevis, founders of the Kern County Land Company. Smaller, less powerful farmers found themselves somewhere in the middle.

At the time, there were three newspapers in the county, according to historian Harland Boyd: *The Kern County Californian*, the *Kern County Gazette*, and the *Morning Echo*. All were published in Bakersfield.

The Californian, owned by Albert C. Maude and edited by Richard Hudnut, supported the Haggin-Tevis interests. And if readers weren't aware of *The Californian's* persuasion, George Wear of the rival *Gazette* made sure they did, for Wear called Hudnut the "mouthpiece" of the landowners and their manager, William Carr.

The *Gazette* was on the side of Miller and Lux. It was published by John Linthicum; however, the *Californian* accused Linthicum of being "into cahoots" with Julius Chester. One of Bakersfield's first merchants, Chester was known to represent San Francisco investors and in the 1870s had been the owner-editor of the *Californian*.

Then, in 1886, the year the dispute was finally settled, a third entrant leaped into the journalistic fray: the *Morning Echo*. The newcomer, which stayed on the scene until 1927, when it was acquired by *The Bakersfield Californian*, was financed by a group of independent farmers who favored state legislation and regulation of water rights. The *Echo's* first editor, a young lawyer named Sylvester C. Smith, later was elected to the state Senate.

At the beginning of Kern County's media history, however, there was only one newspaper: *The Havilah Courier*, from which today's *Bakersfield Californian* traces its roots.

George A. Tiffany, a printer from San Jose, published the *Courier's* first edition in Havilah on August 18, 1866, five and one-half months after the county was established. Said author Barbara Boyd Voltmer in *Kern County's Courier: 1866-1876*, "The need for a newspa-

Sunny Scofield, far right, who produced and hosted the widely watched local TV show, "Sunny Today," for more than nine years, went to London in 1970 to interview the Duke and Duchess of Bedford.

lished in Bakersfield: The *Bakersfield News Observer,* published by Joseph Coley; *El Mexicalo,* with Esther Manzano at the helm; and Raul Camacho's *El Popular.* There also are three Spanish language radio stations in the county: KWAC, owned by Ed Hopple; Steve McGavren's KAFY; and KXEM, with Frances Torres as general manager.

Surprisingly, television arrived in Kern County in 1932, one year before the first radio stations, when the Schamblin brothers, owners of the Pioneer Mercantile Company, produced the first telecast west of the Mississippi.

The experiment was short-lived, however, and in 1933 the Schamblins obtained a license for radio station KPMC. Earlier that year, the McClatchy family, owners of the Fresno Bee, established KERN, the county's first radio station.

Twenty years later, in 1953, television became a permanent and significant part of Kern's media. KAFY-TV (now KBAK-TV) came first, followed a few months later by KERO-TV. KGET (originally KLYD-TV, then KPWR-TV) went on the air in 1958. Financial backing and staffing for the stations came from a number of investors and broadcasters — Gene DeYoung, Ed Urner, Ken Croes, Ed Andress, Bryan Coleman, among others.

Although the technology had improved considerably by the 1950s, television still was in its infancy. Still photos, which arrived via Greyhound bus from Los Angeles, were the only visuals on news shows. And every-

per in a mining community, particularly a county seat, was real and earnest." Charles W. Bush, a medical doctor, was the first editor.

Although Tiffany lasted only one month, his paper continued, and Augustus D. Jones took over in December 1866. (The ownership during the intervening months is somewhat of a mystery.) Jones, an officer in Kern's Democratic Central Committee, used his position and his paper to further his political aspirations. He was elected coroner while running the *Courier* but lost his bid for a seat in the state Assembly.

Accurately predicting that Bakersfield soon would become the county's hub, Jones moved the *Courier* and its equipment down from the mountains. Without missing an issue, it appeared for the first time in Bakersfield on December 22, 1869, as the *Kern County Weekly Courier.*

The paper went through a series of name changes and acquisitions over the next 30 years. Alfred Harrell, who then was Kern County Superintendent of Schools, became the owner and publisher in 1897. *The Californian's* ownership has remained with the family right up to the present. Berenice Fritts Koerber, Harrell's granddaughter, is president of the corporation, whose chief executive officer is Jerry K. Stanners. Robert Bentley has been managing editor since 1983.

At least two other families have played prominent roles in the county's newspapering history: the Johnsons, former publishers of the *Tehachapi News,* now owned by William Mead; and the Reeds, founders and present owners of the *Arvin Tiller* and the *Lamont Reporter.* The Reeds also own the *Delano Record.*

In the past decade, three newspapers serving particular ethnic segments of the community have been estab-

> ## Accurately predicting that Bakersfield soon would become the county's hub, Jones moved the *Courier* and its equipment down from the mountains without missing an issue.

thing, including the commercials, was done live, a situation that led to some surprising and often amusing slips of the tongue.

As it moves into the 1990s, television is much more sophisticated — in a technical as well as a business sense. The present network affiliations, owners and managers of the three stations are: KBAK (ABC) Burnham Broadcasting, Frank Gardner; KERO (CBS) McGraw-Hill Broadcasting, Ron Mires; KGET (NBC) Ackerly Communications, Ray Watson. The respective news directors are Rick Snyder, Walt Brown and Gaylen Young. Soon there will be a fourth station, headed by Dorothy Owens, who currently is involved in the management of Buck Owens Enterprises. She is Buck's sister.

Taken as a whole, Kern County's media includes three daily newspapers, approximately 20 weeklies and at least three magazines; three television stations; 24 radio stations. And just as it was at the beginning, the situation is highly competitive.

Happily, over the years there has been a vast change for the better in terms of ethics and professional qualifications. Two professional organizations, the Kern Press Club and the Kern County Broadcasters, provide annual scholarships for college-level students. Since 1978, the Press Club has given annual awards to individuals in all areas of media. The journalism awards program was initiated in 1978 by Steve Talbot, who then was news director for KERO-TV.

Some of the best and the brightest in the business can be found in both the management and staff of Kern's wide-ranging media. Kern County's uniqueness in terms of geographical size and political activity, as well as the international attention it receives because of its oil-agriculture economy and as the home of the Naval Weapons Center and Edwards Air Force Base, makes it a valuable training ground for journalists.

As journalism educator Charles Katzman used to tell students, "Once you learn to cover City Hall here, you can cover it anywhere."

Adamo, Felix — Felix Adamo, a photographer for *The Bakersfield Californian,* twice has won two first place awards from the National Press Photographers Association: in 1980, for a four-shot sequence of a drag boat crack-up at Lake Ming and, in 1985, for the Kern Canyon rescue of a car accident victim.

Adams, Charlie and Mike Derryberry — This KBAK-TV reporter-photographer team won a Golden Mike award from the California Radio and Television News Association for their "best spot news" coverage of a drag boat racing fatality at Lake Ming.

William J. Burris — The KERO-TV producer-director's promotion announcement, "CPR: Training for Life," won the American Heart Association's 1986 California Media Award. In 1985, Bill Burris received the national Broadcast Promotion and Marketing Executives Gold Medallion Award for "We've Got the Touch," especially memorable for the swimmer diving into the letter "O".

Chappell, Charles — Mississippi-born Chuck Chappell covered the courthouse beat for *The Californian* for three years until he was called to active duty with the Army Reserve shortly before Pearl Harbor. He served as a public relations officer on General MacArthur's staff for some time in Australia. After the war, he became city editor, then managing editor, of the old *Los Angeles Daily News*. After the paper ceased publica-

tion, he joined McDonell Douglas (then called Douglas Aircraft) and, among other duties, wrote speeches for Donald Douglas, Sr. Chappell, a resident of San Marino, California, retired in 1977 and is an active member of the Los Angeles Press Club.

Cheski, Cynthia — *The Californian* staff writer received the 1987 Guild Service Award from The Newspaper Guild, a union representing 40,000 newspaper workers in the United States and Canada. The award includes a $1,500 scholarship for labor studies.

Chipman, Bernice Harrell — A witty and intelligent writer, Bernice Harrell Chipman for many years contributed a weekly column, "What Do You Think?" to *The Bakersfield Californian.*

The daughter of publisher Alfred Harrell and his wife, Virginia, Chipman was born in Bakersfield in 1887. Following her marriage in 1911 she made her home in San Francisco, where she was a civic leader, but retained strong ties with her hometwon and took an active interest in the newspaper until her death in 1967.

"She certainly was a woman ahead of her time," said Lawrence Weill, one of Chipman's contemporaries. "In those days, women did not participate as they do now, but she always did."

Chipman served on the boards of all the major arts groups in San Francisco and was president of such civic organizations as the Family Welfare Agency and the League of Women Voters. Earl Warren, then the governor of California, appointed her to a two-year term on the state Welfare Board.

She was instrumental in the creation of a replica of the *Havilah Courier* office at Pioneer Village and in 1966 was named honorary chairman of the Kern County Centennial celebration.

"Bernice was sophisticated with a sense of what was

*Two men who appreciate the importance of finance — Joseph L. Coley publisher of the **Bakersfield News Observer**, and Governor George Deukmejian — exchanged views at a political fund-raiser recently.*

right at the right time," said her friend, Marie Clerou Barnett. "She was sort of New Yorkish, sort of Paris — and sort of Havilah."

Christie, Casey — While working for the *Kern Valley Sun,* Casey Christie, now with *The Californian,* received a first place award from the California Newspaper Publishers Association for "Mud Flood," a fanciful picture story showing Kernville area youngsters playing in the mud.

Coley, Joseph L. — In 1975, Joseph Coley, the owner and operator of the Observer Group of Newspapers, began publishing the *Bakersfield News Observer,* the city's only newspaper specifically for the black community.

And he admits it has been an uphill battle. "Starting a newspaper is the hardest thing I've ever done," Coley says. "For a black person in this community, it has been very hard."

Three years ago, he launched two papers in the Los Angeles area, the *LA Bay* and its separate San Fernando Valley edition. Before the end of 1987, he plans to establish papers in the Monterey-Salinas area, in Fresno and in Modesto.

KERN COUNTY MUSEUM

Pioneer TV and radio personality George Day had a host of friends and they set up a memorial fund in his honor. The money has helped Bakersfield College maintain its KBCC-FM radio broadcasting curriculum.

A veteran of 22 years of military service, Coley was one of the first blacks in the Navy to be selected for aviation technical duties. In 1986, he was appointed to the state Republican Central Committee. He is the first black to hold such a position. The publisher's wife, Ellen, is involved in the business operation of the newspapers.

Cox, Bob and Ronald Campbell — These *Bakersfield Californian* staff writers received an "Oscar in Agriculture," a national competition sponsored by the DeKalb Corporation, for their series, "The Government's Steele Web."

Drury, Allen — Allen Drury, who grew up in the Porterville area, worked for both the *Tulare Bee* and *The Californian,* before writing his Pulitzer Prize-winning novel about the Washington political scene, *Advise and Consent.*

Day, George — The 50s generation remembers George Day as the first host of the afternoon show on KERO-TV. One of Bakersfield's best-known broadcasting personalities, Day also was a popular radio disc jockey.

His daily TV program provided a forum, during the movie breaks, for just about any organization in the community with something to promote. He had a sort of whimsical charm that made viewers feel they were a part of the new medium.

Day, whose real name was Daisa, left KERO in 1957 following a salary dispute. He subsequently hosted shows on both KBAK-TV and KLYD-TV (now KGET). After his death, a group of his friends set up a golf tournament in his memory in 1975. Proceeds from the George Day Memorial Fund have amounted to nearly $40,000 since that time. The money has been donated to the Bakersfield College radio station, KBCC-FM, where the funds have provided scholarships and electronic equipment for the 900 students who have passed through the college's broadcasting classes in the past 10 years. Broadcasting professor Ron Dethlefson says the fund "has preserved the station and the broadcasting curriculum at Bakersfield College during a time of minimal support from normal tax revenue."

Day, Jim — Jim Day went to work at *The Bakersfield Californian* in 1923 as a sports and general assignment reporter. He retired 44 years later as managing editor. For 15 years, the Victoria, British Columbia native — he previously had worked for the *Victoria Times* and the *Seattle Post-Intelligencer* — followed the championship Bakersfield High School Drillers all over California. He also covered the courthouse, wrote lively accounts of such oddities as the Taft mouse invasion and contributed to the editorial page. A fine photographer, his pictures were the first local ones to appear in the paper. He set up a photo department, and designed *The Californian's* first engraving plant.

Readers knew Jim Day best, or felt that they did, through his daily "Pipefuls" column. Using a personal, anecdotal style, the editor focused on individuals. On any given day, the contents might range from the doings of national notables to the achievements of everyday people in the community or perhaps two of Day's chief interests, hunting and fishing. Although some insiders thought it a bit too laudatory, "Pipefuls" was the kind of column people liked to read and just about everyone did.

Day exerted a strong influence on the newspaper's style during his long tenure as editor. He had a love for words that bordered on infatuation and in matters of grammar and sentence structure he was a stern disciplinarian.

Harrell once refused to grant a certificate to Mary Hunter Austin, declaring that, while her abilities in language and grammar were acceptable, her knowledge of mathematics was "deplorable."

Deaver, William — A former owner-editor of the *Mojave News,* Bill Deaver now lives in Washington, D.C. where he is an administrative aide to Rep. Charles "Chip" Pashayan of Fresno.

Fox, Charles — In 1908 Charles Fox started *California Oil World* in Bakersfield. It has been continuously published since that date. Now called the *Pacific Oil World,* it is the only oil trade publication in existence. Jack Rider is the current publisher.

Gutcher, Ann — In 1957, Ann Gutcher — or as she was known to viewers, "Miss Ann" — launched "Romper Room" on KERO-TV. In the early-1960s, the popular children's show moved to KLYD-TV (now KGET) with Gutcher as the host. She also was a "substitute teacher" for Romper Room producer Bert Claster on his shows in Kansas City and San Francisco.

From 1966 to 1974 Gutcher worked for KBAK-TV as director of Community Club Awards and public affairs director. She was the host of a 30-minute live talk show daily for seven years. She recalls that among her more fascinating guests were the Mercury cougar, which stretched itself across her feet, and Art Buchwald, "who captivated me and took complete control of the show."

Gutcher went on to become public information director at Bakersfield College and later held a similar position at Kern High School District. She later was vice president in charge of marketing for American National

Bank and is a past president of the Kern County Board of Trade. She now heads her own public relations agency.

Harrell, Alfred — Throughout his long life Alfred Harrell was one of the most respected members of the community, first as Kern County Superintendent of Schools and ultimately as publisher of *The Bakersfield Californian.*

KERN COUNTY MUSEUM

Alfred Harrell, who bought **The Bakersfield Californian** *in 1897, started a newspaper dynasty that still continues. The paper is now owned by his granddaughter and great-grandchildren, the Fritts family.*

As superintendent of schools, from 1887 to 1898, Harrell initiated examinations for pupils and strengthened the requirements for teachers. (He once refused to grant a certificate to Mary Hunter Austin, who later became a noted author, declaring that, while her abilities in language and grammar were acceptable, her knowledge of mathematics was "deplorable.") He also is credited with the establishment of the first high school in the county, in Bakersfield in 1893.

The Merced native came to Kern County as a schoolteacher in the Wasco area in 1883 and got his first taste of printer's ink in 1889, as an interim editor of the *Kern County Gazette.* Then, in 1897, at age 34, he bought *The Californian.* It was the start of a family ownership that continues to the present.

A tall, dignified man — silver-haired in his later years — Harrell was highly visible in the community. He spearheaded the formation of many organizations, ranging from the first Board of Trade in 1903 to the Kern County Historical Society in 1929. Actively involved in the operation of the paper until almost the time of his death, Harrell encouraged the community's growth and development, both in the editorials he

Familiar Faces
on
Locally Produced Shows

Norma Anglen — "Food for Thought," KERO-TV

Jennifer Barefield — Morning show, KBAK-TV

Sandra Bayes — Host of KERO-TV show

Hazel Davis — Noon talk show, KPWR-TV (now KGET)

Kay Ferguson — Noon talk show, KERO-TV

Ted Fritts — Nighttime show, KBAK-TV

Mary Gregg — Cooking show, KBAK-TV

Ann Gutcher — "Romper Room," KERO-TV and KLYD-TV;
afternoon show, KBAK-TV

Lucia Marvin — Host on KBAK-TV

Raylene Merman — Cooking Show, KERO-TV

Mitchell, Harry — "Meet Mitchell" KERO-TV

Sunny Scofield — "Sunny Today," KERO

June Stiern — "Coffee Time" KERO

Vivian Tucker — "Midday Bakersfield," KGET

Steve Walsh — Noon show, KPWR-TV; currently publishes Bakersfield Lifestyle Mag.

wrote and in the tone of the news sections.

The publisher could be courageous too. In the 1920s, when the Ku Klux Klan was active in Taft, *The Californian* printed the names of all those involved. One was a member of the Kern County Board of Supervisors.

Today, Harrell's granddaughter, Berenice Fritts Koerber, is president of the corporation. His great-grandsons, Donald Fritts and Alfred T. Fritts, are the publishers. In recent years, Harrell's great-granddaughter, Virginia Fritts Cowenhoven, has taken an increasingly active role in the newspaper and in the Fritts Family Foundation.

Harte, John — *The Californian* staff photographer's heartwrenching photo, "A Family's Horror," won the 1985 "Mark Twain Award" from the Associated Press (California-Nevada-Arizona-Hawaii region) and also was named best spot news photo. The same picture took a first from the California Newspaper Publishers Association. John Harte also has received the California School Boards Association "Golden Apple Award."

Henley, Beth — Beth Henley was *The Californian's* women's page editor at a time when social activities were the primary interest of females. And she covered just about all of them.

Henley was very much a part of her beat, an involvement which occasionally had its negative aspects, as she acknowledged in an interview.

"A lesson on how to lose friends and lose influence is

to be had from judging. Baby shows, floats, essays, speeches, Christmas parades, Miss Kern County candidates, scrapbooks, pies, cakes, crazy hats — one makes three friends with each encounter and innumerable non-friends."

Still, the editor was held in high regard by members of women's organizations and recognized as a powerful influence, particularly in the arts community. One producer of amateur theatricals said, "You knew that if you didn't get a good review from Beth Henley you were dead."

Henley's 45-year career began in 1922 when she went to work for the *Morning Echo,* which was acquired by *The Californian* in 1927. It ended abruptly on the evening of April 27, 1967 when she was killed in an automobile accident while on the way to a sorority meeting.

Henson, Herbert Lester, Jr. — For nearly 10 years, starting in 1953, "Cousin Herb's Trading Post" was the most popular show on local television. And viewers quickly made "Y'all come," Herb Henson's musical signature, part of their own vocabulary.

The locally produced country western show, which appeared nightly on KERO-TV, provided the first television exposure for such rising stars as Buck Owens, Merle Haggard, Billy Mize, Fuzzy Owen and Bonnie Owens. Audiences liked the show, both for its cornball humor and the interplay between the piano-playing Henson and his guests. Henson also was manager of radio station KUZZ — the call letters reflect his nickname, "Cousin Herb."

The Illinois native suffered from heart disease and at the time of his death had been off the air for about six months. Henson died in 1963 at 38, but he left a lasting imprint on local television and country music.

Hopple, Edwards — When Ed Hopple, with his partner, Gordon Sherwood, established KWAC in 1963, it was Kern County's first Spanish language station and one of about eight in California. As Hopple puts it, "We sort of Daniel Boone'd it."

Initially, the station was Spanish for half of its broadcast day and black programming for the remainder. (Maria Elena, Carlos Zapiain and Esteban Lopez-Sierra, all of whom previously had shows on other local stations, were among the first on-air people hired.) The reason half the programming was in English is that advertisers felt there was no "Spanish" market. They soon learned they were wrong and KWAC has become enormously successful.

The station also was a pioneer in convincing entities such as the California Highway Patrol and the American Heart Association they should produce public service announcements in Spanish.

In February 1986, Hopple, Sherwood and Robert Duffy launched another new venture, KIWI-FM, the county's first classical music station.

Each Christmas, Hopple and his wife, Catherine, provide Bakersfield residents with a spectacular display of colored lights and moving figures in the frontyard and on the roof of their two-story home.

Kane, Walter — Walter Kane, who was hired by *The Californian* in 1922 as a $25-a-week advertising salesman, retired 45 years later as its chief executive.

His official title was secretary-treasurer. But, as the newspaper said in announcing Kane's retirement in 1967, "since the death of ... publisher-editor Alfred Harrell in 1946, (Kane) has come to be regarded by the public, as well as *The Californian's* employees, as the publisher, and his name is synonymous with the newspaper's."

Kane, now 87, is a past president of the California Newspaper Publishers Association and the Associated Press Association of California-Nevada. He served on the board of directors of the California State Chamber of Commerce and was chairman of the first Kern County Business Outlook Conference in 1958.

Katzman, Charles — "Charlie Katzman knows everybody" was a phrase people often used to describe the Bakersfield College journalism department chairman, who also was the director of public information for the college and Kern Community College District. And in many ways it was true.

A native of Russia, who fled the Ukraine with his family in 1921 when he was 12, Katzman's associations were developed during a long career that culminated in Bakersfield, a city he came to love. Before moving to Kern County in 1966, he had been a reporter for the Los Angeles City News Service, an assistant to Mayor Fletcher Bowron, a professor in the UCLA School of Journalism and public information officer for the LA County Superior Courts. As a member of the International Press Institute he was acquainted with some of the world's top editors and publishers. These friendships formed a vast pool of speakers for his classes at Bakersfield College as well as at meetings of Kern Press Club.

Katzman, who died in 1979 four years after his retirement, had an anecdotal style of teaching that some students found confusing. But many more found it rewarding and, in 1974, the California Newspaper Publishers Association named him "Junior College Journalism Teacher of the Year."

Knutson, Carl D. — As a producer-director, the KERO-TV production manager received the American Heart Association's 1979 California Communications Award for his 30-minute documentary on by-pass heart surgery. A "first" in local television, Knutson donned a mask and gown to film an actual surgery, performed by

Three local giants of journalism — Bill Rintoul, Jim Day, and Ralph Kreiser — reminisced at a banquet in 1975 when Day and Kreiser were made life members of the Kern Press Club.

cardiologist Dr. Bruce Frazier at San Joaquin Community Hospital.

In 1972, while on active duty with the U.S. Naval Reserve, Knutson was the liaison between the military and the civilian press for the Apollo 16 space mission. He spent his two-month hitch aboard the USS Ticonderoga. The aircraft carrier recovered the spacecraft — and astronauts Charles Duke, Thomas Mattingly and John Young — in the South Pacific, following their 20-hour exploration of the moon. Through a special arrangement, and in addition to his official duties with the Navy, Knutson sent films and audio tapes back to his station, giving Kern County viewers first-hand coverage of the historic event.

Kreiser, Ralph — A respected newsman and historian, Ralph Kreiser was, among other things, the editor of *The Bakersfield Californian's* award-winning Centennial edition in 1966. The massive issue celebrating the county's 100th anniversary remains one of the best sources on its history. During his lifetime, Kreiser was honored by many organizations, including the California legislature and the Kern Press Club, for his contributions to the state, the community and his profession.

Kreiser spent 22 years — in three separate stints — at *The Californian.* At different times he was county editor, sports editor, city editor, editorial writer and assistant managing editor. Before joining the staff in 1936 he

A proud voice for Hispanic causes, Esther Manzano publishes **El Mexicalo,** *the Spanish-English newspaper based in Bakersfield. She also founded the Hispanic Chamber of Commerce.*

worked for papers in Southern California, including the *Los Angeles Times.* After one of his departures from *The Californian,* he was wire services editor for the *San Jose Mercury.* On another hiatus, he was assistant director of the Kern County Museum.

A man with keen intellect and unusual foresight, Kreiser made this prediction in 1962:

"Bakersfield is in a period of suspension. With the decline of oil as the No. 1 source of revenue for the county, Bakersfield is faced with the problem of becoming a city with an industrial base for its economy or continuing its dependence on agriculture. The latter's future depends so much on the availability of water that prognostication is not easy."

Kummerfeld, Donald D. — The chief operating officer (since 1979) of media magnate Rupert Murdoch's News America Publishing Company, Donald Kummerfeld attended Delano High School. He is the son of the late Theodore Kummerfeld, a one-time Wasco potato farmer.

"You knew that if you didn't get a good review from Beth Henley you were dead."

The 53-year-old CEO, who has degrees from the Harvard Business School and the London School of Economics (he's also a former New York City budget director), believes that he and Murdoch have much in common. "We are both entrepreneurs," Kummerfeld says. "Newspaper publishing is a business and we run it like a business."

Long, Elaine — While a news anchor/reporter at KERO-TV, Elaine Long tied for first place with a reporter from KGO San Francisco in a nation-wide television news feature competition sponsored by the National Commission on Working Women. She also was recognized by the California Society of Professional Journalists, Sigma Delta Chi, for her report on spina bifida. Like many of her colleagues at Channel 23, she has won numerous other professional awards. Long now is with WTSP in Tampa, Florida.

Manzano, Esther H. — In 1980, Esther Manzano became the publisher of *El Mexicalo,* a Spanish-English language weekly newspaper based in Bakersfield. Initially, the staff included herself and her son, Tony. She now has 12 employees.

For her, the toughest part is selling the advertising space to a somewhat reluctant business community. "Even after seven years of establishing ourselves," she says, "it's tough."

Manzano was the first Hispanic woman appointed to the Kern County Civil Service Commission and is the founder of the Hispanic Chamber of Commerce. She was a leader in the establishment of the county's first activity centers for senior citizens in Delano in the 1970s, lobbying before the state legislature and the Kern County Board of Supervisors. A gerontology specialist, she has taught courses in the subject at Delano High School, her alma mater, and at one time was information and referral specialist for the Bakersfield College senior citizen program.

She and her husband of 35 years, Tony Manzano, have raised 22 children — two of their own, five foster youngsters and 15 nieces and nephews. For many years, her mother, Angelina Talamantez, owned and operated El Gato Negro, a restaurant in Delano.

Matthews, Mark — Now on the news staff of KGTV in San Diego, former KERO-TV newsman Mark Matthews won awards in competition with the top Southern California markets for his coverage of the 1983 floods in Kern County. His work, and that of Jonathan Mumm (now with KXTV, Sacramento) and Channel 23 news photographers Carlos Gonzales and Paul Black, received Golden Mike awards from the Southern California Radio Television News Association and the Associated Press California-Nevada region.

Noel, Lynn — Director of public affairs at KERO-TV since 1973, Lynn Noel is the only black who holds a management position on any local television station and one of the few female executives in any Kern County media.

Noel represents McGraw-Hill Broadcasting, the station's owner, at annual conferences of the National Urban League, a pioneer forum on race relations founded in 1910. Its purpose is to secure equal opportunities for blacks and other minorities in all areas of American life.

At KERO-TV, she also initiated the Minority Affairs Committee, a group of citizens who meet monthly with the station management to provide input about the minority community in Kern County.

KERO-TV public affairs director Lynn Noel represents McGraw-Hill Broadcasting, the station's owner, at annual conferences of the National Urban League. Here she is chatting with Senator Robert Dole of Kansas.

Nordquist, Brian — The KERO-TV sportscaster's series on steroids was awarded a Golden Mike in 1984 by the Southern California Radio Television News Association. The entry won in the open division against major Southern California stations. Sharing the award was news photographer Carlos Espinoza.

Patton, John — For his series, "Cancer in Firefighters," the KBAK-TV reporter received a first place award from the Associated Press Radio-Television Association in 1985.

Press, Larry — Sports columnist Larry Press came to *The Californian* 33 years ago as a reporter, after attending Ohio University, and a brief stint as a one-man sports department at the *Casper* (Wyoming) *Tribune-Herald.* Football, particularly the Bakersfield Renegades, was the hot topic. One of the first sources he cultivated here was former Bakersfield High School coach Paul Briggs, whom Press had known in Casper.

Since then, the tall, slender and energetic Press has devoted himself to covering local sports of every kind

---

The toughest part is selling the advertising space to a somewhat reluctant business community. "Even after seven years of establishing ourselves, it's tough."

---

and is the newspaper's most widely read columnist. (He has turned down job offers from the *Washington Post* and the *San Francisco Examiner.)* He also travels around the country, reporting on Super Bowls, spring training sessions and a host of other sporting events.

In his typical staccato style, Press recalled just two of his many career highlights.

"Most memorable interview in Bakersfield: Casey Stengel, when his Cadillac broke down on the Ridge Route and he had to stay overnight.

"Most memorable single event: Jim Ryun setting a new world record for the mile run, 3:51.1, at the AAU National championships at Memorial Stadium in June 1967."

Although his colleagues often are awed at the speed in which Press turns out copy, he maintains it isn't as easy as it looks. In an interview with managing editor Robert Bentley, published on Press's 30th anniversary, the columnist said, "A column is as personal as a toothbrush and as public as a pay phone. It is usually an exercise in agony."

Rahn, Keith — For 13 of his 37 years at *The Californian,* Keith Rahn's beat was the Superior Courts. In 1971 the Kern County Bar Association honored him with its Bench and Bar Award. The veteran newsman is one of only two members of the press to be so honored by the legal profession. (Jim Day was the first in 1962.) Rahn was the charter president, in 1967, of Kern Press Club.

Rahn covered two of the most notorious murder cases of the 1960s — the trial of bandleader Spade Cooley, who killed his wife in a particularly unpleasant manner, and that of the kidnap-murderers of Rosemarie Riddle, a child the couple abducted from a Shafter labor camp. Recalling that period, the softspoken Rahn said, "Unfortunately, the ones you remember are the more horrendous crimes."

In addition to handling the higher courts (Bob Jones had the municipal court beat at the time), Rahn also covered the Board of Supervisors and all other county offices. In 1970, he was named city editor. Rahn retired in 1986 as an assistant managing editor of the editorial page and says he's attempting to improve his golf game. He and his wife, Judy, make their home in Bakersfield.

Reeder, Philip — Since his graduation from Shafter High School in 1965 and Bakersfield College two years later, Philip Reeder has become active in the television industry, mainly with KNBC in Los Angeles. In the past three years, the writer, producer, director has won three Emmys for his work, including "The Open Air Asylum," named Best Documentary in 1985. In 1986, he received the Chicago International Film Festival Award for "I Forgot to Say Goodbye," and has been recognized also by the American and New York film festivals.

Now married and living in Van Nuys, Reeder says, "I think of Shafter often: Saturday mornings, summer nights and the smell of alfalfa alongside the canal banks. These are good memories for a barefooted Okie kid from Euclid Avenue."

Rider, Jack M. — Jack Rider is the publisher of *Pacific Oil World,* the nation's second oldest oil magazine, which was begun as California Oil World in Bakersfield in 1908. Charles Fox was the founder and first editor. On his death, Fox's wife moved the publication to Los Angeles in 1917. The monthly journal's name was changed to *Pacific Oil World* in 1971. Since 1976 it has been based in Brea, in historic Orange County oil country, where it continues publication as the only West Coast oil magazine.

Rider grew up in Delano, serving as a sports stringer for *The Bakersfield Californian* until the late 1940s while he attended Delano High School and Bakersfield College. He graduated from the University of Southern California with a degree in journalism and has been associated with the publishing scene ever since. He has been honored as one of the outstanding graduates of USC's School of Journalism.

Rintoul, William — Most people in Kern County know free-lance writer Bill Rintoul as the six-days-a-week "Oilfields" columnist for *The Bakersfield Californian.* It isn't hard to understand, considering that he's

Don Rodewald's crew cut and ready smile typify his all-American image. A favorite local radio and TV performer for years, he has also served as public information director at Bakersfield College.

been doing it for 38 years.

But during those same 38 years, the Taft native has written five books — three factual and readable nonfiction works about the oil industry and two collections of short stories. He also wrote the text for a Standard Oil of California's 100th anniversary publication.

His short stories have appeared in a dozen or more literary magazines; one originally published in *Carolina Quarterly* is included in the anthology, *California Heartland.* Two stories published in *Roustabout,* one of his collections, were translated into Russian and included in an anthology titled *I Believe In Humanity,* published in 1986 in Moscow.

Highly respected in the oil industry, Rintoul is a contributing editor for *Pacific Oil World,* and has written for the *San Francisco Chronicle, Los Angeles Times,* and *Tulsa World.* His magazine pieces on an array of topics have appeared in many magazines, ranging from *Sports Illustrated* to *The Nation.* He still uses a 1950s-era Royal Standard typewriter, given to him by his wife, Frankie Jo Rintoul.

A graduate of UC Berkeley, Rintoul has a master's in journalism from Stanford. Even though his grammar is faultless and his vocabulary boundless, his writing and his everyday speech are flavored with expressions drawn from the Taft oilfields where he worked as a youth. Take, for example this excerpt from an interview with Gerald Haslam in which Rintoul said:

"The advantage of working as I've worked is, I'm my own boss. The disadvantage is a total lack of security. There isn't any safety net. It's like working in the rig-building gang. You didn't wear a safety belt because you couldn't move around up there like you had to; but like they said, you only fall once."

Rodewald, Don — Don Rodewald's easy-going manner has made him a favorite of radio listeners and television viewers for 36 years, both as a professional broadcaster and as director of public information at Bakersfield College.

The East Bakersfield High School and University of the Pacific graduate became well-known to KERO-TV viewers as host of the afternoon show on KERO-TV. He held the position for 17 years, from 1957 until he joined the BC staff. During that time he also directed the news and other locally produced shows, including "Romper Room" and "Cousin Herb's Trading Post."

Rodewald, who clings tenaciously to the same crew-cut hairstyle he sported when he was hired for his first radio job with KWSO in Wasco, maintains that he was something of a Dr. Jekyll and Mr. Hyde during his TV days.

"When I was in front of the camera, I was laid-back, smiling, happy-go-lucky and just doing my thing," he said in an interview with *Renegade Rip* staff writer Deborah Mish. "When I was in the director's chair, I was like a dictator. I liked things neat, orderly and precise."

Yet KERO-TV production manager Carl Knutson describes his former colleague as "the All-American Good Guy," and few would disagree.

Rodewald retired from Bakersfield College in June, and he and his wife, Shirley, intend to spend their time traveling.

"Saturday mornings, summer nights and the smell of alfalfa alongside the canal banks. These are good memories for a barefooted Okie kid from Euclid Avenue."

Salamacha, Judy — As the director of public affairs and promotion for KGET-TV since 1984, Judy Salamacha has coordinated a number of public service campaigns notable for their broad and positive impact on the community. Each was a team effort, involving Ray Watson, the station manager, and members of the news and marketing departments.

The campaigns included "The Driver," an anti-drunk driving project for which KGET received a commendation from the National Highway and Safety Commission; "Sober Graduation," recognized for its effectiveness by the California Highway Patrol; and "Just Say No," an anti-drug project that involved a parade of 3,300 people and led to the establishment of similar campaigns in six elementary schools.

Salamacha served as president of the Kern County Board of Trade in 1986-87 and is a past president of Bakersfield Branch, American Association of University Women.

Saunders, Mae — Like most of the reporters of her day, Mae Saunders covered everything from plane crashes to musical concerts. During her 46 years at The *Bakersfield Californian,* she interviewed dozens of celebrities, including George Bernard Shaw, whom she captured as he strode along the platform at the Santa Fe train station.

Saunders was one of the organizers of the Community Council of Metropolitan Bakersfield, a group that supported day camps for underprivileged children and recreation for senior citizens. She was equally active in her profession, particularly in the Bakersfield Newspaper Guild. Saunders was instrumental in establishing a retirement program for *Californian* employees but did not live to enjoy the benefits. The Mae Saunders Memorial Pension Fund is named in honor of the one-time women's page editor.

A graduate of the University of California at Berkeley, Saunders got her first journalistic training as a newspaper and yearbook staffer at Bakersfield High School and Bakersfield College.

The Schamblins — Frank, Charles and Leo Schamblin, the sons of Pioneer Mercantile Company founder Gustavus Schamblin, were the broadcasting pioneers in Kern County, both in television and in radio.

Way back in 1932, the first television broadcasts west of the Mississippi emanated from the Schamblin brothers' experimental television station on East 21st Street in Bakersfield. Frank Schamblin, who enjoyed inventing things in his backyard shop, assembled the equipment and made it operable. Ralph Lemert was chief engineer for the locally produced shows.

The station attracted the attention of Lee DeForest, known as "the father of modern radio" for his invention in 1906 of an electron tube that was crucial in the development of radio. DeForest visited Bakersfield often during the station's short life and acted as a consultant.

Owing to the limited technology available at the time, the Schamblins soon abandoned the idea of television and switched to radio. In 1933, T.A. "Pete" Beaty, business manager of the Pioneer Mercantile Company, appeared before the Federal Communications Commission in Washington, D.C. to obtain the license for radio station KPMC. It was the second station to go on the air in Kern County. The first, KERN, was launched the same year by the McClatchy family, publishers of the Fresno Bee newspaper.

Beaty said later, "We really wanted to call it KERN, but the McClatchys had already applied for those call letters and they won out. So we used KPMC, for the Pioneer Mercantile Company."

The Schamblins owned KPMC until 1978, when it was purchased by the present owner, Dan Speare.

Schweitzer, Karl — In addition to numerous awards from professional organizations, KERO-TV news reporter Karl Schweitzer, a Bakersfield native, received a

$1,000 fellowship in 1986 for national defense reporting from the National Radio/Television News Directors Association. (He also is a member of the News Brothers, a local rock music band, along with KGET newsman Kevin Keeshan. Incidentally, Keeshan is a nephew of Bob Keeshan of Captain Kangaroo fame.)

Scott, Jim — The KERO-TV anchor/reporter has received a number of awards for agricultural reporting and in 1985 was the first television newsman to be honored by the California Farm Bureau as "State Ag Reporter of the Year."

Scott, Kim — KGET reporter Kim Scott and photographer Tracy Swackhamer received a first place for "Best Reporting" in the 1985 Tri-State United Press International awards for their coverage of the child molestation cases in Kern County.

Smith, Burleigh — Burleigh Smith is considered the dean of television news here and with good reason: During his 34 years in Bakersfield, the personable KERO-TV News anchor has worked for all three stations.

Like many of the other TV pioneers, Smith got his start in radio. But his was a unique beginning, for as a teen-ager the native Texan had his own station, KTHT.

News anchor Burleigh Smith, one of the most familiar faces on local television, happily greets the crowd as grand marshall of a Veterans Day parade in downtown Bakersfield.

The call letters stood for "Kome to Hondo, Texas." The studio was his bedroom. The antenna was hooked to a telephone line, for a range of about one mile. Smith said, "I used to put a record on the phonograph, get in the car and drive like hell along the telephone line so I could hear my station. I even thought I was a celebrity."

From 1939 to 1954, before he was hired by KERO (now KGEE) radio, the veteran broadcaster worked for the ABC network in Los Angeles and for stations in Texas, New Mexico and Alaska. Smith has left television on two occasions since coming to Bakersfield. He worked one year for an advertising agency and from 1970 to 1973 was Supervisor Milton Miller's adminis-

trative assistant. Smith returned to KERO-TV in June 1973 as news anchor. He has been there ever since.

Smith, Jack — *Los Angeles Times* columnist Jack Smith probably has done more to give a clear picture of what Kern County is all about than any other journalist.

You get the idea that he likes the place, and that, of course, is because he knows the territory. A little known fact is that the first column he ever wrote — it was called "Jackpot" — appeared in the *Renegade Rip* 40 years ago when he was editor of the Bakersfield College student newspaper.

Smith spent the early years of his youth in Bakersfield but missed being born there due his mother's preference for sea breezes. (He was born August 27, 1916 — in Long Beach because "it was thought to be too hot to be born in Bakersfield in August.")

After graduation from high school in Los Angeles, and two voyages as a scullion in the Merchant Marine, he enrolled in Bakersfield College. He got his first professional experience, from 1937 to 1939, as a reporter on *The Californian.* His wife, the former Denise Bresson, is a member of a French family who were early settlers in the Pond-Delano area. And Jack's aunt was Shafter Branch librarian for many years. He twice has been a speaker at the Business Outlook Conference.

Smith served in the Marine Corps as a combat correspondent in the Pacific Theater from 1944 to 1945. Before joining the *LA Times* in 1953, he worked for the *Honolulu Advertiser,* the United Press wire service, the *Los Angeles Daily News* and the *Los Angeles Herald Express.*

Sommerfeld, Timothy R. — Now with WJBK-TV in Detroit, Tim Sommerfeld received United Way of America's 1986 Communication Award for his public service announcement for United Way of Kern County, which he did as a producer-director for KERO-TV.

Stanners, Jerry K. — The chief executive officer and member of the board of directors of *The Bakersfield Californian,* Jerry Stanners first came to Kern County as the president and CEO of Perelli-Minetti Winery. He previously was the executive officer of several companies owned by Dart Industries Inc.

The University of Illinois graduate and former U.S. Army captain and aviator is the president of Associated Press Association of California-Arizona-Hawaii-Nevada.

A number of organizations in the community have benefited from Stanners' expertise. He has served as president of the Bakersfield College Athletic Foundation, Southern Sierra Council, Boy Scouts of America and California Living Museum. He is a member of the Cal State Bakersfield Foundation and serves on the advisory council of the School of Business and Public Administration. An executive committee member of the Kern County Business Outlook Conference, he is active in seeking and encouraging new business for the county.

At 52, Stanners is an ardent, and active, track and field competitor. In 1986, he broke 18 records in the 50-59 age group. His specialties are the 110-high hurdles, pole vault, high jump and triple jump.

Swackhamer, Tracy — KGET photographer Tracy Swackhamer received a first place in the 1986 Tri-State United Press International "Best Spot News Videography" awards for her coverage of the rescue of Meryl Rouss, a paraplegic Cal State Bakersfield professor who survived three days after his van went off the road on Highway 158. She also was recognized for her work on the Magna Chemical spill with a "Best Spot News" from the Southern California Radio and Television News Association in 1985.

Swenson, Steve E. — A legal affairs writer for *The Californian,* Steve Swenson was appointed to the California State Bar Association's public affairs committee and served as its chairman in 1986-87.

Thomason, Jimmy — Jimmy Thomason became Bakersfield's first country-western disc jockey in 1948. He was hired by Ken Croes, manager of radio station KERO, who happened upon Thomason in the Lucky Spot, a tavern on Edison Highway. As Thomason said in an interview nearly 40 years later, "That's when country music moved from Edison Highway to Chester Avenue."

Thomason, who got his start at 15 as a band boy with Bob Wills and His Texas Playboys, broke into television in 1953 as the host of his own show on KBAK-TV. He left one year later but returned to do another show

*Leaping over obstacles is a way of life for Jerry Stanners, chief executive officer of **The Californian.***

PETER A. LUGO

from 1956 to 1958, and in 1966 began an eight-year stint with KERO-TV on the "Jimmy Thomason Show." His guests during the early years included Buck Owens and Merle Haggard.

Trihey, Michael — *The Californian's* Mike Trihey is the recipient of the California State Bar Association's 1986 Golden Medallion Award for legal affairs writing.

Watson, Raymond A. — In years of service, Ray Watson is the longest-tenured chief executive in Kern County television. Presently the vice president and general manager of KGET, a position he assumed in 1983, Watson held a similar post with KERO-TV from 1975 to 1981. Between his two Bakersfield assignments, he headed KMGH-TV in Denver.

Under his leadership, KGET changed network affiliations (from CBS to NBC) and has moved from the No. 3 position in the market to No. 1 in an 18-month period. The station has held the first spot since November 1984.

A graduate of the University of Southern California and a certified public accountant, Watson is the founder of Broadcast Credit Association, an organization representing the credit interests of more than 600 broadcasters nation-wide. He has served on the board of directors of the California Broadcaster Association and the Broadcasting Financial Management Association.

Watson is a current board member and past president of the Kern View Foundation, the fund-raising organization of Kern View Hospital. In the 1970s, he spearheaded the foundation's successful "Kern View House" project. He was the 1977 campaign chairman for United Way of Kern County and is an active member of the Bakersfield Rotary Club.

Young, Gaylen — KGET's Gaylen Young has been recognized by the regional Veterans of Foreign Wars for his documentary, "Agent Orange," which informed Kern County citizens about the chemical's effect on Vietnam veterans. Young, who co-anchors (with Gail Asayama) the Channel 17 news, also received a Golden Mike award in 1985 for "Best Newscast" from the Southern California Radio and Television News Association.

Hank Pfister, Jr. traveled the international pro tennis circuit for several years, ranking 19th in the world at the height of his career. Pfister now shares his expertise with other players as one of the pros at the Bakersfield Racquet Club.

Talented, Wilda Mae Turner was one of the world's greatest female softball pitchers. In 1975 she became the first woman inducted into the Bob Elias Hall of Fame.

Steve Strelich owned and operated Strelich Stadium for professional boxing and wrestling matches for years. He was also famous for having been one of actress Mae West's bodyguards.

132

10
Champions All

"We seem to raise a hard-nose, tough kind of kid...athletes get great support and encouragement locally."

Larry Press, *The Bakersfield Californian*

Before the turn-of-the-century, organized sports in Kern County were limited to horseshoe tournaments, croquet games and impromptu buggy races. And in Bakersfield, there were the spirited baseball contests between the two volunteer fire departments — the Eurekas and the Alerts.

By the early 1900s, the picture had changed considerably and much of the activity was centered at Kern County Union High School (now Bakersfield High School).

Football rapidly gained a prominent place under the guidance of the legendary Dwight Griffith. The coach ultimately led the Drillers to seven state championships. In succeeding years, four Drillers would become All-Americans — Don Robesky, Burr Baldwin, Frank Gifford and Jeff Siemon. Kern's fifth All-American, Vern Burke, played for North High.

The athletic programs at KCUHS set a pattern for community-supported sports activities at all high schools in the county, including Garces, a private parochial school, as well as those at Bakersfield College and, subsequently, Cal State Bakersfield. The early training provided by countless Kern County coaches, as well as strong support from other segments of the community, has produced a remarkable number of top athletes in every major sport.

Kern County's love affair with auto racing has its roots in competitions that began when horseless carriages still were an exciting novelty. In the early days, endurance was one of the primary qualifications. As journalist Bill Rintoul so aptly put it in recounting the historic 212-mile Washington's Birthday Race of 1912, "The question wasn't who would win the race. It was who, if anyone, would finish it."

The two-lap race, organized by H.C. Katze and the Kern County Automobile Racing Association, drew 15 drivers. It started at 19th and H streets and proceeded, mainly on dirt roads, through the west side oilfields — Maricopa, Taft, Fellows and McKittrick — then back to Bakersfield by way of Buttonwillow.

After a grueling 5 hours, 33 minutes and 59 seconds (and despite having landed his Stutz in a ditch near Rio Bravo), Jack Bayze emerged the winner. The Kern County deputy sheriff's prize was the silver Lakeview Cup and $1,000.

One year earlier, the famous Barney Oldfield set a world record at the Bakersfield Speedway in his 300-horsepower Christie. His time, 46:24 seconds, was the fastest ever on an oval track. The crowd went wild, according to a report in the *Morning Echo,* but the race car driver was somewhat reticent about taking a bow. "Fred Malone and P.H. Glasglow picked up Oldfield on their shoulders and carried him to the timers' stand, where Barney slid off and sat down on the fence with his back to the crowd."

Boxing was a popular attraction as well. And 98-year-old Lawrence Weill recalls that Jack Johnson, world heavyweight in 1908, fought one of his first professional matches in Bakersfield.

Tennis, a sport that has produced a number of top-ranking players here, began to come into its own in the 1930s at the courts of Bakersfield's Jastro and Beale parks.

Lake Lovelace, now 92, was the prime mover in convincing the city it should build the courts. He also

"Mr. Tennis" of Bakersfield, Lake Lovelace founded the Bakersfield Racquet Club and coached many players, including Dennis Ralston, who have achieved international fame.

brought such champions as Bill Tilden and Jack Kramer to play exhibition matches in the 1930s. Nearly 30 years later, it was largely through Lovelace's efforts that the United States Tennis Association chose the Bakersfield Racquet Club for the site of the U.S. Davis Cup Team's match with Canada in the 1960s. Few American cities have hosted the Davis Cup play at any level. (Not to be overlooked is that eight national track and field championships have been held at Bakersfield College's Memorial Stadium.)

Recreation opportunities of every kind abound in Kern County and they attract local as well as out-of-town sports enthusiasts. Taxpayer-supported programs and facilities have been built up over a long period. Much of the leadership has come from appointed and elected officials in the county and in various communities.

Among the pioneers are Alex Park, who established recreation councils in outlying areas in the 1940s; Herbert Evans of Taft, a long-time Kern County recreation superintendent — Evans Lake at Buena Vista is named for him; Frank Stramler, head of the county's parks and recreation department; Herman Riese, who headed the city of Bakersfield's recreation department from 1957 to 1973; Don Harrelson of the North Bakersfield Park and Recreation District; Tehachapi's Walter Dye; and several members of the Board of Supervisors, including Stanley Abel, Roy Woollomes, Vance Webb and Floyd Ming.

Thousands of golf enthusiasts have benefited from the guidance of such professionals as Jimmie Haggerty, Chet Foss and George Miflin, at county-owned courses, and from that of several long-time pros at private links, including Al Seanor and Rolly Allen at Stockdale Country Club, and Babe Lazane of Bakersfield Country Club.

One sport that has shown phenomenal growth in a short time is soccer. The first games, involving about 75 players, were organized in 1975 by Bakersfield residents Michael Holdsworth, Derek Holdsworth and others. Today, there are about 8,000 participants in leagues affiliated with AYSO (American Youth Soccer Organi-

Bill Colm, Sr. won the U.S. Golf Association Senior Amateur championship in 1975. He has also won the International Seniors Championship at Gleneagles, Scotland, three times.

zation) and another 2,000 in the more competitive CYSA (California Youth Soccer Association).

In the late 1970s, after the passage of Proposition 13, a group of parents formed an organization called SOKS (Supporters of Kern Soccer) for the purpose of establishing the sport in area high schools. The $120,000 which the group raised was used by Kern High School District and Garces High School to implement the program. (In 1986, teams from West High School and Garces won Central Valley championships.)

Presently, the group is working to establish a new soccer complex between Hart Park and the California Living Museum, on land leased from the county. Among the ongoing leaders in the soccer movement are Ann Enge, Dan Imes, Bob Hoffman, Bill Tensley, Hank Hinse and Dr. William Baker.

Taken as whole, these athletic programs and their leaders — in both the public and the private sectors — are the vibrant core for Kern's impressive roster of champions.

Apsit, Marger "Migs" — Migs Apsit spent nearly 25 years at East Bakersfield High School, as head football coach and athletic director. And the Illinois native brought with him solid experience.

In the early 1930s Apsit played professional football. He was pitted against such greats as the Chicago Bears' Red Grange. Apsit, now 78, says with a chuckle, "We got paid too — a hundred bucks a game."

Hundreds of former high school students, athletes and non-athletes alike, fondly remember the coach and his wife, Tiny, for their U.S.A. tours. Each summer, from 1958 to 1972, the couple shepherded a busload of youths across the country, stopping at nearly every scenic attraction along the way.

Beatty, Homer — A standout quarterback for the Bakersfield High School Drillers in the 1930s, Homer Beatty gained fame as an end at the University of Southern California. He then turned professional, playing for the Los Angeles Bulldogs. Returning to his hometown in the mid-1940s, Beatty first coached the Drillers, then went on to lead the Bakersfield College Renegades to a 12-0 record and, in 1953, a Junior Rose Bowl championship. He left BC to go to Santa Ana College where he had good teams and later coached at Los Angeles State. Beatty's overall coaching record: 185 wins, 36 losses and two tie games.

Bishop, Gil — A veteran coach, administrator and track official, Gil Bishop was a prime mover in the development of Bakersfield College's athletic program for more than 25 years.

Bishop was BC athletic director from 1954 to 1973. During that time he was instrumental in bringing eight national championship track meets to Memorial Stadium. The competitors, most of whom were from out-of-town, praised both the facility and the treatment they received here. One of the highlights of his career came

"We got paid too—a hundred bucks a game."

in 1976 when he served on the staff for the Olympic Games in Montreal.

A man of many talents, Bishop was active in radio while a student at San Jose State and was sports editor of the college paper. He continued that interest in Bakersfield, doing radio and television shows. (A very green Frank Gifford made his first TV appearance on Bishop's program.) For 15 years, he was the public address announcer at Memorial Stadium.

Bishop retired in 1973 as assistant superintendent of the Kern Community College District. Since then he has been a retirement consultant for about 23 school districts. He and his wife Roberta, are Bakersfield residents.

Blick, Richard — Richard Blick won an Olympic gold medal in Rome in 1960 as a member of the U.S. swim relay team. Blick was an outstanding athlete at Bakersfield High School — in football and basketball as well as swimming. As a basketball player at North Central Illinois College, he led the team to a national NAIA title and was a high scorer in AAU competition. Blick now coaches in Northern California.

Boyd, Freddie — A basketball star at East Bakersfield High School and Oregon State, Freddie Boyd went

A prime mover in the development of Bakersfield College's athletic program, Gil Bishop was on a first-name basis with many noted sportsmen, including star John Wayne.

Freddie Boyd was a professional basketball player for seven seasons with the Philadelphia 76ers. He is now the boys' basketball coach at Garces High School. Here Dave Fanucchi congratulates him.

on to play seven seasons with the Philadelphia 76ers. Although a knee injury caused his retirement from professional play, Boyd is still active in the sport as the boys' basketball coach at Garces High School.

Callison, Johnny — In the eyes of many sports fans, Johnny Callison is the best baseball player ever to come out of Bakersfield. As an outfielder for the Philadelphia Phillies, he combined speed, batting power and fielding acumen.

Signed by the Chicago White Sox upon his graduation from East Bakersfield High School in 1957, Callison was traded to Philadelphia three years later. He spent 10 season with the Phillies and finished his career with the New York Yankees. His overall batting average was :264, with 226 home runs and 840 runs batted in. It was his homer that won the 1964 All-Star game for the National League.

Now a resident of Philadelphia, Callison underwent successful heart bypass surgery in 1986.

Carvajal, Rudy — The athletic director at Cal State Bakersfield since the campus was established in 1971, Rudy Carvajal has been the guiding force in gaining financial support for its sports program. He was instrumental in the development of the Roadrunner Founda-

Professional Athletes

Baseball

		(High School)
Johnny Callison	Philadelphia Phillies	East
Bill Cowan	Chicago Cubs (and other teams)	East
George Culver	Cincinnati Reds	North
Manuel Fierro	Cleveland Indians (Triple A)	Delano
John Hale	Oakland Mariners	Wasco
Junior Kennedy	Cincinnati Reds, Chicago Cubs	Arvin
William "Buckshot" May	Pittsburgh Pirates	BHS
Curtis Meacham	Brooklyn Dodgers	BHS
Steve Ontiveros	San Francisco Giants, Chicago Cubs	BHS
Dave Rader	S.F. Giants, Cardinals (and other teams)	South
Jim Tyack	Philadelphia A's	BHS
Bernard "Frenchy" Uhalt	Chicago White Sox	BHS

Basketball

Freddie Boyd	Philadelphia 76ers, New Orleans Jazz	East
Lonnie Shelton	Seattle Super Sonics, Cavaliers	Foothill

Football

Marger "Migs" Apsit	Green Bay Packers, Boston Redskins	
Homer Beatty	Los Angeles Bulldogs	BHS
Theo "T" Bell	Pittsburgh Steelers, Tampa Bay Bucs	BHS
Frank Gifford	New York Giants	BHS
Don Johnson	Philadelphia Eagles	BHS
Joe Hernandez	Washington Redskins; Canadian League	Garces
Russell Letlow	Green Bay Packers	Taft
Brent McClanahan	Minnesota Vikings	BHS
Ken Ruettgers	Green Bay Packers	Garces
Doug Rogers	San Francisco Forty-Niners	Highland
Grayson Rogers	Seattle Sea Hawks, L.A. Raiders	Highland
Jeff Siemon	Minnesota Vikings	BHS
Charlie Smith	Oakland Raiders	BC
Jerry Tarr	Denver Broncos	BHS
Dick Witcher	San Francisco Forty-Niners	BHS
Louis Wright	Denver Broncos	BHS

tion, a non-profit group that annually provides 85 percent of the athletic program's budget. Tenneco Oil Corporation donated six soccer fields, which also are used by AYSO teams. Other recent additions are the $1.5 million John S. Hillman Aquatic Center and the John Antonino Sports Center. Before assuming his position at CSB in 1971, Carvajal was assistant athletic director at the University of California at Berkeley.

Castillo, Ruben — A highly ranked featherweight and junior lightweight boxer for nearly 10 years, Ruben Castillo earned four championship match challenges and fought a close 15-round bout with Salvador Sanchez of Mexico but lost the decision. Castillo grew up in Bakersfield and attended South High School before transferring to high school in San Diego. He now is pursuing a career in broadcasting and acting and is involved in a youth anti-drug campaign.

Collis, Gerry — As Bakersfield College football coach from 1967-1985, Gerry Collis led the Renegades to five Metropolitan Conference titles, three Potato Bowl victories and a Junior Rose Bowl win. Collis played football at Denver University and was in the New York Yankees minor league organization. He presently is director of the Bakersfield College Athletic Foundation.

Highly ranked featherweight and junior lightweight boxer Ruben Castillo is now pursuing a career in broadcasting and acting.

Dunn, Natalie (Taylor) — Roller skating champion Natalie Dunn Taylor won her first title, the Tiny Tot junior's, at the age of 7 and advanced through the junior ranks to win the women's figure skating championships three times. In 1976, she became the first American to win the world women's crown in Rome, turning in an almost flawless performance despite the fact she had suffered a broken kneecap only a few months before. She is one of the few female skaters — on rollers or ice — ever to attempt triple salchows and triple mapes (toe loops). At the time of her win, Dunn said proudly, "Not

The first American to win the women's world roller-skating championship — in Rome, 1976 — Natalie Dunn Taylor began her career at "Skateland," the rink which her parents, Mr. and Mrs. Omar Dunn, owned.

even Dorothy Hamill (the champion ice skater) does that."

Dunn learned to skate when she was 2, receiving her instruction from her parents, Mr. and Mrs. Omar Dunn, who then owned Skateland.

Elias, Bob — A popular radio broadcaster known for his dedicated coverage of local sports, Bob Elias often had discussed the idea of establishing some sort of permanent display to recognize the achievements of Kern County's top athletes. Herman Riese, who then was recreation superintendent for the city of Bakersfield, said that a few days after Elias' death, he and several members of the Bakersfield Jockey Club were discuss-

Bob Elia

Name	Principal sport/activity	Inducted
Marger "Migs" Apsit	East High coach, athletic director	1981
Burr Baldwin	All-American — USC	1969
Georgene Bihlman	Skier, BC coach	1979
Ken Barnes, Jr.	Champion skeetshooter	1973
Homer Beatty	BHS, BC, LA State football coach	1971
Theo "T" Bell	BHS football; Pittsburgh Steelers	1985
Gil Bishop	BC athletic dir.; Olympics staff	1973
Richard Blick	BHS Swimmer; Olympic Gold Medalist	1977
Freddie Boyd	Philadelphia 76ers	1981
Paul Briggs	BHS football coach	1977
Floyd Burcham	Sports benefactor	1984
Vern Burke	All-American — Oregon State	1978
Jim Bush	BHS, BC, Cal track; UCLA coach	1975
John Callison	Philadelphia Phillies	1967
Manuel Carnakis	Champion powerboat racer; Marine Hall of Fame	1979
Dr. Romaine Clerou	Team physician	1980
Gerry Collis	BC football coach	1982
Bill Colm	California Golf Hall of Fame	1986
Bill Cowan	East High baseball; Chicago Cubs	1987
George Culver	North High, BC athlete; Cincinnati Reds	1974
Sherilyn Doyle Curti	Taft High; national champion archer	1983
Bob Engel	National League umpire	1975
Mike Fanucchi	Garces, St. Mary's football; intnl. rugby	1986
Ray Frederick	Delano High baseball, football coach	1968

Name	Principal sport/activity	Induct
Jack Frost	BC football coach	19
Joe Galante	Regional handball	19
Alex Germanetti	Softball star	19
Frank Gifford	All-American - USC; New York Giants	19
Claude Gilbert	BC, San Diego State, San Jose State coach	19
Don Glover	Pro bowler; ABC Masters title	19
Dwight Griffith	BHS football coach	19
Les Haney	National Softball Hall of Fame	19
J.B. "Cap" Haralson	UCLA star, BHS coach, Olympics official	19
Theo "Spud" Harder	BHS, Stanford football	19
Joe Hernandez	Garces, BC football; NFL, Canadian league	19
Don Johnson	BHS, BC, Cal football; Philadelphia Eagles	197
H.W. "Pat" Kelly	High school coach, official	197
Junior Kennedy	Arvin High; Cincinnati Reds, Chicago Cubs	198
Leamon King	Delano High track; Olympic Gold Medalist	196
Al Kirkland	BHS, BC, USC football; international rugby	198
John Kovacevich	World champion speedboat racer	19
Russ Letlow	Taft High, USF football; Green Bay Packers	19
John Loustalot	Football, all-round sports enthusiast	19
Lake Lovelace	"Mr. Tennis"	196
Sing Lum	Over-65 track recordholder	19
Jack Lynch	Taft High, Stanford tennis	19

ing whether just sending flowers to the sportscaster's funeral was an appropriate way to honor Elias.

Riese recalls that he said, "Flowers are one thing, but if you want to remember Bob, let's set up a hall of fame. Larry Press was the president, and he said, 'Since you brought it up, you be the chairman.' And that's how it started." Also instrumental in its formation was Moss Henken, who still is active in the ongoing project.

In its 21 years of existence, the organization has in-ducted 85 members at its annual banquet. Recognition plaques and other memorabilia are housed in a display case in the lobby of the Bakersfield Civic Auditorium.

Engel, Bob — Bob Engel, a pioneer professional base-ball umpire, now is in his 22nd year in the National League. The Atascadero native played baseball at Ba-kersfield High School and Bakersfield College and spent a long umpiring apprenticeship in the minor

Hall of Fame

ame	Principal sport/activity	Inducted
m Lynn	Pioneer baseball team organizer	1967
illiam "Buckshot" May	Kern County's first pro baseball player	1984
ent McClanahan	South High, Arizona St.; Minnesota Vikings	1980
ve Marion	BHS, Wyoming University football	1972
rtis Meacham	BHS, Oregon football; Brooklyn Dodgers	1976
ck Mears	Two-time Indy 500 winner	1980
ger Mears	Race car driver	1986
lly Moore	BHS tennis; natl. junior champion	1977
rel Mulkey	Champion bronc rider; Cowboy Hall of Fame	1970
e O'Brien	Shafter harness racing champion	1968
nny O'Neill	BC sports publicist	1983
eve Ontiveros	BHS baseball; S.F. Giants, Chicago Cubs	1985
on Patterson	Taft High discus, shotput; NCAA	1968
nk Pfister, Sr.	BHS, BC tennis coach	1982
orge Poloynis	BHS, BC track; handball	1978
ve Rader	South High football; S.F. Giants catcher	1987
nnis Ralston	BHS tennis; Wimbledon winner at 17	1967
rman Riese	City/county rec. supv., track official	1986
on Robesky	All-American — Stanford	1967
arlie Sarver	BHS, BC, Cal football, baseball	1976
e Seay	South High, CSB wrestling coach	1981

Name	Principal sport/activity	Inducted
Lonnie Shelton	Foothill, Oregon St.; NBA All-Star	1982
Jeff Siemon	BHS, Stanford All-American; Minn. Vikings	1976
George Snider	Indy driver	1976
Lonnie Spurrier	Delano High track; 1956 Olympics	1969
Steve Strelich	Pro wrestler/boxer; sports promoter	1971
Jerry Tarr	BC, Oregon U. football; Denver AFL	1976
Natalie Dunn Taylor	National champion roller skater	1978
Orlando Torigiani	Buttonwillow hydroplane racer	1987
Jack Trout	BHS, USC track, football	1973
Wilda Mae Turner	First woman pro softball manager	1975
Jim Tyack	BHS, BC athlete; Philadelphia A's outfielder	1974
Bernard "Frenchy" Uhalt	BHS football; Chicago White Sox	1974
Claude Varner	World ranking featherweight	1983
Jim Warren	Drag racer; March Meet title-holder	1983
Art Williams	First black umpire — National League	1981
Dick Witcher	Shafter football, JC All-American, Forty-Niners	1971
Louis Wright	BHS, BC, Arizona, San Jose; Denver Broncos	1981
Robert C. Young	BHS, BC, UCLA track; Olympic Medalist	1982

leagues. An umpiring crew chief for several seasons, Engel has officiated in All-Star games, post-season playoffs and the World Series.

A former president of the Major League Umpires Association, the official is known for his candor. In an interview in April of this year, he was asked if an effort was being made by leaders in professional baseball to recruit more black umpires. "No, but I'm sure it will happen," Engel responded. "As long as they're quali-fied, it shouldn't make any difference if they're black, white or green."

In the off-season, Engel is the show manager for the annual Kern County Boat, RV and Sports Show.

Fierro, Manuel — Manuel Fierro was the first Hispanic in Kern County to become a professional baseball player in 1947 when he was signed by the Cleveland Indians. The Delano High School graduate first was a member of the Indians' Bakersfield team, then played two years of Triple-A ball with Albuquerque.

Fink, Myrl — In Taft sports circles, Myrl Fink is affectionately known as the "Voice of the West Side." He has been announcing softball games for the West Side Recreation District for the past 33 years — first at Franklin Field and now at the new recreation complex. In his distinctive, high-pitched voice, Fink provides personal insights into the players — perhaps their earlier activity in Little League — or offering congratulations when one receives a college scholarship. The 71-year-old retired postal worker spends his weekday mornings delivering meals to 47 senior citizens in the area as part of a recreation district program.

Frederick, Ray — For many years the baseball and football coach at Delano High School, Ray Frederick inspired many youths, particularly minorities. During his tenure, the Tigers' baseball team won 15 league titles.

Friedman, Gloria — In May of this year, Gloria Friedman was named Division II "Coach of the Year" for women's tennis. The selection was made by 189 coaches nationwide. During her 13 years as head women's tennis coach at Cal State Bakersfield, Friedman's teams have won seven conference titles. She also is associate athletic director for administration at CSB.

The Bakersfield High School graduate is married to Superior Court Judge Gary Friedman. She is the daughter of Ethel Pananides and the late Nicholas Pananides, an astronomy professor at Bakersfield College.

Frost, Wallace D. "Jack" — Jack Frost, the coach of the Bakersfield College Renegades for 22 years, had an impressive career at UCLA before coming to Kern

---

"Rafer Johnson is quiet dignity personified."

County. At the university he played varsity football and baseball and was a featherweight boxer. The Jack Frost League, a football organization for youths, is named for him. The coach died in 1986.

Gifford, Frank — The world knows Frank Gifford as one of television's (ABC) outstanding sports broadcasters; Kern County knows him as a youth from Oildale who seemingly has made the American dream a reality.

Gifford's success as a sportscaster was preceded by a star-studded career in football that began when he was at Bakersfield High School and Bakersfield College. An All-American at USC before entering the professional ranks with the New York Giants, the halfback was named All-Pro and inducted into the Pro Football Hall of Fame.

During the time he was with the Giants, Gifford held a number of jobs in Bakersfield during the off-season.

Frank Gifford, an All-American at USC and a star with the New York Giants for several seasons, was among the original nine athletes inducted into the Bob Elias Hall of Fame in 1967. Currently he is an ABC sports announcer.

In 1960, he was featured nightly on KLYD-TV (now KGET) on the Frank Gifford Sports Revue, plus a single 15-minute show each week following the ABC television fights. He also did a series of commercial spots for Great Western Savings.

The football great was among the initial nine athletes inducted into the Bob Elias Hall of Fame in 1967 and also acted as master of ceremonies. But he is remembered even more, by aficionados of the annual event, for his appearance as a guest speaker in 1976, along with his irrepressible Monday Night Football sidekick, Dandy Don Meredith.

Gifford now makes his home in New York and still keeps in touch with a few close friends here whom he has known since his high school days.

Gilbert, Claude — Now the head football coach at San Jose State University, Claude Gilbert is one of the nation's leading college coaches in won-lost percentage. He led the Spartans to the PCAA championship and a victory over Miami of Ohio in the California Bowl in 1986.

The Oklahoma native grew up in Bakersfield and attended Bakersfield High School, Bakersfield College and San Jose State. He stayed with football all the way, despite suffering a broken leg two consecutive years at San Jose.

Prior to assuming his present position at San Jose,

Gilbert coached at Tulare and Shafter high schools and Southwestern College in Chula Vista. He then became assistant coach under Don Coryell at San Diego State, assuming the position of head coach when Coryell was tapped by the Chargers.

Griffith, Dwight M. — (See "The Plus Factor")

Haralson, James Burnett "Cap" — J.B. Haralson got his nickname, "Cap," when he was captain of the UCLA Bruins' football team in the 1920s. An all-round athlete, Haralson earned four letters in four sports at the university, a record equalled only by Jackie Robinson.

Haralson was chiefly responsible for the planning and design of Bakersfield College Memorial Stadium. Its original brick track was made of crushed bricks he obtained from the many Bakersfield buildings that were destroyed in the earthquakes of 1952. At the time it was built, in 1955, he was superintendent of athletics for the Kern County High School and Junior College District. Under his aegis, the first three AAU national championship meets were held at Memorial Stadium.

A native of Covina, he came to Kern County in 1924 as assistant coach of football and basketball at Bakersfield High School. In 1930, he was named head track and field coach. In that position, Haralson led the Driller tracksters to successive regional titles for the next 15 years and a California championship in 1939.

Although Cap's chances of competing in the 1922 Olympic Games were good (the javelin record he set at UCLA stood for 20 years), an ear infection, which led to a mastoid operation, prevented him from doing so.

More than 40 years later, he did participate but in a different way, as assistant manager of the U.S. track and field team at the 1964 Olympics in Tokyo. He subsequently was appointed manager of the team for the 1968 Olympics in Mexico City but did not live to fulfill what probably would have been the high point of

Olympic Decathlon winner Rafer Johnson, the national coach for Special Olympics, spends a good part of his time giving encouragement to young athletes in Kern County.

Olympics Athletes/Officials

Barbara Andrews	High diver—1964, 1968
John Azevedo	Wrestler—1980
Gil Bishop	Staff—1976
Richard Blick	Swimmer—1960 Gold Medal
Bill Chisholm	50,000 meter walk—1932
Joe Gonzales	Wrestler—1984
J.B. "Cap" Haralson	Track team manager, official
Rafer Johnson	Decathlon—1956 Silver Medal; 1960 Gold Medal; Final Torch Bearer, 1984
Leamon King	100 meter relay team—1956 Gold Medal
Charlie Morton	Cycling team captain—1936
Dr. John Pulskamp	Weightlifting—1960, 1964
Joe Seay	Freestyle coaching staff—1984
Lon Spurrier	800 meters high jump—1956
Jim Turner	Swim team coach—1960
Robert Young	400 meter relay—1936 Silver Medal

his long career. On April 14, 1967, shortly after returning from Colorado where he had been scouting high altitude training sites for the athletes, Haralson died at home of a heart attack.

The coach and his wife, Louise, had three daughters: Elaine Brewer and Mary Sowers, who live in Bakersfield, and Anita Gifford, who teaches sports to special education students in four high schools in the Manhattan Beach area.

Johnson, Rafer — A native of Kings County, Olympic decathlon champion Rafer Johnson has strong connections with Kern County.

He was an executive with Contel for a number of years, and his active support of Special Olympics, a sports program for handicapped youngsters, led to Bakersfield's Peter Pan School being renamed in his honor. Dee Olson, the founder of Kern County Special Olympics, says, "Rafer will always take the time to stop and squat down and talk to any child. He is quiet dignity personified."

Johnson has been president of California Special Olympics for the past three years and is the organization's national head coach.

A versatile natural athlete, he won a silver medal in the 1956 Olympics and the gold medal for his decathlon performance at the 1960 Olympics in Rome. He thrilled the world again at the 1984 Olympics, when he carried the torch on its final stretch to the top of the Los Angeles Coliseum. Jack Maguire, the late chairman emeritus of Contel who hired Johnson, was among the thousands of spectators that day.

King, Leamon — Most people think of Leamon King as an Olympic gold medal winner, which he is. The

After winning an Olympic Gold Medal at Melbourne in 1956, Leamon King entered the field of education and first taught kindergarten. He now is a fifth grade teacher at Terrace School in Delano, his hometown.

champion sprinter took the gold as a member of the U.S. relay team in Melbourne in 1956.

But the Delano High School and University of California graduate says that for him, the biggest moment in his outstanding track career came one year earlier when he beat Fresno State's Mike Augustini in the 220 yard dash at Berkeley "To me," says King, "that was the one race that meant everything. I won the race I wasn't supposed to win."

King, who now teaches fifth grade at Terrace School in Delano, explained that all during high school he rarely had lost a race. But in King's freshman year at Berkeley, Augustini beat him in the 100 yard dash at the West Coast Relays in Los Angeles. It was a tough defeat for King. "For a whole year, I didn't want to run against Augustini again."

But he did, at a meet between Fresno State and Cal at the Berkeley Stadium, with 18,000 people in the stands. This time, King was victorious in the 100 as well as the 220 yard dash. After King finished the 100, the event he was noted for, his coach, Brutus Hamilton, urged the runner to warm up for the 220 yard dash. Even though King felt he wasn't up to it, he entered the race and beat Augustini a second time. "I ran against Augustini many times after that," King said, "but he never beat me again."

King now lives in Bakersfield. His only athletic activity at present is bicycle touring — to places like San Diego and Las Vegas. "I do it because it's a challenge to

ride that far," King says, "and to keep my weight down, which is a losing battle."

Lovelace, Lake — Without a doubt, 91-year-old Lake Lovelace, the founder of the Bakersfield Racquet Club, is responsible for more tennis champions than any other person in Kern County.

Starting with Louise Snow in 1946, five have played at Wimbledon. The others are Sally Moore, Dennis

Tennis champion Marianne Werdel has won at least 15 junior titles, more than any other U.S. player in her age group. She also has played at Wimbledon.

Ralston ("The best player ever to come out of the Racquet Club," says Lovelace), Camille Benjamin, Marianne Werdel — winner of at least 15 junior titles, more than any other U.S. player in her age group — and Hank Pfister, Jr. In all, Racquet Club players have won more than 100 national championships, a record that is equalled by few, if any, other club in the country.

Lovelace initiated the idea for the Racquet Club in 1944; it became a reality in 1948. His foresight is evident when you consider that at the time there were only four such clubs in the entire state. Support for the club was gained in a somewhat pedestrian manner. With his characteristic wry humor, Lovelace said, "We just went after them door-to-door like the people who sell washing machines, you might say."

The tall and lean coach was the principal architect for the club, structurally and in establishing the kind of family atmosphere that is a unique feature of the facility. Known as "Mr. Tennis," he does more than merely teach people how to play the game. Jack Lynch, who has known Lovelace for 60 years, says, "Lake has been a terrific influence on the lives of so many young players. It's not just knowing how to hit a tennis ball — he's influenced them in how to live. He is a philosopher as well as a tennis coach."

Lum, Sing — This retired Bakersfield farmer proved that age is no barrier when it comes to sports: Sing Lum became a competitive runner at age 65. By the time he was 70, he had set national and international records in his age division for the 100 and 200 meter dashes. The Panama District's Sing Lum School is named for him.

Lynn, Sam — The man for whom Sam Lynn Ballpark is named came to Bakersfield from Tennessee in 1916 and, in 1922 established the local Coca-Cola Bottling Co. Lynn was active in forming amateur baseball teams, especially those for young people, and took an equal interest in civic affairs. He also was one of the organizers of the California State Baseball League. Dorothy Taber and Berniece Mosconi, the daughters of Lynn and his wife, Odelia, are residents of Bakersfield.

McClanahan, Brent — An outstanding runner and pass receiver, Brent McClanahan had an eight-season career with the Minnesota Vikings. He previously starred at Bakersfield's South High School and at Arizona State.

Since his retirement from professional football, McClanahan has returned home and currently is the director of the Bakersfield Boys and Girls Club. Like his parents, Melton and Christina McClanahan, he also is active in other community organizations on a volunteer basis.

Age is no barrier for Sing Lum, a retired Bakersfield farmer who became a competitive runner at age 65. He has since set national and international records in his age division for the 100 and 200 meter dashes.

Mears, Rick — Twice the winner of the Indianapolis 500 (in 1979 and 1984), Rick Mears personifies Kern County's 75-year mystique with auto racing, one that traces its beginnings to the early day long-distance road races in which the famed Barney Oldfield was a frequent competitor.

Mears, who rose from the dirt track and off-road ranks, got his start in motorcycles and dune buggies. In 1978, his rookie year at the 500, he electrified Indy watchers when he became the first driver to qualify at over 200 mph.

Known for his pleasant, cooperative manner, Mears has been a tremendous goodwill ambassador, both for auto racing and for Bakersfield. The young driver comes from a racing family. His parents and his brother, Roger Mears, all are active in the sport.

Pfister, Hank, Jr. — At the time of his highest ranking, tennis professional Hank Pfister, Jr. was 19th in the world. He now is a part-time pro at the Bakersfield Racquet Club, where he was "born." His father, the late Hank Pfister, Sr. trained the star for his pro tour and was the founder of the Bakersfield Tennis Patrons. The

Rick Mears is famous as a two-time winner of the Indianapolis 500 — in 1979 and 1984. His parents and his brother, Roger, are also active in auto racing.

elder Pfister achieved an impressive record as a tennis and basketball coach at Bakersfield High School and Bakersfield College.

Olson, Dee — The owner of one of the busiest advertising agencies in Bakersfield, Dee Olson also is the founder of Kern County Special Olympics. She has been active in the athletic program for handicapped youngsters for the past 19 years.

Her involvement began in 1969 when she took six swimmers to the California Special Olympics games at Long Beach. (Her mentally retarded son, Jeff, now 21 and a stand-out Special Olympian, was three at the time, too young to participate.) Presently about 450 youngsters, county-wide, participate in the year-round program that includes track and field, gymnastics, floor hockey and swimming. Olson has been the swim coach since the beginning and is one of its chief fund-raisers, often speaking to service clubs to help gain support for Special Olympics current budget of $35,000.

One of her earliest supporters was Olympic decathlon champion Rafer Johnson. And it was Olson who led the campaign to rename Peter Pan School in his honor.

Olson says of work with the handicapped, "To take a child who thinks he has nothing, to see him grow and begin to feel that he is a member of the human race — it's a nifty, nifty feeling."

Ralston, Dennis — Dennis Ralston, who grew up at and around the Bakersfield Racquet Club, was the first to carry Bakersfield's tennis reputation to a national and international level. At 17 he teamed with Rafael Osuna of Mexico to win the doubles at Wimbledon. He was the top-ranked U.S. singles player for three years in the 1960s and for five years was captain of the Davis Cup team, of which he also was a coach.

A graduate of Bakersfield High School, where he also played basketball, Ralston attended USC before turning professional. Although he once had a reputation for his temperament, the 44-year-old athlete has mellowed over the years. (His coach and mentor, Lake Lovelace says, "He was a saint as compared to Connors and McEnroe. Denny was never rude to umpires but he could never stand to lose. He didn't take it out on anyone but himself.")

Now in his seventh season as coach of the men's tennis team at Southern Methodist University tennis team, Ralston also has been Chris Evert's personal coach for the past seven years.

Riese, Herman — Under Herman Riese's 26-year tenure as superintendent (1957-73), the city of Bakersfield's recreation program was recognized as one of the most outstanding in the state.

Riese was known for his persistence in persuading the City Council to provide the funds for increased programs and facilities. Recalling his bouts with the council, Riese says, "You fought fire with fire."

As superintendent, he enthusiastically developed a variety of programs in cooperation with the schools and other organizations. The Wisconsin native was instrumental in forming the Jack Frost League. He also initiated the idea for the Bob Elias Hall of Fame and worked with J.B. "Cap" Haralson in bringing the first national track and field meets to Memorial Stadium.

Robesky, Don — Kern County's first All-American, Don Robesky, was an outstanding guard for the Bakersfield High School Drillers before going on to Stanford, where he played in the Rose Bowl games of 1926 and 1927. From 1934-42, Robesky served as the line coach at Bakersfield College.

Seay, Joe — Now the head wrestling coach at Oklahoma State University, a Division I school, Joe Seay developed the wrestling program at Cal State Bakersfield and for the first 12 years was its only coach. He led the Roadrunners to seven NCAA Division II titles, five of them consecutive. Seventeen of his athletes were Division I All-Americas and 70 earned the title of Division II All-America. Two of his wrestlers — John Azevedo and Joe Gonzales — made it to the Olympics. Seay was on the coaching staff of the U.S. Olympic freestyle team in 1984.

Shelton, Lonnie — One of the fastest big men (6-foot-8, 250 pounds), in professional basketball, Lonnie Shelton enjoyed a successful NBA career that included playing on the Seattle SuperSonics 1979 world championship team. In 1982, he played in the NBA All-Star game and was named to the league's all-defensive second team.

An all-round athlete at Foothill High School, Shelton was a national high school record-holder in discus and was offered a football scholarship at USC. He chose

All-Pro Minnesota Vikings linebacker Jeff Siemon was an 8-letter athlete at Bakersfield High School and an All-American at Stanford.

BOB ELIAS HALL OF FAME

Lonnie Shelton, one of Bakersfield's finest all-time athletes, is best known as a member of the Seattle SuperSonics 1979 world championship basketball team. He now lives in Bakersfield.

basketball and Oregon State instead, then turned pro in 1976 with the New York Knicks. Now retired and living in Bakersfield, Shelton ended his career with the Cleveland Cavaliers.

Siemon, Jeff — All-Pro Minnesota Vikings linebacker Jeff Siemon first showed his athletic prowess at Bakersfield High School, where he earned eight varsity letters in football, basketball and baseball.

At Stanford, where he was named an All-American, he played on two conference championships teams: in 1970, when Stanford beat Ohio State and in 1971, in which the team defeated Michigan in the Rose Bowl.

After joining the Vikings, Siemon was voted to the All-Pro team in 1973. He played in the 1974 and 1975 Super Bowl games.

In 1973, he received the Vineland Trophy, an award that recognized him as Kern County's outstanding sports personality for that year. He has also been honored by the Fellowship of Christian Athletes as its "Man of the Year." Siemon now lives in Minneapolis and is engaged in religious work.

The athlete is the son of Dr. Glenn Siemon, a Bakersfield ophthalmologist, and the grandson of Alfred Siemon, a long-time mayor of the city.

Strelich, Steve — Probably the most colorful and likeable promoter ever to enliven the local sports scene, Steve Strelich was the owner and operator of Strelich Stadium on Golden State Highway in Bakersfield. For several decades, the arena was the setting for professional boxing and wrestling matches. (It now houses the Victory Outreach Church.)

A native of Colorado, Strelich grew up in Yugoslavia. As an adult he made many trips there and on one occasion met with Marshal Tito. Strelich's personal career included professional wrestling and boxing, dance and swim marathons, auto racing, sky diving and channel swimming. He once was Mae West's bodyguard.

The sports promoter took a strong interest in the community at large and was the sponsor of many activities for youths.

Turner, Wilda Mae — Softball champion "Willie" Turner started her career at age 11 in Bakersfield, playing for the Mears Lumber Company team. At 14, she competed in the World Softball Tournament and, by the time she was 16, in 1938, had struck out more than 2,000 hitters. She pitched six seasons for the Parichy Bloomer Girls of Chicago and in 1952 became the first woman to manage a professional team. She completed her career with an 0.14 earned run average. In 1975, Turner became the first woman inducted into the Bob Elias Hall of Fame.

Watkins, Dennis — Taft native Dennis Watkins is a two-time winner (1981 and 1984) of the PRCA National Rodeo Finals team roping competition.

Williams, Art — In 1972, Art Williams became the first black National League umpire. Nearly 20 years earlier, the Bakersfield High School graduate was the first black pitcher signed by the Detroit Tigers. However, an arm injury in 1956 caused his retirement from professional play.

Returning home, Williams got his first experience as an umpire when he served as an official for his son's Little League. In succeeding years he called the balls and strikes for local high school and college games. With the encouragement of his wife, the former Shirley Roberson, the Arkansas native resigned his job with the city in 1969 and enrolled in umpire's school in Florida. After first working in the minor leagues, he was a National League umpire for five years. He retired in 1977, two years before his death.

Throughout his career Williams encouraged young people to engage in sports and was a frequent speaker at schools and before community groups.

Wright, Louis — A 12-season veteran defensive back for the Denver Broncos, Louis Wright has played in both the team's Super Bowl games. He has been named to the Pro Bowl five times, the last time at age 34.

A football and track star at Bakersfield High School, Wright was an outstanding athlete as well at Arizona State, Bakersfield College and San Jose State. He now lives in Denver but visits his hometown frequently.

Flanked by the flags of China and the United States, the students of the Bakersfield Chinese School posed for this picture with their teacher, a Mr. Gee, upper right. The school, which still exists today, began in 1912 when potato farmer Yen Ming hired the instructor from San Francisco.

Bakersfield delegates to the National Association of Colored Women's convention in 1950 included, front row, Cleora Frazier, Laura Olivia, Alberta Dillard, Addie Lowrey; back row, Francis Owens, Beatrice Dantzler, Pearl Winters and Hattie Bagsby.

Books on the history of Italy were presented to the Cal State Bakersfield Library in 1975 by Ben Sacco, center, Italian vice consul for Kern County. Benton Scheide, library director, and Vincent Ponko, Jr. accepted the gift.

Carrying on the business their father, Santos Gamez, started in East Bakersfield in 1922 are Esther Gamez, Lillie George and Rachel Gamez. The sisters are the owners and operators of the Mexicali restaurants.

11
Rich Roots

"May we never forget them
and the heritage they have left us."

Mary Grace Paquette, *Lest We Forget*

Kern County's cultural heritage, as well as its economy, has been richly enhanced by the diversity of its ethnic groups.

Today, the descendants of those first families — particularly those of Hispanic, Chinese, Basque, Italian, Greek, Black American or Filipino origin — share their roots with all other members of the community in annual festivals and celebrations.

Such festivities were limited in the early days, however. Hard work and long hours left little time for play.

And some worked exceedingly hard in getting established. Nearly all of the early Chinese, for example, came here in the 1870s as laborers on the railroads. When that work was finished, many began to farm small plots of land.

Starting in the 1850s, those of Mexican descent, along with members of American Indian tribes who had been here for centuries, formed the chief supply of labor for farms and ranches. In the mountainous Kern River Valley, two of the better-known Indians were Jose Chico, chief of a tribe in the Kernville area, and Steban Miranda. Among the famous vaqueros on the Tejon Ranch south of Bakersfield were Jose Jesus Lopez, Antonio Araujo, Sr., and his son, Tony, and Arnold Rojas, who wrote several books and was known as "the last of the vaqueros."

Today, Hispanics in Bakersfield, Delano and Lamont commemorate two important events in Mexico's struggle to win independence: Cinco De Mayo (the Fifth of May) and Mexican Independence Day in September.

Many early French immigrants became merchants and also were involved in the sheep industry, as were most of the Basques. The majority of the early Italians were engaged in farming, as were those who traced their roots to the Slavic countries.

Black Americans first arrived in large numbers in the valley region of the county in 1884. More than 100 black families were brought here from South Carolina by James B. Haggin and William Carr to plant and harvest cotton in the Wible Road area. The Kern County Land Company founders provided the families with housing and salaries of $10 a month for male workers, $8 for women, and about $4 for children.

However, due to poor yields, the landowners abandoned the cotton crop after only one year. Many of the blacks left the area. About a dozen families remained and found other occupations. One of these was William Henry Pinckney. He first served as a butler at the home of Dr. L.S. Rogers at 18th and H streets, the present site of Judd's clothing store. Pinckney later worked on a Tehachapi cattle ranch and at a dairy in the Bakersfield area.

Youngsters dressed in the costumes of old Mexico enhanced this colorful float in the Lamont community's observance of Cindo De Mayo in 1987. Observances of the important date in Mexican history also are held in Delano and Bakersfield.

THE BAKERSFIELD CALIFORNIAN

A tenor trombone player, Pinckney played in a band made up of black musicians. The group took part in the celebration that marked the arrival of the Santa Fe Railroad in Bakersfield in 1898.

In more recent times, the black community has celebrated its heritage with annual Black History parades and pageants.

A few Japanese settled in the farming areas of Kern County in the early 1900s. Russian families began farming near Shafter in 1912. About the same time, people of German descent began settling in the area.

Beginning about 1920, natives of the Philippines came to the Delano area as farm workers. Today, the Filipino community forms one of the city's largest minority groups. Their annual celebration is Philippine Weekend.

Nearly all ethnic groups have formed associations to help keep their heritage alive — for themselves and for younger generations. Among these are the Ani-Yun 'Wiya, an American Indian group; the Bakersfield chapter of the National Association of Colored Women's Clubs; Le Club Francais (French Club); Italian Heritage Dante Association; the Daughters of the British Empire; the German Lodge; and several lodges that represent the Scandinavian countries.

Many of Kern County's most prominent leaders are descendants of the early ethnic groups. But today, some are the first generation of their family to settle here. And, as can be seen in the biographical sketches that follow, more than a few have served as strong role models for their compatriots.

Aguirre, Juan — Now the executive chef of Stockdale Country Club, Juan Aguirre got his start there as a youth — not as a cook but as a pot washer. That experience, however, helped Aguirre land his first cooking job at the old Cy's Coffee Shop on Union Avenue after telling the owner, "I had just worked at the country club."

The chef, who is of Mexican descent, was born on his parents' farm in Santa Maria. The eldest of five children, he often cooked for the family. Then his specialty was handmade tortillas. Now he is noted for his elegantly prepared meals and creative ice sculptures.

In 1970, Aguirre was named "Chef of the Year" by the Chef de Cuisine of California, the first time the award had been given to a chef outside the Los Angeles area. He later received a similar award from the association's Bakersfield chapter, which he helped found. Aguirre has taken a leading role in promoting professional standards. He helped establish the apprentice cooks program at Bakersfield College and has been a part-time instructor there for four years. (Two apprentices work for him at Stockdale.) The chef is area coordinator for the American Culinary Federation's Western Region, which includes the southern parts of California and Nevada, as well as Arizona and New Mexico.

The chef and his wife, Mary, whom he met when both were students at Arroyo Grande High School, make their home in Bakersfield.

Antonaros, John George — George Antonaros, who was born in Greece, came to the United States in 1906 and opened a grocery business in Fellows the following year. Five years later, he returned to his native country to bring his wife, Harriet, and their daughter to America. By 1921, when the couple opened a grocery store on Baker Street in East Bakersfield, their family was complete with seven children: Fannie, Irene, Anthony, Nikita, John, Phryne, and Callie.

Although he was appreciative of the opportunities that living in America provided for him and his family, Antonaros had a deep devotion to his ethnic and spiritual background. His descendants have been instrumental in the growth and development of St. George's Greek Orthodox Church, as well as the community festivals sponsored by the church.

John Antonaros joined his father in the grocery business after his graduation from Bakersfield High School in 1936. In 1967 he and his wife, the former Bessie Kazas, opened John T's Pipes and Tobaccos Shop in Valley Plaza Regional Shopping Center. The Antonaroses also have a store in the Solano Mall in Northern California. Their innovative merchandising techniques

Stockdale County Club executive chef Juan Aguirre has been at the forefront of promoting professional standards among culinary workers in Kern County.

have made them the subjects of many articles in trade journals.

Aubin, Jean Pierre — A native of France, Jean Pierre Aubin established the Parisian Bakery, in the early 1900s, one of Bakersfield's oldest bakeries. The bakery founder's sons are Emile Aubin, a stockbroker with Dean Witter, and George Aubin, a retired Bakersfield Californian printer. His daughter, Mary Hylton, also is a Bakersfield resident.

Pierre Laxague, the owner since 1944, changed the name to the Pyrenees French Bakery to reflect his Basque heritage. When Laxague erected a new structure on the East 21st Street site in 1961, the original building was moved to Pioneer Village.

Calaustro, Elena — Elena Calaustro has served as president of the Filipino Community of Bakersfield for four years. During her tenure, the organization has formed a youth group, established a scholarship program for Filipino students and expanded its services to senior citizens, particularly by helping them with immigration and tax matters. A native of the Philippines, Calaustro twice has been recognized by the Kern County Board of Supervisors for her service to the community. She is a past president of both the Bakersfield and Oildale Business and Professional Women's Clubs, Community Round Table and the Women's Auxiliary of Veterans of Foreign Wars, Arvin Post.

Cappello, Faust — A chef and a farmer, Faust Cappello was born in Italy in 1903 and came to the United States in 1921. Joining his elder brothers in Gallup, New Mexico, he began his restaurant career as a dishwasher in the Harvey House there. Three years later he got a job at the Palace Hotel in San Francisco and helped prepare a banquet for 2,000 in honor of President Warren Harding. According to Cappello's wife,

Lena, the president was ill and so did not attend the dinner. Harding died a short time later.

In 1926, after working at several restaurants in Hollywood, Cappello joined his brothers, Albert and Angelo, in Mojave. Eventually, they owned three restaurants there. During World War II, Faust operated the Officers Club at the U.S. Marine Corps Station in Mojave. He began farming in the Bakersfield area in 1951 with his brother-in-law, John Antongiovanni. Three years later he formed an agricultural partnership with his son, Jerry Cappello, and son-in-law, Don Tendrup. Faust Cappello died in 1986.

Carson, Irma — Irma Carson, now a patrol sergeant, was the first black female officer in the Bakersfield Police Department and the first female detective assigned to the major crimes division. In 1974 she was named "Officer of the Year" and in 1985 was included in Who's Who in Black America. A graduate of Bakersfield College and Cal State Bakersfield, Carson is serving her second term on the Bakersfield City School District board and was president in 1982-83. That year she received the California Alliance of Black Educators' Distinguished Service Award. She was appointed in 1987 to the State Superintendent of Schools Advisory Council on black affairs.

Carson is active in many local organizations, including the Community Alcohol Counseling Center, American Business Women's Association and the Black History Committee.

Childs, James Henry — James Childs is the first black to serve as vice mayor of Bakersfield. Since 1977, he has been the personnel officer at Kern Medical Center. He joined the hospital staff in 1960 as a nursing attendant and after becoming a licensed vocational nurse worked for 12 years in emergency services. A Navy veteran, he is a graduate of Bakersfield College and Cal State Bakersfield. Childs is listed in Who's Who in American Politics and in 1976 was a delegate to

Irma Carson served as coordinator of the Rev. Jesse Jackson's presidential campaign committee in Kern County and was on hand to greet Jackson when he spoke at Civic Auditorium.

149

the National Democratic Convention in New York.

As a city councilman, Childs has been instrumental in encouraging blacks to establish businesses on Lakeview Avenue in southeast Bakersfield and in promoting the location of a county Human Services office in the area. He is a past president of the Kern County Employees Association. Many organizations have honored Childs for his community service, including the Cal State Bakersfield Afro-American Student Union and the League of United Latin American Citizens. He and his wife, the former Johnnie Fite, are the parents of six children.

Choo Lai — Choo Lai, known in Bakersfield as the "father of Chinatown," came to Kern County in the late 1860s. Over the years he apparently accumulated considerable property and was highly respected by members of the Chinese community. At the time of his death, in 1908 at the age of 74, the *Morning Echo* said, "All Chinatown is in mourning for [Choo Lai] is the one man to whom residents of that part of the city looked for assistance and advice." His elaborate funeral was preceded by a musical band.

The pioneer Chinese was instrumental in the construction of the Sam Yup Association building. He was the father of Rose Kimm (Mrs. George Kimm Sr.).

The City of Fuchau was the first Chinese store to offer American goods and clothing.

Chow, Leland — A native of Selma who received his dental training at Portland University in Oregon, Dr. Leland Chow was the first Chinese dentist in Bakersfield. Chow has been active for many years in the Camellia Society and is often asked to judge shows in many other cities. He is an officer in the Ying On Club and other organizations, including Ducks Unlimited.

Choy, K.C. — K.C. Choy came to Bakersfield in the 1920s and opened the City of Fuchau department store, near 19th and Eye streets. His establishment was the first Chinese department store to offer American clothing and goods. The merchant later moved his business to 19th and L streets and renamed it Choy's Store.

Choy served for many years as president of the Chinese Benevolent Association. In 1949 he spearheaded a campaign to provide the money for its first building. The structure at 21st and N streets now houses the Chinese Confucius Church and the Chinese School. Choy's son, Lawrence, who died several years ago, was associated with his father in business. Both of his other sons are architects. Eugene, and his son, Barton, have their office in Los Angeles, while Allan works in Bakersfield.

De La Rosa, Lupe — A native of Mexico, Lupe De La Rosa keeps her heritage alive by teaching others the dances and culture of various Mexican regions. She is an instructor at Cal State Bakersfield and has formed a dance troupe made up of her students. An entertaining and energetic dancer herself, De La Rosa also has presented instructional programs for children in area schools, under the auspices of Young Audiences.

Dillard, Alberta — (See "The Plus Factor")

Edwards, Lynn — Lynn Edwards, born on a farm in Old River, retired from the Kern County Fire Department in 1984 as a captain. Presently, he chairs the board of the Martin Luther King Community Center as well as the Bakersfield Senior Center. He also is a director of Southeast Bakersfield Enterprise Zone and its Community Advisory Council.

In the 1970s, he was president of the McKinley School PTA. He also was a Boy Scout leader and a member of the Camp Fire board.

A graduate of Bakersfield High School, Edwards also attended Bakersfield College. He worked in the construction industry for five years after his World War II service in the Navy. Before joining the fire department in 1962, he was employed for 10 years by the U.S. Postal Service.

Everly, Anne — Anne Everly aptly has been referred to as "a one-woman crusade." A nurse at Mercy Hospital for many years, Everly has been one of the driving forces in the hospital's outreach program in the southeast Bakersfield minority community, where she makes her home.

Starting in 1984, the nurse began working a reduced shift at the hospital so she could spend several days a week helping Sister Frances Webster of Catholic Social Services develop the outreach program. With energy and enthusiasm, coupled with a no-nonsense approach, Everly has involved area residents in the project. In addition to serving hot meals from the hospital kitchen — a table set up on a vacant lot on Lakeview Avenue — Everly and other leaders have helped form basketball teams for youths and initiated a tutoring program for schoolchildren.

Fang, Fabian — Dr. Fabian Fang, a Ph.D. in chemistry, was the first chairman of the chemistry department at Cal State Bakersfield. He has been active on the Asian Studies Committee and as an advisor to the Asian Students Club for many years. Fang has assisted students from overseas in finding housing. He often meets the young people when they arrive at Los Angeles International Airport.

Through the professor's efforts, the Chinese Consulate donated 20 artifacts to the Kern County Historical Society. The gift from the Chinese government was made in connection with the dedication of the Chinese temple at Pioneer Village.

Francisco, Zedore — A well-known black farm labor contractor, Zedore Francisco and his family began farming in the Old River area in 1936. The Louisiana native later acquired a large amount of rental property in southeast Bakersfield. George Gholston, who later became the familiar voice of "Collector's Corner" on KPMC, was Francisco's main bus driver in the labor contracting business.

Galtes, Pablo (Paul) — One of Bakersfield's first merchants, Paul Galtes opened a store in Bakersfield in 1871 and soon began to prosper. In 1878, when a fire destroyed many buildings in the town, he rebuilt in brick an entire block on Chester Avenue. Galtes, whose first wife died in 1869, married Marianne Laxague, a French Basque.

The couple brought several members of Marianne's family to Bakersfield within the next 10 years. Her niece, Marie Inda, married Jean B. Berges, a Frenchman and a leading liquor merchant who had a store in the Weill building. Louise Inda, Marianne's sister, married Faustino Mier Noriega, who was born in Spain and first worked as a sheepherder for Haggin and Tevis. Author Mary Grace Paquette notes, "The Noriega wedding was to be the indirect cause of the beginning of large-scale migrations of French and Spanish Basques to Kern County, for, in 1893, Faustino Noriega and a French Basque associate, Fernando Etcheverry, built the Iberia Hotel (later called the Noriega Hotel) in Kern City." It was the first of the Basque hotels in East Bakersfield and became the center of social activities in the area.

Gamez Family — Bakersfield's Mexicali restaurants began about 65 years ago when Santos Gamez, a native of Durango, Mexico, saved enough money from his railroad earnings to open a succession of businesses in front of the family home at 419 Baker Street. (The site now houses the Mexicali's business office and central kitchen.)

Gamez first had an open air sno-cone and hot dog stand and later opened a Mexican-style restaurant. His children worked in the business, after school and on summer vacations. Today, the popular three-restaurant chain is still a family business, with Gamez's three daughters, Rachel Gamez, Lillie George and Esther Gamez at the helm. Rachel, president of the corporation, also is president of the Cal State Bakersfield Roadrunners, an athletic department support group. In addition, she is a member of the Bakersfield Symphony board and is active in other organizations.

Ghilarducci, Joe and Natalina — In the 1930s, Joe and Natalina Ghilarducci opened Ghilarducci's Market in Buttonwillow, which has become well-known for its good service and excellent meat. Carrying on the tradition are their sons, Leo and Art Ghilarducci.

Joe Ghilarducci went into the grocery business almost as a last resort, says his granddaughter, Cynthia Fox. "My grandfather came here from Italy when he was 16," she said. "First he worked for the railroad, then for Miller & Lux. Then he tried farming and that didn't work. So he opened a grocery store."

His wife, the former Natalina Antongiovanni of Tehachapi, ran the store for many years after her husband's death in 1955. Now 83, she retired several years ago.

Gilbert, Elydia — In the 1960s, Elydia Gilbert was known as "the Indian lady" at Pioneer Village. Her mother was a Yokuts; her father, a member of a southwest desert tribe. Gilbert told stories of Indian life and culture to children who visited the museum on school tours.

Giminiani, Mike — Old-timers in the Pumpkin Center area south of Bakersfield claim that the settlement's name came about indirectly because of Mike Giminiani. In 1919, he opened a grocery store and fruit stand on the present site and his brother operated a barber shop. Non-Italians found the name Giminiani difficult to pronounce, so when a large orange pumpkin was painted on the barber shop window one autumn, people started calling the place Pumpkin Center.

A native of Italy, Giminiani came to Bakersfield in 1911. After working for a time on the Canfield Ranch,

After working at a variety of jobs in Kern County, Italian-born Joe Ghilarducci found his niche when he and his wife, Natalina, opened a market in Buttonwillow.

he purchased a Model T Ford and began operating an auto stage line that originated in Bakersfield and served the communities of Buttonwillow, Shafter, Wasco and Caliente. He purchased the four-passenger vehicle from George Haberfelde Ford for $960 — on credit. He was required to park the car in the auto dealer's lot at night until the full amount was paid.

Giminiani was named honorary mayor of Pumpkin Center in 1941. He retired in 1963 and moved to Pismo Beach, where he died in 1981 at the age of 89. Many of his descendants still live in the community he founded.

Hanson, Dugan — A Piute Indian, Dugan Hanson is a well-known storyteller in the Ridgecrest area. He is employed as a welder at the Naval Weapons Center at China Lake.

Jeppi, Frank — (See "The Plus Factor")

Lee, Bill — (See "The Plus Factor")

Leong Gee Ping — The father of Rice Bowl co-owner Bill Leong, Leong Gee Ping came to Kern County in

1874 as a laborer for the Southern Pacific Railroad. After farming for a time, he opened a store on 18th Street in Bakersfield. The senior Leong learned to read and write English at the Salvation Army school and worked part-time as a bill collector for Pacific Gas & Electric in the Chinese community. He also operated the Eastern Cafe at 18th and G streets.

McClanahan, Christina and Melton, Sr. — The McClanahans long have been active in the black community and in other civic affairs. Both are graduates of Bakersfield College, where Melton McClanahan was an outstanding member of the Renegades football team. (Brent McClanahan, one of three children, formerly starred with the Minnesota Vikings.) A retired Kern County Sheriff's deputy, he has coached teams for the Carver YMCA, Little League, Junior Baseball Association and the Jack Frost Football League. He served 12 years as Jack Frost director, including two terms as president. A past president of his Kiwanis Club, he received the Distinguished Presidents Award for District 33 in 1975.

Christina McClanahan presently is a member of the Cal State Bakersfield Advisory Board and the Southeast Enterprise Zone board. She served eight years on the Kern County Fair board. She is the daughter of Arthur and Martha Williams, who farmed in the Buttonwillow area. In 1965, the Williamses were members

---

Matlock is the only black, the only law enforcement officer, ever to receive the Kern County Bar Association's Bench & Bar Award.

---

of a two-month tour of India, sponsored by the Farm Leaders Exchange Program of Farmers and World Affairs, a Philadelphia-based organization.

Maitia, Frank — Bakersfield restaurant owner Frank Maitia, a French Basque, came to Kern County in 1930. After working as a sheepherder for 12 years, Maitia had saved enough money to go into business. He bought the French House on East 21st Street and renamed it the Basque Cafe. In 1962, Maitia and his son, Frank Jr. built the present Maitia's Restaurant on Union Avenue. The Basque Cafe was sold to Raymond and Yvonne Arretche Etcheveste, who operated the restaurant until 1973 when they opened the Chateau Basque on Union Avenue.

Matlock, Harold — A highly respected member of the community at large, Harold Matlock retired in 1979 as chief deputy in charge of the Corrections and Custo-

dial Bureau of the Kern County Sheriff's Department. He is the only black, and the only law enforcement officer, ever to receive the Kern County Bar Association's Bench & Bar Award. Upon his graduation from Bakersfield High School in 1942, he became the first black to receive the Outstanding Senior Service Award.

Matlock, who spent 31 years as a deputy, also taught police administration classes at Bakersfield College. He was foreman of the 1979-80 Kern County Grand Jury and is the past president of many organizations, including the Kern County Peace Officers Association, Camp Fire (he was a national board member in 1975), and Westchester Kiwanis. Matlock and his wife, Fern, are Bakersfield residents.

Matsumoto, Robert J. — A major residential builder and developer in Kern County for more than 20 years, Robert Matsumoto came to Bakersfield at the age of 11 in 1947. During World War II, he and his family were interned for three years in a camp at Poston, Arizona, along with other West Coast Japanese. Earlier, his father had been a rice grower in the Imperial Valley. After coming here, the senior Matsumoto worked as a landscape gardener.

Upon his graduation from Bakersfield High School, Robert Matsumoto received an appointment to the U.S. Military Academy by Harlen Hagen, then the congressman for our area. After completing his work at West Point, Matsumoto served for five years as an officer in the U.S. Army. Resigning his commission as a captain, he returned to Bakersfield and entered the real estate business as an associate in Charles Webster's realty office.

Matsumoto formed his own company, Great Western Builders, in 1964. (His wife, Twyla Matsumoto, a former schoolteacher, has been the office manager and also acts as an interior design consultant for the company's properties.) Great Western became one of the first to begin buying lots from Tenneco West when it began developing property in southwest Bakersfield. Matsumoto since has built hundreds of homes and apartments in such subdivisions as West Park, Pepper Tree, Highland Oaks and Laurelglen. He also has built residences in Ridgecrest and Lancaster. In 1986, Matsumoto constructed the new Southwest Branch Library on Ming Avenue.

Nagatani, Tsurumatsu — Tsurumatsu Nagatani, one of the first Japanese to come to Delano, found himself unwelcome: he was run out of town at gunpoint shortly after he arrived in 1905. Courageously, Nagatani returned in 1912 and stayed until 1943, when he and his family, along with other Japanese, were placed in an internment camp for the remainder of World War II.

In 1945 Nagatani came back for good and resumed farming with his sons. In 1974 the pioneer was honored by his fellow citizens on Japanese Cultural Heritage Day. One of his sons, Dr. James K. Nagatani, an active member of the community, has practiced dentistry in Delano since 1950.

Ono, Joe — Joe Ono, the owner of Evergreen Nursery in Bakersfield, grew up on his family's farm in the

Elizabeth Ordiz and her mother were interned at Manzanar during World War II.

Lamont area. He graduated from high school in Poston, Arizona, where the Onos, and other Japanese, had been interned at the beginning of World War II. He then joined the Army and served until 1947. Returning to Bakersfield, Joe and his father opened the present business on H Street. To learn more about landscape gardening, Joe commuted to UCLA, where he took courses from a Japanese landscape architect. His son, Lindsay, who is associated in the business, graduated from Cal Poly, San Luis Obispo, with an ornamental horticulture major.

Yoneo Ono, one of Joe's brothers, worked in the business for several years after receiving his degree in landscape design from the University of Connecticut. He later joined the Bakersfield Planning Department and taught courses in his field at Bakersfield College. He subsequently worked for the Fresno Planning Department. Now retired, he operates a landscape consulting service in Fresno.

Ordiz, Elizabeth and Bennie — Elizabeth and Bennie Ordiz have been community leaders in Delano for many years. Originally farmworkers, they saved their money and bought real estate. Now semi-retired, they own and operate a nursing home.

A third generation Californian, Elizabeth is Filipino and Japanese. (Both she and her mother were interned at Manzanar during World War II.) She long has been active in the Filipino Community, an umbrella group for several Filipino organizations, and is a past president of the Soroptimist Club. She also serves on the city's personnel board.

Bennie was a Tenneco West crew foreman for 20 years. He acts as a court interpreter for non-English-speaking Filipinos and is involved in many civic organizations. The couple's son, Danny Ordiz, a Bakersfield architect, has been chairman of Delano's Filipino Weekend for the past two years.

Quon, Benson — Born in China, Benson Quon is an authority on Chinese customs and protocol. He often is consulted for advice on "good and bad days" for weddings, funerals and other events. Quon's beautiful calligraphy is highly valued. The two couplets on the door of the Chinese temple at Pioneer Village were written by him as well as the name over the door.

Solomon, Gabriel — A member of a pioneer black farming family, Gabriel Solomon became a prominent attorney in Bakersfield. He now practices in Los Angeles.

Sue Hee — Sue Hee came to Bakersfield from Canton, China in 1868. A tall, well-built man, he drove teams of horses at various ranches, including those of Colonel Thomas Baker and William Tibbet. He was proficient in martial arts and performed for the community on holidays.

Ellen Baker and Rebecca Tibbet taught Sue how to read and write English. He became an interpreter for other Chinese at court hearings and served in that capacity at the famous trial of the outlaw, Bill McKinney. He also farmed on what is now 18th and Q streets and in the Sunset Avenue area.

The Chinese pioneer donated land next to his home on 22nd Street (presently owned by Pacific Bell) for the construction of the Sam Yup Association building. Sue's daughter, Mary Ming, says that it was in this building that Sun Yat-sen, the Chinese revolutionary leader, stayed when he was trying to raise money here for his cause.

Toliver, Tyree — A leader in the black community for many years, Dr. Toliver is the pastor of St. John Baptist Church. He was instrumental in securing the funds to construct the $3 million St. John Manor, the facility at Fourth and P streets which provides housing

Youngsters of Filipino descent participate each year in Philippine Weekend in Delano. Originally a two-day affair, the event now includes a variety of activities over a period of several weeks each July.

for senior citizens and handicapped individuals. Toliver's church also operates a credit union for its members.

Tyler, Carolyn E. — The pastor of Caine Memorial African Methodist Episcopal Church, Rev. Tyler has initiated many programs in the black community since coming to Bakersfield in 1983. In 1985, she was selected as one of 15 females, nationwide, for "Black Women Who Make It Happen," a program sponsored by Frito-Lay. Prior to coming here, she was instrumental in the founding of a child care center and mental health service organization in Indio. In the 1960s, Tyler was involved with Dr. Martin Luther King Jr. - in the civil rights movement in the southern states. She and her husband, Cary B. Tyler, are the parents of six children.

Dressed in traditional costumes, these young Greek dancers from Bakersfield perform exhibitions throughout California. Soula Schoell, who was born in Greece, is their instructor.

Tyler, Carolyn E. — The pastor of Cain Memorial African Methodist Episcopal Church, Rev. Tyler has initiated many programs in the black community since coming to Bakersfield in 1983. In 1985, she was selected as one of 15 females, nationwide, for "Black Women Who Make It Happen," a program sponsored by Frito-Lay. Prior to coming here, she was instrumental in the founding of a child care center and mental health service organization in Indio. In the 1960s, Tyler was involved with Dr. Martin Luther King Jr. in the civil rights movement in the southern states. She and her husband, Cary B. Tyler, are the parents of six children.

Valdez, Luis — An internationally known playwright and director ("Zoot Suit," among others), Luis Valdez was born in Delano, second in the family of 10 born to his migrant farm worker parents.

After his graduation from San Jose State University in 1964, Valdez returned to his hometown, where he founded El Teatro Campesino as a dramatic voice in support of Cesar Chavez and the United Farm Workers. Since 1969, the theater group has been based in San

Juan Bautista. The troupe has toured the United States and Europe, presenting Valdez's bilingual interpretations of Hispanic culture and contemporary issues. El Teatro Campesino has performed on several occasions at Cal State Bakersfield and in Delano, where Valdez's cousin, George Caraveo, is a former Delano city councilman.

Valos, George — A former Kern County schools teacher and administrator, George Valos was a prominent member of the Greek community and, with his wife, Mary, was active in the affairs of St. George's Greek Orthodox Church. It was Valos who initiated the church's annual wine festival. He also was well-known as a leader in the East Bakersfield Progressive Club. For many years, he was the chief coordinator of the club's annual Easter egg hunt for children at Jefferson Park.

Winters, Pearl Lowery — Pearl Lowery Winters, whose spacious two-story home stood for many years on H Street near Dracena Street in Bakersfield, was a gifted black singer who gained a wide reputation around the turn-of-the-century. After hearing the contralto perform at a concert, President William McKinley is said to have called her "the nightingale of California."

El Teatro Campesino has toured the United States and Europe, presenting bilingual interpretations of Hispanic culture and contemporary issues.

Wong, Earl and Alice — During the years they were the owner-operators of grocery and liquor stores in Bakersfield, Earl Wong, who died several years ago, and his wife, Alice, were prominent members of the community.

Earl was active in Rotary, the Masons and Shriners. He was president of the Chinese School board of directors. During World War II, he led many fund-raising efforts, including one elaborate party at which a Chinese princess, Der-Ling, was the honored guest. An amateur magician, he often performed for local groups, with his wife as his assistant.

The Wongs' son, Erwin, was killed in a plane crash during the war, and Alice was president of Gold Star Mothers. She also headed the Chinese Women's Club and in the 1970s was named a "Beautiful Activist" by the Broadway Stores. The couple's son, Delbert Wong, is a retired Los Angeles County Superior Court judge.

Wong, Violet Leong — When the Chinese Women's Club was organized in 1946, Vi Wong became the first

Recipients of the Italian Heritage Dante Association Columbian Award

Louis Agnetti	1964	Gino J. Fanucchi	1976
Frank Jeppi	1965	Lido Sandrini	1977
Guido Martini	1966	Joseph J. Trino	1978
Joseph Giumarra	1967	Ben Sacco	1979
James Petrini	1968	Jimmie Icardo	1980
Ugo Sandrini	1969	John Lencioni	1981
Arnold T. Cattani	1970	John Antonino	1982
Antonio Perelli-Minetti	1971	Ilo Scatena	1983
Harry Amenta	1972	Livio Palla	1984
Augustine Sorci	1973	Gino Chicca	1985
Arthur F. Tognini	1974	David Fanucchi	1986
Joseph A. Di Giorgio	1975		

president. (The other officers were Jessie Jing and Thelma Chow.) Initially, the club provided New Year's baskets for the elderly in the Chinese community in Bakersfield. In 1950, the members established a scholarship program which over the years has assisted many Chinese students in completing their college educations.

After her graduation from Bakersfield High School in 1932, Wong became the private secretary of Grace Nicholson, the owner of the Asian Pacific Museum in Pasadena. And Wong rode on the prize-winning Celestial Dragon float in the 1935 Rose Parade.

Vi and her husband, Harold, have owned and operated a market at Morning Drive and Edison Highway for many years. Their son, Dee, is in the produce business. Dee's wife, Linda Wong, who was born in China and grew up in Hong Kong, came to the United States in the 1960s. After completing her education at Bakersfield College and San Jose State, she was a staff writer for *The Bakersfield Californian* for 13 years.

Young, Henry M. — One of Kern County's early civil rights leaders, Henry Young once recalled that when he was a youth, blacks were barred from many facilities, including public swimming pools. He and several friends broke that particular color line in the 1940s at Hart Park. Although the lifeguard told the youths to leave the pool, they refused. "That was the end of that," Young said. He added, "Nothing was ever easy. Pressure was what made things change."

A decorated World War II veteran, Young was a past commander of the American Legion's 15th district, which includes 27 posts in Kern and Tulare counties. He also was a national vice chairman and state commissioner for the Legion. He served on the Bakersfield City School District's affirmative action advisory committee, the Kern County Grand Jury, the Juvenile Justice Commission and was active in the NAACP (the National Association for the Advancement of Colored People.) In 1975 he was grand marshal of the Black History parade.

A retired heavy equipment operator for the city of Bakersfield, Young died in 1981. His wife, Roberta, a retired Kern County Library employee, still lives in Bakersfield.

Jack Albertson was guest star at the opening of Cal State's Dore Theater.

Delano-born Benita Valente is a gifted soprano who has concertized all over the world.

Bakersfield Symphony's music director and conductor John Farrer achieved international notice in 1986 when he conducted the London Philharmonic.

12
Star Quality

"Asleep beneath a singing tree,
I dreamed I shared its destiny.
We stretched our sky thrust arms afar,
And strove as one to touch a star."

Ardis Walker, *From Wild Rootage*

Kern's pioneers were innovative in satisfying their thirst for the fine arts and other entertainments.

In a word, they were creative.

For example, enterprising lads like Rush Blodget, who later wrote about his experiences in *Little Dramas of Old Bakersfield,* got their first exposure to art by sneaking into the Arlington House at 19th and Chester to take a peek at the scantily clad figure in the gilt-framed oil painting above the bar.

And in all parts of the county, wherever a hall of any size was available, and someone to play the fiddle, there were dances.

In the Kern River Valley, families came from the surrounding hills to whirl the night away at hotels in Kernville and Havilah. The evening's revelry ended when the musicians struck the opening notes of "Home, Sweet Home," but the party often continued the next day with a banquet for all.

At the sprawling Tejon Ranch south of Bakersfield, where Hispanic traditions were strong, fiestas that often lasted a full week marked the completion of the annual sheep-shearing operation.

Around 1890 a number of theaters, each dubbed by their owners with the more grandiose title of "opera house," arose in Bakersfield. Local talent as well as traveling troupes of players performed everything from musical revues to Shakespeare on the stages of George Scribner's and Philip Niederaur's establishments.

Culture, or at least a recognition that there was a lack of it, became firmly established in Bakersfield in 1896 when a group of 18 women formed the Woman's Club of Bakersfield. Their aim was to encourage the development of women's interests in literature, science and the arts. Members read and discussed a wide range of topics — the lives and works of established authors, international trade with Japan and hygiene in the home. Lucretia Stevens was the founding president of the club, which today remains the oldest organization of its kind in the county.

During the next decade, women in the Glennville area formed a Literary Society to help enrich the lives of their youngsters. Groups with similar purposes soon were launched by the women of Delano, Shafter, Wasco, Taft and Kernville. All of these trailblazing organizations, along with the public schools — always a hotbed of creative activity — provided a strong stimulus for artists in every field.

Spurred by the little theater movement that swept the country in the early part of the 20th century, or perhaps by the magical images they saw on the screens of Frank Panero's theater in Delano or the Banducci

157

Carol Elieff, Gertrude Beach, and Marilyn McArthur enlivened the action in the rollicking Bakersfield-based musical, "For the Love of Maggie," written by composer Ann Agabashian and lyricist Barbara Gardner.

and Lemucchi families in Bakersfield, enthusiastic amateurs formed dramatic groups during World War I and the years following.

Neighborhood backyards were the settings for some of the early shows. Others, directed by Alma Campbell, were held under the auspices of the Ancient Egyptian Order of Sciots and the Woman's Club. Gladys McKee, a lifelong supporter of all the arts, and Walter Mortensen, founder of the insurance agency that bears his name, played the title roles in "Adam and Eva," a 1922 production.

The Bakersfield Community Theater, now the oldest continuing little theater in California, was born in 1924. The premiere starred Geraldine Peacock in "The Hottentot," under the direction of Ted Brown. Also in the cast were Stephanie Massey and her soon-to-be husband Dr. Chris Stockton, and Vera Gibson, who later served for many years as Kern County Clerk.

Like arts organizations the world over, the fledgling theater wouldn't have made it without financial backing from the business community. Happily, a quartet of "angels" appeared in the form of Arthur S. Crites, Henry A. Jastro, Henry J. Brandt and Asa Dimon. Nearly 40 years later, BCT would have its own playhouse,

thanks to "For the Love of Maggie." In the 1970s, such leaders as Earl Stine, Richard K. "Stubby" Newman, Roger Benischek, O.D. Williams, John DiMundo and architect Joe Licastro would be the driving force behind the refurbishment of the playhouse.

Bakersfield Civic Light Opera, founded in the late 1960s by Jim Fillbrandt, Georgianna English and Ron Steinman, is noted for the quality of its productions and for giving hundreds of performers and technicians an opportunity to display their talents. Choral directors Kathleen Grainger Nicholas and Darrell Cates, and music directors John Briscoe and Ken Fahsbender also have provided leadership.

The Kern County Music Association, now the Bakersfield Community Concert Association, had its beginnings in the 1920s. Its founding executive board was made up of Mrs. T.L. Cummings, Mrs. J.B. Wendell and Phelps Jewett.

The first concerts were held in the old Kern County Union High School auditorium on 14th Street, just south of the Santa Fe Railroad's main station and switchyards, which "sometimes forced the visiting artist to compete with the trains for audience attention; generally, the artist came in second," said the late David E. Urner, founder of Urner's Appliances and an active supporter of the music association.

In 1946, the Kern Philharmonic Association, now called the Bakersfield Symphony, was organized with Harry Gardner as its founding president. Bakersfield High School music instructor Harold J. Burt was a leader in its development and many of the first musicians were his students or those of Wesley Moore, director of the Driller Band.

The Bakersfield Symphony is an 85-member orchestra made up of paid professionals led by resident conductor/music director John Farrer. The symphony attracts top guest artists, ranging from Ella Fitzgerald to Andre Watts. Among community members who have provided leadership and financial support in the past decade are Wendall and Betsy Kinney, Robert Abrams, Sid Chapin, Pete Jones, Richard Leask, Ted Fritts, Al

WINI DAVIS

The Arts Council of Kern has attracted many dedicated volunteers, including Eloise Lambert, Dorothy Nobles, and Gretchen Reinecke. Here they prepared for a lobby display at Civic Auditorium in 1976.

Stanley, Charles Francis, Gertrude Sill, Eleanor Weinberger and Maggie King.

Residents of the desert area are afforded high caliber musical performances through the Indian Wells Valley Concert Association and the Desert Orchestra, Delano, which provides scholarships to students through its Music Memorial, has enjoyed the guidance of a number of individuals, including Charlotte Chichester.

Country western music, a heritage of the Dust Bowl migration of the 1930s, is a vibrant part of Kern's entertainment history. Superstars like Buck Owens and Merle Haggard, along with hundreds of others in the field, got their start playing in clubs and on television shows in Bakersfield.

Visual art has shown a steady development in the past 40 years. Charles La Rue Smith was instrumental in the establishment of the Bakersfield Art Association in the 1940s. Bernice Jarrett, a junior high school art teacher, was another leader. (Delano educator Charlotte Chichester was active in her community and in Bakersfield.) Members of the association voluntarily

staffed the Cunningham Memorial Art Gallery, Bakersfield's municipal art museum, from the time it opened in 1956 until 1986, when its operation was assumed by the Bakersfield Art Foundation, with Kathy Leverett as founding president.

The Arts Council of Kern, founded in 1977 by a committee headed by Gretchen Reinecke, now the western region representative for Young Audiences, is the umbrella group for about 200 fine arts groups in every part of the county.

Yes, Kern County has come a long way in the arts over the years. In their wildest fantasies, the regulars at the Arlington House saloon could never have imagined that, a century later 45,000 people would view Armand Hammer's priceless collection of art at Cal State Bakersfield's Todd Madigan Gallery in 1987.

The biographical sketches that follow highlight some of the top achievers in the arts.

Agabashian, Ann — The Bakersfield business community knows Ann Agabashian as the co-owner, with her husband, Rudy Agabashian, of House of Comfort, but the arts world knows her as the composer of "For the Love of Maggie," a rollicking musical that has raised substantial amounts of money for the Bakersfield Community Theater and the city's Chamber of Commerce.

The show, first performed in 1959 outdoors at the Stockdale home of Helmuth and Jutta Cordes, is based on a true-life romance of a 19th century Rosedale "remittance man," Lord Sholto Douglas, the third son of the Marquis of Queensbury, and Addie Loretta Mooney, a showgirl from Tehachapi.

Barbara Gardner, who later became an administrator at the University of Southern California, wrote the show's lyrics. Gloria Zigner, now the owner of a Newport Beach public relations firm, handled the promotion.

The first fully staged production of "Maggie" in 1960 inaugurated BCT's theater on South Chester Avenue. It has been presented twice at the Civic Auditorium: in 1966 as part of Bakersfield's centennial celebration and in 1981 as a benefit for the Chamber of Commerce. Ken Secor and Phyllis Adams were the coproducers for the show, which netted $30,000 for the chamber's building fund.

"Maggie" had its genesis in the "Ballad of Frank Gifford," a segment the collaborators created for Bakersfield Memorial Hospital's first "High Fever Follies."

Agabashian recalls that "The first line was, 'Everything's great in Bakersfield,' and after that, everything just fell into place."

Jack Albertson — Jack Albertson, winner of both a Tony and an Oscar for "The Subject Was Roses" and an Emmy for "Chico and the Man," long will be remembered for being the guest star at the gala opening in 1979 of Cal State Bakersfield's Doré Theater. The Albertson Room, the area between the theater and the Todd Madigan Art Gallery, is named in his honor. The actor, a friend of Jack Frankel, then president of the college, was accompanied by his wife, Margo Albertson, who at the time was a member of the California State University System board of trustees.

Angell, Sir Norman (originally, Ralph Norman Angell Lane) — Ralph Lane, as he was known to Bakersfield area residents, organized the Rosedale Amateur Dramatic Club, which flourished briefly in 1894. The company was made up of Lane's fellow settlers in the Rosedale area. Lane, who was 20 at the time, later returned to his native England, where he became an internationally known pacifist, economist and writer, using the name Norman Angell. He invented The Money Game, a series of card games designed to teach the elements of economics. Lane subsequently was knighted and in 1933 was awarded the Nobel Peace Price.

Argersinger, Charles — Now a nationally known composer-conductor and a professor at DePaul University in Chicago, Charles Argersinger played a vital role in shaping the jazz program at Cal State Bakersfield that presently is being carried on in able style by Doug Davis. While at CSB from 1979 to 1982, Argersinger completed two albums featuring student musicians. "Both received great play on Los Angeles jazz stations," said Jerome Kleinsasser, chair of the fine arts department. Argersinger composed many of his pieces in Bakersfield, including "Rage Cage," "Salsa 'n Peppers," "Mandala" and "No Clams Allowed." One of his pieces, the five-part "Pysche," premiered at Carnegie Hall in 1981.

Armstrong, Karen — A Cal State Bakersfield theater arts graduate, Armstrong is a production stage manager in theater and television in New York City. She is the daughter of Donna Armstrong and Dr. Frank Armstrong.

Austin, Mary Hunter — A singular individual with a mystical bent that bordered on the eccentric, Mary Austin lived in Kern County only a short time: from 1888 to 1893, with intermittent visits up until 1906.

But her experiences here — and in the Owens Valley — and the material she gleaned from those experiences, proved to be the source for most of what she later wrote and published. Two of her best known works are *Land of Little Rain* (1903), a poetic series of essays about the high desert that catapulted her into instant fame, and *The Flock* (1906), which includes an account of the legendary sheep drive to Wyoming conducted by Jose Jesus Lopez, major-domo of the Tejon Ranch.

While living on the Tejon, Mary Austin gathered tales of folklore and history from Edward Fitzgerald Beale, the ranch's founder. In many ways, Beale was her mentor, stimulating her writing ambitions and her intellectual curiosity. "There was nothing General Beale did not know, or had not seen, or had not been a party to, since Pio Pico's time," she wrote in her autobiography, *Earth Horizon*. He released her "from the black spell of her wanting to know."

Austin roamed the Tejon freely, listening to the stories of John Vineyard Rosemeyer, proprietor of the ranch store, as well as those of various Indians, shepherders and vaqueros. Equally important to her later writing was the strong communion she felt with her surroundings. Like Beale, she "married the land" in her heart.

Later, while serving as tutor to the children of Darius Pyle at the Mountain View Dairy in the Panama-Old River area, the future author heard tales about such famous landowners as James B. Haggin, William Carr and Henry Miller. Several characters in Austin's books bear a strong resemblance to those historic figures. She also lived in Bakersfield; one of her first published short stories, "The Conversion of Lew Sing," is based on a Chinese truck gardener who raised his crops on a small plot near 19th and L streets.

While living in Bishop during the early days of the Owens River-City of Los Angeles water battle, Austin wrote an article in support of the Owens Valley interests and remained an environmental activist for the rest of her days.

Austin came to know all of the top writers. In England, where she gave a speech to the Fabian Society, she had tea with George Bernard Shaw. And the respected literary critic Carl Van Doren said in his introduction to the 1950 edition of *Land of Little Rain,* "Everybody who talked with Mary Austin knew at once that there was greatness in her."

Despite her worldliness, her spirit remained tied to the southwest. Austin lived her last years in Santa Fe,

Stage and screen actor Robert Beltran studied drama at Bakersfield College and Fresno State. He helped stage the highly successful 1983 summer production of "Lone Star" in the backyard of Narducci's Cafe.

Artist Lynn Taber-Borcherdt is admired for her gold-leafing technique in depicting ancient fairy tales. She is the daughter of Harold and Dorothy Taber, and granddaughter of pioneer Coca-Cola dealer Sam Lynn.

New Mexico, where she died in 1934. The next to last day of her life she spent giving a poetry reading at a benefit to raise money for native Americans of the area.

Beltran, Robert — Even though he's a hot commodity in Hollywood, stage and screen actor ("Zoot Suit," "Eating Raoul," "Lone Wolf") Robert Beltran keeps close ties with his friends and family in Bakersfield.

In the summer of 1983, Beltran helped Larry Thomas, whom he has known since the second grade at Mount Vernon School, George Carson III and Hank Webb stage a first-rate summer production of "Lone Star" in the backyard of Narducci's Cafe. The drama played to sell-out audiences during its run. It also attracted a number of non-paying spectators — namely, the residents of the hotel next door who watched the performances from their second-floor window sills.

Larry Thomas, who starred as Che in Bakersfield Civic Light Opera's 1986 production of "Evita," said the show at Narducci's was a collaborative effort. "Robert had to leave for El Paso to film a movie with Chuck Norris five days before 'Lone Star' opened. He was our artistic eye. He'd say, 'This works . . . this doesn't work and here's why'."

Beltran, who studied drama at Bakersfield College and Fresno State, recently appeared in "We Don't Need To Show You No Stinking Badges" at the LA Theater

Center. His latest motion picture, "Gaby," stars Liv Ullman and Robert Loggia. His mother, Aurelia Beltran, lives in Bakersfield, as do his grandparents.

Benischek, Roger — Now teaching at Fairleigh-Dickingson University in New Jersey and designing sets for off-Broadway shows in his spare time, Roger Benischek created outstanding settings for numerous Bakersfield Civic Light Opera Association productions and Bakersfield Community Theater, particularly for "Cabaret." He also put in many hours, and acquired many donations of material, in the refurbishment of BCT's playhouse.

Betty, Stafford — A professor of philosophy and religious studies, Stafford Betty has written one novel, *The Rich Man* (St. Martin's Press), and, with artist Sylvia Zimmerman, a fanciful tale titled *Sing Like the Whippoorwhill,* published this year. While doing research for *The Rich Man* in India, Betty met the world-famous humanitarian, Mother Teresa.

Borcherdt, Lynn Taber — Aptly described as an "artist magician," Lynn Taber-Borcherdt uses the medieval technique of gold leafing to enhance her contem-

"They mirror the basic patterns of the pysche; the problems we all share in our individual journeys through life."

porary depiction of ancient fairy tales. Taber-Borcherdt, who had a one-woman show at the Tucson Museum of Art in 1986, says of her paintings: "They mirror the basic patterns of the pysche; the problems we all share in our individual journeys through life."

The daughter of Bakersfield residents Harold and Dorothy Taber, Lynn lives in Arizona with her husband, sculptor Fred Borcherdt. She is the granddaughter of Sam Lynn, pioneer Coca-Cola bottler for whom Sam Lynn Ball Park is named.

Brown, Ann — For nearly five years, Ann Brown has been the driving force behind Cunningham Memorial Art Gallery, Bakersfield's municipal art museum. She is recognized as a talented printmaker but even more so as the one person who has united artists, arts supporters and city officials in taking tangible steps to provide Bakersfield with an accredited art museum. The impetus came from a study by Bay Area arts consultant Robert Bailey, which was presented to the City Council in 1984. Brown was instrumental in securing a grant from the Skaggs Foundation that provided Bailey's fee. As volunteer gallery director for four years, she upgraded the Cunningham's exhibits and initiated a docent program that provides guided tours and workshops for hundreds of schoolchildren each year. She also has created a number of distinctive logos for local organizations, including the one for Beautiful Bakersfield.

Mort Brown, Ann's stockbroker husband, is a country western music fan. Nonetheless, he and his company, E.F. Hutton, are active supporters of the fine arts. In 1986, the elegant party which opened Hutton's new headquarters was a benefit for arts organizations in the community.

Bryan, Diane Lang — An accomplished clarinetist who received her early training in Bakersfield schools, Diane Lang Bryan is the founder of the Beethoven Festival. The musical event, which features top local artists as well as nationally known ones, originated in Tehachapi but now is held each summer in Bakersfield and is governed by a board of directors. Bakersfield College professor James Mason is music director.

Calhoun, Eleanor — Item from the *Kern County Californian,* March 8, 1890: "Miss Eleanor Calhoun, who may be called a daughter of Kern County, is sup-

Jo Ann Castle achieved national fame as the energetic piano player on the Lawrence Welk TV show. As Jo Ann Zering, she began her career in Bakersfield at age 3, singing and dancing for $5 a show at local lodges.

porting Coquelin, the French actor."

Given the Victorian sensibilities of the era, you have to wonder if that single sentence in the newspaper's "Social and Personal" column shocked its readers, who may have thought Nellie Calhoun of Tehachapi was financing a gigolo. Actually, what the unknown item writer meant was that Calhoun was appearing on stage, in Paris, with Coquelin Aine, the star of the Comedie Francaise.

The by-then world-famous actress had made a giant leap from a childhood of near poverty in a remarkably short time. In 1867 she had been a student of Louesa Jewett Crites at Old Town School. *In Pioneer Days in*

Kern County, Louesa's son, Arthur S. Crites, said that, since textbooks were scarce, and because "Nellie had a good voice and was adept at learning," his mother often called upon her to read to the other students. Her father, Ezekiel Calhoun, Kern County's first district attorney, was a "truly Southern gentleman of the old type but ill fitted to cope with the conditions of the West . . . The family was in dire distress for even the necessities of life most of the time."

The Calhouns later moved to San Francisco and became acquainted with Phoebe Hearst, who recognized Eleanor's talent and paid for her professional training. Phoebe's son, William Randolph Hearst, became smitten with the actress and wanted to marry her. Somewhat prophetically, his mother squashed any idea of marriage because Eleanor was "of the theater."

Eleanor Calhoun, who was considered one of the great tragedians of her day, later married a Serbian prince.

Camp, Robin Eschner — A young artist whose prints and posters are sold all over the nation, Robin Eschner Camp is especially well-known for her sensitive watercolor interpretations of flowers and plant life. (Her prints were featured on a calendar printed by the Junior League for its 1986 "Holidays of Magic.") Camp, whose studio is in San Francisco, is the daughter of Bakersfield residents Stanford and Virgina Eschner.

Castle, Jo Ann — Jo Ann Castle, for 10 years the bouncy blonde piano player on the Lawrence Welk Show, began her career at age 3 in Bakersfield, where she was known as Jo Ann Zering. "I'd sing and dance at the lodges in town — the Elks, the Moose. Sometimes I got $5," she said in an interview with *The Californian's* Steve Hall. Jo Ann got her first break on the Tex Williams Show when she was 13 and made her television debut on the Spade Cooley Show. Seven years later, Welk hired her as a replacement for Big Tiny Little. Castle left the show in 1969 and had a series of personal misfortunes. Following the death of her severely retarded 15-year-old daughter, she was the national spokeswoman for United Cerebral Palsy. Castle now is a country-western entertainer.

Cunningham, Marion Osborn — To most people, Marion Osborn Cunningham is the person for whom the Bakersfield's 31-year-old municipal art museum, Cunningham Memorial Art Gallery, is named.

To the art world, she is best known for her imaginative silk screen prints of San Francisco street scenes. In its review of a memorial exhibition of her work following her death in 1948 — she died at age 39 as a result of a brain tumor — the *San Francisco Chronicle* described Cunningham as "one of the most gifted artists San Francisco has ever known."

The sights and sounds of Chinatown especially intrigued the artist, and she incorporated many of the "amazing shapes" she found in herbalists windows — such as seahorses and mandrake roots — into the serigraphs she created in her glassed-in studio on Telegraph Hill.

Her works are in the collections of the Metropolitan Museum of Art in New York, Cleveland Museum of Art,

Conductor Phillip C. Dodson is well-known for presenting memorable performances of requiem masses and other classical vocal music for more than 25 years. He is music director at Bakersfield Christian Life Center.

San Francisco Museum of Art, the De Young Museum, Los Angeles County Library, the U.S. State Department and the Cunningham Memorial Art Gallery. The gallery which bears her name was established in 1956 with a gift from her family. Her parents, Mr. and Mrs. Walter Osborn Sr. (he once was the city attorney) came to Bakersfield in 1911; Marion's brother is retired Superior Court Judge Walter Osborn Jr. Her sister Priscilla Mueller, a harpist, is the wife of the late Calvin Mueller, Bakersfield College music instructor.

Dodson, Phillip — Under the energetic direction of Phillip Dodson, the Masterworks Chorale has presented first-rate performances of requiem masses and other classical vocal music for more than 25 years. The community chorus also has recorded a long-playing album. Dodson is the music director at Bakersfield Christian Life Center and was instrumental in securing the church's large pipe organ.

Doré, Frances B. — Cal State Bakersfield's Doré Theater is named for Frances Dore, the wife of an oilman. The $500,000 bequest from her estate helped attorney Curtis Darling, as chairman of the CSB Foundation, to persuade the stage college board of trustees to provide the balance needed for the construction of the theater, which opened in 1979.

Farrer, John — Bakersfield symphony music director/conductor John Farrer gained international prominence in 1986 as guest conductor of the London Phil-

harmonic. And this year, Farrer was one of 10 conductors, nation-wide, to participate in a special New York Philharmonic program directed by Zubin Mehta. Farrer also is a member of the American Symphony Orchestra League's Artistic Affairs Committee. As the Bakersfield Symphony's music director since 1976, Farrer has been a key figure in the orchestra's growth and development. He is married to concert pianist Bonnie Bogle Farrer, a graduate of Juilliard.

Fiser, Barbara — A Bakersfield resident who makes her living as an artist, Barbara Fiser's work is represented in many collections throughout the country. She is a generous supporter of Cunningham Memorial Art Gallery and has worked diligently to promote professional standards in the arts.

Galbraith, Georgie Starbuck — "Her poetry explodes at the end and galvanizes you like a friendly scorpion with a kindly sting in its tail." That's how *The Californian's* Beth Henley described Georgie Starbuck Galbraith's witty verses. Few would disagree.

The poet, who spent almost all of her 70 years in Bakersfield, began writing in 1938. During her lifetime her work appeared in more than 100 national publications, ranging from *The Saturday Evening Post,* in which her work appeared 255 times, to the *Wall Street Journal.*

Public though her poetry was, Georgie Starbuck Galbraith was an intensely private person, virtually a re-

Georgie Starbuck Galbraith saw her poems published in more than 100 national magazines and newspapers, including The Saturday Evening Post and The Wall Street Journal.

163

Four dynamos — Merle Haggard, Pete Jones, Rafer Johnson, and George Valos — planned a concert to benefit four local service clubs. (Photo on wall is of country music legend Bob Wills.)

cluse for the last 20 years of her life. Both her wit and her reticence come to the fore in the copy she wrote for the dust jacket for *Have One On Me,* her only published book:

"I live alone in an amiable clutter of books, manuscripts, pictures and junk. I garden; or at any rate, I dig nut grass. I'm thinking of starting an organization called Nut Grass Anonymous."

Still, classmates recall that Galbraith took an active part in drama and other activities at Bakersfield High School and Bakersfield College.

Much of Galbraith's work is reminiscent of Dorothy Parker. "Her aphorisms have been notable and endlessly quotable," said Jim Day in his "Pipefuls" column.

At her best, Georgie Starbuck Galbraith shows the influence of 19th century American poet Emily Dickinson. As her cousin Roxanne Starbuck, an employee of the Cal State Bakersfield Library, astutely observes: "Like Emily Dickinson, Georgie's poetry was her 'letter to the world.'"

Green, Florence — Florence Green, the first woman elected to the Ridgecrest City Council, now is a resident of Los Angeles, where she is a grants consultant, But

she hasn't forgotten her hometown. Due to her efforts, the Maturango Museum in Ridgecrest received a $75,000 grant from the Irvine Foundation, which made possible the construction in 1986 of a new building for the facility.

Green, who produced many of Cerro College's and Community Light Opera Theater's most memorable productions, returned to the desert community in March 1987 as producer-director of a locally written musical, "Rasputin."

Haggard, Merle — Considered by nearly all of his peers the best country western singer in the business, Merle Haggard is one Bakersfield native who's parlayed bad times into good ones. As writer Nat Hemphill puts it, "Merle Haggard's songs come straight up from the gut ... If you listen to the lyrics of his songs (like) 'Mama Tried' and 'Hungry Eyes,' you are hearing Merle Haggard's life."

Haggard was born in Bakersfield in 1937, two years after his parents migrated from Oklahoma. Until his father got a job with the Santa Fe Railroad, the entire family did farm work to survive. From the time he was 14, shortly after his father's death, until he was 23,

Merle was in and out of jail for everything from armed robbery to passing bad checks. Then in 1960, after serving two years in San Quentin, the singer returned to Bakersfield. He began playing at the Blackboard and clubs on Edison Highway and on Cousin Herb Henson's television show. The rest is history.

In the 1970s, the entertainer built a spacious split-level home (with an electric train running through it) at the mouth of the Kern River Canyon. During that time, he performed a sell-out benefit concert that started late, owing to a traffic jam outside the Civic Auditorium. Music store owner Pete Jones, who initiated the event, said the $10,000 net proceeds were divided among the Boys Club, Special Olympics, Kern Press Club and the East Bakersfield Progressive Club.

Haggard now lives in Shasta, California and, except for concerts and recording sessions, spends most of his time bass fishing.

Yet the hurt and the hard times are still there, in the throaty, rough-but-gentle voice (that nearly every singer in the business tries to imitate) and especially in his own songs. One man's pain is often another's pleasure. Merle Haggard has "pleasured" millions the world over.

"For as long as I can remember, I have read everything and anything. A book was never very far away, and I learned to vacuum the floor, to iron and even to dry dishes with a book propped before me."

Hall, Elizabeth — A Bakersfield native, Elizabeth Hall, who at one time was Shafter Branch librarian, now is a widely published author and behavioral science journalist. Her classmates at Bakersfield High School and Bakersfield College knew her as Harriet. Since becoming a professional writer, she has used only her middle name, Elizabeth.

She is a former editor of *Psychology Today* and *Human Nature,* the author or editor of a dozen or more books on psychology and parapsychology, and has done a number of films in association with Peter Drucker. Two of her books earned National Media Awards from the American Pyschological Foundation.

An avid reader from the time she was very young, Hall once said, "For as long as I can remember, I have read everything and anything. A book was never very far away, and I learned to vacuum the floor, to iron and even to dry dishes with a book propped before me."

The author now lives in Waccabuc, New York. Her brother, Norman Hall, is director of engineering at KERO-TV.

Haslam, Gerald — A writer enriched by his Oildale roots, Gerald Haslam is gaining solid recognition for his work, most recently in a critical study that California State University, Long Beach professor Gerald Locklin wrote for Boise State University's *Western Writers Series.*

The series' impressive roster includes such well-known writers as Wallace Stegner, Bret Harte, Sam Shepard and John Gregory Dunne. Locklin favorably compares Haslam to Mark Twain, particularly in the Sonoma State University professor's use of the vernacular. Haslam's writing, beginning with *Okies* in 1975, strongly reflects his boyhood in Kern County. He writes about farmhands, roughnecks, and just plain folks, affectionately but with a piercing honesty that gets to the heart of the matter.

Haslam has a number of publications to his credit, including a fine anthology of western writers (*California Heartland,* Capra Press), which he co-edited with James D. Houston. In 1988 the University of California Press will publish Haslam's *The Great Central Valley: California's Heartland* and Capra plans to release a new collection of his short stories. He also is one of five editors of *History of the American West* (Texas Christian University Press, 1987), a 10-year project sponsored by the National Endowment for the Humanities and the Western Literature Association.

He and his wife, the former Jan Pettichord, also a native of Oildale, make their home in Petaluma.

Helmick, Carl and Shirley — Known in Ridgecrest as "Mr. and Mrs. Music," the Helmicks are active in all facets of the music community in Kern's desert. As key people in the Indian Wells Valley Concert Association series, they have been instrumental in bringing quality professionals to the area. A music teacher, Shirley Helmick was violinist Anne Akiko Meyers' first instructor. Carl Helmick is a research physicist at China Lake Naval Weapons Center.

Hodges, Keith — A fashion designer whose 1986 collection was featured in "People for People," an AIDS-research benefit at the Pacific Design Center in Los Angeles (with "Murder She Wrote" star Angela Lans-

---

"I remember when I used to charge a set of strings with Pete on Friday and pay for them Monday after a weekend gig."

---

bury as honorary chair), Keith Hodges is the son of Mr. and Mrs. Colbert Hodges of Wasco.

In a *New York Times* interview, Liza Minnelli, one of the notables the designer has clad, praised Keith Hodges' work as "simple but extraordinary . . . a combination of something that Chanel might have designed and someone like [Marchesa] Casati might have worn."

Hylton, Andrew — Film and television costume designer Andrew Hylton credits Bakersfield College's Mary Lou Wilson and Foothill High's Peggy Pauley for his early training and inspiration. "Doing your research — that's what the education process is all about. And then you can bring in your knowledge and share it with

Violinist Anne Akiko Meyers, a child prodigy, has performed with the New York Philharmonic and the Los Angeles Philharmonic orchestras. Currently she is a student at the Juilliard School of Music in New York.

somebody else." Repaying the favor, Andy returned to Foothill in March 1987 to assist with the alumni production of "Our Town."

The 36-year-old Hylton's credits include the films "Blade Runner," "Starman," "Annie" and "Raging Bull." On television, his designs have appeared on "The Carol Burnett Show," "The Thorn Birds" and "Dynasty."

Kerzie, Ted — Cal State Bakersfield art professor Ted Kerzie has had a number of one-man shows in Los Angeles and New York galleries. He has gained international acclaim for his large, post-modernist paintings. The unusual technique he developed incorporates multiple strips of computer-punched paper, which, in his more recent work, also reveal subtle images of exotic jungle flowers and animals.

Ketterl, George — George Ketterl, a member of the fine arts faculty at Cal State Bakersfield, recently exhibited his work in a one-man show at a major Los Angeles art gallery. The exhibit received favorable reviews in the *Los Angeles Times* and *Art News.*

Logan, Karl — This 1967 Bakersfield High School graduate and fashion designer markets his line of women's clothing nation-wide. His company, Karl Logan Inc., based in Hollywood, grosses between $300,000 and $400,000 annually. Logan, whose parents are Bakersfield residents Cleve and Ada Jones, describes his designs as "very modern, very clean . . . as sleek as possible . . ."

Madigan, Maris and Todd — At the time of his death Todd Madigan was actively engaged in seeking contributions for the construction of an art gallery at Cal State Bakersfield. Subsequently, the Todd Madigan Art Gallery was named in his honor. In January and February 1987, nearly 45,000 people viewed the Armand Hammer Collection at the gallery, undoubtedly the finest collection of art ever presented in Kern County.

At the opening, Maris Madigan said, with shining eyes, "Todd would have been very happy." A member of the Dorian Society, a support group for the college's fine arts department, Maris Madigan has contributed much to CSB. But, like her husband, she is a very private person and prefers anonymity for what she does.

Artist Leo Nowak's versatility has ranged from painting Superman comics and World War II battle scenes to creating art for an advertising agency. He is listed in Who's Who in American Art.

CHRISTIAN STEINER

Buck Owens, internationally known country western star, is also a successful businessman who owns radio station KUZZ/KKXX and the weekly publication, The Kern Shopper. He has raised thousands of dollars for local charities.

Madison, Guy — A television and film actor who got his first break as the fresh-faced sailor in "Since You Went Away," Guy Madison, then known as Robert Moseley, worked as a telephone lineman following his graduation from Bakersfield High School in 1940. He later appeared in westerns and on television as "Wild Bill Hickok." Now retired, Madison lives in the Riverside area.

Meyers, Anne Akiko — Violinist Anne Akiko Meyers, who began her training at age 4 with Ridgecrest's Shirley Helmick, has come a long way in a short time.

At 16, she has played twice as soloist with the New York Philharmonic under Zubin Mehta and also has performed with the Los Angeles Philharmonic. On television, she has been a featured artist on Johnny Carson's "Tonight" show, "That's Incredible" and in documentaries produced by ABC and CBS. Ann currently is a full scholarship student at the Juilliard School of Music in New York.

In February 1987 she gave a recital at the China Lake Naval Weapons Center Theater, where she made her orchestral debut at age 8. At the recent concert, Anne dedicated her encore piece to her first teacher, Shirley Helmick, saying, "She not only taught me music, she taught me love."

The violinist is the daughter of Richard S. and Yasuko Meyers. Now the president of Western Oregon State College in Monmouth, Oregon, he formerly headed Cerro Coso Community College.

Nowak, Leo — During his lengthy and still-active career 79-year-old Leo Nowak has gone from being an artist for the first "Superman" comics to painting the desert tortoises he and his wife Gloria Nowak shelter on their ranch at Inyokern.

His bulging art portfolio shows the range of his work: speakeasy scenes from his clarinet and saxophone-playing days in Cleveland, action-packed jungle pictures done when he was a battalion artist during World War II, advertising art created during the 25 years he spent with Stamps-Conhaim Newspaper Service, and his present love, historic and contemporary western art.

A former field representative for Assemblyman Phil Wyman, Nowak also contributes conservative political cartoons to *The Daily Independent* and is listed in *Who's Who in American Art.*

Osborne, Mary (Scaffidi) — Jazz critic Leonard Feather has praised guitarist-singer Mary Osborne for her "exceptional beat and aggressive swinging style." Cal State Bakersfield's Doug Davis calls her "Bakersfield's jazz treasure."

Osborne, a North Dakota native, has known and played with all the greats — Beryl Booker, Coleman Hawkins, Buddy Rogers, Joe Venuti, Dick Stabile and

"Bakersfield has remained my spiritual home. I was fortunate in being guided by such distinguished teachers as Ruth Emerson and Clarence Cullimore"

Russ Morgan, to name a few — in New York and throughout the country.

And she has earned their respect. In the jacket notes for Osborne's album "Now and Then" (Stash Records, 1980), pianist Mary Lou Williams described her colleague as "the most amazing woman I know on guitar. And in terms of blues feelings and jazz roots, she really has it."

Osborne was one of the stars of CSB's jazz festival this year. She also performs with her husband, Ralph Scaffidi, a trumpet playing bandleader and former member of the CBS Orchestra in New York. They also appear with their son, Pete Scaffidi, a bassist who also is a member of the Bakersfield and Tulare symphonies, and with their daughter, Susan Scaffidi, a jazz singer and member of the KKXX/KUZZ news team.

Owens, Buck — At 57, country western star Buck Owens owns a vast business enterprise that includes lucrative radio stations in Bakersfield (KUZZ/KKXX) and Phoenix, and a weekly publication, the *Kern Shopper.* It was not always thus for the entertainer who music store owner Pete Jones says is one of the shrewdest businessmen he's ever known.

Owens has been Jones' customer, and friend, for 35 years. Buck says, "I remember when I used to charge a set of strings with Pete on Friday and pay for them Monday after a weekend gig."

"Victor Pesina started with me in 1973 when we did 'King of Glory' for the First Baptist Church. I offered free ballet lessons to any man who could dance."

Responding in kind, Pete said, "He'd load up his old truck with his gear and his boys . . . come back after a trip and buy a few more pieces."

The lean times are far behind for the poor boy from Sherman, Texas, whose family piled into a mattress-topped 1933 Ford to make the trek to the San Joaquin Valley in 1937. He has 55 albums to his credit and with his red-white-and-blue guitar in the forefront, has performed at Carnegie Hall, the Palladium in London and other theaters all over the world. For 17 years he was the star of the television show, "Hee Haw" and in the 1960s was named "Country Western Star of the Decade."

During the 1970s, Buck Owens was highly visible in Bakersfield, riding in his steer-horned Buckmobile in parades and in connection with his annual rodeo that raised thousands of dollars for local charities. In recent years he has been less active publicly, although he is well-known in the business community.

Owens, Rod — Nationally known in the fashion industry, Rod Owens operates showrooms in Los Angeles, at the California Mart, and in New York, where he has an apartment in Manhattan. The fashion promoter once was associated with the noted motion picture designer Helen Rose in marketing her special collections. A graduate of Bakersfield High School (1939), Bakersfield College and UCLA, Owens is the brother of Dr. Charles Owens, a Bakersfield physician.

Paradise, Phil — A painter and sculptor who has exhibited at some of the nation's foremost galleries —

the Los Angeles County Museum of Art, the Art Institute of Chicago and the Whitney Museum of American Art, among others — Phil Paradise's desire to become an artist was awakened when he was a student at Bakersfield High School.

"Bakersfield has remained my spiritual home," he says. "I was fortunate in being guided by such distinguished teachers as Ruth Emerson and Clarence Cullimore in those early years, and in being advised by (principal) Herman Spindt."

Paradise, now 82, has been director of fine arts at Chouinard Institute, art director and production designer for Sol Lesser Productions at Paramount Studios, and director and part-owner of Greystone Galleries in Cambria. He is a past president of the California Watercolor Society and a member of the National Academy of Design.

The artist has designated that, upon his death, a large collection of his serigraphs will be given to Cunningham Memorial Art Gallery.

Penningroth, Phil — Television audiences nationwide have seen the work of Tehachapi playwright Phil Penningroth within the past four years. Two of his teleplays, "Silence of the Heart" and "Promises to Keep," were featured as the CBS Movie of the Week. Another, "When the Bough Breaks," appeared as the NBC Movie of the Week.

Penningroth's first big break came in 1981 when his screenplay, "Ghost Dancing," was presented at the Na-

---

"I persist in the belief that Bakersfield can become more cosmopolitan, in that it will begin to support and encourage the arts."

---

tional Playwrights Conference at the Eugene O'Neill Theater Center in Waterford, Connecticut. The play, which concerns the battle over Owens River water rights, subsequently received the ABC Theater Award and, in 1983, became the ABC Theater Special. His plays also have been produced locally and at the Dallas Theater Center. The playwright was alcohol program administrator for the Kern County Department of Mental Health from 1973 to 1985 and has written a number of journal articles on that subject. He now is a full-time writer.

Pesina, Victor — Dancer Victor Pesina, now with the internationally known Stuttgart Ballet, was discovered by Martha Knight, director of the Bakersfield Ballet Theater.

"Chet Seltzer told me once he wrote under the name Amado Muro because who'd believe the kind of story he wanted to write if it was written by a guy named Chester Seltzer."

"He started with me in 1973 when we did 'King of Glory' for the First Baptist Church," said Knight. "I offered free ballet lessons to any man who could dance. Victor was 17 then; he had never danced before."

Pesina performed in Knight's productions for three years before receiving a scholarship to the San Francisco Ballet, where he was a member of the company for three years. In 1986 he returned to do a reprise of his 1976 role in "Roumanian Rhapsody" for his former teacher in a production in the Beale Park amphitheater. A few months earlier, Knight and several of her students had been in Washington D.C. to see Pesina perform, under the direction of the Stuttgart's artistic director and prima ballerina, Marcia Haydee.

"I asked Victor then if he would do the summer show for us," she recalled. "We fitted his costume in the parking garage at the Kennedy Center and I came home and finished it."

An accomplished dancer herself — she once was a member of the Oakland Civic Ballet — Martha Knight has taught hundreds of young students during her 31 year career in Bakersfield. She is especially noted for the imaginative choreography and splendid costuming of her shows. She is married to optometrist John L. Knight.

Raborg, Frederick R., Jr. — A much-published free lance writer, Fred Raborg recently has gained new stature as the editor and publisher of *Amelia,* a Bakersfield-based literary journal with an international circulation.

Reviewing *Amelia* for the *Library Journal,* literary critic Bill Katz said: "The editor strives, and succeeds, in offering readers a widely different cross section of American creative power . . ."

Raborg is assisted in his endeavors by his wife, Shafter native Eileen Bradshaw Raborg, a printer for the Hoven Company. Fred admits that establishing a literary journal isn't easy. "I persist in the belief that Bakersfield can become more cosmopolitan, in that it will begin to support and encourage the arts. Unfortunately, if an art form is to succeed here, it first must prove itself on the broader field. *Amelia* is no exception."

Raborg publishes mainly the work of nationally known authors. However, a number of Kern County writers have appeared in *Amelia,* including Nancy Edwards, William Rintoul, Gerald Haslam, Lester Cash, Phil Waterhouse, Juanita Phillips, Pat Lemm, Pam Cobb, Jennifer Resch, Harry Wilson and Gregory Powell.

Raborg's personal publication credits are extensive — more than 200 short stories and nearly 1,000 poems. He has received numerous awards, some carrying fascinating bonuses. In 1973, in connection with a *Guideposts* prize, he won a trip to New York and spent time with Dr. Norman Vincent Peale and Catherine Marshall. The essay he entered in The USA-The Netherlands 200 Foundation competition garnered him a trip to Amsterdam and an introduction to Queen Beatrix.

The author began his writing career at age 12 in Virginia as a newspaper columnist. A graduate of Bakersfield College, Raborg earned his B.A. in English at Cal State Bakersfield and has taught courses in professional writing.

Delano High School teacher Chester Hayden first recognized Valente's outstanding vocal ability when she was in her junior year.

Reep, Edward Arnold — A painter, teacher and author whose impressive career spans 40 years, Edward Reep had the enviable task of designing the painting studios at California Institute of the Arts with an almost unlimited amount of founder Walt Disney's money.

"Think blue sky, Walt always said," recalled Reep, who then was chairman of the school's painting department and previously held a similar position at Chouinard Institute.

Reep's work has been exhibited at New York's Whitney Museum of American Art, the National Gallery in Washington D.C. and the Los Angeles County Museum of Art, among others. He has authored two books.

The artist was among the lecturers who provided training for the docents for the Armand Hammer exhibit at the Todd Madigan Gallery. He and his wife, Pat, moved to Bakersfield in 1985. Their daughter, Susan Reep, an administrator at Medi Center, is married to Mark Smith, an architect for the county.

Rippey, Clayton — The art work of former Bakersfield College professor Clayton Rippey is owned by Wakayama Castle in Japan, PepsiCo, Chevron U.S.A., Tenneco, Dance Magazine, The Bakersfield Californian, Valley Plaza Regional Shopping Center and Mexicali Restaurants. He also designed the Renegade pylon at the northwest corner of the Bakersfield College campus.

Since his first one-man show in Bakersfield in 1947, Rippey has exhibited in galleries throughout the United States, in Mexico and in Europe. The late Todd Madigan, and his wife, Maris, who now represents Rippey, built the Cezanne Gallery specifically to exhibit the artist's work. A painter, sculptor and muralist, Rippey often writes free verse to accompany his work.

Many Kern County artists have benefited from Rippey's instruction at BC. Now retired, the artist and his wife, Marcia, live on Orcas Island in the state of Washington.

Robertson, Cliff — This Cliff Robertson grew up in Shafter and has risen to fame, not as an actor but as a model. The blond and brawny Robertson was featured in Nordica ski-equipment ads appearing in the November and December 1986 issues of *Gentlemen's Quarterly* and in *Life, Playboy* and *Los Angeles* magazines. Robertson's mother, Marge, lives in Shafter.

Robinson, Ethel — A long-time drama instructor at Bakersfield High School and Bakersfield College, Ethel

---

Ardis Walker eloquently puts into words the mystical feelings many of us share about the wilderness—his "constant source of inspiration."

Robinson earned respect both for her inspirational qualities and for the high standards she set. Frank Wattron, who was her student and later her colleague, assumed her position at Bakersfield College upon her retirement in 1954. He looked upon Robinson as his mentor. "Robbie," he says, "was the greatest."

Seltzer, Chester (Amado Jesus Muro) — "Chet Seltzer," says writer Bill Rintoul, "told me once he wrote under the name Amado Muro because who'd believe the kind of story he wanted to write if it was written by a guy named Chester Seltzer."

Rintoul became friends with Seltzer when the short story writer, whose stature has increased since his death in 1971, worked on the copy desk at *The Bakersfield Californian.* Considered something of an eccentric, Seltzer usually dressed, to the dismay of his managing editor, in the same manner as the inhabitants of the Rescue Mission, where he spent his off-duty hours.

Yet the unfortunates were the kind of people Seltzer preferred. The people he met during his vagabond life are the people about whom he wrote.

In his introduction to the posthumously published *The Collected Stories of Amado Muro,* Rintoul said of his friend: "Seltzer rode freight trains, worked in the crops, went to sea, lived on skid rows, sometimes worked on newspapers — and from the time he was 20 until he was 56, when he died in El Paso, wrote short stories that may be the best that have been written in this country about men on the road and in the fields, at the missions, and in the villages of Mexico."

Seltzer, whose father was Louis B. Seltzer, the influential editor of the *Cleveland Plain Dealer,* was a conscientious objector during World War II and served time in prison because of his belief in pacifism.

Stanley, Alfred — Al Stanley, a retired executive of the Joslin Co. in Chicago and former violinist, is undeniably one of the Bakersfield Symphony's most dedicated volunteers.

Despite his characteristic lightheartedness, Stanley, formerly a consultant to American National Bank, is serious about helping the Symphony. "Now and then work in the arts might seem a bit discouraging and uphill, but eventually things come together and it is all worthwhile."

Stanley was the symphony association's treasurer for

Ruth Emerson Stutzman was the cheerful, talented teacher of several generations of art students at Bakersfield High School. She was also a driving force in the formation of the Cunningham Memorial Art Gallery.

FELIX ADAMO/THE CALIFORNIAN

*Chuck Roberson, John Wayne's stuntman for most of the star's career, is the subject of Glennville author Bodie Thoene's book **The Fall Guy**. Roberson raises quarter horses on his ranch south of Bakersfield.*

many years. He currently is secretary and probably does more odd but needed jobs for the symphony than even he can count. Each year a Kern County student's musical career is furthered by a scholarship which Al and his wife, June, established in memory of their daughter.

The son of missionary parents, Stanley was born in China. His woodcarving of the Last Supper graces the altar of Bakersfield's First Congregational Church.

Stine, Earl — Affectionately known as "Uncle Earl," Stine has been one of the backbones of Bakersfield Community Theater for more than 25 years. He has served in every behind-the-scenes role imaginable — from being the treasurer to sweeping out the theater — and has been a cast member in many productions, as well as a director. (At a celebration in 1986 honoring him on his 25th anniversary with BCT, Stine was presented with a director's chair inscribed with his name.) He was instrumental in securing several large grants for the refurbishment of the theater in the 1970s.

Strelich, Alison Nigh — Alison Nigh-Strelich's touching documentary on Bakersfield dance instructors John and Jean Soiu and their work with brain-damaged children and adults was nominated for a 1986 Academy Award. The film is the basis for a planned motion picture starring Dick Van Dyke.

This year, John Soiu received the Beautiful Bakersfield Committee's Humanitarian Award. Alison is married to Tom Strelich, whose play, "Neon Psalms" won first prize in the 1985 CBS/Foundation of the Dramatists Guild New Plays Program. A systems analyst for General Research Corporation in Los Angeles, he is the son of Tom and Virginia Strelich, both of whom are teachers and writers.

Lawrence Tibbett, the son of a Bakersfield sheriff, was a world-renowned baritone with the Metropolitan Opera Company from 1923-50. He also appeared in light opera and films, and on radio and on Broadway.

Stutzman, Ruth Emerson — Several generations of Bakersfield High School art students have benefitted from the teaching of Ruth Emerson Stutzman. A cheery, active person almost until the time of her death at 92 in 1986, and an accomplished painter, she also was instrumental in the formation of Cunningham Memorial Art Gallery.

Thoene, Bodie — Actor John Wayne once said, "Bodie Thoene has that rare kind of talent that captures the people and the times."

The Glennville resident first became acquainted with

171

the "Duke" when she wrote *The Fall Guy,* a biography of Wayne's stuntman, Chuck Roberson, who now lives on his ranch south of Bakersfield. The book later was made into a television series starring Lee Majors.

Bodie recently turned her hand to novel writing. *Gates of Zion* (Bethany Press, 1986) is the first in a planned trilogy. The author got her start as a paid professional at age 14 free-lancing for The Bakersfield Californian and has written for national magazines.

Tibbett, Lawrence — A sell-out crowd greeted Metropolitan Opera star Lawrence Tibbett on his first return to Bakersfield in 1926. David E. Urner who recalled the event 40 years later said the local-boy-who-made-good "lived up to every expectation." Tibbett, a principal baritone with the Met from 1923, when he debuted as Levitzky in "Boris Godunov," until his retirement in 1950, was born in Bakersfield. His birth-

Annual performances at Civic Auditorium of "The Nutcracker," co-produced by dance director Cindy Trueblood and the Bakersfield Symphony, are joyful experiences for scores of aspiring young dancers.

ALAN FERGUSON

place, the site of the present-day Pioneer Nursery, is commemorated by an historical marker.

Tibbett also was popular as a performer in light opera, films, on radio and Broadway, where he appeared in "Fanny" in 1956, four years before his death at age 64. The singer, who added an extra "t" to his name, was the son of Will Tibbet, the deputy sheriff who died in a shoot-out in Bakersfield with James McKinney, an outlaw, in 1903.

de Trevino, Elizabeth Borton — Born in Bakersfield in 1904 and a resident of Mexico since 1935, "Beth" Borton, as she is known to her contemporaries, is the author of 12 books. In 1966 she received a Newbery medal, the highest award in children's literature,

for *I, Juan de Parejo.* The original manuscript of another of her juvenile books, *A Carpet of Flowers,* is held by the Kern County Library. The daughter of attorney Fred Ellsworth Borton, she is the sister of Judge P.R. Borton.

With the simple eloquence so characteristic of all of her writing, Trevino explained her philosophy in a biographical sketch for *Something About the Author:* "I am a profound believer in peace and in all efforts to broaden understanding and love among all peoples, all races, all faiths. In every one of my books ... I trust that the message of love comes through."

Trueblood, Cindy — Co-producer, with the Bakersfield Symphony, of Bakersfield's annual "Nutcracker" ballet, Civic Center Dance Theater director Cindy Trueblood has trained hundreds of young dancers. In addition, she's given them the opportunity, through the "Nutcracker," to perform before audiences of 2,500 or more at the Civic Auditorium.

One of her students, Niklas Zisk, was accepted this year as a student in the Houston Ballet Company's training academy. The 15-year-old Foothill High School student excited Bakersfield Civic Auditorium audiences as the prince in the December 1986 "Nutcracker." His parents are residents of Bear Valley near Tehachapi.

Valente, Benita — Earlier this year, a *New York Times* critic praised Benita Valente as "a rarity among sopranos today."

During an impressive 27-year career — she won the Metropolitan Opera national auditions in 1960 and joined the Met's roster of stars in 1973 — Valente has performed all over the world.

In 1981, when she was guest soloist with the Bakersfield Symphony, Valente received a jubilant homecoming in her native Delano. The community can congratulate itself as well, for it was instrumental in encouraging her career. Delano High School teacher Chester Hayden first recognized Valente's outstanding vocal ability when she was in her junior year; the town's Lions Club provided her with her first scholarship, making it possible for her to study at the National Music Camp at Interlochen, Michigan.

Valente was one of the stars of the gala celebrating the 1986 re-opening of Carnegie Hall. The performance, which included such musical luminaries as Leonard Bernstein, Zubin Mehta and Issac Stern, was presented this year as a two-hour CBS television special.

Walker, Ardis — The 85-year-old poet laureate of the Kern River Valley who sings of the Sierra Nevada, Ardis Walker eloquently puts into words the mystical feelings many of us share about the wilderness — his "constant source of inspiration ... a quiet singing that had gained rootage in my subconscious."

Walker, whose great-uncle was Joseph Walker, the famous scout and explorer, was born in Keyesville in 1901. He pursued, successfully, a career in engineering on the East Coast for a number of years but the call of the wild pulled him inevitably back to his birthplace.

Since his return, Walker has published numerous volumes of poetry, including *Buena Vista*, which is artfully enhanced by Gregory Iger's photographs, and *From Wild Rootage*, highlighted by Roy Purcell's sensitive sketches.

Both the poet and his wife, Gayle, are active environmentalists and act as advisers to the Kern Valley Wildlife Association in its efforts to protect the giant sequoias on the Kern Plateau.

Walker, Marguerite — Retired Cal State Bakersfield art professor Marguerite Walker continues to share her expertise with the community. In 1987, she instructed docents for the Armand Hammer Collection exhibit at the college's Todd Madigan Gallery. Primarily a teacher of art history, Walker first came here as a member of the faculty of Fresno State's Bakersfield Residence Center.

Watkins, Carleton — A masterful 19th century photographer, Carleton Watkins recorded some of the most aesthetically pleasing pictures ever taken of the San Joaquin Valley. His photos illustrated a Kern County Land Company brochure distributed at the Chicago World's Fair in 1893. The booklet was designed to encourage people to buy land in "the greatest irrigated farm in the world."

Ardis Walker, the poet laureate of the Kern River Valley, is an active environmentalist who writes lyrically of the Sierra Nevada. He has published numerous volumes of poetry.

Watkins photographed many California scenes, including some of the earliest ones of Yosemite. The largest collection of his work is in the Library of Congress.

In the 1970s, an 8-inch thick album of his Kern County photos was stolen from the Beale Memorial Library. The theft went unnoticed for some time. The library eventually recovered the historic document when the thief attempted to sell it to the Huntington Library in San Marino, California. Now kept safely in the Beale Library vault, the album's estimated value is $10,000.

Wattron, Frank — Truly a man for all seasons, Frank Wattron's long career in the arts has ranged from acting at the old Pasadena Playhouse to creating metal sculptures, one of which won a first at the 1964 California State Fair. (He learned the techniques of metal work as a welder's helper in the oilfields in the 1930s, while attending Bakersfield College.)

A poet and a playwright, his play, "Green Valley," a charming fantasy originally titled "The Earth of Eldon," debuted in 1948 at Harvey Auditorium under the direction of Bakersfield High School drama teacher Ellen Landes Osborn; Peter Gilli created the imaginative props. Since being published, the play has been produced in all 50 states and in Canada.

Wattron, who has a Ph.D. in drama and speech from the University of Southern California, retired from BC in 1977 as associate dean of instruction. In an interview that year, he philosophically assessed education's role in encouraging the arts:

"Whatever the idea of what college means to a community, the hopes and aspirations of the society toward fulfillment, all that is embodied in education, particularly the liberal arts. It is part of the mystical quality of Western civilization."

Watts, Jane — Through her Poet and Printer Press, Bakersfield College English instructor Jane Watts has published a number of books notable not only for their content but for their quality of design. A fine poet herself, Watts specializes in printing the work of local and regional writers. The pen and ink drawings of BC art professor Al Naso add a humorous and refreshing bit of whimsy to Watts' books.

Winslow, Sylvia — A popular painter of desert scenes, Sylvia Winslow was named founding curator of Ridgecrest's Maturango Museum when it was established in 1962. A wing of the museum's new structure is named for the artist, who now is in her 70s.

She first came here when she and her husband, Slim Winslow, a cowboy, rancher, stunt rider for western movies and an early member of the Screen Actors Guild, homesteaded land in the Kern River Valley. To help pay the bills, and until Slim got a job working for the Navy at China Lake, Sylvia Winslow began painting. Her work has been exhibited at the Los Angeles County Museum of Art and at the Palace of the Legion of Honor in San Francisco.

When disaster struck in the form of a train wreck on March 1, 1960, Marian Bruce, Lucille Garlow, Lucille Snyder, Opal Payne and Ruth Spink were among the American Red Cross workers who responded. The Kern Chapter was chartered in 1918 by the Woman's Club of Bakersfield.

Proudly mounted on their horses, Boy Scout Troop 37 gathered in downtown Bakersfield for this 1927 picture. Although the first council was formed in 1919, Boy Scout activities in Kern County began as early as 1914.

13
Catch the Vision

"From possibility to reality."

Woman's Club of Bakersfield Motto

Kern County's spirit of volunteerism dates back to the days of the first settlers, when helping your neighbor was paramount to survival.

One of the first service organizations in most communities was the volunteer fire department. In Bakersfield, Col. Thomas Baker, the town's founder, maintained a wagon loaded with barrels of water, which he kept near his home at 19th and M streets. The volunteer firefighters among the village's 500 inhabitants sprang into action as soon as they heard the alarm. Instead of a clanging bell, however, the alert was sounded by striking an iron wagon wheel rim — suspended from a tree near Baker's house — with a sledgehammer. For many years the volunteer brigade served as the community's only fire protection.

Organized religion was an important aspect of early life in Kern County. The long and colorful history began when Father Francisco Garces, the second white man to pass through Kern County in 1776, conducted services for the Indians.

The first churches established in Kern County were located in Havilah, the county seat. Services and classes were conducted by a Catholic priest and a Presbyterian minister in 1864 and 1866. Soon afterwards, one of the circuit riders who made regular visits was Father Daniel F. Dade, a 50-year-old priest from Pennsylvania. He later established St. Joseph's Catholic Church in Havilah.

Before a regular minister of the gospel could be found, William Gill Mills, a 44-year-old Havilah storekeeper, conducted Episcopal services in Justice P.T. Colby's courtroom. Later, the Rev. Joseph H. Cornwall, a 35-year-old native of Arkansas, conducted Protestant services.

One of the first churches established in the county was the Cumberland Presbyterian Church, built in 1867 at Glennville.

The first Catholic Mass in Bakersfield was held by Bishop Thaddeus Amat on October 1, 1871, in the Pablo Galtes store. The site of the first Catholic Church in Bakersfield was purchased in November, 1878, at 17th and K streets. Julius Chester, who helped raise money for the community Methodist Church, was on the Catholic Building fund committee. The church was officially made a parish in 1884, headed by Father Patrick M. Bannon.

St. Paul's Episcopal Church was founded in 1879 in Bakersfield under D. O. Kelley. The Rev. H. H. Clapham, rector from 1884 to 1892, was said to be largely responsible for the first church building, erected in 1886 at the corner of 17th and Eye streets.

The Cain African Methodist Episcopal Church was

organized in Bakersfield in 1879. The First Methodist Church was built in 1903 at the corner of Truxtun Avenue and H Street.

Elder J. M. Gilstrap, who practiced dentistry by day and preached at night, launched the First Christian Church in Kern County in 1887. The meetings were conducted in a large tent at the corner of Truxtun Avenue and K Street.

Next to religion, the early citizens of Kern County sought knowledge and culture through educational and literary groups, and brotherhood and support through service, vocational and fraternal organizations.

The first literary association was formed in 1866 in Havilah to provide early Kern residents literary, social and cultural outlets. Known as the Havilah Library Association, the group first met in 1866, in Justice P.T. Colby's office. R. d'Heureuse, C. W. Bush and H. D. Bequette were appointed to draft the by-laws.

J. W. Freeman, who presided over the first meeting, pointed out that such a group would be a "great inducement for many who had no pleasant home firesides." Freeman also noted that the club would form a retreat free from the influence of the "evil doer who stalks abroad, ready to seduce the unwary from the path of morality and usefulness."

Benjamin Brundage, who later was appointed to the Beale Memorial Library Board, was one of several Havilah residents elected to the library association's first governing board.

In 1868 the First Odd Fellows Lodge was established in Havilah.

Four years later, 14 master Masons met in Brundage's office to form a lodge of the Free and Accepted Masons in Bakersfield. Petitioners of the early charter include L.S. Rodgers, S.M. Judd, Oliver T. Chubb, Jacob Weil and William P. McCord. Thomas Baker was a leader in promoting Masonry in Bakersfield as were Alphonse Weill, H.A. Jastro and H. Hirschfeld. The lodge laid the cornerstones of many early buildings, including the first Kern County courthouse.

Mommie Dearest author Christina Crawford, guest speaker at a 1979 joint meeting of Rotary Clubs, is greeted by Owen Goodman, Rev. Jack Peacock, Brad Ritter and Ed Shuler.

In 1894 the women of Kern City, now known as East Bakersfield, formed a library association headed by Mrs. P. Gillespie. A lot on Baker Street was purchased from Dixon Dougherty, and social events were held to raise money for a library. Later that year the men of Kern City asked to join the enterprise, and the Kern Library Association was formed. J. W. Shaffer was elected president. Other officers were Kittie Kennedy, W. V. Matlock, and T. W. Dorgan. In 1896 the association turned its library and reading room over to the city, making Kern City Library the first publicly-supported library in the county.

The Salvation Army was founded in 1890, when Captain T. W. Rees and Lt. G. W. Wade were assigned the task of starting operations. Today the corps has more than 200 soldiers. The Salvation Army has always been on hand whenever disaster has struck in the community, as evidenced at the time of the 1952 earthquake.

The Bakersfield Elks Lodge 266 was chartered in 1894. The first exalted ruler was F. Cook Caldwell, a Bakersfield physician. The Bakersfield Aerie No. 93 Fraternal Order of Eagles was established in 1900. Early leaders included Fred Gunther and Henry A. Jastro.

Following World War I, the Frank S. Reynolds Legion Post was formed. Thomas W. McManus was the first commander.

The Legion's Cecil Thompson Post No. 63 of Fellows was organized in 1919, largely through the efforts of Thomas L. Cavett.

From these roots, today the vision of volunteerism expresses itself in more than 1,500 non-profit organizations county-wide. Fifty percent of the county population volunteers at least three hours per week.

The County of Kern uses volunteers through the Probation Department and the Department of Human Services. Helen Rurup, volunteer coordinator, speaks with great love and affection about Goldie Whitley, Erv Sasman, Gail Paap, Patti Reed, Lucile Wake, Rosalyn Strauss, Frances Holmes, Mae Nix and all the many other people who volunteer through foster families, A. Miriam Jamison Children's Center, Friendly Visitors, Special Friends and Transportation Aids. Others do clerical work or help in implementing programs. Annually the department presents the Love Award to signify the meaning of being a volunteer. The 1987 recipient is Betty Newman.

This chapter represents a sampling of those who have "caught the vision" and will pass that vision on to future generations. All volunteers in Kern County know that the past creates a fertile future when vision and charity merge.

Alliance on Family Violence — The Alliance on Family Violence was founded in 1979 by a group of therapists who recognized the plight of battered women and sought to provide them with counseling, shelter and educational services.

The Alliance has grown from a single dwelling providing services to six individuals to a four-unit complex serving 24 individuals. Most recently, a Family Counseling Service Center has begun providing preventive treatment for women, men, children, families and couples. Mae Stewart and Jo An Jones worked as agency directors for the first two years.

Many individuals are involved in making this organization a success. Jeri Voge and Gay Lynne Natho, attorneys, have given great insight into the legalities for advocating change, both in our local District Attorney's office and in Sacramento.

Today, the Alliance has an active board of directors whose 1986 president is Anne Hutton. Through funds secured by the Office of Criminal Justice Planning, the Alliance has developed a Rural Outreach Program for battered women, providing service in Taft, Tehachapi, Kernville, Lake Isabella and Frazier Park. Karla Necessary has single-handedly gone into these communities, bridging the gap between service and the isolated battered woman.

Trish Joslin started with the Alliance in the summer of 1982 as a volunteer and six months later became the shelter coordinator. Joslin has personally touched the lives of more than 4,000 women and children.

American Cancer Society — The Kern Unit of the American Cancer Society was begun in 1951. The founders included Phil Pifer, Barbara Shields, Hugh Jewett, John Wilt, Gladys McKee and Dr. Lucille B. May. The unit covers the entire geographical area of Kern County with specific branch activities in Arvin (Corinne Cattani), Delano (Helen Cole), and Ridgecrest (Rose Varga).

Several individuals have "made history" in the Kern Unit. They include: Dr. May, whose efforts began the Reach to Recovery Visitor program; Gladys McKee, who got the "Free Wheelers" program off the ground; Hugh Jewett, a prime mover from the beginning, went on to become the California Division's first president. Jon Van Boening served as the California Division fund-raising chairman for 1984-86. Van Boening is a founding member of Couples Against Cancer. Connie Frasch organized the fund-raising effort that resulted in the Kern Unit being the first in California to own its own building. Frasch also motivated members to start the Discovery Shop, the unit's thrift store. Others include: Elizabeth Bell, Kern Unit executive director for more than 10 years; Helen Weill, first representative director to the California Division Board; Curt Carter, instrumental in getting the Kern Unit building; Helen Cole, branch chairperson in Delano for nearly 35 years; Corinne Cattani, who has chaired the Arvin branch for 35 years. Rose Varga, "Mrs. Volunteer" in Ridgecrest, has headed that branch for the last five years. Dr. and Mrs. Daiber were originally very active in service to cancer patients in Ridgecrest; Marge Daiber has been in charge of all the memorials in the Ridgecrest area for the past several years.

American Heart Association — John Cove, the director, believes in reaching out to the community through education to teach people the causes of cardiovascular disease and the ways individuals can protect

their own health. Members of the first board of directors in 1953 were Drs. Ralph Burnett, Marion Barnard, L. N. Osell, Jack Hayes, Richard Dickmann, Robert Scherb, Juliet Thorner, James Stanton, R. T. Cunningham, and attorney V. P. DiGiorgio.

Most recently Diana Mestmaker, whom Cove calls "a dynamite woman," has spearheaded the Dance For Heart fund-raiser, which this year netted $30,000.

Dr. Neil Arbegast has been a prominent force in the creation of Mended Hearts, a support group for heart surgery patients. Arbegast, along with Dr. Bruce Frazier, Dr. William Schmalhorst, Allen McGinnis and Ann Gutcher, was instrumental in the early 1960s in forming a funding committee that ensures continued financial stability of the Heart Association. Gutcher went on to represent the chapter at the state level.

Barbara Logan, Margaret Pryor, Dr. Craig Saunders and Dr. Owen Haig led the way in advancing several projects. Harvey Hall developed the CPR program; Marilyn Arbegast mobilized the volunteer bank.

In 1985, a branch of the chapter was started in Ridgecrest by Dr. Robert Jones, who now serves on the state board. The 1987 president of the Ridgecrest chapter is Dr. Dan Kus.

American Indian Council —Since its beginnings in 1977, the American Indian Council's primary goal has

Youngsters learn about health education from such American Cancer Society volunteers as Carrie Kirschenman Camp. The Kern Unit allocates 23 percent of its budget for educational outreach.

been to coordinate programs to meet the health, cultural and community needs of the American Indian. According to John Feliz, director since 1978, Kern County has more than 160 tribes represented in this council. Feliz has spoken twice before the Senate Select Subcommittee on Indian Affairs. He says, "The United States government has had 18 treaties with the Indian Tribes and refused to ratify any of them." One quarter of the national Indian population is in California.

Ernie Albitre, Ron Lopez, Carmen Peebles and Joaquin Aguerria were movers behind the growth and development of the board of directors. Wadie Johnson, a

Cherokee who lost his leg in Okinawa, is considered an inspiration for the group.

Dr. Homer Montalvo of Cal State Bakersfield set up an aviation program for Indian children to build character and self-esteem. One of Montalvo's students, Patricia Guerrero, 15 when she started the program, is now putting herself through Cal State by working as a commercial pilot for Sierra Flite Service.

American Lung Association — The purpose of the American Lung Association of Kern County is to prevent and control lung disease. The organization is dedicated to eliminating smoking by the year 2000, and, in addition, plays an active role in improving air quality in Kern County.

Dr. Tom Larwood has been a leader in the American Lung Association of Kern County (formerly National Tuberculosis Association) for many years. Larwood, known as a "gem" in the association for his volunteer work, guided many of the group's education projects, such as the migrant health program. He is also active in valley fever research. According to Larwood, much of his time was spent in attempting to prevent consolidation of the Kern County office with other state and national offices. As a result of the efforts of Larwood and others, the Kern County office has maintained its own branch.

J.W. Freeman pointed out that the club would form a retreat free from the influence of the "evil doer who stalks abroad, ready to seduce the unwary from the path of morality and usefulness."

Ann Farrell's past work with the association shows the great spirit of volunteerism. In November of 1981, Farrell walked through the door of the association's office to make a donation, encountered the new "part-time" director hopelessly submerged in enough full-time work for three people, and made a commitment to the organization. She threw herself into association work, sometimes working 25 to 30 hours a week as a volunteer. Farrell maintains her California license, although retired from her 28-year position as a supervising public health nurse at the Kern County Health Department.

Arthritis Association — In 1981 Dode Perrin and Irene Sorenson formed the cluster group that established the Arthritis Association. Perrin became the first director; Sorenson, the administrative assistant. The first president was Jere Sullivan Jr. Members of the first board of directors included Hazel Reed, Lee Sattley, Dr. Martin Berry, Barry McCown, Bill Lazzerini Sr. and Jacque Parish. This team laid the foundation for an organization "dedicated to improving the quality of life for those living with arthritis."

Virginia Miller, a past president and current advisor to the board, has been one of its guiding lights, along with Jim Banducci, affectionately called "the godfather" by the association staff.

Judy Combs, current director, initiated the innovative "Buy A Guy Bachelor Auction", held in June of this year. Brave souls who placed themselves on the auction block included Tom Coleman, Woody Bryant, Hale Costerisan, Tom Fallgatter, Joey Garza, Frank Gipson, Tom McCormick, Loren Stroope and Art Rockoff. Russ Allen acted as auctioneer.

The association hopes to construct a therapeutic pool available for use by arthritis sufferers as well as victims of cystic fibrosis, strokes, the visually and hearing impaired, multiple sclerosis and other maladies. Beverly Steveson recently donated $100,000 to begin the drive to raise $450,000 for the project.

Assistance League — In 1956, Ruth Ann Montgomery, teaching school in Kern County, became aware that some children were not attending classes because they had no clothes to wear. She decided to do something about it. She began by collecting clothes and passing them out to the children. Then, Wini Davis joined Montgomery in the effort and Diane Adams donated her garage to store the clothes. And thus was born the Assistance League of Bakersfield and its main project, Operation School Bell, so named by Wini's husband, Tom Davis. In 1959 the local league became affiliated with the National Assistance League. Now 24 other chapters nationwide have opened projects based on "Operation School Bell." Today, the league clothes 2,500 children annually through their thrift store called Bargain Box.

Mary Ann Boynton was the first president of the Assistance League auxiliary, Ayudantes, (helping hands) started in 1970. The group of young mothers have as their main project the "Country Fair." The funds they raise provide hygiene kits for children.

In 1984, a second auxiliary, Las Amigas was formed with Ann Greenberg as first chairperson. Composed of people who work more than 20 hours per week, this organization acts as a funding arm for Assistance League. Dorothy Neuman and Genevieve Craig were the founders.

Current president of Assistance League, June Laramore, speaks with great pride about the organization. "Bargain Box started out in the back of a filling station at California and O streets in 1959." Now 80 active women keep this organization busy at their large headquarters, 1216 O Street.

Bakersfield Community House — This project began in 1959 under Junior League president Mary Lou Raney, with headquarters on Truxtun Avenue. One of the many early supporters of Community House was

To meet a critical need in the community, Dodie Perrin and Irene Sorensen formed the group that launched the Arthritis Association. Perrin retired as executive director in 1986 and now lives in Carpinteria.

Henry Brandt. Brandt offered to match the Junior League's $25,000 for the construction of a building. Hugh Jewett donated $5,000, and $20,000 came from the Arkelian Foundation. On March 3, 1966, the new building, located in Central Park, was dedicated and given to the city to be run by a community board of directors. The first board president was Richard Frasch.

Bob Spawn, involved from the beginning of Community House, has contributed to the organization's funding foundation.

Arline Pratt and Barbara Macnair became the angels of Community House with their tireless work on the bazaar. Held annually at the holiday season, this event now nets approximately $20,000 per year.

Today, Community House provides its 560 members with a variety of programs. As Avery Allen has said so many times, "It's a place to go and something to do when you get there".

Beautiful Bakersfield Committee — To help create a more positive image of her city, then-mayor Mary K. Shell encouraged the formation of the Beautiful Bakersfield Committee in 1982. Bob Clerico, the first president, headed a board that included Graham Kaye-Eddy, Stella McMurtrey and Romayne McMahan. Bettie Howell subsequently served two terms as president and was instrumental in the committee's growth and development.

Over the past five years, the committee has taken a leading role in encouraging beautification projects. Its major event is the annual awards dinner. Jan Duncan, who has been involved since the beginning and served as president in 1986-87, chaired the first dinner. (William Helms is the current president.) The awards are given in 14 categories to honor individuals, organizations and businesses whose efforts have helped improve the community and its image.

In November 1986, Duncan, representing Beautiful Bakersfield, and Jim Turner, lieutenant governor of Kiwanis Division 33, cochaired the benefit opening of J.C. Penney's new store in Valley Plaza. The department store split the $20,000 proceeds from the event between the A. Miriam Jamison Children's Center, where the Kiwanis Clubs are developing a park, and California Living Museum.

National Association of Colored Women's Club — Formed nationally in 1776 by an Act of Congress, this organization was the first in the world organized to help educate blacks, men as well as women, so that they could enter the mainstream of society. California's central district has eight clubs - two in Hanford, two in Fresno, and one each in Delano, Wasco, Bakersfield and Barstow. The Bakersfield organization was founded in 1906.

Lena Jones from Delano developed the education program and helped sponsor scholarship programs for young people in the Delano-McFarland area. In Bakersfield, Katherine Smith has been active in program development and education. The National Association of Colored Women's Club is the oldest black organization in Kern County.

Boys and Girls Club of Bakersfield — The Boys and Girls Club of Bakersfield was incorporated in 1966. Brent McClanahan is the current director.

The club's parent organization, Boys Club of America, was headed originally by former President Herbert Hoover. The local club, at 800 Monterey Street, serves 1,400 boys and girls, aged 6 to 18, yearly. Its aim is to develop strength of character and good citizenship through social, cultural, recreational, physical and educational programs.

Carol Lee is one of the many volunteers who give their time to the Bargain Box, the Assistance League's thrift shop.

179

Founders of the club were David S. Fairbairn, who then was chairman of the Board of Supervisors, Otto Olofson and Thomas W. Curran. Hired as director was Nello Panelli. The original board also included Manuel Ruiz, Robert Lumis, George Lusich and Harold Moore.

In 1984, the Boys Club of Bakersfield organized "Run To The Torch," which kicked off a two-day run from Bakersfield through western Kern County into Paso Robles to meet the official Olympic Torch Relay enroute to Los Angeles for the opening ceremonies of the XXIII Olympiad. Participants included Mary K. Shell, Leonard Anaya, Brian Jones, Laurie Kempen, Aurin Lahiri, Tim Lemucchi, Ray Maranda, Chris Meeks and Trish Reynolds. Brian Jones represented Taft and ran the torch into the King City area.

Bernice Harrell Chipman Winners

Ovillah Hort	1967
Gladys McKee	1968
Faye Gribble	1969
Dorothy Taber	1970
Sunny Scofield	1971
Ella Surgener	1972
Adeline Frasch	1973
Marge McCoy	1974
Bessie Rose	1975
Maggie King	1976
Belle Ruppe	1977
Helen Trammel	1978
Leta Buerkle	1979
Goldie Loveland	1980
Sibyl Koontz	1981
Stella McMurtrey	1982
Nellis Johnson	1983
Louise Henderson	1984
Lenna Jennings	1985
Alberta Dillard	1986

Alfred Harrell Man of the Year Award Winners

Norman Crouse	1984
Dr. Joseph Anderson	1985
Fred Dukes	1986

Boy Scouts of America — Southern Sierra Council — In March, 1914, L. S. Robinson organized Troop 1, the first troop in the council and possibly the first troop in California. One of the first scoutmasters was Arthur J. Myer. Some of the Scouts from this early troop still residing in this area are Orville Colburn, Henry Mack and Harold Owens.

In 1919 a group met to organize the Bakersfield Council, which, in 1922, was to become the Kern County Council.

During the 1920s, Scout troops were formed in Taft, Delano, Wasco, and other communities, involving approximately 450 boys. W. J. Schultz was the first council president; and Roland Dye, the first Scout executive. In 1952 the council built its present office at 2417 M Street. Inyo and Mono counties became part of the council; in 1965, the name was changed to Southern Sierra Council.

California Living Museum — CALM is a concept of environmental education that combines botanical gardens, zoos and natural history with emphasis on plants and animals native to California. CALM began in 1976 as the vision of one person, Michael D. Hopkins. In early 1979, the board of directors was formed with Dr. Thomas H. Banks as president. The remainder of the board consisted of Frank Ghezzi, Louise Henderson, Frank Rosenlieb, Vicki Araujo, Mel Ashland, James Barton, Dale Bender, Shannon Blackburn, Marzee Cunningham, Jack Hundley, Don Fritts, Robert Hutchinson, Lenna Jennings, Adele Nickel, Susan Maitia, Fred McAtee, Kay Meek and Faye Walters. The Junior League of Bakersfield developed a docent program at CALM, coordinated by Ann Wright and Dolores Hoffman. Its first members included Sandy Banducci, Kathy Clark, Shirley Clerou, Florine Davis, Constance Dickson, Lou Evans, Lani Gianquinto, Kathy Hannah, Claudia Keith, Mary Lewis, Susan Maitia, Mary Moreland, Brenna O'Meara, Ilene O'Neil, Judy Reed, Elaine Thomson, Jan Thomson, Ruth Thrasher, and Susan Weaver. Lars Helgeson, a science coordinator for the Kern County Superintendent of Schools, worked with Laura Stockton, Laurie Brooks, Bob Schneider, and Ron Hughes to provide instructional materials for the program.

In 1982 Ginny and Wayne Kirschenmann donated the old DiGiorgio home to CALM. The two-story structure is being refurbished for use as an education facility. The estimated cost of the remodeling, $180,000, has been significantly reduced, thanks to the support of the community.

Director Kevin Hunting says, "CALM would not be in existence were it not for the literally thousands of volunteers and supporters of the new museum." These include the Bakersfield Rotary Club, Kiwanis Clubs, the Junior League and countless individuals.

Camp Fire Council of Kern County — Camp Fire provides opportunities for young people which help them realize their potential so they can function effectively as caring, self-directed individuals responsible for themselves. Its programs respond to the needs and interests of boys and girls up to age 21. These include club membership, camping and outdoor activities, guidance in self-reliance and child care facilities.

Nationally, Camp Fire was organized in 1910. (Its motto, Wo-He-Lo, combines the first letters of "work, health, love.") Viola Blodget served as the first leader of the Kern group, which began in 1915 and received its national charter in 1929. Eldora De Mot was the first director of the summer camp, organized in 1924. (From 1927 to 1980, the council used Camp Yenis Hante for its summer programs.)

The council was incorporated in 1939, during Mrs. A.C. Dimon's presidency. In the next 20 years, the organization would be guided by such leaders as Helen

Weill, Gene Winer and Jim Burke. Jeanne Glascock organized the group's 50th anniversary celebration. A totem pole was erected at Pioneer Village as a part of the commemoration.

School principal Margaret Dennis helped establish the Metropolitan Area's Project, which brought the Camp Fire program to girls in low-income areas. Student teachers were recruited and trained to supervise the youngsters' activities. Marge Sugden ably served the council as executive director from 1967 to 1984.

Harold Matlock, a dedicated volunteer who served for 25 years on the board of directors, including a term as president, was honored with the Gulick Award, the highest honor Camp Fire can give to an adult. In 1975, boys were added to the Camp Fire program, and it became the country's largest co-educational organization.

Chicanos Unidos For Progress — Started at Bakersfield College campus under Ruben Imperial, this group was formed as a coalition in 1971 to look at the educational needs of the Chicano at Bakersfield College. In 1978-79 Chicanos Unidos For Progress was reorganized into a separate entity whose goal was to increase the educational and cultural awareness of Mexican-Americans. Manuel Gonzalez was instrumental in arranging applications and programs for scholarship recipients. Duane Gulf and Ernie Patino were involved in the formation of CUP. Patino, originally from Lamont, organized MECHA at Arvin High School. John Ortiz has been active in promoting the traditional celebration of the 16th of September, Mexican Independence Day.

CUP has long been a clearing house for information concerning the Hispanic community. Strong support for the organization came from Ann Valez of Lamont, Ray Gonzalez and Fred Munoz.

In the early 1970s Julian Filoteo developed the idea of Project Adobe. This house, built at Pioneer Village

Bakersfield attorney Bruce Bunker, shown here at a 1968 awards presentation, is a long-time supporter of Camp Fire.

TOM JADWIN

with volunteer labor, is used to display the historical background of the Hispanic community.

Child Guidance Clinic — The Henrietta Weill Memorial Child Guidance Clinic provides mental health treatment and prevention services to children and families in Kern County. In 1946, Blanche and Irma Weill founded the clinic as a tribute to their late mother. The Weill sisters were graduates of Kern County Union High School and the University of California, and their level of advanced education was unusual for the time. Blanche received a doctorate from Harvard and Irma received her master's degree from Smith College.

In the early 1950s, Dr. Antonio Perelli-Minetti Jr. acted as the first medical director of the clinic, working for five years as a volunteer. In 1986, the clinic set up the Blanche and Irma Weill Award for outstanding contribution to the emotional well-being of Kern County's children. The first recipient was Margaret Gannon, followed in 1986-87 by Bonnye Deal.

The clinic is funded in part through its auxiliary group, Child Guidance Guild, founded in 1958 by Charlotte Ramirez. To provide a more stable source of income for the clinic, the group opened the Guild House in 1963 on Chester Avenue and later moved to its present location, the elegant Barlow house where Guild members serve gourmet lunches. Since its founding, 200 Guild women have raised a total of $500,000 for the clinic.

The Delano Guild was started in 1960. First president was Georgann Perelli-Minetti. In 1986, during Jana Campbell's presidency, the Delano Guild contributed $24,000 to the clinic.

The initial support for the clinic came from such volunteers as Mrs. Hugh Nation, Hazel McCuen, Margaret Gannon, Dr. Thomas Reese, Bonnye Deal, Senator and Mrs. Walter Stiern, Robert Strauss, J. K. Thrasher, Milton and Betty Younger, J. M. Sudarsky, Judge Gerald Davis, Glen Brown, Dr. John Almklov, Millie Ablin, Carol Sharpe, Harry Chicklenis and Dr. Joseph Nunez, who served as president in 1986.

Children's Home Society of California — Children's Home Society of California was founded in 1891 by Dr. and Mrs. J. R. Townsend, medical missionaries whose only child had died in Jamaica. The San Joaquin Valley District, with its headquarters in Bakersfield, was established in 1947. Ann Smart, director of voluntary services, says, "The society serves as an endearing, enduring advocate of the rights of all children through public education and information."

Two group homes in the Bakersfield area focus on special needs of children with mental disabilities: Camino Primavera is a home for adolescents classified as mildly retarded or educationally handicapped; Eisenhower Street houses an older group of teenagers who are mildly or moderately retarded. Each residence can accept up to six children. Each child has an individual program plan which is reviewed monthly.

Don M. Mitchell is the San Joaquin Valley's district director, and Raymond Duquette is chairman of the district board. Gordon Turl served this year as Bakersfield area president.

Children's Home Society relies greatly on its volunteers, such as Nancy Carr, Susan Christiansen and Lou May, president of the San Joaquin council of auxiliaries.

Through a contract with the Kern Regional Center, approximately 250 children and their families are served by the society's social workers.

Community Action Against Drug and Alcohol Abuse — CAADA is a non-profit organization concerned about the increase in drug and alcohol use among our youth. The organization developed from "the chemical people", a nationwide outreach program dealing with school-age drug and alcohol abuse.

CAADA cooperates with schools, community agencies and young people to create an atmosphere in which the use of drugs and alcohol is no longer the social norm.

In March of 1985, a group of four students — Steve Cochran, Amy McMurtrey, Michele Herrington, and Rick Adams — returned from a conference in San Diego and developed STAND, a peer group whose goal is to prevent substance abuse, suicide, and other problems by increasing each student's self-awareness and ability to be socially responsible.

Diane Sellers has been the driving force behind the formation of CAADA. She now serves on the California Board for Drug-Free Youth, and she is also an advisor to STAND. Susan Peebles is the 1986-87 president of CAADA.

Community Connection for Child Care — Community Connection for Child Care, originally the Child Care information Service, was established in 1978 as a result of a community conference at Bakersfield College, which identified the need for a central clearinghouse to disseminate child care services information. The agency was a vision of Carol Sharpe, then the chair of the Family and Consumer Education Department at Bakersfield College. (Barbara Hoyt, Share's predecessor, had been the department's guiding force for many years.) She continues to be an active member of the advisory council and a representative of the community on state committees related to child care services. A CETA (Comprehensive Education and Training Act) grant provided start-up monies.

In 1980, the agency was funded by the California State Department of Education, Office of Child Development. The original purpose of the Child Care Information Service was to encourage and support parental choice in the selection of child care services. The philosophy was and continues to be that all children have the right to adequate and safe care, and that it is the responsibility of parents to determine their family's needs. Under the direction of Sharron Goldstein, in the first years of operation, the agency provided information regarding available licensed child care for working parents. It also developed a consumer guide for selecting quality care and started a toy lending library. Under the auspices of Bakersfield College, monthly seminars were developed for child care centers. Other programs are Respite Care, Employer - Supported Child Care, Phone Friend, Alternative Payment, Child Care Employment Fund, and others.

By 1984 the agency, which had grown to six employ-

ees and was logging 250 requests per month, opened an office in Ridgecrest. The following year, Wendy Wayne became the director and the agency began serving Inyo and Mono counties. Today, the agency serves Kern, Inyo and Mono counties from five offices located in Bakersfield, Ridgecrest, Bishop and Mammoth Lake. Funding sources include county, state, federal grants, and private foundation money.

The agency now receives approximately 400 requests for child care referrals and responds to almost 2,000 calls per month.

Community Connection has received continual support and guidance from an advisory council comprised of 24 community members. Diane Hendrickson has chaired the council for the last two years. She is also the director of the Cal State Bakersfield Children's Center.

Girl Scouts - Joshua Tree Council — Prior to 1947, the Girl Scouts in the Bakersfield area consisted of several lone troops meeting independently from the national organization, Girl Scouts of the U.S.A. In 1947 the Bakersfield council of Girl Scouts was formed.

Nadine Kennedy, who worked as a volunteer, coordinated and delivered program services to troops through a growing network of volunteers. The council's mem-

---

One of Montalvo's students, Patricia Guerrero, is now putting herself through Cal State by working as a commercial pilot for Sierra Flite Service.

---

bership rapidly grew, and professional staff was hired in 1950.

Girl Scouts' growing interest in outdoor camping led the council to enlist the aid of the Kiwanis Club of Bakersfield to explore the possibility of establishing a resident camp. Under the leadership of Clyde Trammel and William Patton, the Kiwanis located a site in the Greenhorn Mountains, and 305 volunteer workers were recruited to help construct and finance Camp Mountain Meadows.

In January 1954 the Bakersfield council merged with Girl Scout councils from Taft, Indian Wells Valley and several other small communities to form Girl Scouts — Kern County Council. Construction on the camp began in May with all materials and labor donated. The camp was opened in July. Eighty girls and 19 staff attended camp that first summer.

The council continued to grow and was renamed Girl Scouts - Joshua Tree Council, symbolizing the numerous Joshua Trees found throughout the desert regions. "To date, the council, spanning 16,000 square miles, remains one of the fastest-growing councils in the world's largest organization for girls and women with membership rising to 5,800 for girls, and 2,800 for adults," says Mary Pagliaro, 1986 president of the board of directors. Executive director is Joan McDonald.

For the Girl Scouts' 75th Anniversary in 1987, the council's activities included an open house at its new service center, with desserts made from Girl Scout Cookies by local members of Chefs de Cuisine of Greater Bakersfield.

Golden Empire Gleaners — The Gleaners was founded in February 1985, by a group including Patrick Haenelt, Gordon Fisher, John E. "Jack" Hunt and Jerry Todd. The Gleaners' purpose is to help alleviate hunger in Kern County by working through 90 agencies and 150 volunteers. John P. Lynch, the president, says the organization strives to avoid wastage of food. "We must use the surplus to feed the hungry. No one should go without food in this county." Father Craig O'Neill has given great encouragement to the organization. Myrtle Bauchman, Lena Cherry and Cliff Beecher are three of the many indispensible volunteers. More than 65,000 pounds of food per month are being distributed, according to Lynch. The Gleaner's 1987 budget is $160,000.

Haven Counseling Center/Kern Child Abuse Prevention Council — Origins of the current Kern Child Abuse Prevention Council and Haven Counseling Center date to March 2, 1973, when "The Battered Child Sub-Committee" of the Family and Children's Advisory Committee to the Kern County Welfare Department (now Human Services) was formed. The committee's objectives included the provision of maximum protection under the law to abused children and the framing of legislation to change California law regarding children's dependency. Approximately 20 individuals - including Welfare Department and law enforcement representatives, as well as court and hospital personnel, participated in this committee. At first, the group focused primarily on legislative and medical issues.

In January 1978, Al Marquam was hired by the Welfare Department to serve as administrative assistant to the committee. Later that year, the committee's name was changed to the Kern Child Abuse Prevention Council.

One year later, attendance at council meetings had increased to well over 100 people. By October, discussions were underway to merge with another corporation, Kern Haven, Inc., to co-sponsor Haven House.

At the same time that KCAPC was underway, a group of community people with similar goals was striving to establish Haven House, which was incorporated in 1978. The first board of directors was led by president Betty Wickersham. Other members included William Rasmussen, Charlotte Vaughan, Josie Koelzer, Roy Dull, Carolyne Edmondson, Jeanne Anderson, Wendy Wayne, Dr. Juliet Thorner, Mary Brooks, Margaret Ireton, Neil Koenig, Bill Stone, Sharron Wennihan, Terri Jamieson, Barbara Jewett, Lani Smith, Charlotte Brandt, Staci Apsit, Mary Anne Fritts, Gary Olson, Claude Bentz, Earle Gibbons and Marilyn Coleman.

In January of 1979, the group moved to 217 H Street, their first of many residences. Funding from the United Way began in 1981.

When Haven House moved to 730 Chester Avenue in December of 1984, its name was changed to Haven Counseling Center. The building was purchased by Kern County Community Development. Mona Covey served as president in 1986-1987.

Junior League of Bakersfield — The Junior League is an international organization of women committed to promoting volunteerism and to improving the community through educational and charitable action. The organization was started as the Community League in 1952 by Elizabeth Lewis and Ann Sacre, assisted by Barbara Thrasher Robesky, Reba Green, Elizabeth Grant Reynolds, Allison Sedgewick, Isabel Taylor, Barbara Jones and Dorothy Jameson.

Reba Green served as the first president with an initial membership of fifty. Elizabeth Lewis, Ann Sacre and Patricia Rieber made up the executive committee.

In 1965 under the presidency of Kay Sherman, the Community League was accepted as the 207th member League in the Association of Junior Leagues.

Today, the Junior League has 400 members. More than one million volunteer hours have been given to the community. The League has supported agencies and organizations with monies totaling well over $500,000.

Well-known for its fund-raising abilities, the League has launched many creative events over its 35-year history. With the funds raised, the League is able to develop, implement and fund community projects formed and staffed by Junior League volunteers. These projects are eventually turned over to other community boards.

Kern County Cystic Fibrosis — Kern County Cystic Fibrosis was formed by Tom and Gail Burch after the birth of their daughter, Heidi. Unable to get any

Celebrating the 37th anniversary of Girl Scouts in 1949, members donned international costumes.

GIRL SCOUTS — JOSHUA TREE COUNCIL

183

information from the National Cystic Fibrosis Organization, they decided to make sure no other family would have to live without the information they felt they needed.

Tom Burch says, "Kern County Cystic Fibrosis, along with its affiliation with the National Cystic Fibrosis Foundation, continues to strive for enough money to make doctors want to work on a cure for our disease. In 1980, the total budget for the national organization was $3 million. Now it requires $8 million just to keep the research programs going."

Kern County Cystic Fibrosis first raised funds — $4,000 — in 1977, in a bike-a-thon which had only 50 participants.

The Burches have been the mainstays of the local organization, co-ordinating all fund-raising events. They also have been active in public information activities.

The single most supportive group for KCCF has been the Bakersfield Active 20-30 club, which over the years has helped raise more than $30,000. Also, they have provided camperships and transportation for some of the local cystic fibrosis children who otherwise would not have had the opportunity to go to summer camp, an experience which is the highlight of the year for most of the youngsters.

Kern County Society for Crippled Children and Adults — The Society for Crippled Children and Adults of Kern County was founded in 1947 by the Bakersfield Rotary Club. The Kern County Shrine Club and the Kern County Chapter of the National Foundation of Infantile Paralysis also gave funds to start the society.

Henry Eissler was the first president; other officers included H.O. Westbay, Doyle Miller and Walter L. Thornton. Guy Greenlee is the current president, succeeding H. Russell Taylor, who served for 15 years.

One of the society's volunteers, Pauline Heimforth, has worked six hours each week for the past four years. Her husband, Glenn Heimforth, also served for many years.

The society provides four community programs: speech therapy, equipment loans, summer camp for orthopedically-handicapped and hearing-impaired children, and transportation funds to out-of-town medical facilities.

The society receives funding from businesses, clubs, organizations, individuals and United Way.

Kern Eye Foundation Eye Bank — The Kern Eye Foundation, incorporated in 1966, obtains, preserves and transports eyes so that eye surgeons can perform corneal transplants. The Kern Eye Bank acts as a depository of consent forms for people who wish to donate other organs for transplant.

Agnes Herren, the executive director since 1966, says strong support has been provided by Dr. David Evans, Dr. Gregory Stainer, (the medical director), Dr. Hosein Mohammadi, as well as by Harold Nelson, Joseph "Bud" Scott, Gene Truax, Joseph Giuffre, Dr. Ron Morton and Dale Anderson.

Mercy Hospital has provided space and equipment for the Eye Bank. Sister Phyllis Hughes, the hospital's

At a benefit for the Kern Child Abuse Prevention Council held in 1987 at Rio Bravo Tennis Ranch, Norma Peal welcomed actress Karen Black, guest speaker

WINI DAVIS

chief executive officer, is outstanding in supporting the foundation's efforts, as is Sister Placida.

Financing of the Kern Eye Bank's corneal tissue to recipients is provided through memorial donations and gifts from corporations and other organizations. Soroptimist International of Bakersfield has long been a strong donor.

Vision screening, glaucoma screening and counseling are provided on request. More than 1,500 school children are screened for vision problems each year.

La Loma Council — The Council was organized to serve the Mexican American community through outreach and educational programs that help build social and cultural awareness within the La Loma community.

Augie Flores, the first Hispanic employed by the county Probation Department, maintains an excellent rapport within the community.

La Loma Council president Rosie Negrete oversees programs ranging from food giveaways and immigration services to agency and service referrals. Connie Nieto is the current KCEOC outreach advisor.

Others actively involved with the Council are Al De La Rosa, Frank Espinosa and Ken Garcia.

Lori Brock Children's Museum — Lori Brock Children's Museum was an outgrowth of a program started in Arvin in 1955 by Margaret Ann Frick. Desiring for her own children more enrichment opportunities than were available at the time, she organized the Saturday Adventurers program, a series of educational programs given by volunteers who were highly qualified in the fields of art, science and the humanities.

This idea met with such success that Frick approached the Junior League of Bakersfield (at that time known as the Community League) to sponsor additional groups to make similar experiences available to children. Ultimately many hundreds of children were en-

Junior League of Bakersfield sustainer Mary Wakefield coordinated one of the clinics for children at the Avon Futures Tennis Tournament. The 1980 event at Laurel Glen Tennis Club was sponsored by the Junior League.

rolled throughout Bakersfield in a series of learning activities.

The success of the Saturday multi-subject programs spawned the organization of additional groups in the areas of art, literature and music. The idea was to show that learning could be an adventure, and more effective when instruction was coupled with hands-on experiences. The feasibility of a facility which could expand these experiences was explored by the Junior League. Key figures in the Museum Development Committee were Mary Smith, Dorothy Ernst and Ken Secor. A leading factor in the acquisition of funds was the generosity of John Brock, Sr., who donated the proceeds from the opening of his Valley Plaza store and the downtown store Bicentennial Party. The remainder of funds came from donations by the Junior League and the community at large.

The development committee requested permission from the Brock family to name the museum in honor of their daughter, Lori, who had been killed in an automobile accident in 1972.

The dream became reality when on October 6, 1976, the building, built by contractor Fred Macomber and designed by Leonard Schroeder, was dedicated. Carol Jones served as the first president of the new Lori Brock Junior Museum board.

The museum has gained a reputation among educators for quality enrichment experiences, resulting in a capacity school tour program.

Instrumental in this growth was Barbara Jewett, who volunteered early, then became coordinator of children's activities, and finally executive director.

The museum added to its physical plant in 1987, thanks to grants from several civic organizations and foundations.

Mexican-American Opportunity Foundation — Founded in 1963, this agency serves the economically disadvantaged and unskilled through education and training. "We train thousands of individuals, regardless of age, sex or ethnic background. Working with a string of agencies as a cohesive unit, we strive to place individuals in the labor market," says Richard Prado, the director.

Clients are referred through Employers Training Resource by its director, Tim Christensen, and Pete Parra, assistant director.

MAOF target groups are the unskilled, drug and alcohol abusers, the handicapped, senior citizens, and those with no past work experience.

Lupe Alamaraz served as board chairman this year.

Muscular Dystrophy Association — MDA's purpose is to allow the muscular dystrophy patient to live life to the fullest. A current goal is to develop a clinic

Junior League Projects 1952-1987

Symphony Forums
Handicapped Girl Scout Troop
Memorial Hospital Gift Shop
Saturday Adventurers
Pre-school Vision Screening
Drugs Are Like That Film Project
Lori Brock Children's Museum
PACE - Parenting and Childhood Enrichment Project
Victim Witness
Beautiful Bakersfield Clean City Program
Kern General Hospital Toy Loan Library
Community Workshop

Bakersfield Community House
Young Audiences
Volunteer Center
Mercy Hospital Orientation Puppet Show
Haven House
Make Today Count
Teen Involvement
CALM Reptile House and Docent Program
Marcy Hospital Therapeutic
Kaleidoscope
Kids on the Block
CALM Education Center

here in Kern County to offer rehabilitiation, physical therapy and support groups, according to Liz Howard, executive director.

MDA represents over 40 diseases, and the Kern County unit serves over 200 families annually.

The Harley Davidson Ride For Life, a popular event sponsored by Tex and Pat Thorpe, is one of its major fund-raisers.

Perhaps the most visible community event is the annual Jerry Lewis MDA Labor Day Telethon. Local broadcasting of the event started in 1970 in the studios of KERO-TV. The telethon settled in its final location at the Kern County Fairgrounds in 1978. Jerry Foust acted as master of ceremonies in 1970 and continued until 1982, serving one year with a broken leg. Larry Edwards was the producer for ten years. for the past seven years Carl Knutson has produced the event.

Rusty Shoop, Lynn Sage and Robin Mangarin hosted this year's telethon.

Raising $158,505 last year, the telethon relies on hundreds of volunteers and months of long volunteer hours for its 22 continuous hours of fundraising. Says Knutson, "The support from the community is excellent. Without the donations of time, equipment, maintenance, repair, food and services, the event would never happen."

Red Cross (American) — The Kern Chapter of American Red Cross was chartered in 1918 by the Ba-

---

The philosophy was and continues to be that all children have the right to adequate and safe care.

---

kersfield Woman's Club, with some of the prominent citizens of Kern County helping it form, including the Haberfeldes, the Brocks, the Stierns, the Karpes, the Bakers, and the Currans.

Many people have helped the Red Cross over a period of years. Lucy Stiern Johnson, Senator Stiern's aunt, left money in her estate that enabled the Red Cross to purchase its current building at 239 18th Street.

Key support for Red Cross over a period of years has come from various organizations such as the Lions Club, which for the last 35 years has taken night duty from 5 p.m. to 8 a.m. Both Frances Nairn and Charlotte Mobley gave more than 40 years of community service. One of the longest volunteers for Red Cross is Bill Rasmussen, with almost 50 years of service in water safety instruction and fund-raising.

Other active participants over the years include attorneys Bob Patterson and Jere Sullivan, Judge and Mrs. John Nairn, Dr. and Mrs. Sam Schreiber, Dr. M. C. Barnard II (an officer in the Red Cross at present), Dr. Marion C. Barnard and Dr. James Barnard (both

Nicholas Anderson, 1987 poster child for the Kern County Society for Crippled Children and Adults, is joined by Linda Hartman, fundraising coordinator; Guy Greelee, president; and Rusty Shoop, honorary campaign chairman.

are former chairmen), Buck Owens and Dorothy Owens, John Barber, the DiGiorgio family, and William Balch. Agnes Chipps has assisted with Service to Military Families for 15 years. Jean Curtis has volunteered for 30 years and Barbara Logan for 25 years. One of the oldest volunteers is Pluma Cullen, who, at 84, gives four days a week. Vivian Westerfield has been a Red Cross volunteer for 25 years. Other long-time volunteers include Steve Schilling of Clinica Sierra Vista, Kirk Wilson of the District Attorney's office, and Harold and Fern Matlock. Muriel Hanchett, with 38 years of service, presently is volunteer program chairman. Disaster chairman is Fred Shaffer, assisted by his wife Altah. Safety services chairmen are Charles DeSimone and Robert Gardiner. Program Development on newer projects such as AIDS and Senior Citizens (programs like Red Cross Calling, Safety in Your Home and How to Earthquake Proof Your Home) is headed by Dr. Sam Schreiber and Dr. George Ablin. The Bob Karpe family, and Les and Lucy Connor have been generous to Red Cross. Del Gardner is this year's chairman.

Sister City Projects — Three Kern County communities have Sister City programs. Bakersfield/Wakayama, Japan Sister City Project, was the pilot program of the Women's Division of the Bakersfield Chamber of Commerce. Heeding President Eisehower's call for World Peace through learning other people's cultures, they applied to the State Department to enter the "People to People" project, Sister City Division. Adeline Frasch coordinated this program in 1964 and is still active. (She is affectionately known as "Mamasan" by the people of Wakayama.)

When it was initiated, Tony Ishiyama, born in Bakersfield and a boyhood friend of Don Hart, was living in Wakayama. Calcot executives Tom Akers and J. Russell Kennedy were exporting cotton to Wakayama. So, with these initial ties, Wakayama was chosen as the Sister City.

The first official visit to Japan was made by Mayor and Mrs. Gene Winer, Mr. and Mrs. George Barnett, Mr. and Mrs. Walter Kane and Adeline Frasch. Wakayama Mayor Takayaki died in office shortly after the program began. Mayor Shozo Ujita was elected to the office and serves in that capacity today.

The mayor of Bakersfield is always the official head of the Sister City Project, which was incorporated in 1966. Mayor Tom Payne and his wife headed the delegation that went to Wakayama in 1985.

The Bakersfield Sister City Project is well-known for its youth programs. Dave Urner, a charter member of the program, says, "Our youth program received the Reader's Digest International Award for most comprehensive program for a city our size."

Delano sponsors three Sister City projects. Its first was Asti, Italy, initiated 25 years ago by Dr. Cliff Loader, a consistent supporter of the program. Since that time, three more cities have been "married" to Delano. Jacona, Mexico is co-ordinated by Carlos Ortiz, Alice Duarte and Eva Garcia. The program was set up by Al Espinosa, and his late wife, Mary, leaders in the Latin-American Citizens Organization.

Delano's "Sister" exchange with Kalibo, the Philippines, organized by Mayor Leonard Velasco, is co-ordinated by Elizabeth Ordiz.

The one with Arida, Japan, is coordinated by Junko Hicks. The Rotary Club of Delano was instrumental in the formation of this program and continues to be the force behind all activities and events surrounding

PETER ESPINOSA

"Top Sergeant" Frank Espinosa heads Tops Army, an anti-drug abuse program for youngsters.

"We must use the surplus to feed the hungry. No one should go without food in this county."

Arida. Dr. Rachel Espinosa is chairperson of the Sister City program.

Ridgecrest's Sister City project with Tepatitlan, Jalisco, Mexico, started in 1974 through the leadership of Rex Shacklett.

Dan Ledesma, current president, says the two cities have developed an extremely close bond, based on cultural exchange and enterprise.

Currently the two cities have combined efforts to build a Kiosk at the Kern County Regional Park in Ridgecrest.

Board members include Vince Avalos, Marge Fulton and Dick Cruise. Hector and Mena Leon also have given much time and effort since the beginning of the project.

Society For the Prevention of Cruelty to Animals/SPCA — "When the SPCA started almost 40 years ago, the society couldn't afford to feed all the animals, so some of the members took turns, each providing enough money to feed the entire kennel for a month," says director Ann Reilly.

Among those who regularly fed the animals, helped care for the sick, and were instrumental in placing many of the homeless animals were Mr. and Mrs. R. L. Blake, Mr. and Mrs. William Quinlan, past president Genevieve Howell, Mrs. Jack O'Brien, Charles Tracy, Dorothy Wilder and Mrs. G. A. Volonterio.

In more recent years, Mary Cox and Tom Tutton have greatly assisted the SPCA, particularly in making the move in 1978 from the old facility in Oildale to the new one on Edison Highway. Gay DeTuncq has also contributed hours of work at the shelter, as well as serving on the board of directors.

Starlight Foundation — Formerly called Grant A Wish, this program strives to make dreams come true for chronically and terminally ill children in Kern County. Grant A Wish was initiated by Delta Theta Tau Sorority, Theta Eta Chapter, in 1983. In 1985 the organization became a chapter of the Starlight Foundation. Their aim is to improve the quality of life of a child who is ill and to provide the child and family with special joyful memories.

The core people for this project were Judy Combs and Monica Parks. Starlight foundation has granted 80 wishes to children throughout Kern County. Linda Douglas is in charge of finance and fund-raising. Debbie Ferguson started the Candlelighters, a support group for parents whose children have cancer.

United Way of Kern County — United Way was incorporated in Kern County in 1963, with Robert Ho-

Beautiful Bakersfield Awards
1983-1987

1983

Estuardo Aguilar
Rosie Garza
Morris Rosenburg
Floyd Burcham
George Palmer
Marjorie Rump
Girl Scout Pixie Troop 197

1984

Charlotte Johnson
Mike Hopkins
Reverend Ralph Belluomini
Kevin McAtee
Delpha Nichols
Dorothy Hill

1985

John J. Kovacevich
Richard Bailey
Ted Haring
B.B. Butler
Judy Combs
George W. Nickel, Jr.
Geneva Burns
The Bakersfield Californian
Lori Brock Children's Museum
James L. Burke
Ice House Plaza
Rose Marie Blozer
City of Wasco
Keywonettes

1986

John S. Etcheverry
Ken Reed
Kern Agricultural Foundation
Dr. H. Parley Kilburn
Hazel Haag
Francis Holmes
The Facade Improvement Program, City of
Bakersfield, and Downtown Business
Association
Kiwanis Club of South Bakersfield
Richard Nuckles
Kress Building
Toby and Janet Mazzie
City of Taft
Wings for Life
The Bakersfield Symphony

1987

Leo N. Whitecotton
John Bidart, Sr.
The "Collateral Loan Group" —
   Rubin Brothers Loans
   Globe Loan and Jewelery
   M.A. Griffin and Sons
Kern Adult Literacy Council
Frito-Lay
Leo B. Hart
Chris Brewer and Don Pipkin
Bakersfield Cash Register
Johnny Soiu
Dennis and Karen DeWalt
Janet Thompson
City of Arvin
Jim Turner
Todd Adams

ven as president. "Our fundraising goal for 1987 is $2,100,000, according to Gerald Beggs, executive director. As many as 1,000 volunteers do the solicitation for contributions, 71 percent of which comes from individuals and 29 percent from companies. Dr. Claude Benitz has served as allocations committee chairman for several years.

Volunteer Center — The Volunteer Center began in 1971 as a Junior League project, with an $8,000 budget over a two-year period. In 1973, United Way funding was received, and Polly Huggins became the first director of Volunteer Center, Joan Dezember, the first board president. The Volunteer Center promotes volunteerism as a means of fostering increased citizen involvement in the community, and thus enabling public and private non-profit agencies to enhance or maintain needed human services. Current director is Georgia Herald. Each month the center presents a silver bowl sponsored by the Carnation Company to the individual who best represents the spirit of volunteering. The first recipient, in 1972, was Emma Buckmaster, a retired teacher.

The Bernice Harrell Chipman Woman of the Year Award and the Alfred Harrell Man of the Year Award are presented in conjunction with the Volunteer Center.

YMCA (Young Men's Christian Association) — The YMCA of Kern County, incorporated in 1935, is dedicated to the belief that fellowship united with a strong commitment to Christian principles will foster a healthy, prosperous and peaceful society. Incorporators were Howard Dickson, J.F. Faber and Leonard Dahlquist. (Cliff Scott was advisor to the first Hi-Y club.)

Initially, the Y had a camp at Portuguese Meadows and had its headquarters on 19th Street in Bakersfield. Both were destroyed as a result of the 1952 earthquake.

A new camp at Poso Heights was acquired in 1957. The 220-acre site was sold to the Y, interest free, by Lillian Stegeman.

Howard Dickson worked long and hard to fund the camp. Camp Dickson as it now is known, is one of the finest youth recreation areas in the state. The YMCA headquarters building, at 22nd and P Streets, is dedicated to Charles and Lola Scharpenberg, who provided the majority of the money for its construction.

In 1959 the gymnasium was funded through a general campaign.

Charles Stone started as director in 1948 and is well-known for his 17 years of dedicated service. Upon leaving the Y, Stone went on to spend nine years fundraising for 18 Y groups as a member of the national staff.

Stone says, "Hundreds of dedicated individuals have given above and beyond since 1935. It would take an entire volume to name them all. After all, the Y is people, not buildings".

The current director is Paul Andresen, known as "the best Y director around." Current president is Brent Dezember, who gains support from stalwart volunteers like Bill McKenney, John Lake, Gene Oldershaw, Mark Engelien and Warren Minner, who was honored as the Outstanding Volunteer of 1986. Eloise Nelson and Maxine Simpson are always there when needed.

The current budget, approximately $500,000, is raised through contributions, United Way funding, memberships and fees. More than 7,000 people made use of the programs and facilities of the Y last year.

As the first director of the Volunteer Center, Polly Huggins, left, was central to the growth and development of the center, which promotes citizen involvement in the community. Also pictured are Delores Hoffman, Mrs. Earnie Hailey, John Burtchaell and Harlan Mann.

The Bakersfield Sister City delegation received a banner welcome from the citizens of Wakayama, Japan, when they arrived in 1963. Kern County is linked with other countries through the Sister City programs of Delano and Ridgecrest.

A scholarship program exists so that no child is ever turned away because of lack of ability to pay.

The vision of Howard Dickson and others in the early years continues today.

YWCA (Young Womens Christian Association)
— At the end of World War II, members of the USO wanted to continue serving the community, so together they planned and organized the YWCA and by July 10, 1946, 1,600 women had signed their names to the charter at the Bakersfield Inn.

President in the early years included Marne Shreve, Leta Clanin Buerkle and Freda Frank. Buerkle was designated by the national organization to "start the ball rolling" in organizing the Y and has been a dynamo of devotion ever since, serving two presidencies and becoming a life member.

Beatrice Cumby was the first black member and a dedicated volunteer.

The YWCA is a cooperative project of all women in the community doing things together — laughing and playing, learning and planning — to meet their practical and spiritual needs.

Over the years, the Y has worked with hundreds of young women, through comprehensive youth programs and activities. Recently the YWCA formed a coalition with the Junior League to offer training to the community.

R.H. Anderson gave the lot at 17th and M streets. Clifford Harding designed the building, and Mr. and Mrs. A. H. Karpe donated the seed money for the building campaign.

On April 2, 1967, ground-breaking ceremonies were held on the present location of the YWCA.

For more than a century the members of the Weill family have been at the forefront of the growth and development of Kern County. In this early photo, pioneer merchant Alphonse Weill and his wife, Henrietta, share a warm moment with one of their daughters and a family pet.

Bakersfield restaurant owner Bill Lee, wearing a cap, spearheaded the fund-raising campaign for the construction of a school in his home village in China. Completed in 1986, it was the first new structure built in the community in more than 400 years.

At the 65th reunion of his Kern County Union High School graduating class in 1973, Chief Justice Earl Warren recalled that he once had been expelled from school for being late to class. Mary Ann Ashe, a member of a pioneer family, is seated at Warren's left.

14
The Plus Factor

"The best thing we can do...is to make an effort
to think of the other fellow's interest
as well as our own."

Henry J. Brandt

This final chapter is reserved for movers and shakers who share a common element that might be called "the plus factor," an intangible ingredient that puts them above and beyond the rest.

These individuals, like all the others in the book, are ones who have made significant contributions to the county's growth and development over the years. Many have had an impact that has been felt throughout the country and, in some cases, the world.

Yet the lives of the "Plus Factor" people and their works particularly exemplify our definition of movers and shakers: Those who have vision and foresight, the ability to inspire others and a dogged determination to make things better for themselves and others.

Several of the individuals whose vignettes appear in the following pages have faced what many people would consider insurmountable odds in terms of education and ethnic origin.

Many of those who were pioneers had little, if any, formal education and perhaps because of that went on to become staunch supporters of the public schools.

Those who have been highly successful in a financial sense often worked for many years at menial tasks in order to save enough money to buy land or to open their own businesses. In later years, many shared their wealth with the community by donating substantial amounts to a variety of organizations.

Others arrived in this country knowing only a few words of English. Yet they quickly recognized that if they were to make their way in their adopted country, they would have to learn the language, and they did so.

Those who were looked upon as "different," because of their color or ethnicity, worked hard to gain acceptance in the community. Once they had become established, they helped pave the way for others of similar backgrounds.

More than a few have been the champions of what, at the time, were unpopular causes. And in doing so, they exhibited the particular kind of courage needed to attain victory, not just for themselves but for all humanity.

And that, perhaps more than anything else, distinguishes the people in this chapter. They are humanitarians, the kind of people who give of themselves unstintingly, expecting little in return. Their chief satisfaction is the pleasure they receive from having helped their fellow citizens.

For example, when Bill Lee was asked what he derived personally from gathering the funds to build a school in his native village in China, he seemed surprised at the question. Then, as a warm smile spread slowly across his face, the Bakersfield restaurant owner replied, "Just the pleasure of doing it."

Collectively, the "Plus Factor" movers and shakers are an example for all of us to follow. They have shown us what it takes to be the very best that it is possible to be.

Brandt, Henry J. — Henry J. Brandt was one of the most influential businessmen in Kern County during his long life and one of its most generous philanthropists.

Like many other pioneers, he worked hard to attain that status.

Born in Denmark, Brandt was 15 when he arrived in the United States in 1896. Three years later he came to Bakersfield and began working as a blacksmith. For the next 10 years he followed that trade and also farmed in the Fruitvale area. By then he had saved enough money to go into the pipeline construction business.

Using teams of mules — he had as many as 500 of the animals at one time — Brandt delivered pipe to oil companies throughout the Central Valley and as far north as the Bay Area. One major project, which took nearly three years to complete, involved the laying of a pipeline from Texas to Missouri.

In 1916 he organized the Brandt Investment Company, and within a few years became one of Bakersfield's major subdividers. Among other projects, he developed Lincoln Park between Alta Vista and Union avenues, and the Sunset and Holtby tracts, south of Bakersfield High School. (Brandt and his wife, the former Pearl Maynard, built a spacious home at 729 Oleander Avenue.) He also owned three dairies and continued in that business until 1944.

Nearly every business-related organization benefited from his leadership, including the Kern County Board of Trade, the Civic Commercial Association (a forerunner of the Bakersfield Chamber of Commerce), Board of Realtors and Rotary Club. He was highly involved in other non-profit organizations.

Brandt, whose formal schooling had been limited, became a strong supporter of education. He served on the high school board of trustees and set up a scholarship fund for college students. (His son, Louis J. Brandt, now 82, graduated from Stanford in 1929 before joining his father's business.)

During his lifetime, he contributed large amounts of money to the building funds of the Salvation Army, YMCA, YWCA, Assistance League and Bakersfield Community House. Brandt died in 1969 at the age of 88.

He once said, "The best thing we can do for Bakersfield is to make an effort to think of the other fellow's interest as well as our own, to work together and to have more tolerance for each other's ideas."

Henry Brandt's life personifies the statement.

Dillard, Alberta — When Alberta Dillard came to Bakersfield from Oklahoma in 1944, she had a degree in home economics from Langston University and a family to support — two daughters and a niece.

Henry J. Brandt, a native of Denmark, worked as a blacksmith for about 10 years after he arrived in Bakersfield in order to save enough money to go into business for himself. A kind and generous man, Brandt became one of the city's most prominent leaders.

Getting a job was no easy matter, however, for in those days there were few, if any, school jobs open to blacks.

So Dillard did the next best thing: she became involved as a volunteer and soon was elected president of the Lincoln Junior High School PTA. Ultimately, she would hold a similar position with the Bakersfield Council and the Seventh District PTA.

Her PTA activities brought her to the attention of John L. Compton, who then was superintendent of the Bakersfield City Schools District. With Compton's support and encouragement, she finally gained employment in the schools in 1950. Dillard says now, "I broke the color barrier when I was hired as a cafeteria manager at Potomac School (now Bessie Owens)."

Later, after continuing her education at Bakersfield College, Cal State Bakersfield and UCLA, Dillard became a classroom and library teacher assistant. In 1973, she received the California State Employees Association's "Outstanding Employee" award.

The Girl Scouts is just one of the many organizations that have benefited from the inspirational leadership of Alberta Dillard. In this photo Ann Penner presents the volunteer with a certificate of appreciation.

When she reached mandatory retirement age in 1973, Dillard took another job as food service manager for the Kern County Economics Opportunity Corporation, a position she still holds.

Throughout her career, Dillard has maintained her role as a volunteer. In 1987 she was recognized for her community service with the Bernice Harrell Chipman "Woman of the Year" award. She is the first black to receive that honor.

A Girl Scout leader for 22 years, she organized the first inter-racial troop, which was made up of girls from six schools. She was the first black to become a member of the Girl Scouts board of directors and served for 18 years. In 1987, Dillard was honored with the Thanks Badge, the highest honor that can be given by the Girl Scouts.

In addition, she has participated in the county's foster parent program since 1944. Long active in the affairs of Cain African Methodist Episcopal Church, she is a member of the board of directors of the church's newly formed child care center.

Known as a soft-spoken yet determined woman, the 81-year-old Dillard has been an inspiration to many people. In a speech she gave earlier this year to a Business and Professional Women's convention, she summarized her philosophy: "I believe in the intrinsic value of the individual and the contributions each person can make to better the world we live in."

Espinosa, Mary Zaragoza — Mary Espinosa forged a trail that has helped many Hispanics in Delano over the past 40 years.

One of those is Alice Duarte, a secretary at the Bank of America for 22 years and president of the community's Cinco De Mayo celebration. Duarte explained that when Espinosa went to work for the government rationing board in 1943 she opened the door for other Mexican-Americans.

"Mary Espinosa was one of the first brown faces you saw on Main Street," says Duarte. "She was the first Hispanic to be hired for a clerical job — way back in the 1940s. She was a real role model for me."

An outstanding student, Espinosa was the first Hispanic to graduate from Delano High School as a California Scholarship Federation gold seal bearer. She later became a notary public and helped many Spanish-speaking people with immigration and other legal matters. Espinosa, according to her friends, rarely charged for her services.

In the mid-1940s, she was instrumental in forming the Latin-American Citizens Association. The organization came into being as a result of an incident involving Danny Melendez, a Delano resident who was serving in the military.

Home on leave during World War II, Melendez bought a ticket at the local movie theater, then took a comfortable seat in the loges, a section where minorities were not allowed. Upon being told by the management that he would have to move to another seat, Melendez refused. Legal action brought by LACA, as it is commonly known, resulted in the abandonment of the policy.

Mary Espinosa was an early role model for Hispanics in Delano and was noted for her ability to work with all segments of the community in creating better understanding of the needs of minorities.

Espinosa, who died in 1980, was recognized as a leader in the community at large. Among other things, she worked with Dr. Clifford Loader, then mayor of Delano, in developing the Sister City program with Jacona, Mexico.

She and her husband, Al, a former Delano police officer who since has remarried, were involved in the formation of several other organizations, including the annual Cinco De Mayo celebration. The couple's daughters, Yolanda and Rosemary, are residents of Bakersfield.

Grauf, Paul J. — In early December 1986, Paul Grauf sat down to write his Christmas cards, his checkbook close at hand. By the time he had finished, he had reduced his balance by $85,000, for inside each of three greetings — those to the American Heart Association, American Cancer Society and Arthritis Association — he had tucked a check for $25,000. A fourth card to the American Lung Association contained one for $10,000.

The 80-year-old retired printer suffers from arthritis and is blind in one eye. He lives in an old house that is

Taking in homeless dogs and making major financial contributions to health agencies has a become a way of life for retired printer Paul Grauf who prefers to give away his money rather than using it to enhance his own comfort.

CASEY CHRISTIE/THE CALIFORNIAN

dwarfed by a motel on one side and a retail business on the other. But he prefers to give his money away rather than live a more affluent lifestyle.

Grauf began building his financial estate many years ago when he was employed as a printer for *The Bakersfield Californian.* "I would save up a little money, like $1,000, then buy land with it," he said. "I bought land when it was cheap, rented it out, invested a little and then sold most of the land."

He began his philanthropic activities in 1966, after the death of his wife, Erminie. He set up a bank account in her memory, now called the Paul J. Grauf Memorial Fund. Initially, it benefited seven charitable organizations. By 1983, the fund's principal had grown to $600,000, and currently the interest is divided among more than 30 organizations.

A relatively solitary person, unused to publicity, Grauf found himself the center of attention when he made his Christmas gifts last year. He was interviewed by newspaper and television reporters. And the four associations that received his holiday gifts hosted a luncheon in his honor.

At the luncheon, Grauf accepted their thanks with tears in his eyes. Later, in a private moment, he explained his reasons for allowing the organizations to make a public announcement of his generosity: "I thought maybe what I have done would give other people the same idea."

Griffith, Dwight M. — Affectionately known as both "Goldie" and "Griff," Dwight Griffith coached the Bakersfield High School Drillers from 1908 to 1948. And he did it very well.

It was Griffith who started the tradition of excellence in football that has become a Bakersfield trademark, one that endures to this day. Under the Iowa native's dynamic leadership, the Drillers became a powerhouse feared throughout California. In the years when California had a statewide playoff system, the Drillers won seven state championships and 18 San Joaquin Valley titles. The coach also formed the Big B Society, the school's lettermen organization.

Among the top players who benefited from Griffith's training were George Williamson, Don Robesky, Homer Beatty, Burr Baldwin, Charlie Sarver and Frank Gifford.

Griffith was hired to coach all sports and to head the school's mathematics department. Over the years, additional coaches were added to the athletic staff, but Griff taught higher math throughout his career.

A short, wiry individual, the coach had a number of mannerisms reminiscent of actor James Cagney. Griff could be as feisty in the classroom as he was on the playing field and tended to be especially tough on those students who were members of the football squad.

In springtime, he often tucked a tiny pink rosebud in his lapel. Striding down the hall to his classroom he had a smile and a warm greeting for everyone he passed. But a short time later, his high-pitched voice could be heard throughout the building as he berated students who had failed to complete their homework. Following the tirade, Griffith often would put his feet on his desk and take a short nap.

Still, he was respected — even revered.

Drillers coach Dwight M. Griffith, who became a legend in his own lifetime, started the tradition of excellence in football that has become a Bakersfield trademark.

Real estate executive Bob Karpe played for Griffith in the 1940s and also was one of his math students. (A star tackle for the Drillers and later for the University of California Golden Bears, Karpe is a former president of the multi-billion dollar Government National Mortgage Association — Ginnie Mae.)

Karpe puts it succinctly when he says, "Griff was the father of it all. Withouth him, there would not have been a Cap Haralson, a Frank Gifford, a Gil Bishop, or any of the rest. If I had done nothing else in my life, just being on the Drillers would have been enough."

Griffith Stadium, the Drillers home field, was built during the coach's reign and named in his honor.

Hart, Leo B. — In 1939, when Leo B. Hart was elected Kern County Superintendent of Schools, the problem of providing adequate education for the children of migratory farm workers had become acute.

Between 1935 and 1940 the population of Kern County increased 70 percent. The rapid increase was due mainly to the influx of refugees from the Dust Bowl. And there was strong resentment from much of the established population against these individuals, whom they derisively called "Okies."

"The children looked like war refugees from a distant country, and in a way they were," notes Cal State Bakersfield history professor Gerald Stanley. "Their

hand-me-down trousers and skirts didn't fit. Rope and twine were used to hold the clothing up. All the kids looked undernourished and in need of medical attention."

At first, Hart tried to place the migrant youngsters in existing schools but met stiff opposition. One of his former students says, "A lot of very influential people in the county thought Leo was a communist or a revolutionary or worse."

Undeterred, the superintendent solved the problem by creating the Arvin Federal Emergency School on a 10-acre site next to the government's camp for farm workers. Its first students, Hart recalls, were "50 poorly clad, undernourished and skeptical youngsters."

After hand-picking his teaching staff, Hart set about securing what he needed to construct the school — at no expense to the county and with the help of the students themselves. As the school grew so did the children's self-esteem. In addition to their classroom lessons, they learned the skills of carpentry and raised their own livestock and vegetables. Before long, they became as self-sufficient as the school itself.

The school soon gained national attention as one of the finest educational projects of its kind in California. Hart also was innovative in developing facilities and programs. He often would invite associates to schools in isolated areas for weekend outings, during which he and his "crew" would add such improvements as cupboards and kitchen sinks. A noted communicator, he kept people informed about activities in the schools through a monthly newsletter and weekly radio program. He also was a leader in providing special education for handicapped students.

Hart retired as superintendent in 1946 to accept a position as an educational consultant to the Korean

Educator Leo B. Hart's caring attitude is evident in this photo taken about 1940 at the Arvin Federal Emergency School, the facility the superintendent set up for children of Dust Bowl migrants.

government. He returned to Kern County in 1949 and served as superintendent of the Pondham Union School District until 1959 when he retired to his farm near Shafter.

More than a few of the pupils at the Arvin Emergency School have become valuable members of the community. Among his alumni are Jim Wren, now a teacher at West High School; Janice Newton, the first female painting contractor in Kern County; supermarket owner Bill Johnson; and Bob Rutledge, owner of Bob's Bait Bucket.

Recalling his time at the school, Rutledge says, "Leo's philosophy was that nobody should be wasted. That philosophy was shared by our teachers and, as I look back, by the students too. He was one of a kind."

Heller, Carl, Jr. — Dr. Carl Heller devoted his life to serving his nation, his community and humanity at large.

As a research chemist at China Lake Naval Weapons Center, Heller made many contributions to the field of chemistry in the areas of ordnance and atmospheric pollution abatement, and most particularly in the field of chemiluminescence.

One of his colleagues, Dr. George A. Neece, has said, "It's difficult to estimate how many lives have been and will be saved by the light sticks Carl helped to develop." In 1983 Heller was presented the Meritorious Civilian Service Award, the highest honor that can be granted by a base commander.

"It's difficult to estimate how many lives have been and will be saved by the light sticks Carl helped to develop."

Heller joined the Naval Weapons Center civilian staff in 1952, after serving with the Marine Corps. He participated in the World War II battle at Iwo Jima and later was part of the occupation force in Japan. A native of New Rochelle, New York, Heller subsequently earned a bachelor's degree in chemistry and in 1950, a doctorate, from New York University.

A lifelong bachelor, the chemist became a father figure for many youths in the Ridgecrest area through his work with the Boy Scouts. (Heller received the Silver Beaver award in 1983.) He founded the community's Explorer Post and was one of the first to urge the national Boy Scouts organization to open Explorer membership to girls as well as boys. The post was instrumental in developing a ski patrol in the Shirley Meadows area. Heller also gained a national reputation as a first aid instructor for the American Red Cross.

An avid backpacker and outdoorsman, the scientist drew much spiritual strength and joy from mountain-

In addition to gaining stature as one the Naval Weapons Center's top scientists, Dr. Carl Heller organized the China Lake Mountain Rescue Group. During his 25 years of leadership the volunteer unit saved more than 250 lives.

eering. He taught community college courses in moutaineering so that others could safely enjoy that pursuit.

Perhaps his most outstanding contribution came about through his leadership of the China Lake Mountain Rescue Group, of which he was a founding member. During his 25 years of activity the group participated in 400 rescue operations and saved the lives of nearly 250 individuals. Heller was known nationally for his work in that field and was the first president of the California region of the Mountain Rescue Association.

Heller died of cancer in 1984. By special permission, his ashes were scattered from a Navy search-and-rescue helicopter over the Sierra Nevada he loved so well. The China Lake Mountain Rescue Group has submitted a request to the government that a peak in the Sierra be named in Heller's honor.

Jeppi, Frank — When a 13-year-old Italian boy named Frank Jeppi stepped out of the steerage section of the ship that had carried him from Sicily to New York in 1905, he passed through Ellis Island without much in his favor except hope and ambition.

He had no friends here, almost no money and the only word he knew in English was "hello." Though he had relatives in Baltimore, he declined to stay with them because they spoke Sicilian. He wanted to learn English.

That plucky young adventurer became one of the most successful businessmen Kern County has ever produced.

In his first years in America, Jeppi held all kinds of menial jobs in order to survive. In South Carolina, he began as a "squincher" (his word for a lowly employee who does everything, including sweeping out the office) and soon learned to be a cotton classer. A few years later he was hired by George H. McFaddin, then the largest cotton broker in the world, and sent on the road to Texas and California. While the other salesmen stayed at the best hotels and took taxis everywhere, Jeppi slept in cheap rooming houses and walked or thumbed rides to his appointments. When his boss asked why his expense account was so low, Jeppi replied, "That's your money I'm spending, not mine."

Sent to Bakersfield, he liked the people and the climate and decided to strike out on his own as a cotton broker. Later he formed the partnership of Jeppi and Simpson. Eventually he branched out into the cotton ginning business and at one time was sole or part owner of five gins. He financed numerous cotton farmers so they would use his gins.

In partnership with W.B. Camp for many years, Jeppi also engaged in growing cotton, potatoes and other crops on Calolina Farm. In addition, he had vineyards near Delano.

When he started buying oil properties, a local saying became popular: "If you want to make money in oil, pick a lease next to any land that Frank Jeppi owns."

Still active at 94, Jeppi smiles as he says, "People talk about how lucky I've been. What they don't know is how hard I've worked all my life."

An American citizen since 1916, he sailed to France in World War I and saw action at Verdun as an ordance sergeant.

Jeppi is one of the founders of the Italian Heritage Dante Association and received its Columbian Award in 1965.

His philanthropy has been quiet but extensive. He is one of the major donors to Mercy Hospital, the Bakersfield Rotary Club and the Rotary International Foundation, and the Boy Scouts.

In his birthplace of Cefalu, Sicily, he is considered a patron saint, for he has supported several orphanages, hospitals and old people's homes, given money to ease suffering after earthquakes and floods, and helped countless young people with scholarships.

Honored by two presidents of Italy, Jeppi has been given the Star of Solidarity Medal and awarded the title of Commendatore (Knight Commander), the second highest honor the Republic of Italy bestows.

Lee, Bill — Bamboo Chopsticks owner Bill Lee was born in China and came here in 1920. And although he has become a solid American citizen, he never has forgotten his homeland.

Lee has returned to his village in Loong Ping many times and over the years has done much to help the villagers. During the widespread famine that swept China at the close of World War II, millions were dying of starvation. Relief from established agencies was slow in coming. A communication from his sister, May, alerted Lee and other family members in the United States of the desperate situation.

"May told us they couldn't wait for the agency to provide food — the whole village would die," Lee said later. "We had to get the money to her direct and immediately."

There were about 600 living in the village at the time. About one-fourth were saved by the $6,000 sent by the Lees.

Forty years later, Bill Lee, who got his start in the

restaurant business at age 11 raising bean sprouts in a dark corner of his father's Star Cafe on 20th Street, would launch his crowning achievement. He decided that Loong Ping needed a schoolhouse and set out to gather the funds to accomplish the task.

In many ways, his idea was a revolutionary one, for there had been no new buildings in the village for more than 400 years. Upon his request, village officials supplied him with the names of 56 district families now living in the United States. Lee wrote each one, asking their help. His letters resulted in gifts of $25,000. The balance needed for construction — $60,000 — came mainly from Lee himself.

The school opened in September 1986. The grateful

HENLEY'S

Frank Jeppi, one of Kern County's most successful cotton brokers and financiers, came to the U.S. in 1905. After hearing Americans pronounce his family name, Geppi, so it was almost like "guppy," he changed the spelling to Jeppi to sound as it does in Italian.

villagers wanted to name the structure in Lee's honor but he refused. He preferred to call it Shing Ping, a phrase that means the "school from overseas." And to the people of China, Lee says, "overseas" means America.

"Long after I am gone," said the 76-year-old restaurateur, "no one will remember who Bill Lee is. But with the name, 'overseas school,' the people in Loong Ping will always know that it came from here — from the United States."

Although he was honored that the citizens of Loong Ping wanted to name their new school for him, Bill Lee preferred that it be called — in Chinese — "the school from overseas."

McKee, Gladys Downing — Gladys McKee was the kind of community leader who, in addition to presiding at meetings, pitched in to help with the chores. When she was well into her 70s, McKee volunteered her services as a Cancer Society "free wheeler," providing transportation on a weekly basis for cancer patients who were unable to drive themselves to clinics where they received treatment for the disease.

McKee came to Bakersfield in 1922 as the bride of Dr. Keith S. McKee. And for the next 60 years she devoted her time to dozens of fine arts, civic and charitable organizations. She used a unique filing system to keep her many interests in order: a collection of about 20 wicker baskets and tapestry tote bags, each containing the materials related to a particular organization in which she was involved.

She also was a tireless, and successful, fund-raiser for many non-profit groups. Describing her technique, and her philosophy, McKee once said, "I've begged for everything — Cancer Society, Community House, Woman's Club, Musical Association, Kern Philharmonic . . . If I had a fairy godmother who would give me a million and a half dollars, I'd give it to charity. I wouldn't use it for me."

An academically trained actress — she attended the Chicago College of Drama — McKee had a strong interest in the fine arts. She took lead roles in Bakersfield Community Theater productions and in 1937 was instrumental in the formation of the Kern County Musical Association. She later recalled that the association had many problems in its first season.

One of these problems involved the appearance of Marian Anderson, a world-famous operatic singer, who also happened to be black. The site for the concert had to be moved because the auditorium had a policy prohibiting blacks from using its facilities. To avoid any problems in Anderson's overnight accommodations while in Bakersfield, McKee made the singer's reservation in her (McKee's) name.

But upon learning of the arrangements, Anderson refused to stay at the hotel. Instead, she spent the afternoon before the concert as a guest in the McKee home.

The daughter of a Quaker father and a Scotch Presbyterian mother, Gladys McKee began each day by reading passages from the Bible. "I think we're guided to do things," she said. "I have a great belief in God. You can look up when you can't look anywhere else."

Stiern, Walter W. — During his 27 years of public service, retired state Senator Walter Stiern has gained the respect of nearly everyone with whom he has come in contact — on both sides of the political fence.

A dominant figure in the state Senate for nearly his entire career, Stiern was first elected in 1958 and re-elected thereafter until his retirement in 1986. His legislative accomplishments would fill many pages, but Stiern says that his role in education has meant the most to him personally. He was the co-author of the 1960 Master Plan for Higher Education in California. This provided a new and comprehensive approach to the orderly growth of higher education in the state. Ultimately, the plan resulted in the establishment of California State College, Bakersfield, the 19th and last campus in the system.

He also was responsible for laws that created a program for the construction of community colleges; increased both the number and the monetary value of state scholarships; set up a separate board to govern

A gracious and energetic lady, Gladys Downing McKee was the kind of community leader who never asked more of others than she did of herself.

community colleges.

Stiern, who maintains that he was not an outstanding student at Bakersfield High School, credits his experience at Bakersfield College, and later at Washington State College where he earned his degree in veterinary medicine, for turning his life around.

Throughout his distinguished career, the senator has been guided by the values instilled in him by his father, William W. Stiern, who taught industrial arts at Bakersfield High for many years.

Gloria McLean, Walter Stiern's staff assistant for 27 years, says, "The senator's father always told his sons that once they established themselves financially, they should do public service," McLean said. "And that's what they did — Walter in the Senate, Richard as a city councilman, and Robert in the county Probation Department."

In many of his decisions, Walter Stiern was guided as well by the desires of his constituents, with whom he never lost touch. His is a distinguished record that has left an indelible imprint, one that will last for generations to come.

"I learned many things from my father, but the most important was that an education is the most precious possession you can have."

Warren, Earl — The most famous lawyer — and possibly the most famous person — who received his early education in Bakersfield was Earl Warren, Chief Justice of the U.S. Supreme Court from 1953 to 1969.

Warren graduated from Washington School and from Kern County Union High School (now Bakersfield High School) where he played clarinet in the band. He was once expelled from school for being late to class, which caused a dramatic crisis, since he had a major role in that evening's senior class play.

The Chief Justice, then retired, recalled the event with amusement in 1973 when he returned to Bakersfield for the 65th reunion of his high school class. That evening he addressed 2,000 people in the quad at Cal State Bakersfield. The occasion was the graduation of the college's third class, numbering 411.

Warren's father, Methias Varren (the name was later changed to Warren), was a Norwegian immigrant. The elder Warren was killed in a still unsolved murder in East Bakersfield in 1938. Earl's mother was born in Sweden.

When his son was born in 1891, Methias Warren almost immediately began to set aside funds for the boy's education. The Chief Justice later told a reporter, "I learned many things from my father, but the most

State Senator Walter W. Stiern, a primary force in the establishment of California State College, Bakersfield, shared some words of wisdom at the groundbreaking ceremonies of the campus in 1969.

important was that an education is the most precious possession you can have. I remembered this lesson when I was pondering the writing of the desegregation decision."

Before his appointment to the Supreme Court by President Eisenhower, Earl Warren had been district attorney of Alameda County, attorney general of California and a three-term (1943-1953) governor of the state. In 1948 he ran for vice president on the Republican ticket headed by Thomas Dewey.

Though Warren never had been a judge, he accepted the post of Chief Justice and the "Warren Court" became both celebrated and controversial for its social activism. Among its most far-reaching decisions were:

• *Brown v. Board of Education of Topeka, Kansas,* 1954, which declared segregation in public schools unconstitutional

• The one-man-one-vote ruling in 1963, which forced states to reapportion legislative and congressional districts to make them more equal in population

• *Miranda v. Arizona, 1966,* which expanded the rights of the accused in criminal cases when the court ruled that police must warn suspects of their right to be silent and to have a lawyer present even before being questioned.

At President Lyndon B. Johnson's request, Warren headed the commission which investigated the 1963 assassination of President John F. Kennedy.

Warren's admirers say he will rank in history with

19th century Chief Justice John Marshall, who established the court's authority as the ultimate interpreter of the Constitution.

His detractors find his views on social leglislation too extreme.

Yet, as an article in *True* magazine pointed out, "Remember that his uncle, a Norwegian immigrant, worn down by hard work, died of malnutrition and tuberculosis.

"If you think that he leans too far in the direction of government medicine," the writer continued, "remember that he was crippled financially when his daughter Nina (Honey Bear) contracted polio in 1950. He told me that before she recovered from the disease, he spent more money on medical bills than he derived from his entire income as governor of California."

Many far-reaching decisions were made while Earl Warren was Chief Justice of the Supreme Court. Some observers believe that he will rank in history with 19th century Chief Justice John Marshall. Warren received his early education in Kern County.

Earl Warren died in Washington, D.C. in 1974 at 83 and was buried in Arlington National Cemetery. A marble bust of his likeness adorns the Great Hall of the Supreme Court.

Weill Family — In Kern County, the Weill family is something of an institution. For every one of its members undeniably has contributed in great measure to the growth and development of the county's economy, as well as in the areas of education, mental health and the fine arts.

Their contributions began more than a century ago when Alphonse Weill, a native of France, came to California at the age of 17 and settled in Havilah in the early 1870s. He brought with him a limited knowledge of English, a few books and a fervent desire to work hard and make a good life for himself in his new country.

After clerking in a store there, Weill moved to Bakersfield and soon opened his own business. From a small general store, it grew into a major department store, which was owned and operated by the family until 1952.

Weill soon became a driving force in the community's growth and development, and among other things, was the first president of the Board of Trade when it was formed in 1903. His wife, Henrietta, was elected president of the Woman's Club in 1903 and was instrumental in the formation of the first Red Cross chapter. She also initiated the first kindergarten and assisted in the establishment of a shelter for neglected children.

The Weill's daughters, Blanche and Irma, both were pioneers in the field of early childhood education. The Henrietta Weill Child Guidance Clinic, which since has served hundreds of emotionally disturbed children, was established in 1946.

For most people in Kern County today, 98-year-old Lawrence Weill and his wife, Helen, are the best-known members of the family. Lawrence Weill has contributed

DENNIS FOSTER

Lawrence Weill donned a top hat for a celebration at Pioneer Village that marked the 100th anniversary of his family's home. The structure, which the Weills gave to the museum, originally stood at the southeast corner of 17th and H streets in Bakersfield.

so much — and for so long — that it is difficult to recount all of his accomplishments for he is a mover and shaker supreme.

During his active years in the department store, he employed many high school and college students in the area. For many years, three percent of the store's annual sales were given to the Oracle, the Bakersfield High School yearbook, and the school's mechanics club. He was a national director of the Boys Clubs of America. In 1985 the Bakersfield College Downtown Center was renamed the Weill Institute in his honor.

An aviator during World War I, Weill was instrumental in the establishment of Kern County's first airport and was a member of the airport commission. He served as president of a score of business, civic and arts organizations.

Well-known for his wit, wisdom and excellent recall, Weill long has been a prominent source of information on Kern County history. In 1984 the Kern County Historial Society published his book, *Lawrence Weill's Bakersfield.*

Helen Weill, whom Larry Weill married in 1932, has been equally active in the life of the community. Like her husband, she has a strong interest in the arts and over the years has provided enjoyment for many through her dramatic interpretations of plays and musicals.

Larry Weill once was asked why, after his retirement, he and Helen chose to remain in Bakersfield. Without a moment's hesitation, he answered, "Why, because our friends are here."

Yes, indeed.

Bibliography

Bailey, Richard, *Heart of the Golden Empire: An Illustrated History of Bakersfield.* Woodland Hills, California: Windsor Publications, 1984

Bann, Robert T., *The Shafter Pioneers.* Shafter, California: The Shafter Press, 1963.

Barras, Judy, *The Long Road to Tehachapi.* Tehachapi, California: Tehachapi News, 1976.

Boyd, William Harland, *A California Middle Border: The Kern River Country,* 1772-1880. Richardson, Texas: The Havilah Press, 1972.

Delano, Land of Promise, Jim Thornton, Chester Bruszewski, Cecil Dyar, Ken Graydon and Harry Hofman, eds. Delano, California: Delano Historical Society, 1965.

Harrington, E. Ross, *A History of the Office of the Kern County Superintendent of Schools.* Bakersfield, California: Kern County Historical Society, 1969.

Heffernan, William J., *Edward M. Kern: The Travels of an Artist-Explorer.* Bakersfield, California: Kern County Historical Society, 1953.

Hine, Robert V., *In the Shadow of Fremont: Edward Kern and the Art of Exploration,* 1845-1860. Norman, Oklahoma: University of Oklahoma Press, second ed., 1982.

Indian Wells Valley Handbook, Lorraine McClung, ed. Ridgecrest, California: China Lake-Ridgecrest Branch of the American Association of University Women, fifth ed., 1979.

Inside Historic Kern, W. Harland Boyd, John Ludeke and Marjorie Rump, eds. Bakersfield, California: Kern County Historical Society, 1982.

Kern County Centennial Almanac, Howie Wines, ed. Bakersfield, California: Kern County Centennial Observance Committee, 1966.

Morgan, Wallace W., *History of Kern County,* California. Los Angeles: Historic Record Company, 1914.

Paquette, Mary Grace, *Basques to Bakersfield.* Bakersfield, California: Kern County Historical Society, 1982.

Paquette, Mary Grace, *Lest We Forget: The History of the French in Kern County.* Bakersfield, California: Kern County Historical Society, 1978.

Powers, Bob, *Kern River Country.* Los Angeles: Westernlore Publications, 1976.

Powers, Bob, *South Fork Country.* Los Angeles: Westernlore Press, 1971.

Rintoul, William T., *Spudding In: Recollections of Pioneer Days in the California Oil Fields.* San Francisco: California Historical Society, 1976.

Stanley, Gerald, "Children of the Grapes of Wrath," in *Delta Chi Quarterly,* vol. 83:3, Winter 1986-87. Iowa City, Iowa: The Delta Chi Fraternity.

Thompson, Gerald, *Edward F. Beale & The American West.* Albuquerque, New Mexico: University of New Mexico Press, 1983.

Voltmer, Barbara B., *Kern County's Courier, 1866-1876: A Newspaper in a Period of Economic and Political Transition.* Bakersfield, California: Kern County Historical Society, 1968.

Where the Railroad Ended, Barbara Richardson, Jane Randolph, Gary Girard, Betty LeCourse, eds. Delano, California, 1974.

Who's Who in Kern County, Wilson & Peterson, eds. Bakersfield, California: 1940.

Newspapers

The Bakersfield Californian
Bakersfield Morning Echo
Bakersfield News Observer
Tehachapi News

Index

D

E

F

U

V

W

Y

Z